THE OLYMPIC GAMES

Athens 1896 to Los Angeles 1984

THE OLYMPIC GAMES

Optimum Books

Photographic Acknowledgments

Allsport Photographic, Morden: title-spread, 13 left, 18, 22, 29 below, 31 above centre, 36 right, 37, 38 left, 42 above, 43 below, 51 below, 52, 53 below, 65, 69, 77, 91 above, 106 above, 115 above, 115 centre, 115 below, 131 above right, 133, 136, 146 above, 148 above, 151, 160, 164 above, 167, 175 below, 178 above, 179 centre, 181 above, 183 right, 184 below, 185, 186, 187, 191, 194, 195, 198 above, 202 below, 203, 204, 205, 208 below, 209 above right, 210 above left, 210 below, 212 above, 221, 227 above, 232, 238 above, 240 above, 241 left, 242 centre, 244 left, 246 right, 248 left, 248 above, 249 below right, 249 centre right, 249 right, 250 below right, 251 below left, 251 below right, 251 above right, 252 left, 252 above centre, 252 above left, 253 right. Associated Press, London: 163 left. BBC Hulton Picture Library: 10 above, 12 above, 14 below, 15 below, 21 above, 23 above, 23 centre, 23 below, 24, 27 above, 27 centre, 27 below, 28, 29 above, 32 above, 32 below right, 40 above, 40 below right, 41 above, 41 below, 72 above, 75 left, 76 right, 88 below, 91 below, 93, 118, 224, 225, 226, 228 below, 233 right, 233 below. Central Press, London: 8 above, 71 below, 89, 103 above left, 128 left, 131 below, 137 below, 143 above, 234 above, 234 centre, 236 centre, 240 above right, 242 centre left. Colorsport: title spread, 6, 7, 132 below, 166 above, 166 below right, 168, 169 below, 170 below, 171, 172 below, 173, 174 above, 175 above, 176 above, 176 centre, 177 above right, 178 below, 179, 180, 181 below right, 182, 183 left, 184 above, 188 below, 189, 190, 191 below, 192, 193 above, 196, 197, 198 below, 199, 200, 201, 206 below, 207, 208 above, 208 centre, 209 above right, 209 below, 210 above right, 211, 212 below, 214, 246, 247 above, 247 centre, 248 below left, 248 below right, 249 below left, 249 below centre, 249 above right, 249 above left, 250 below left, 250 above, 250 centre, 251 above left, 251 below left, 252 above centre, 252 below centre, 252 above right, 252 below right. Colour Library International, London: 84, 85. Fox Photos, London: 71 above, 232 below. Hamlyn Group Picture Library: 9 above, 15 above, 32 below left, 35 below, 39, 54 above, 61, 130 above, 228 centre. Ed. Lacey, Great Bookham: 126 below, 140, 154 below, 155 above, 157 centre, 158 above, 159 below, 162, 164 below, 165 right, 174 below right, 177 below, 242 above centre, 242 below right, 244 below. Mansell Collection, London: 25, 26, 67 below, 68 below, 79 below. Mary Evans Picture Library: 13 right, 14 above, 16 below, 22 below, 30 below, 34, 42 below, 44, 50, 53 above, 58, 59 above, 60, 63 below, 66 left, 70 above, 76 left, 78. Michael Holford: 9 above, 10 below, 11 above. Illustrated London News: 16 above. Keystone Press Agency: 8 below, 11 below, 12 below, 20 right, 45 above, 47, 54 below right, 55, 56 above, 56 below, 64 below, 66, 67, 70 below, 79 above, 81, 82 above, 83, 92, 95 below, 96 above, 97 above, 98 above, 99 below, 100 above, 101 above, 102 left, 102 right, 103 above right, 103 below, 105, 111 below, 112 below right, 114 below, 116 above, 123 above, 123 below, 124 above, 124 centre, 124 below, 125 above, 127 above, 127 below, 128 above, 129 above left, 129 below, 131 above right, 132 above, 136 below, 137 above, 148 below, 159, 160 below, 170 above, 173 above, 188 above, 230 centre, 236 below, 236 above, 238 below left, 240 centre left, 240 left. Popperfoto, London: 30 above, 36 left, 43 above, 45 below, 51 above, 53 centre, 54 below left, 57, 61 centre, 62, 72 below, 73 above, 73 below, 82 below, 88 above, 96 below, 97 below, 98 below, 100 below, 101 below, 106 below, 119 below, 120, 122 below, 125 below, 126 above, 134 above left, 137 centre, 138 left, 138 right, 139 above, 139 below, 140 above, 141 above, 141 below, 142 right, 143 below, 144 above, 144 left, 144 right, 145, 148 below, 149, 150 above, 152 below, 153 below, 155 below, 156 above, 156 centre, 156 below, 157 above, 157 below, 158 centre, 158 below, 159 left, 159 right, 160 above, 161, 163 right, 165 left, 165 below, 169 above, 176 below, 227 below, 228 centre, 233 above, 234 below, 234 centre, 240 below left, 242 centre right, 242 centre left, 243 left, 244 above right, 245. Pressefoto Muhlberger, Munchen: 163 above, 193 below. Presse-Sports, Paris: 19, 20 left, 21 below, 38 right, 40 below left, 41 above, 46, 48, 49, 59 below, 64 above, 68 above, 95 centre, 108 above, 109, 111 above, 111 below right, 121 above right, 121 above left, 121 below, 127 below right, 130 above, 134 right, 134 below, 135 above, 135 centre, 135 below, 147 below, 152 above, 153 above left, 153 above right, 222, 227 centre, 228 above, 230 above, 230 below, 238 right, 239 below, 239 above, 240 below right, 241 right, 241 below, 242 below centre, 242 above, 244 above left, 244 centre left. Rex Features, London, title spread: 94, 122 above, 154 above, 202, 244 centre. Sporting Pictures (UK) Ltd: 206 above, 212 centre, 213, 215, 252 below, 252 centre right, 253 left. Sven Simon, Munchen: 166 below left. John Topham Picture Library: 33 below, 99 above, 108 below, 110, 112 above, 113, 114 centre, 116 centre, 116 below, 117, 119 above, 238 centre, 238 right.

This edition published by Optimum Books 1983

Prepared by
Deans International Publishing
52–54 Southwark Street, London SE1 1UA
A division of The Hamlyn Publishing Group Limited
London·New York·Sydney·Toronto

Copyright © The Hamlyn Publishing Group Limited 1983
ISBN 0 603 03068 8

Printed and bound by Graficromo s.a., Cordoba, Spain

Contents

Introduction

The Olympic Games is the greatest amateur sporting event in the world. The modern Olympics is based on the sporting festivals held in ancient Greece, in particular on the most famous, that held at Olympia at four year intervals for over 1,000 years.

The ancient games died out in A.D. 393. But in the late 19th century, a Frenchman, Baron Pierre de Coubertin, envisaged their revival. He was inspired by the discovery of the site of the ancient games at Olympia, and his dream was to incorporate the Greek ideal of harmony between physical and intellectual pursuits in a festival of sports and arts, in which amateur athletes from all over the world could compete in friendship. He formed the International Athletic Congress, and one of the first motions passed unanimously in 1894 was: 'the revived Olympic Games shall not admit of money prizes'.

The International Athletic Congress created committees whose duties were to define amateurs and to forward the organization of the Games. One of these committees, the International Olympic Committee, has been responsible ever since for running the Games. A self-recruiting body, its members are co-opted, and the current tendency is to restrict membership to one per nation as the total number rises towards 100. There is a smaller executive board headed by the President, who is elected initially for eight years and may stand thereafter for re-election every four years, and the administrative work is carried out by a general secretariat based in Lausanne, Switzerland.

It can be imagined that the organization of each Games is a complex business. Thus, in order to facilitate all the planning and the accompanying preparations, the I.O.C. awards each Games to a city many years in advance. To date only Paris and London have held two Games, but in 1984 Los Angeles will be staging the Games for the second time, having been the venue in 1932.

In recent years the size of the Games has become its biggest problem for two main reasons. First, the expense of staging the events has grown so much that many cities are precluded from applying. In Montreal in 1976, 88 nations took part (despite 29 others withdrawing for various reasons including political and financial). Costs, which included the building of a main stadium and an Olympic village to house 6,152 competitors, put a burden of nearly $200 million on the Canadian taxpayers.

Second, the attention given to the Games, with millions around the world watching on television, presents unprecedented opportunities for political gestures and acts of terrorism. The black power salute of the U.S. sprinters on the podium in 1968 caused dismay and indignation, but could hardly compare with the student rioting before the

Pierre de Coubertin, the founder of the modern Olympic movement, called Olympia his 'dream city', and his heart rests in this memorial at the site of the ancient Olympics.

Games which led to hundreds being killed or injured, or the tragedy in the Olympic village itself in 1972 when Israeli competitors and officials were held hostage by Palestinian terrorists. Eleven Israelis, five terrorists and a policeman died before the Games was over.

It is difficult to justify the continuation of the Games in the face of such tragedies. Coubertin's ideal of harmony and friendship was not so much tarnished as almost destroyed. But the ideal itself must be considered to be worth fighting for, and to abandon the Games now would be to admit failure.

Where does the Olympic ideal stand today? Coubertin, inspired by a sermon delivered by the Bishop of Pennsylvania, said in 1908: 'The most important thing in the Olympic Games is not to win but to take part, just as the most important thing in life is not the triumph but the struggle. The essential thing is not to have conquered but to have fought well.'

These sentiments would not have applied to the ancient Olympics. The Greeks valued victory almost as much as a triumph of arms on the battlefield. There was cheating and there was bloodshed. Winners were honoured and rewarded.

The concept of 'sportsmanship' is relatively new. It implies many things: modesty and generosity in victory, grace in defeat, scorn of unfair advantage, acceptance of luck (good or bad), and playing to the rules, as administered by umpires, judges and referees who are the unquestioned authorities. All of these qualities were recognized by Coubertin.

Modern sport at the top levels is almost entirely a big-money professional business. Golfers, boxers, footballers, players of baseball, basketball, tennis, all can become millionaires. In many sports athletic services are bought and sold by clubs for enormous sums. Winning is all important and has been recognized as such by competitors and spectators alike – as the use of new concepts such as 'gamesmanship' and 'professional foul' suggests. The antics of boxers at the weigh-in, footballers feigning injury to win free kicks, rugby players 'softening' each other up in the scrums and tennis players constantly questioning line calls are examples of behaviour which offend the true spirit of sport.

The Olympic Games has made great efforts in the face of professionalism to remain amateur and sporting. It is not easy. Perhaps the efforts were too great when Jim Thorpe was forced to relinquish the medals he won in the 1912 Olympics. Paavo Nurmi and Jean-Claude Killy were other Olympic winners whose amateurism was questioned, and Nurmi was prevented from taking part in Los

The altar of Hera, daughter of Rhea and sister of Zeus, at ancient Olympia, where the Olympic flame is kindled from the sun's rays.

The 77th session of the International Olympic Committee took place in Innsbruck in 1976, with the President, Lord Killanin, in the centre, and Willy Daume on the left.

Below: The scoreboard at the Tokyo Olympics, with, in French and English, the words of Pierre de Coubertin which have become an ideal of sportsmanship.

Angeles in 1932. Latterly such practices as college scholarships for athletes in the U.S.A., government posts for Communist athletes in the U.S.S.R. and other Communist countries and commercial sponsoring of individuals throughout the West have caused misgivings.

Perhaps the political value of success, the unofficial medals lists which are published everywhere, the playing of winners' national anthems and the raising of flags have encouraged nations to strive too hard for victory. Much has been made in the West of the intensive squad training of selected young girls in Communist countries like East Germany, particularly for gymnastics and swimming events. In some cases individual athletes appear to have been encouraged to try too hard. There has even been a recent disqualification for blatant cheating.

However, the fact remains that, taking account of the fame that an Olympic medal brings and the dedication required to win it, the standard of sportsmanship in the Olympics remains remarkably high. Whatever squabbles surround the Games from time to time, the competitors still strike friendships with each other which ignore national prejudices and ideological strictures. The electronic scoreboards repeat Coubertin's words, now definitive of the modern Olympic spirit: 'The most important thing . . . is not to win but to take part.' Long may it be so.

The Ancient Olympic Games

The Olympic Games takes its name from the games held at Olympia in Elis in ancient Greece. These were not the only Greek games, others being the Pythian, Nemean and Isthmian Games, but those at Olympia came to be the most important. The Games were part of larger religious ceremonies, and at Olympia was the altar to Rhea, mother of Zeus and known as 'Mother of the Gods'. It is believed that the first Games at Olympia was held about 1370 B.C. On the day of the early Games, men would race for the honour of lighting the sacrificial fire at the altar. The race covered a distance of one stadium (about 202 yards or 185 metres), the winner taking the torch from the priest to light the fire.

One Greek legend tells of how Heracles began the Olympic Games as a celebration of his revenge on Augeias, King of Elis, who had not paid him the cattle promised after Heracles had cleaned his stables as his sixth labour. Another legend suggests that Pelops began the Games after he had won the hand of Hippodameia by defeating her father by treachery in a chariot race.

The Games took a big leap forward in 884 B.C. when Iphitus, King of Elis, arranged a truce, an *ekeheiria*, by which visitors from the cities of Sparta and Pisa, the combative rivals to Elis, were guaranteed safe conduct to the Games. The Games were to be held in the first year of each four-year period known as an Olympiad. The first winner whose name has survived was Coreobos of Elis, who won in 776 B.C., and the Games of that year is regarded as the first of the major Olympiads, and is given the number I in the subsequent records of the ancient Games.

Until 724 B.C. the stadium race was the only 'official' race, although other events took place. In 724 B.C. a second race, the *diaulus*, was introduced over two stadia (405 yards or 370 metres) followed in 720 B.C. by the *dolichus* over 24 stadia (2.76 miles or 4.44 km). There followed in 708 B.C., wrestling and a pentathlon (running, jumping, discus, javelin, wrestling). Then came boxing, chariot racing and the *pancratium*, a brutal mixture of boxing and wrestling.

The scene of the original Olympic Games. The ruins of the sacred enclosure which held the temples of Hera and Zeus and the tomb of Pelops. Just outside were the stadium and the lodgings for distinguished guests.

Below: A Greek vase shows runners rounding the turn post in the Olympic Games, dating from about 470 B.C.

Right: A weightlifter at an ancient Olympic Games, shown on a Greek vase.

Opposite above: A Greek vase shows an Olympic athlete long jumping. Long jumpers of the day carried weights in each hand.

Opposite below: At the ceremony at Olympia in 1964, young Greek maidens lit the Olympic flame at the sacred altar. The torch lit from the flame was carried by a series of runners to the Winter Games at Innsbruck.

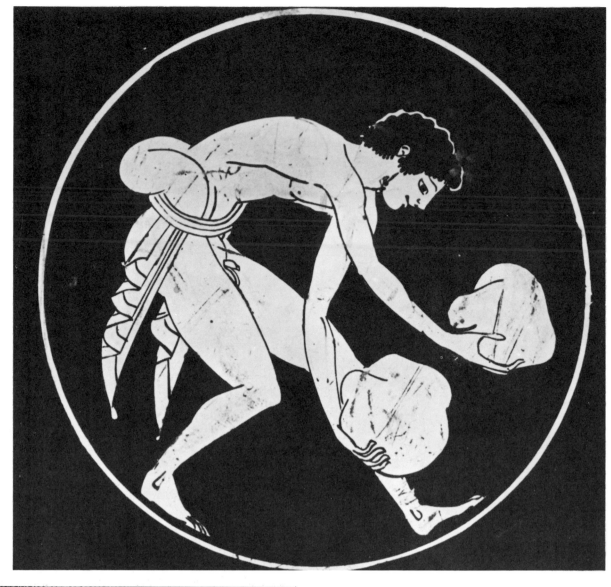

Below: The fierce battle called the *pancratium* in which biting and eye-gouging were about the only activities that were barred.

The duration of the Games was at first of one day only, but with the introduction of new events (there were over 20 during the series of Games) extra days were added until by 632 B.C. the Games lasted five days. At first athletes competed naked and women were not allowed to watch. The winners' prizes were olive branches, signifying vitality.

Soon winners at the Games began to be celebrated by writers and poets, sculptors erected statues to them and athletes were depicted on Greek vases and pots. The Games lost some of its religious significance and became a great festival of athleticism and the arts which reached its peak in the period of Pericles (490–429 B.C.), when Athens was pre-eminent in Greek classical art and intellectualism. The Games were the greatest events of the times, and the great athletes were famous. There were multiple winners like Theagenes from Thassos, a boxer and wrestler in Pericles' time, and later Leonidas of Rhodes, who won the three foot-races in four successive Games. These men reflected what was most admired in Greece.

The ancient Games were of astonishing duration, lasting over a thousand years from 776 B.C., 293 Olympiads in all. Eventually the ideal of harmony between athleticism and the arts gave way to more specifically intellectual pursuits such as philosophy and study. The Romans came and preferred the battles between slaves and animals. The sacred truce was not always observed in the strictest fashion. The worship of the body declined still further with the beliefs of the early Christians. Finally in A.D. 393 the Roman Emperor Theodosius the Great banned all pagan cults and prohibited the continuance of the Olympic Games.

Olympia itself rapidly declined after this, pillaging being followed by a series of earthquakes and floods until only ruins were left. What Olympia had symbolized for over one thousand years lay dormant for just as long, until in the 19th century A.D. the best aspects of the Olympic Games were revived.

Athens

Below top: The organizing committee for the first modern Olympic Games in Athens in 1896. Baron Pierre de Coubertin is seated left.

Bottom: The opening of the first modern Games, with the Greek royal family leading the parade.

Baron Pierre de Coubertin was a French educationalist who held the view in the 1870s and 1880s that the tradition of games-playing and athleticism of the public schools of England was what had made that country one of the greatest powers in the world. He was depressed by the lack of such a tradition in France and felt it was needed if France were to become a strong nation again after the humiliating defeat in the Franco-Prussian War of 1871.

Interest in classical Greece had flourished with archaeological discoveries in the 17th and 18th centuries (a Cotswold Olympic Games had been regularly held in England from 1636 into the 19th century) and further excavations at Olympia led Coubertin to dream of an international festival of sport based on the Games of ancient Greece.

Courbertin expressed his views on visits to the U.S.A. and in 1893 discussed with representatives of the American universities of Harvard, Yale, Princeton and Columbia the formation of an International Athletic Congress to forward his plans. This Congress met at Paris in June 1894, where the Greek 'Hymn to Apollo' was sung. At this Congress Coubertin gained agreement for most of the basic principles for his idea of a revived Games but his biggest difficulty came with the definition of amateurism. Coubertin had long scorned the growing professionalism in sport, and his vision saw amateur sport promoting health and vigour to balance the intellectualism found in French public schools. Much was made of this in the inaugural address of the President of the Congress, Baron de Courcel. Eventually a definition of amateur status was agreed.

Coubertin himself selected the International Olympic Committee, still the organizing body of the Games. Initial attempts to hold the first revival of the Games in Athens in 1896 were hindered by Greek financial problems, but in 1895 a committee was formed in Greece which issued the rules and guidelines and set about raising the money for the stadium and other facilities.

The first modern Olympic Games was opened on Easter Monday, 6 April 1896 by King George I of Greece, although the previous day there had been a ceremony to unveil a statue to Georgios Averoff, a businessman who had made a large financial contribution to the Games. The opening is therefore sometimes given as 5 April, and sometimes as 24 or 25 March, because the Greeks were using the old Julian calendar. This evidently caused confusion at the time, as the 14-man American team, who expected some days to practise, managed to arrive the day before competition started. This error,

however, did not prevent them from winning seven of the nine events held on the first day, most of which were heats. After Crown Prince Constantine of Greece had made a speech and King George I opened the games, the first three events were 100-metres heats. Then came the 'hop, step and jump', now known as the triple jump, and the first modern Olympic champion emerged. He was James B. Connolly, of Suffolk Athletic Club, U.S.A., who jumped 13.71 metres. Some 40,000 in the stadium, including sailors from the USS *San Francisco*, watched him win, together with as many more spectators on the hills around.

A big surprise on the opening day was the defeat of the Greek discus champion, Paraskevopoulos, by American Bob Garrett, who was also to win the shot put. Americans, therefore, won the only two winners' medals awarded on the first day.

At these first modern Games, there were medals for all competitors, including special

silver medals for winners and bronze medals for runners-up. The first two also received a diploma, and the winner a crown of olive, the second a crown of laurel.

As the games proceeded, the Americans confirmed their superiority in athletics, winning nine of the 13 events. The Americans had taken the Games more seriously than the British, who were represented by only eight rather casual competitors. Of the 311 athletes who took part, 230 were from Greece, and the majority of the remainder came from Europe. Apart from the U.S.A. contingent, there was a competitor from Chile and another from Australia, although the Australian, Edwin Flack, was a member of the London Athletic Club. He won the 800 metres in 2 minutes 11.0 seconds and the 1,500 metres in 4 minutes 33.2 seconds.

Outside the athletics events, the French dominated the cycling, Paul Masson winning two events, and the Greeks won two of the three fencing events. The Germans did best in

Far left: Bob Garrett of the U.S.A. caused an early upset when he beat the Greek favourite, Paraskevopoulos, in the discus.

Left: Paul Masson of France is congratulated after one of his two cycling victories in the first Olympic Games.

Athens

The start of the 100 metres. Tom Burke of the U.S.A., the winner, is second from the left and is using the crouch start which, at that time, was used only by the Americans.

Below: An early training picture. Three runners in the 1896 marathon get themselves into shape.

the gymnastics, a tribute perhaps to Ludwig Jahn, who after the defeat of the Prussians by Napoleon at the Battle of Jena in 1806 had opened the first German gymnasium in 1811 to encourage young Germans to find a national ideal in physical training, an ambition which foreshadowed Coubertin's ideal 70 years later. The Greeks also excelled in the shooting, possibly because they supplied 90 per cent of the competitors.

The standard of the Games might be best illustrated by the two British winners. A huge handsome man, Launceston Elliott, who also took part in the wrestling, won the one-handed weightlifting easily, but it was said that after the contest Prince George of Greece lifted the heaviest weight with ease. And the British tennis winner, John Pius Boland, was a tourist who entered because he happened to be in Athens at the time.

The climax of the Games, and the event which caused most excitement, was the marathon. The race, which had not been an event of the ancient Olympics, was suggested by Michel Bréal, a French student of Greek mythology, to commemorate the feat of the Greek messenger, Pheidippides, who ran from the plains of Marathon to Athens with the news of the Greek victory over the Persians in 490 B.C. The Greeks, without an athletics winner in the Games, particularly wanted to win, and supplied 12 of the 16 runners. The race was to be from Marathon to the stadium, a distance of about 40 km.

The foreign runners led at first, among them Edwin Flack, the 800 and 1,500-metres winner. But at 36 km, he was exhausted, and a 25-year-old Greek shepherd, Spyridon Louis, forged ahead to win. There were scenes of extraordinary fervour, and as Louis approached the stadium, Prince George ran to the entrance and joined him on his final lap. It is said Louis was promised free shaves by a Greek barber and free meals by a Greek restaurateur for life.

In the first Olympics, stormy weather caused the rowing and sailing events to be abandoned. The winners received their prizes on the last day of the Games, 15 April (3 April for the Greeks) in pouring rain, which did not dampen the enthusiasm of the crowds for Spyridon Louis, who was cheered in the parade of champions.

The Games had been accompanied by other cultural events, and the whole festive atmosphere of Athens augured well for the revived Olympics.

The finish of the marathon: Spyridon Louis is accompanied on the final lap of the stadium by Prince George of Greece.

Baron Pierre de Coubertin

Coubertin was the idealist whose dream led to the modern Olympic Games. He was born on 1 January 1863 in Paris of an aristocratic family who lived in a private hotel in the city, and he graduated in arts, sciences and law. It was intended that he join the army, but he became interested in educational reform, writing numerous books throughout his life with titles like *French Education during the 3rd Republic* and *English Education in France*. He visited England several times in the 1880s having been impressed with the ideas of Thomas Arnold, the headmaster of Rugby School many years earlier. He concluded that physical culture was an essential part of education, became secretary-general of a committee to propagate physical exercise, and after a visit to North America decided that a movement to popularize international sport would be of great value to education and international harmony. On 25 November 1892 he first suggested the revival of the Olympic Games in a speech at the Sorbonne. Several conferences and committees later he saw his ideal realized, and until 1925 when he retired as President of the International Olympic Committee he was the leading organizer of the Olympics. He married and had two children. He devoted so much of his fortune to pursuing his ideas that he was comparatively poor when he died in Geneva on 2 September 1937. His heart was taken to Olympia, in Greece, where a memorial was erected.

Marathon winner, Spyridon Louis, receives his prizes at the end of the first modern Olympic Games.

Paris

If the 1896 Olympics were a success, the 1900 celebrations were so disorganized that Coubertin himself wondered if the Games would survive. In the euphoria of the 1896 Games the King of Greece had claimed the right of staging all future Games in Athens.

Charlotte Cooper of Great Britain at the Wimbledon tennis championships in 1900, the year she became the first woman to win an Olympic title.

The scene for the Paris Olympics of 1900, where the 500-metres grass track was laid out between trees on the Bois de Boulogne.

Coubertin went ahead with plans to combine the next Games with the Paris Universal Exposition of 1900. Fortunately the Greek claim foundered after a disastrous war with Turkey in 1897 and continuing financial problems for the government.

A succession of disagreements hindered the planning of the Paris Games. The organizer of the Exposition was reluctant to incorporate the Games. When other arrangements were made, the Union des Sociétés Françaises de Sports Athlétiques (U.S.F.S.A.), of which Coubertin was an official, would not support his organizing committee, and Coubertin resigned. Eventually, at the last minute, the first plan was revived, and the Games began on 20 May 1900.

However this Olympic Games was quite unlike the Athens festivities of four years earlier, and the compact Games of today. To begin with, it lasted several months. Secondly, events were organized haphazardly, as separate items in the Exposition, so that it was not clear that a unified Games was taking place at all. There were even professional championships.

A great many sports were represented: association football, athletics, cycling, eques-

trian events, fencing, gymnastics, rowing, shooting, swimming, cricket, croquet, golf, tennis, polo, rugby and yachting.

Of the non-athletics events, the most interesting results came with a British win in the soccer, Upton Park Football Club defeating a top French representative team in the final, and in the cricket, where the French beat the British team, Devon County Wanderers. The swimming events took place in the Seine, the current producing some startling times: Freddie Lane of Australia 'beat' the world record by 13 seconds in the 200-metres freestyle. The swimming also featured an underwater and an obstacle race, neither repeated since. Americans won the golf, French the croquet, British the polo and French the rugby. Britons dominated the tennis, the famous Wimbledon champion Lawrie Doherty winning the singles, and, with his brother Reggie, the doubles. Tennis provided the first woman Olympic champion, Charlotte Cooper of Great Britain, who also won Wimbledon. She took the singles medal and, with Reggie Doherty, the mixed doubles.

The athletics events were held on a 500-metre grass track laid out in the Bois de Boulogne. Trees hampered the discus and hammer and prevented timekeepers seeing the starts of some of the races; the sprints were downhill.

As in 1896, the Americans took the Games more seriously than most, and sent a strong team, mainly from the universities of Pennsylvania, Michigan, Georgetown, Syracuse, Princeton and Chicago and from the New York Athletic Club. They dominated the athletics, winning 17 of the 24 events.

The star of the Games was Alvin Kraenzlein of Pennsylvania who won four events, the 60-metres dash, 110-metres and 200-metres hurdles and long jump. He may have been lucky in the long jump, as the finals were held on Sunday 15 July, and several of the American college athletes had said they would not compete on the Lord's Day. Kraenzlein's rival, Myer Prinstein, who a month earlier had beaten Kraenzlein and set a

world record, scratched from the finals, and was so angry that Kraenzlein competed that he attacked him with his fists afterwards. Prinstein took second place on the strength of his jump which led the heats and he also won the triple jump.

The American world record holder in the 100 metres, Arthur Duffey, pulled a muscle, but Americans Frank Jarvis and Walter Tewksbury finished first and second. Maxie Long of the New York Athletic Club won the 400 metres to complete an American clean sweep of the sprints.

The middle-distance track events were won by the British, although there were again American withdrawals, a fact which also helped Irving Baxter from the University of Pennsylvania, a descendant from Sioux Indians, to win the high jump and pole vault. Rudolf Bauer of Hungary won the discus, beating Bob Garrett, the 1896 winner, who kept hitting the trees with his throws, but Americans won the shot and hammer. Another American, Ray Ewry, with his long legs, easily won the three jumps from a standing start.

On 19 July the French at last won a race: the marathon. It was a badly organized affair in blazing sunshine throughout, starting at 2:30 in the afternoon. After four circuits of the track the runners did a circuit of Paris and returned. Michel Theato, a baker's roundsman who knew the streets well, including, it is suspected, the short cuts, won, and provoked the same sort of enthusiasm that the local man Louis enjoyed in Athens four years earlier. American Arthur Newton, who finished well behind, thought he had won. Dick Grant, also of the U.S.A., was sixth of seven finishers, collapsing at the line over an hour after Theato. Later he unsuccessfully sued the I.O.C., claiming that one of the cyclists cluttering the course had knocked him down as he was about to take the lead.

This Olympic Games was the least satisfactory of all the modern Olympics, attracting little of the attention given to the Universal Exposition as a whole. It was not even clear at the time that the 'Olympic Games' was taking place, the programme and most newspaper reports describing it as the International Championships of the Universal Exposition. Nor are the results to be trusted entirely, as it was not until 1912 that the I.O.C. reconstructed the results and awarded medals, Michel Theato being one winner surprised to discover he had won an Olympic event.

The decision to hold finals on a Sunday created more farce. The pole vault, for example, was re-staged after protests by two of the competitors who had withdrawn from the finals, and Irving Baxter finished third at the second attempt, but he was later reinstated as the winner when French officials decided the original Sunday result would stand.

The excellent American team prevented the Games being a complete disaster. Their supporters often provided half the crowd, and their concerted cheering, college style, astonished the Europeans, who dubbed them a band of savages. The American athletes' crouching style of starting in the sprints also caused interest, and in general the American attitude of thorough organization and preparation combined with an enjoyment in their prowess contrasted with the squabbling and lackadaisical behaviour of the Europeans.

Cooling treatment for Michel Theato of France, on his way to winning a marathon run in intense afternoon heat. Whether he completed the whole course is doubted by some.

Alvin Kraenzlein

Kraenzlein won four Olympic titles in 1900, and he and his room-mates at the University of Pennsylvania, Irving Baxter and Walter Tewksbury, won 14 medals at the Games. Born on 12 December 1876, Kraenzlein pioneered and developed the modern technique of hurdling and held the world record for 200-metres hurdles for 25 years. He also held world records for the 110-metres hurdles and the long jump. He won all three events at the 1900 Olympics, together with the 60-metre dash.

In the late 1890s he won seven United States championships, in the 100 metres, 120-yards hurdles (twice), 220-yards hurdles (three times) and long jump. He was an advocate of physical fitness through moderate living and systematic training, and before the First World War went to Berlin to make preparations for the American team in the 1916 Olympics which was eventually cancelled.

He died on 6 January 1928.

1900

Alvin Kraenzlein of the U.S.A. was the first athlete to make a big impact on a single Games when, in 1900 in Paris, he took four gold medals, winning two hurdles races, a sprint and the long jump, although his long-jump victory resulted in his being assaulted by his colleague Myer Prinstein, who thought he should not have competed on a Sunday.

St. Louis

It had been decided before the first modern Olympics was held that the United States of America would stage the third, and when the I.O.C. met in Paris on 21 May 1901 it had the simple choice of choosing between Chicago and St. Louis. The former was given the vote.

Once again, there were complications. The Louisiana Purchase Exposition, due to be held at St. Louis in 1903, was postponed until 1904, and the organizers, not wishing to compete with the Games, asked for the Games to be transferred to St. Louis and incorporated into the Exposition. Chicago countered with a suggestion that the Games should be deferred to 1905, quite contrary to Coubertin's Olympic concept. President Theodore Roosevelt was asked to arbitrate: he chose St. Louis.

The Games were again attractions in a World Fair, and some of the drawbacks of the Paris Games of 1900 were repeated. There were too many events connected to the Fair, held to celebrate the 100th anniversary of the purchase of Louisiana from Napoleon. All the sports were called 'Olympic', despite the fact that some were professional, some were for schoolboys, some were Y.M.C.A. championships and others were handicaps. Any *truly* 'Olympic' events had to be decided by the I.O.C. later.

It was not surprising that the Europeans, having shown degrees of apathy over the Games held in Europe, should not bother to travel to St. Louis. The number of athletes in the Games dropped by over half compared to Paris: only 625 took part of which 533 were American and 41 were Canadian; the rest, a mere 51, came from elsewhere. Not surprisingly, the athletics events were almost all won by U.S.A. competitors.

The athletics were held between 29 August and 3 September on the track at Washington University. This was a big improvement on the Paris track, being a third of a mile in circumference and with a level 220-yard straight for the sprints.

It was a sprinter who made the biggest

A triple winner at middle distances in 1904 was American James Lightbody, who won the 800 metres, the 1,500 metres and the steeplechase. He also won the team cross-country race over 4 miles (6,437 metres), but his team finished second to another American squad.

Far right: Etienne Desmarteau won Canada's first Olympic medal, for throwing the 56-lb weight, surprisingly beating the triple hammer champion, John Flanagan.

impact in the Games. Archie Hahn, known as the 'Milwaukee Meteor', won the 60, 100 and 200 metres. In the last event, his three opponents in the final were each penalized a metre for false starts, provoked, it was said, by Hahn's own feints at starting.

Three other American athletes won three events. James Lightbody won three middle-distance events, the 2,500-metres steeple-chase, the 800 metres and the 1,500 metres. The steeplechase was the first such event seen in Louisiana, and the spectators cheered at each competitor who landed in the water jump. The 800-metres final was one of the best races of the Games, a German and an American both collapsing from exhaustion at the end.

Harry Hillman won the 400 metres and the 200-metres and 400-metres hurdles; the short-er hurdle race provided a close finish in which the first three crossed the line together. George Poage of the Milwaukee Athletic Club was third in the two hurdle races, the

first black man to reach the first three in an Olympic Games.

The other triple winner was Ray Ewry, repeating his 1900 hat-trick in the standing jumps.

One of the best field-event victories was that of Martin Sheridan, who set a new world record in the discus and beat the Greek competitor into third place. Sheridan threw at least a metre further in a handicap event.

The American monopoly of victories was broken by Etienne Desmarteau, a Canadian policeman, who won the 56-lb weight throw, beating, to everybody's surprise, John Flana-gan, the winner of the hammer in both 1900 and 1904. An Irishman from the New York Athletic Club but representing Great Britain, won the first Olympic decathlon, contesting ten events in one day, and winning four. It was not till 1954 that his name, Thomas Kiely, was added to the Olympic records.

For the third successive time the marathon produced drama. It was the first marathon held in the U.S.A., and a fresh-looking runner called Fred Lorz was first in the

Martin Sheridan of the U.S.A. won the first of three discus titles in 1904 (one of the three was in the Interim Games of 1906). The sock suspenders seem to be an individual fashion. He also won the shot in 1906.

Irish-born John Flanagan won the second of his three hammer-throwing titles for the U.S.A., where he had emigrated in 1896.

St. Louis 1904

Above: Ralph Rose won the shot-put title in 1904 and repeated his win in 1908. He was also second in the 1904 discus.

Right: A German swimmer, E. Rausch, won two freestyle events, the 880 yards and the mile, in the 1904 Games at St. Louis.

stadium and acclaimed the winner. However, it appeared that he had retired exhausted at nine miles, ridden in an automobile for several miles and run the last few miles to the stadium. He was disqualified. The acclaimed winner was Tom Hicks, but he should probably have been disqualified too. The race was again held in the afternoon, in extreme heat with a thunderstorm brewing, with the usual interference from vehicles of all sorts. Less than half the field finished. Hicks was given strychnine tablets and brandy, and was supported by spectators at one stage before collapsing at the line. He recovered in hospital and never ran a marathon again.

Of the other sports, boxing made its first appearance in the modern Olympics. The U.S.A. won all seven classes and provided all the runners-up, too, as they did in the wrestling. However, Zoltan von Halmay of Hungary won the swimming sprints, Germans won other swimming events, Cuba won all the fencing competitions (Ramon Fonst winning foil and épée), and Pericles Kakousis of Greece won the two-handed weightlifting by over 37 kg (60 lb).

The events as a whole were well organized, and it was not the Americans' fault that they were little more than national championships. Unfortunately, the indifference of the rest of the world was not helped by the week of the athletics coinciding with two terrible battles in the war between the U.S.S.R. and Japan, which monopolized newspaper space.

The most unwanted event in the World Fair was an exhibition entitled 'Anthropological Days', in which groups from less 'developed' peoples from around the world were displayed in a parody of the Games. In a programme of pathetic running, jumping, shooting, and so on, a pygmy threw the weight 3 metres. This was reported with disgust to Coubertin, who had remained aloof in Paris. Coubertin saw it as an American attempt at sensationalism, but added prophetically that such charades would lose their appeal when black men, red men and yellow men learned to run, jump and throw as well as, or better than, white men.

Athens Interim 1906

Left and below: Two views of the stadium for the 1906 Olympic Games. The picture on the left shows a gymnastics display taking place. A comparison of the picture below with that on page 15 shows new building at the far end of the stadium.

Bottom: The start of the 100-metres sprint. Archie Hahn, second from the right, was the winner. He had won three sprint titles in 1904

The Greeks had never lost their belief that the Olympics should be held permanently in Athens, and proposed a Panathenaic Games for 1908. Coubertin compromised by supporting a plan for Interim Games in 1906 and 1910. These Games were not given official I.O.C. patronage, and are not numbered in the series of Olympiads, being known as the Interim or Intercalated Games.

The 1906 Games was well organized and supported, with a full programme of sports events, including 25 athletics events at the new Athens Stadium. For the first time the athletics included a javelin event which was won by Erik Lemming, a Swede.

Americans again dominated the athletics, some of the winners of 1904 repeating their victories, notably Ray Ewry, in the standing long jump and standing high jump, Archie Hahn in the 100 metres, Myer Prinstein in the long jump and Martin Sheridan in the shot and discus. Max Decugis of France won the men's tennis title. Charles Daniels of the U.S.A. added to his 1904 swimming victories by reversing the 1904 100-metres freestyle result by beating Hungary's Zoltan von Halmay. Great Britain's Henry Taylor, soon to become the swimming star of 1908, won the 1,600-metres freestyle swim.

The importance of the Games was that it confirmed the public's desire that the Games be an international sports festival in its own right, no longer merely attached to a world trade fair. The standard had been set for the 1908 Olympiad.

London

The 1908 Games was originally given to Rome in preference to Berlin, but once again first plans were thwarted. In 1906 Vesuvius erupted, causing many deaths and ruining the Italian economy; the Italians announced at the Interim Games in Athens that they must withdraw.

After the St. Louis Games, Great Britain, the U.S.A. and Germany had formed National Olympic Committees, and at the Interim Games, Lord Desborough, a fencing competitor, was asked if the British Olympic Association could step in and organize the 1908 Games. This was confirmed.

The expertise of the British at running sporting events, plus the co-operation of the organizers of the Franco-British Exhibition, who agreed to build a stadium, ensured that the Games would be the best-run yet. Nevertheless it was not ideal. For the first time the British competed in deadly earnest, determined to beat the Americans. Coubertin, in his admiration of the British as sportsmen and experienced rulers of many parts of the world, supported the idea that the judges should be British. Unfortunately some controversial decisions and the partiality of the spectators led the Americans to believe

they were badly treated, and there was great bitterness between the two nations.

Twenty-one sports were represented in the Games. For the first time entries were restricted to 12 per country in individual sports and for the first time gold medals were given to the winners.

Athletics and summer sports were held in July; sports such as football and boxing were held later in the autumn. The athletics were held at the new White City track.

From the start the tremendous rivalry between Great Britain and the U.S.A. was evident; each believed in its own superiority and realized that this was the 'crunch'.

The short sprints were won by a South African, Reggie Walker, and by a Canadian, Bobbie Kerr; in each an American was second, and the crowd cheered the victory of the Empire over the U.S.A. The 400 metres provided the biggest controversy and the bitterest feelings of the Games. The four runners in the final were three Americans, J.C. Carpenter, W.C. Robbins and J.P. Taylor (who became the first black gold medalist in the relay), and a lieutenant in the British Army, Wyndham Halswelle. There were no lanes, and Robbins cut across

The start of the 100-metres final in the 1908 Games in London. Reggie Walker of South Africa in the far lane was the winner.

The march-past at the opening ceremony of 1908. The countries paraded in alphabetical order, except that English-speaking countries brought up the rear. The swimming pool can be seen inside the main stadium.

Halswelle to share the lead with Carpenter. In the home straight, as Halswelle challenged, Carpenter ran diagonally from inside, forcing Halswelle out and making him check his speed. The British officials shouted in protest and one cut the tape. After the runners' footprints had been examined Carpenter was disqualified for boring, and the other finalists ordered to re-run two days later. Robbins and Taylor refused, and Halswelle ran alone to win the gold.

Americans won both hurdle events, and, strangely, in the 400-metres hurdles (which was run in 'lanes' in that each competitor had his own set of hurdles to jump), the winner, Charles Bacon, jumped an opponent's hurdle, but as he gained no advantage, was not disqualified. Another American, Harry Hillman, was second.

The middle-distance events provided ample consolation for the sprint defeats for the U.S.A.; Mel Sheppard sprinted home in the 800 metres for a world record, and completed the double in the 1,500 metres. The longer distances were British wins; Emil Voigt won the five miles despite the pain of a badly injured toe, Arthur Russell the steeplechase and George Larner the two walks. The British team provided five of the first seven in the three-mile team race, to win with ease.

Americans won most of the field events, Ray Ewry and John Flanagan ending distinguished Olympic careers with gold medals. Great Britain won the tug-of-war after the Americans retired from the competition protesting against the heavy boots that the British had worn when defeating them in a heat.

The marathon again provided the biggest drama of the Games, and one of the Olympics' immortal heroes. The race was run from

London

Athletes and events at the Olympic Games of 1908:

1. Verner Weckman and Yrjo Saarela, both of Finland, in the Greco-Roman light-heavyweight wrestling final.
2. Stanley Bacon and George de Relwyskow, both of Great Britain, battle for the gold medal in the middleweight freestyle wrestling. Both won a gold, Bacon in middleweight and de Relwyskow in lightweight.
3. Charles Bacon of the U.S.A., winner of the 400-metres hurdles.
4. Charles Bacon and Harry Hillman jumping the last hurdle together in the 400-metres hurdles. The beaten Harry Hillman had won three gold medals in 1904.
5. Reggie Walker of South Africa, the 100-metres winner.
6. The long-jump winner, Francis Irons of the U.S.A.
7. Reggie Walker being chaired after his sprint win.
8. The finish of the 100-metres final: Reggie Walker on the right; James Rector of the U.S.A. next to him; and Robert Kerr of Canada, the 200-metres winner, on the left.
9. The most controversial incident of the Games. A judge broke the tape in the 400 metres before J. C. Carpenter of the U.S.A. could breast it. Carpenter was disqualified for boring, and Wyndham Halswelle of Great Britain, seen on the left, had a 'walkover' in the final because the Americans refused to re-run.
10. Officials inspecting the track where the boring in the 400 metres took place.

OLYMPIC GAMES.

1. W. Weckman (Finland) throws Y. Saarela (Finland), and wins the Greco-Roman (205lb.) Light Heavyweight.   2. S. V. Bacon wins the Middleweight Catch-as-Catch-Can from G. de Relwyskow (both United Kingdom), by two falls to none.   3. C. J. Bacon (U.S.A.), winner of the 400 Metres Hurdle Race.   4. Hillman and Bacon jump the last hurdle side by side.   5. R. E. Walker (South Africa), winner of the 100 Metres Flat Race.   6. F. C. Irons (U.S.A.) cleared 24ft. 6½in., and won the Running Long Jump.   7. Chairing Walker, the South African victor, after the race.   8. R. E. Walker breaking the tape.—After a great race, half a yard in front of J. A. Rector.   9. 400 Metres Flat Race.—Judges break the tape owing to Carpenter boring Halswell, and for which he was disqualified.   10. The crowd inspecting the course at the point the boring took place, and the judges declared race void.

Windsor Castle to the stadium on 24 July, a muggy hot day, and the early pace was too fast. Charles Hefferon of South Africa led from halfway, until, just before the stadium was reached, he was passed by the Italian, Dorando Pietri. As the frail-looking Pietri entered the stadium there was a sudden hush from the 90,000 spectators as he first turned right instead of left and then fell exhausted. He was lifted up, fell again, struggled on to within 50 yards of the finish and collapsed once more. It was then noticed that the second competitor, John Hayes of the U.S.A., who had also overtaken Hefferon, was entering the stadium. Pietri, helped again, got to the line, but was then carried away on a stretcher. Naturally the Americans objected, but Pietri was not disqualified until a doctor testified that he would have been unable to rise without help after his third collapse on the track.

There was great sympathy for Pietri, and to general acclaim he was given a special gold cup by Queen Alexandra at the prize-giving; there was tremendous cheering when his name was called. Strangely his name was mistakenly given in the list of competitors as P. Dorando, and the card given him by the Queen with his cup was so addressed.

Newspapers reporting the event in the main used Dorando as his surname and he is still Dorando in many books. So although the

Left: Erik Lemming of Sweden won the first Olympic javelin competition.

Below: The finish of the 800 metres, with Mel Sheppard of the U.S.A. winning.

Bottom: If one includes the 1906 Interim Games, Ray Ewry of the U.S.A. has won most gold medals, with ten, all in standing jumps (now discontinued). Here he is winning the standing high jump in 1908.

Ray Ewry

In the Olympic Games from 1900 to 1908, including the 1906 Interim Games, there were 10 events for standing jumps: Ray Ewry won them all.

The extraordinary thing about these wins is that as a boy, Ewry was partially paralyzed by polio and confined to a wheelchair. At one time it was thought he would never walk. He was born on 14 October 1873 in Indiana and began doing the standing jump to develop his withered limbs. Tall and lanky, he became so good at it that he joined the New York Athletic Club. His world record for the standing long jump of 3.47 metres (11 feet 4¾ inches) stood until the event was discontinued in 1938. The standing jumps ceased to be Olympic events in 1912. Ewry died on 29 September 1937.

London

Harry Porter of the U.S.A. attempts the high jump. The bar can be seen at 6 feet 2 inches, one inch lower than his winning jump.

Dorando Pietri runs through the streets of London in the marathon on his way, if not to victory, at least to worldwide fame.

Below: The winner of the marathon on the disqualification of Pietri, John Hayes of the U.S.A., is carried round the track on a table by team-mates, disappointed at his reception compared to that of Pietri.

winner John Hayes could justly regret that his name was soon forgotten while the loser's was famous, Pietri could also regret that it was the wrong name!

The most important sport after athletics was the swimming. The star here was Henry Taylor of Great Britain, who won three gold medals, in the 400-metres and 1,500-metres freestyle, and in the relay. Charles Daniels of the U.S.A. set a world record in the 100-metres freestyle, and won his seventh Olympic medal.

Great Britain made clean sweeps of the gold medals in boxing, lawn tennis, racquets, rowing and yachting, and almost won everything in archery, cycling and motorboat racing. An oddity was that the middleweight boxing champion was John Douglas, later better known as J.W.H.T. Douglas, England's cricket captain on a tour of Australia. The rowing was notable for a tremendous race in the eights wherein Leander, respresenting Great Britain, just beat the formidable Belgian crew.

There were women's events in archery, tennis and figure skating (the first time a winter sport had been included in the Games). The men's figure skating event was won by the famous Ulrich Salchow of Sweden, who won a record ten world championships (equalled by Sonja Henie). A nice 'Olympian' gesture came in the high diving. When D.F. Cane of Britain ruptured a blood vessel in a difficult dive and lay unconscious in the pool, he was rescued by Hjalmar Johansson, the Swedish gold medalist. The Swedes later presented Cane with a silver cup as recognition of his talent and bad luck.

Where did the truth lie in the bad feeling between the British and the Americans? The incidents that provoked it were small enough in themselves. The English cheering at Empire victories over Americans was criticized in the New York Press; the London *Times* was scornful of the raucous chorus of 'rah, rah, rah' with which American supporters greeted their wins. It must be said that the failure of the American flag-bearer to dip his flag to the King during the opening ceremony had not commended the Americans to the British public or press. American competitors disliked the fuss made of Pietri, but the English

Henry Taylor of Great Britain, who won two individual gold medals in swimming, is chaired from the pool after helping Great Britain win the freestyle relay.

have always perversely preferred gallant and game losers to winners, and the reaction would have been the same had the second man not been American. The Halswelle controversy arose primarily from the difference in rules between the two countries, although one wonders if the official would have cut the tape so finally if the British athlete had 'fouled' the American.

Part of the trouble possibly lay in the belligerent character of the leading American official, James Sullivan, and his determination to win. He proclaimed that the British officials were 'absolutely unfair' and the American press took up the story. The British Olympic Association published a pamphlet, 'Replies to Criticism of the Olympic Games', which caused the British and American Associations to break off communications.

The British had won overwhelmingly the most medals in the Games, but the Americans had won most of the athletics events, which are easily the most important, so luckily neither side's pride was seriously dented in what Coubertin called the 'muscular duel of champions'.

Apart from this controversy, the London Games was a big success. Lavish entertaining at several banquets for up to a thousand guests from July to October helped keep competitors and officials happy, and the competent and thorough production of all aspects of the Games led the Greeks to drop forever their plans to hold Interim Games between Olympiads.

John Flanagan

John Flanagan was born in Limerick, Ireland, on 9 January 1868. He developed his hammer throwing in Ireland, emigrated to the United States in 1896, became a policeman, and won the American hammer title in 1897, the first of seven. He was the Olympic champion in 1900 and repeated his wins in 1904 and 1908, the only athlete until Al Oerter to win three successive gold medals in a current Olympic event. In the 1904 Olympics he also finished second in the 56-lb weight and came fourth in the discus. He broke the world hammer record, an Irish speciality, 12 times between 1895 and 1909. He died in Ireland in 1938.

John J. Flanagan, in 1908, won his third hammer-throwing title, a feat unsurpassed in a current Olympic event until Al Oerter won four discus titles in the 1950s and 1960s.

Stockholm

Below top: The design of the Olympic Stadium, built for the Stockholm Games of 1912, was admired for its architecture as well as its suitability for running.

Bottom: The entry of the Swedish team at the Stockholm Olympics. The Swedes generally performed excellently.

Stockholm was awarded the 1912 Games in 1909, and the I.O.C. was given the full cooperation of the Swedish government.

A new and beautiful stadium and a 100-metre pool for swimming were built. The Swedes were wholehearted in their preparations. A carnival atmosphere persisted throughout the Games, and there were flags all over Stockholm. The Swedes were rewarded with perfect weather throughout. None of the disputes which marred the 1908 Games occurred, and the Stockholm Games is considered to have come as near as possible to Coubertin's ideal and to have set the standard for all future Olympics. At the opening ceremony on 6 July 1912, 200 Scandinavian gymnasts dressed in white mounted a synchronized display and the march-past of competitors was most impressive.

The new arena was planned by the veteran British groundsman Charles Perry, who had laid out the track for the first modern Olympics in Athens in 1896, and it was rated perfect in every respect, as was the stadium itself with its octagonal towers and arched entrance. Technological advances meant that the finishes could be decided by a photo-finish camera, and there was electrical timing of events. The stadium seated 30,000 spectators, who followed the athletics with mounting enthusiasm and reasonable impartiality.

The Americans regained their superiority in the sprints, winning all the events up to 800 metres. Ralph Craig won both the 100 and 200 metres. The final of the 100 metres was remarkable for the fact that five of the six finalists were American, three of whom took the medals, and for the fact that there were no less than eight false starts (after one of the false starts most of the runners completed the course). Craig had a long Olympic career – he was also a member of the U.S. yachting team in London in 1948, aged 59.

The 400 metres was won by Charles Reidpath, who just beat the German Hans Braun. Braun was unlucky in the 800 metres, a magnificent final. The defending champion was Mel Sheppard, who asked for a time for 880 yards to be taken, as he wanted to attempt both world records. A 19-year-old, Ted Meredith, had been asked to make the pace, but it was Sheppard who went out ahead. Meredith moved level on the back straight, but Sheppard edged ahead again. Round the last bend Braun challenged but was forced wide round the two Americans. He got level but his effort was spent, and Meredith came in the last four metres to beat Sheppard by a metre. It was he who broke the two world records.

The 1,500 metres was another disappointment for holder Sheppard, who was unplaced in a blanket finish. Arnold Strode-Jackson, an Oxford University student, entered as an individual and wore the University colours. Strode-Jackson, a comparative novice,

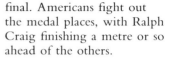

'strode' past the favoured Americans on the outside to win by a metre, with the second and third a tenth of a second behind.

The 5,000 and 10,000 metres announced to the world a new outstanding star: Hannes Kolehmainen, the first of the 'flying Finns'. The 5,000 metres was the race of the Games. The three fancied runners were Kolehmainen, France's Jean Bouin, and Britain's Hutson, but in the actual event the first two led from the start and had the race to themselves. Kolehmainen just led, then Bouin, their stride lengths being so matched that they seemed as one. On the back stretch Bouin put in a sprint and got three or four metres ahead, but in the final straight Kolehmainen slowly closed the gap. Bouin looked round and found the Finn at his shoulder, for a few metres they were together, but Kolehmainen surged ahead at the line to win by a metre or so. It was a new world record.

The 10,000 metres was a different story, Kolehmainen winning with ease. He also won the 8,000-metres cross-country, winning the individual gold and a silver for his team. He set a new world record in a heat of the team 3,000 metres race, but Finland failed to make the final.

Americans took all the medals in the 110-metres hurdles, Fred Kelly winning, and the U.S.A. and Great Briatin shared the relays. Americans took most of the field events, Ralph Rose losing the shot-put title he had held since 1904, finishing second to Pat McDonald, but winning a two-handed shot competition, held only at the 1912 Olympics. Scandinavians took the discus and javelin events, but 'mighty' Matt McGrath, an Irish-born American like his predecessor, Flanagan, won the hammer.

The marathon was a triumph for South African athletes, who filled the first two places, the winner being Kenneth McArthur. But this time the marathon claimed a life, Lazaro of Portugal dying from heart failure in hospital. The news of his condition was kept from the thousands who celebrated the end of the Games by carrying the winner shoulder high to his hotel.

The finish of the 100-metres final. Americans fight out the medal places, with Ralph Craig finishing a metre or so ahead of the others.

The 800-metres final was won in world record time by 19-year-old Ted Meredith from two other Americans, favourite Mel Sheppard and Ira Davenport.

Below: The 5,000 metres was a great battle between two men, Finland's Hannes Kolehmainen, leading here and the eventual winner, and Jean Bouin of France who finished second.

Stockholm

The 1912 Games included, for the first time, a track and field pentathlon, which consisted of long jump, javelin, discus, 1,500 metres and 200 metres. An American Indian, Jim Thorpe, won with ease, winning four of the events and finishing third in the discus. Ferdinand Bie of Norway was second, and Avery Brundage of the U.S.A., later President of the I.O.C., was further back.

A few days later the decathlon began. It was spread over three days, but it was clear from the first that Thorpe would win again. He took four first places, two seconds and four thirds. Thorpe's points, on the method of scoring at the time, were 8,413, nearly 700 points more than the second man, Hugo Wieslander of Sweden. Thorpe also finished fourth in the individual high jump and seventh in the long jump. The following year Thorpe's medals were taken from him because it was found that he had played minor league professional baseball. Bie and Wieslander were awarded the gold medals. Some 70 years later Thorpe was re-instated, and his medals were presented to his family in 1983.

Another new Olympic event, suggested by Coubertin, was the modern pentathlon: shooting, swimming, fencing, riding and cross-country running. It was won by Gustaf Lilliehook of Sweden and Swedes took all the medals to the crowd's delight. The best of the non-Scandinavians was an American army cadet, George Patton, who was given a diploma for finishing fifth, and later achieved fame in the Second World War as General 'Blood and Guts' Patton.

Outside the athletics, the swimming and diving attracted attention. There were dual winners: George Hodgson of Canada in the longer freestyle events, Walter Bathe of Germany in the breaststroke events, and Erik Adlerz of Sweden in the plain and fancy diving. But the star was American Duke Kahanamoku, born in the Royal Palace at Honolulu in 1890, and named after the Duke of Edinburgh, who was visiting at the time. He and two other Americans missed the 100-metres freestyle semi-finals, but were allowed a special race to beat the qualifying time, one of the few incidents which caused controversy in the 1912 Olympics. Kahanamoku broke the world record, and went on to take the gold medal easily.

Throughout the Games the spectators had been delighted by displays of gymnastics, for which 13 nations sent 1,275 men and women. The competitions were restricted to men's individual and team events, both for combined disciplines. Albert Braglia of Italy was the star, winning the individual gold for the second time, with Italy, Hungary and Great Britain taking the medals in the team event. The gymnastics was a huge success, and established the sport in the Olympics.

The soccer tournament, too, in which Great Britain defeated Denmark 4–2 in the

Below top: South African cyclist Rudolph Lewis won the 320-km road race.

Bottom left: The marathon winner, Kenneth McArthur of South Africa, arrives at the tape already garlanded.

Bottom right: The diving pillar at the 1912 Olympics with the finals in progress.

final, was enthusiastically received, and helped spread the game further round the world. The Greco-Roman wrestling was remarkable for long bouts, the light-heavy-weight final lasting nine hours before it was declared a draw, with both men awarded silver medals. One semi-final lasted 10 hours.

After the athletics, a huge banquet was held in the centre of the stadium for officials and competitors. Coubertin made a speech, hoping that the next Olympiad in Berlin would be celebrated with concord.

The Games as a whole was entirely successful, with none of the major squabbling that had spoiled the London Games. Afterwards the American press was to rejoice aloud at American track and field superiority, while the British agonized over their own decline and countered with mutterings about 'professionalism'. In fact, Sweden won most medals, with the U.S.A. second and Great Britain third. The biggest advance was shown by the Finns, who were not happy at having their wins celebrated by the raising of the Russian flag. They were then part of the Russian Empire.

With war threatening Europe, the Games demonstrated clearly the possibility that nations could be friends, and it was the memory of these Games that helped the Olympic movement to establish itself so successfully after the First World War.

Great all-round athlete Jim Thorpe, winner of the pentathon and decathlon in 1912, had his medals taken from him later because of an infringement of the amateur rules.

Six of Jim Thorpe's children receive his medals from the I.O.C. President, Juan Samaranch, centre, at a special ceremony in 1983, after Thorpe's amateur status had been returned. Thorpe had died in 1953.

Jim Thorpe

Jim Thorpe was born in Shawnee, Oklahoma, on 28 May 1888, an Indian whose father was from the Sac-Fox tribe, and he was given the Indian name Wa-Tho-Huck (Bright Path). He went to Carlisle Indian School in Pennsylvania, developed a talent for athletics and American football, and entered the pentathlon and decathlon at the 1912 Olympics. He won both with ease, and he was also fourth in the high jump and seventh in the long jump. Back at Carlisle that year he played his best football, scoring a record 198 points in the season. It was then discovered that he had been paid for playing baseball in a minor league, and his Olympic medals were taken from him, and his name expunged from the records. He also returned over 100 gifts and prizes awarded

him as an amateur. His best events were high jump and hurdles, and after the 1912 Olympics he beat the Olympic champion, Fred Kelly, over the 110-metres hurdles. Barred from amateur sports, he played major-league baseball from 1913 to 1919, and when professional football started in 1920 played six years for the Ganton Bulldogs. In an American poll in 1950 he was voted the greatest athlete of the century. A film of his life, *Jim Thorpe – All American (Man of Bronze* in Great Britain), was made in 1951. In 1971 a petition to reinstate Thorpe as an Olympic champion was signed by 400,000 persons. His amateur status was restored by the American Amateur Athletic Union in 1973 and his Olympic feats recognized by the I.O.C. in 1982. Alas, Thorpe had died a poor man in Carlisle in 1953.

Antwerp

In 1915 Coubertin established the headquarters of the I.O.C. at Lausanne in Switzerland, where he had a home. It was from here that the invitation to Antwerp to host the seventh modern Olympiad was issued in 1919. Antwerp had been considered for the 1920 Games in 1914, and the venue became increasingly appropriate as a consolation to Belgium, devastated by the fierce war that raged within her borders.

The organization proved an almost impossible task for the Belgians, who had only 18 months to prepare. The stadium, pool and other buildings were barely completed, and the damage done to Antwerp and the countryside in general could not be disguised. Judged by earlier Games the facilities were poor, but many of the athletes had fought in the war, and to them any facilities would have been accepted with gratitude. The defeated powers – Germany, Austria, Hungary, Bulgaria, Turkey – were not invited, and the U.S.S.R. declined to take part.

Finland was now free from the U.S.S.R. and the Finnish athletes competed with zest. The Americans, on the other hand, found their usual detailed preparation lacking. The USS *Princess Matoika*, a wartime transport ship, had been hired to transport the athletes. The cramped conditions led the athletes to mutiny; some walked off the ship on arrival and were suspended. Eventually order was restored in time for the opening ceremony on 14 August 1920.

King Albert of Belgium opened the Games, and there was a service in Antwerp Cathedral in memory of those who had lost their lives in the war.

The stadium itself held 30,000 but it was usually only two-thirds full. Perhaps the Belgians were not yet ready to celebrate. The track itself was very poor and inclined to churn up when wet.

The Americans maintained their domination of the sprints, winning gold and silver in the 100 and 200 metres, with Britons taking the bronze medals. Charles Paddock was the star, probably the first to be dubbed 'the world's fastest man', and he won the 100 metres and finished second to Allan Woodring in the 200 metres, where he ran out of stamina near the line. He had the distinctive habit of jumping high at the tape with his arms in the air.

A British-born South African, Bevil Rudd, who was at Oxford University after winning the Military Cross in the war, won the 400 metres from his old opponent Guy Butler of Cambridge University, after a twisted ankle received in the 800 metres earlier had nearly caused him to miss the race.

The 800 metres was won by Albert Hill, a 31-year-old railway guard from Great Bri-

The march-past of nations at the first post-war Olympic Games at Antwerp in 1920. The nations defeated in the war were not invited.

tain, who came in with a run to pass Rudd who caught his foot in a rut in the track on the final bend. Earl Eby of the U.S.A. was second and Rudd third. Hill had served in the army throughout the war, and had the capacity to sleep before races. He completed the best double of the Games in the 1,500 metres, fellow Briton Philip Noel-Baker (winner of the Nobel Peace Prize in 1959) being second and Lawrence Shields, U.S.A., third.

The 5,000 metres, like the race in 1912, was between a Finn and a Frenchman. The Finn was the legendary Paavo Nurmi, making his first Olympic appearance. This time it was the Frenchman, Joseph Guillemot, who sprinted away up the straight, avenging the 1912 defeat of Bouin. Guillemot had been gassed in the war; Bouin had been killed.

Nurmi had his revenge in the 10,000 metres, reversing the placings. The marathon had almost been dropped from the Games, the I.O.C. having authorized its omission at the request of the Belgians and Britons. It was run, and was a triumph for Hannes Kolehmainen, who won by 12.8 seconds from Jari Lossman of Estonia, the smallest winning margin of all Olympic marathons. Kolehmainen's time was a world record, and he ran more than 572 metres further than the official marathon distance set in 1908 but not standardized in the Olympics until 1924.

The hurdles races were again a triumph for American technique. The 110-metres hurdles was won by Earl Thomson of Canada, the world record holder, who learned his skill at Dartmouth University. Americans were second and third, and filled all three medal positions in the 400-metres hurdles, won by Frank Loomis.

Percy Hodge of Great Britain, who had evolved a technique of his own in the steeplechase, won with ease. Paavo Nurmi turned out again in the 8,000-metres cross-country, winning the race and leading Finland to victory. A brilliant Italian walker, Ugo Frigerio, won both walks. Scandinavians won the pentathlon and decathlon: Eero Lehtonen of Finland, the former; and Helge Lovland of Norway, the latter.

The field events, apart from Great Britain's win in the tug-of-war, were shared by the U.S.A., Finland and Sweden, with the Finns taking all the javelin medals. Frank Foss of the U.S.A. cleared over four metres in the pole vault for an impressive win. Paddy Ryan continued an astonishing tradition in the hammer in which all the Olympic champions so far were Irish-born Americans.

The events in the pool were also dominated by Americans and Scandinavians. Duke

Top: Albert Hill of Great Britain completed a double victory in the 800 metres and 1,500 metres in 1920. Only Peter Snell in 1964 has since achieved this feat.

Above: Frank Loomis of the U.S.A. takes the last hurdle on his way to a 400-metres hurdles gold medal.

Antwerp

Kahanamoku repeated his 1912 100-metres freestyle win, and his Hawaiian compatriot Warren Kealoha won the 100-metres backstroke. Norman Ross of the U.S.A. won the longer freestyle races and Sweden's Haken Malmroth achieved a breaststroke double.

The U.S.A. had sent a strong women's squad to the Olympics for the first time. They won all three swimming events and Ethelda Bleibtrey alone won three gold medals. Aileen Riggin, a 14-year-old American schoolgirl, won the springboard diving.

Great Britain won the water polo, but the team was physically attacked by the defeated Belgian finalists, and the home crowd rioted.

It was the third gold medal in the event for the British captain, Paul Radmilovic.

Boxing attracted an international entry for the first time, and five countries supplied winners. Two American winners became famous in the professional sphere; Frank de Genaro became world flyweight champion and Eddie Eagan became the New York State Boxing Commission chairman.

The rowing was notable for an American victory in the eights where the crack British Leander crew was defeated, and for two gold medals which were won by John Kelly, one of America's greatest oarsmen and the father of Grace Kelly, later Princess Grace of

Below: Percy Hodge of Great Britain, out on his own, as he wins the 3,000-metres steeplechase.

Below right: Paddy Ryan becomes the third hammer-throwing champion to have been born in Ireland but to win for the U.S.A.

Monaco. In the single sculls Kelly just beat Jack Beresford, Britain's famous oarsman, in an exciting race.

Italy won five of the six fencing events, with Nedo Nadi winning two individual and three team gold medals. One of the immortals of tennis, Suzanne Lenglen of France, won two gold medals; the U.S.A. shocked France by winning the rugby final 8–0; and the soccer final was a disaster when the Czechs

walked off after a series of bad decisions culminated in one of their players being sent off – the home team, Belgium, was awarded the match.

There was a long shooting programme in which the U.S.A. did well, with the Scandinavian countries not far behind. Norway dominated the yachting, Finland and Sweden the wrestling.

On the whole the Games was very much a

Two lawn tennis gold medals were won at Antwerp by Suzanne Lenglen of France, one of the greatest-ever women players.

Antwerp

Right: Duke Kahanamoku of the U.S.A., who was born in Hawaii, won swimming medals at three Olympics, including the 100-metres freestyle gold in 1920.

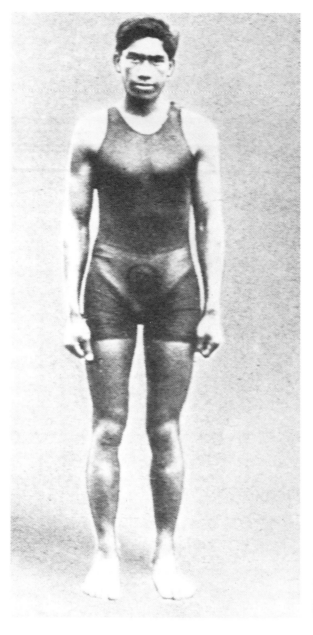

Far right: The Italian fencer, Nedo Nadi, was perhaps the best-ever. Despite the interruption of the war he won six Olympic gold medals, including five at the 1920 Games.

post-war austerity affair, but the Belgians did as well as anybody could hope, and helped re-establish the Olympics after an eight-year break. For the first time American supremacy in the track and field events had been challenged: it was a remarkable achievement for relatively small Finland to win as many gold medals as the U.S.A. It was noticeable that Scandinavians were performing well in events inside and outside the stadium.

The nationalistic fervour exhibited by the U.S.A. and Great Britain since 1908 had not escaped Coubertin's notice, and in 1913 he declared the publication of league tables of results to be 'un-Olympic'. This did not deter the newspapers from compiling them.

There had been a powerful movement in Great Britain before and during the 1920 Games to make it Britain's last. As the inventors of many of the world's modern sports, Great Britain already possessed a full sporting programme, and interest was greater in parochial affairs such as Test matches and the Football Association cup final than in the Olympics. Consequently Olympic expenses were borne largely by a few wealthy men, the public being unwilling to subscribe. It was suggested that the poorly funded British team had no chance of competing equally in such a wide variety of sports outside track and field, where it was felt that the British attitude was truly amateur, whereas some other nations' attitudes were almost professional. The British dilemma regarding amateur attitudes was explored in relation to Harold Abrahams and the 1924 Games in the Oscar-winning film, *Chariots of Fire*. The British Olympic Council's official report of the 1912 Stockholm Games had included this sentence: 'The Council would suggest that this country should cease to be represented at future Olympic Games unless that representation is worthy not merely of the athletes themselves, but of the nation in whose name they will compete.' Theodore Cook, the English

member of the I.O.C., reminded the Editor of *The Times* of this in 1920, and urged that Great Britain should take no further part in the Olympic movement. There was a counter-movement, of course, led by many of the 1920 team, who in time-honoured fashion also addressed a letter to the Editor of *The Times*. Luckily for everybody the latter's view prevailed.

Coubertin had it right as usual in his speech after the Games: 'These festivals are above all festivals of human unity.' It was not always to be so, but it was an ideal worth striving for.

Hannes Kolehmainen

Born on 9 December 1889 in Kuopio, 'Hannes' (short for Johannes) Kolehmainen was the first great Finnish distance runner, the inspirer of a long line of men like Nurmi, Ritola, Haegg and Viren, who became known as the 'Flying Finns'. Kolehmainen's greatest wins were in the 1912 Olympics, where he won every race he entered, taking gold in the 5,000 and 10,000 metres, winning the 8,000 metres cross-country and setting a world record in the 3,000 metres team race. He broke the world record for 5,000 metres later in 1912, and went to the United States in 1913, where in five years he won seven national

championships and set many American all-comers records, including a world record for 20,000 metres. In 1920 he won the marathon in the Antwerp Olympics, and then set further world records at 25,000 and 30,000 metres. He retired to run a sports shop in Helsinki. He won four individual Olympic Gold medals and one silver team medal, but there is no doubt that he would have won three or four more gold medals had the 1916 Games not been abandoned. At the Helsinki Olympics in 1952, he and Nurmi, possibly the two greatest distance runners of all time, lit the two Olympic flames. He died in Helsinki on 11 November 1966.

Hannes Kolehmainen, the first of the outstanding Finnish distance runners, enters the stadium in 1920 to end a superb Olympic career by winning the marathon.

Chamonix

Some winter sports had been included in earlier Olympics. Figure skating had been held at London in 1908 because London had a suitable rink, and figure skating and ice hockey had been in the programme at Antwerp in 1920.

At the I.O.C. meeting in 1921 the following motion was passed: 'The Congress (of National Olympic Committees) suggests to the International Olympic Committee that in all countries where Olympic Games are held and where it is also possible to organize winter sports competitions, such competitions should be put under the patronage of the I.O.C. and arranged in accordance with the rules of the international sports associations concerned.'

Thus the Winter Olympics were born, and in 1922 Chamonix, France, was chosen as the first venue. The Games was only recognized as Olympic in retrospect, however, being called at the time the Chamonix International Winter Sports Week.

In 1925 it was decided that the I.O.C. would sanction a special cycle of the Olympic Winter Games, to take place in the same years

Above: At the first Winter Olympics at Chamonix in 1924 Herma Plank-Szabo of Austria won the women's figure skating title.

Right: Thorleif Haug of Norway won three gold medals in Nordic skiing, both cross-country races and the combination.

Far right: The individual ski-jumping title was won by Tullin Thams of Norway.

as the Summer Games, and to be called the first, second, third Winter Games etc. At the I.O.C. meeting in 1926, it was agreed that the Games which had been held in 1924 would be known as the first Winter Olympics.

Sixteen countries sent nearly 300 competitors, 13 of them women, to contest 14 events at Chamonix. The Winter Games are always dependent on the weather, and at Chamonix it was nearly a disaster. On 23 December 1923 there was no snow at all; on 24 December it was over a metre deep, and 36,000 square metres had to be shifted from the skating rink. A week before the start on 25 January 1924 rain turned the speed-skating stadium into a lake, but luckily the freeze came just in time, and the Games began without a problem.

The Nordic skiing was a clean sweep for Norway. Thorleif Haug won the two races with fellow Norwegians winning three of the four minor medals. Tullin Thams won the 60-metres ski jump with Norwegians in the minor places, and Thorleif Haug won the gold for the Nordic combined, again from his compatriots. As Haug won the bronze in the ski jump, he has a unique collection of medals. Unfortunately his ski-jump win was marred as several ski jumpers were hurt in practice due to the frozen state of the snow.

The individual figure-skating gold medals went to two of the established stars of the sport. Gillis Grafstroem, a world champion who had won the gold at Antwerp, won the men's for Sweden, and Herma Plank-Szabo of Austria, the world champion, won the women's. Norway's champion, an 11-year-old who was to become supreme, Sonja Henie, finished well down the list.

Surprisingly, Norway was vanquished in the speed skating, winning several lesser medals in each event but without winning a gold. Charles Jewtraw of the U.S.A. won the 500-metres sprint, and Finns won the other three events, Clas Thunberg getting two golds and a silver behind Julius Skutnabb. Thunberg was also given a gold medal for his combined performance, the only time this medal has been awarded.

Left: Two Finns won four speed-skating gold medals. Julius Skutnabb (left) won one and Clas Thunberg (right) won three.

The four-man bobsleigh event was won by Switzerland's second crew from Great Britain's second crew and Belgium's first. There were many serious crashes which eliminated several crews, British and French sledders breaking limbs.

The ice hockey was followed with great excitement, although it was one-sided, the Canadians being in a class of their own, winning all their matches by big scores.

Baron Pierre de Coubertin presented the medals to the winners at the closing ceremony.

Action in the ice-hockey match between Canada and the U.S.A. The Canadians were supreme in early ice-hockey competitions.

Paris

At the request of Baron de Coubertin the eighth Olympiad was held in Paris. Coubertin was near retirement, and wished to wipe out the memory of the badly run Games of 1900. Paris was the first city to hold two Olympic Games (Los Angeles in 1984 is the third). Coubertin also looked further ahead, and the I.O.C. meeting of 1921 selected Amsterdam for 1928 and Los Angeles as likely for 1932. It was agreed at this meeting that at future Olympics the winners' names should be set in the walls of the stadium. Another innovation was the new Olympic motto: *citius, altius, fortius* (faster, higher, stronger), coined by a French monk, Father Henri Didon.

The plans of the I.O.C. regularly seemed destined to be thwarted, and the Seine flood in the winter of 1923 threatened another disappointment, but the problem was overcome. In fact one of the hardships of the Games was the intense heat, which reached 45°C (113°F) when the 10,000 metres was run.

The athletics started on 5 July in the Colombes stadium. Huts were built round the stadium for the athletes, foreshadowing the later Olympic villages.

The 100 metres provided one of the great races of the Games, and defeat for the U.S.A. for only the second time. Harold Abrahams had been eliminated in the second round in 1920, but had learned a lot about dedication from the Americans. Against the background of strongly voiced English sentiments on the spirit of amateurism and the iniquity of the

Above: Harold Abrahams of Great Britain won the 100 metres in the 1924 Olympic Games. Jackson Scholz of the U.S.A. (centre) was second, and Arthur Porritt of New Zealand (left) was third.

An illustration by George Leroux of the progress of a race in the 1924 Olympics.

American's systematic training which had rumbled on since the 1912 Games, Abrahams asked the foremost coach of the day, Sam Mussabini, to train him to win the title. It was an attitude which brought him into conflict with the Cambridge University authorities, and he was accused of unsporting behaviour. In the Games, he won each of his races in the new Olympic record time of 10.6 seconds, and won the gold medal convincingly.

The Americans gained revenge in the 200 metres, where Abrahams ran poorly in the final. Jackson Scholz, who had been second in the 100 metres, won the 200 metres from Charlie Paddock, with Eric Liddell of Great Britain third.

Eric Liddell, whose story was coupled with that of Abrahams to make *Chariots of Fire*, was Great Britain's 100-yards champion and record-holder (his 9.7 seconds in 1923 stood until 1958). He was the son of a Scottish missionary and was born in China, and his strong religious views prevented him from contesting the 100 metres in Paris, as he knew the heats were scheduled for Sunday, a day on which he would not race. Instead he decided to concentrate on the 200 metres and 400 metres. He was not at his best when third in the 200 metres, the winning time being slower than his British record the year before, but in the 400 metres, a rare event for him, he was inspired, setting off at top pace and maintaining it for an easy win in world record time. Liddell was also a rugby union international. He returned to China the year after his great win, and died in a Japanese concentration camp in 1945 when only 43.

Great Britain also won the 800 metres, Douglas Lowe winning from Switzerland's Paul Martin.

In the 1,500 metres the star of the Games, Paavo Nurmi, won the gold medal, running with his watch in his hand (there were no lap times then) and looking machine-like as his even pace seemed to take nothing out of him whatever. Having run heats of the 1,500 and 5,000 metres on the previous two days, Nurmi turned out for the 5,000 metres final little more than an hour after winning the

Above: Jackson Scholz of the U.S.A. won the 200 metres, with Charles Paddock, second, making his usual leap for the tape on the left. Eric Liddell (451) was third.

Eric Liddell won the 400 metres in world record time in 1924. His story and that of 100-metres champion Harold Abrahams was the subject of a film, *Chariots of Fire*, in the 1980s.

Paris

1,500 metres. Ville Ritola, Nurmi's great countryman, tried to tire Nurmi by setting a strong pace, but Nurmi came through to win by two metres, with the Swedish runner, Edwin Wide, half a minute behind the two leaders.

The following day Nurmi won his heat of the 3,000-metres team race. He then won the 10,000-metres cross-country, leading Finland to a team victory. Next he and Finland won the 3,000-metres team final. Second to Nurmi in these three races was Ville Ritola, but in the 10,000 metres, run earlier in the Games, he did not have Nurmi with whom to contend. Six weeks before he had beaten Nurmi's 10,000 metres world record, and the Finnish selectors had left the race to him, no doubt thinking that Nurmi had enough to do. The race was run in heat described as 'like a furnace', but Ritola reduced his world record by 12 seconds and won comfortably by over half a minute. It was said that an aggrieved Nurmi did a training run even faster, but this is possibly legend, although he was later to recapture the world record. Ville Ritola also won the 3,000-metres steeplechase in another world best time. But the Finns were not finished yet, for the 35-year-old Albin Stenroos won the marathon by nearly six minutes.

Ugo Frigerio, Italy's stylish walker, won the 10-km walk to add to the two golds he had won at Antwerp, and the only other winner in track and field not to be American, Finnish or British was Anthony Winter of Australia, who won the triple jump with a world record.

American dominance was only slightly dented in the two hurdles races, where they won three medals instead of their customary five or so. They provided both winners, Dan Kinsey and Morgan Taylor, and Taylor in the 400-metres hurdles would have claimed a world record but for knocking over a barrier, which under the rules of the time precluded a record.

World records were set, however, in both relays, both won by the United States. There were dual winners for the U.S.A. in Harold Osborn, high jump and decathlon, and Clarence Houser, discus and shot. Houser was the first discus thrower to perfect the rotating technique now universal, and his Olympic double is the only one apart from Garrett's in the 1896 Games. Fred Tootell of the U.S.A. at last broke the monopoly of Irish-born hammer winners, but Matt McGrath was second. Jonni Myyra of Finland repeated his javelin victory of 1920, as did his countryman Eero

The Olympic oath is sworn by the French athlete, Geo Andre, at the 1924 Olympics. The oath was first sworn at the Antwerp Games of 1920.

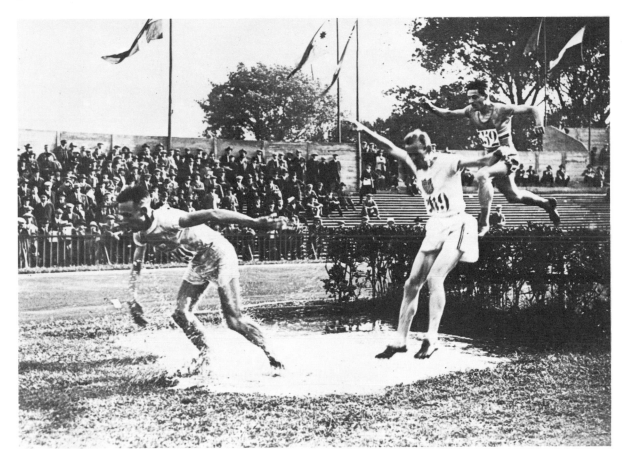

Left: Ville Ritola of Finland, the eventual winner, leads the field over the water in the 3,000-metres steeplechase, followed by E. Rick (U.S.A.) and L. Muskat (Hungary), neither of whom won medals.

Lehtonen in the last track and field pentathlon of the Games. American William DeHart Hubbard won the long jump, but could not beat the mark of Robert Le Gendre the day before in the pentathlon. Le Gendre was so annoyed at not being selected for the American long jump team that he determined to show them wrong in the pentathlon. He broke the world long jump record, but it earned him only a pentathlon bronze. American supremacy in the pole vault was maintained with 17-year-old Lee Barnes winning after a jump-off.

The swimming was a triumph for the U.S.A., who won all but three titles. Some exceptional swimmers made their first appearances. Johnny Weissmuller (U.S.A.), in the 100-metres freestyle, beat into second place the man who had won the event in 1912 and 1920, Duke Kahanamoku, and added the 400-metres freestyle gold, beating Arne Borg of Sweden and Andrew Charlton of Australia. 'Boy' Charlton, only 16 years old, beat Borg in the 1,500-metre freestyle, reducing Borg's new world record, set in the heats, by over a minute, and winning by 34.8 seconds.

Albert White (U.S.A.) won both springboard and highboard diving events, and Aileen Riggin lost her springboard diving title to Elisabeth Becker (U.S.A.), but by getting a bronze in the 100-metres backstroke became the first woman to win medals in swimming and diving. Gertrude Ederle (U.S.A.), who won two bronze medals, became the first woman to swim the English Channel two years later.

Harold Osborn of the U.S.A. on his way to winning the high jump in 1924.

Paris

The home country, France, was forced to win most of her medals in cycling and fencing, sports in which the French have specialized. Lucien Michard, who won the 1,000-metres cycling sprint, was later four times world professional champion and one of France's best-known riders. Armand Blanchonnet and France were easy winners of the individual and team road-races. Roger Ducret was France's fencing star, winning the foil and two team golds.

In the boxing, the two American winners, flyweight Fidel LaBarba and featherweight John Fields, were two more Olympic champions who went on to win world professional titles. LaBarba won his from Frank de Genaro, the Olympic champion of 1920. The biggest boxing story was in the middleweight class. Great Britain's Harry Mallin, one of the world's greatest amateur boxers, 'lost' a controversial quarter-final against Frenchman Roger Brousse, whose tactics brought several warnings. Apart from it being a generally bad decision, Brousse had bitten Mallin violently on the chest in the last round, an incident missed by the referee (who for the first time in the Games was outside the ring). Luckily other officials had seen it and the teethmarks were obvious, so the decision was reversed, but not until all the English-speaking nations had threatened to withdraw in a body. Mallin beat his fellow-Briton John

Elliott in the final to become the first boxer to retain an Olympic title.

The rowing saw John Kelly win a third gold medal when he and his team-mate, Paul Costello, retained the double sculls for the U.S.A., but Kelly had lost his U.S. single sculls title and was thus unable to repeat his thrilling 1920 race with Great Britain's Jack Beresford. Beresford comfortably won his first Olympic gold. The U.S.A. won the eights gold medal again; Benjamin Spock, the famous baby-book author, was a member of the crew.

The last Olympic tennis tournaments were held and provided a clean sweep for the U.S.A. Suzanne Lenglen declined to take part and 18-year-old Helen Wills won two gold medals, as did Vincent Richards and Hazel Wightman, whose name is perpetuated by the Wightman Cup.

Rugby was also an Olympic sport for the last time, and the holders, the U.S.A., surprisingly were the last winners, and are thus current Olympic champions, a fact well-known to sports quizmasters.

The Americans did best at freestyle wrestling, but the Scandinavians swept the board at Greco-Roman. Norway won two of three yachting golds; France and Italy shared the weightlifting.

The Paris Games was a great success in one way with six world records and two world

Johnny Weissmuller of the U.S.A. (centre) after winning the 400-metres freestyle in 1924. He is flanked by two other swimmers who won Olympic gold medals, Andrew 'Boy' Charlton of Australia (left) and Arne Borg of Sweden (right).

best performances set in track and field events. It was well supported by the public, but still made a healthy loss for French tax-payers.

The Finns were again the stars of the Games, Nurmi and Ritola being in a class of their own. The U.S.A. easily won the most medals, with Finland, France and Great Britain next, but on the running track the Finns were best. Nations were as jealous as ever of their comparative performances. *The Times* correspondent, complaining of the unwieldy programme, pointed out that weightlifting counted 22 times as much as the 100 yards (*sic*) and continued: 'Does anybody believe that weightlifting is 22 times as important as being the fastest runner in the world, or that the winning of the 100 yards (*sic*) deserves less than one-two-thousandths of the Olympic glory?' Abrahams, of course, had won the 100 'yards'. On the other hand, and less logically, the New York *Evening World* correspondent wanted fewer distance events, to reduce the threat of Finland to U.S. mastery.

The Games was again marred by ugly incident. The boxing controversy has already been mentioned, but there were also free fights in the rugby where the methods of American football did not mix with French ideas of rugby, and in the fencing, where the French, Italians and Hungarians squabbled. There was further trouble at the men's singles tennis final and at a water polo match where the crowd demonstrated against the Americans.

All this led *The Times* to run a story headed 'Olympic Games Doomed' and an editorial 'No More Olympic Games'. The charges against the Games were 'miscellaneous turbulence, shameful disorder, storms of abuse, free fights, the drowning of national anthems . . . persistent hostility to the Americans.' It was suggested that nobody would ask the British public to subscribe to sending a team to other Games, and it was expected that the Americans would take a similar line and that 'the death knell of the Olympic Games has, in fact, been sounded.'

This view was not born of disappointment, for the British had done well, and there were American and French voices to support *The Times'* sentiments.

Coubertin was not among them, pointing out that 50 hoodlums in a crowd are enough to cause trouble, a fact which British soccer followers discovered in the 1970s and 1980s. Coubertin, the dreamer, dreamed on. 'I dream of the 26th and 28th Olympiads in the years 1996 and 2004,' he said.

After the Games, he retired as President of the I.O.C. (he was 61), but remained a member until his death.

Clarence Pinkston of the U.S.A. in the springboard diving of 1924. He won two bronze diving medals in 1924, having won gold and silver in 1920.

Oscar and Alfred Swahn

No father-and-son pair can have such a remarkable Olympic record as Oscar Swahn, born in Tanum, Sweden, on 20 October 1847, and his son Alfred Swahn, born in Uddevalla on 20 August 1879. They were both outstanding riflemen. The elder Swahn was already 49 when the modern Olympics began. He did not compete until the 1908 London Olympics when he was 61, he and his son both taking part. Oscar, the elder, won an individual gold medal and a team gold and bronze; Alfred, the younger, won a team gold. In 1912 Oscar won team gold and individual bronze, Alfred individual and team gold. In 1920 Oscar (aged 73) won his last medal, a team silver, Alfred individual and team silver and a team bronze. In 1924 Oscar qualified for the Paris Games (aged 77) but was too ill to go, Alfred won individual bronze and team silver and bronze. That ended their Olympic careers: a joint haul of six gold, four silver and five bronze medals. Oscar died on 1 May 1927, Alfred on 16 March 1931.

St. Moritz

Opposite: Sonja Henie of Norway won the first of her three figure-skating gold medals in 1928, after competing as an 11-year-old in 1924.

Winter sports were enjoying a big advance in popularity in the 1920s. The 1924 Winter Olympics had been a success, and everything looked set for a further step forward in St. Moritz in February 1928. Nine further countries took part in the Olympics, making 25, and the number of competitors increased to 495, 27 of them women. Unfortunately, dramatic changes in the weather caused difficulties for the organizers. Once again the Scandinavian countries did best, with Norway leading the way.

In the Nordic skiing events, Johan Grottumsbraaten of Norway easily won the 18-km cross-country in which he was followed home by two other Norwegians. He completed a double in the combined event (18 km and ski jump), which again provided a clean sweep of the medals for Norway. Grottumsbraaten had taken a silver and two bronze in 1924. The 50-km cross-country was held in very heavy weather and took 4 hours 52 minutes 03 seconds, over an hour longer

than in 1924. It was won by Per Erik Hedlund, who led home two fellow Swedes. The ski jumping was won by Alf Andersen of Norway, but a Czech, Rudolf Burkert, took the bronze, setting a record as the only central European to win a Nordic skiing medal before 1956.

In the figure skating, Gillis Grafstroem of Sweden won his third successive gold medal in the men's event, beating Willy Boeckl into second place for the second time. The women's event went to the not-quite-16-year-old Sonja Henie of Norway, the first of three wins. She had added an artistic element to the freestyle phase, and was the star of the Games. The pairs gold medal went to a French couple, Pierre Brunet and Andrèe Joly, who were to marry and repeat their win in 1932.

The speed-skating gold medals were shared by Finland and Norway, the 500 metres itself being shared by Clas Thunberg of Finland and Bernt Evensen of Norway, who beat

Johan Grottumsbraaten of Norway won two Nordic skiing gold medals in 1928 including the combined medal, and won another in 1932.

48

skaters from Finland, Norway and the U.S.A., who each won a bronze, by 0.2 seconds. Thunberg repeated his win in the 1,500 metres, and Ivar Ballangrud of Norway won the 5,000 metres. Evensen won silver and bronze in these events. The 10,000 metres was abandoned after a sudden thaw, when the favourite, Evensen again, was being led by Irving Jaffee of the U.S.A., who was to win in 1932. Heavy rain caused the cancellation of all the events on 15 February, but a frost set in to allow the Games to proceed.

The thaw caused the four-men bobsleigh event to be reduced to two runs instead of four, and of the 23 teams the U.S.A. II bob, driven by William Fiske, won the gold from the U.S.A. I bob, driven by Jennison Heaton, with Germany II third.

There was a skeleton tobogganing event, in which competitors lay chest down on a sliding seat on a toboggan of two steel runners with a platform. A St. Moritz speciality, it was held on the Cresta Run, and Jennison Heaton won for the U.S.A., with his brother, John, second and the Earl of Northesk of Great Britain third.

The ice hockey event was another comfortable exercise for Canada, who were placed straight into the last four, where they were joined by Sweden, Switzerland and Great Britain. Canada beat the others with ease, scoring 38 goals to nil.

The Winter Olympics had again proved successful, without the controversies which had so far figured regularly in the Summer Games. There were, of course, fewer countries competing, with smaller teams, and the main competitors knew each other well through frequent competition.

The biggest advance in 1928 occurred at the conference table where Sir Arnold Lunn, a great British pioneer of Alpine skiing, persuaded the Fédération Internationale de Ski, of which he was a council member, to include experimental downhill and slalom competitions in future Games. In fact Alpine events, which now attract as much attention as any other events, were introduced into the Olympics in 1936.

Amsterdam

The Amsterdam Games of 1928 was another step forward in the history of the Olympics. For the first time women took part in track and field athletics. There were just over 3,000 competitors, 290 of them women, from 46 nations. The Germans, Austrians, Hungarians and Bulgarians were back, Germany with a large squad of about 300. The U.S.S.R. remained aloof and announced its own Games. The French government refused to finance a French team, but were shamed into doing so by François Coty of the cosmetics empire who began a subscription.

A new stadium to hold 40,000 spectators was built, and the Games was enthusiastically attended. The French boycotted the opening ceremony and almost the Games itself, because of the anti-French and pro-German remarks of a gateman whom the Dutch organizers were slow to remove.

The Games opened on 28 July and the track events were remarkable for the almost complete eclipse of the Americans in races in which they had previously enjoyed near-monopolies. The 100 metres and 200 metres were both won by Percy Williams, a Cana-dian just turned 20 years old. In the shorter sprint he was away first after three false starts and led throughout to win from Jack London of London, Great Britain, and George Lammers of Germany. In the longer sprint he came with a strong finish to win from another Briton, Walter Rangeley, and another German, Helmuth Koernig. The Americans, who had won 12 of 16 gold medals in previous sprints, were medal-less.

American pride was salvaged in the 400 metres by a footballer from Syracuse, Ray Barbuti. Barbuti may have been a little lucky to win, as James Ball of Canada ran too far in his lane, not realizing that he could 'break' for the inside. Ball just failed to catch Barbuti in a desperate finish.

The 800 metres was another smooth win for Great Britain's Douglas Lowe, who retained his title won in 1924. An unlucky runner in the 800 metres was the German record-holder, Otto Peltzer, who was below his best through injury, but Lowe beat him later in a special challenge match.

Finland won the 1,500 metres again with one of their lesser known athletes, Harri

A soccer player, Henri Denis, swore the Olympic oath at the opening ceremony in Amsterdam in 1928, following the current practice of holding his country's flag by one hand.

Larva, who ran an even-paced race, like Nurmi, and spurted powerfully in the straight to pass a Frenchman, Jules Ladoumègue, who appeared to have the race won. Another Finn, Eino Purje, was third.

The great Finnish double-act of Ville Ritola and Paavo Nurmi was supreme again in the longer races. Ritola surprisingly won the 5,000 metres comparatively easily from Nurmi, but Nurmi showed his supremacy in the 10,000 metres, with Ritola second. The Swede, Edwin Wide, was third in each case. Poor Wide can reflect that his one silver and three bronze medals in 1924 and 1928 would have been four gold without Ritola and Nurmi, and he would be acclaimed as one of the immortals of the track.

Nurmi and Ritola turned out again in the 3,000-metres steeplechase, and showed they were human. Nurmi, who was a novice at the water jump, attempted, in a heat, to leap from the top of the hurdle, landed on his back in the muddy slime, and ruined his watch. He lost 40 metres, and thereafter walked through the water. He still won the heat. Ritola was little better despite having won the event in 1924. Their lack of technique was exposed in the final; Ritola retired, but Nurmi finished second, although ten seconds behind. It made little difference to the Finns. Toivo Loukola won and Ove Andersen was third to complete a clean sweep of the medals.

The Americans did better in the hurdles than the flat sprints, filling the minor places in each. A South African, Sydney Atkinson, the silver medalist of 1924, won the 110-metres hurdles from Stephen Anderson and John Collier, and a Briton, Lord Burghley, the 400-metres hurdles from Frank Cuhel and Morgan Taylor, the 1924 winner. Lord Burghley's win was most popular, and later, as the Marquess of Exeter, he was a long-serving British official and a member of the I.O.C.

The sprinting in depth of the U.S.A. was vindicated in the two relay races, each being won comfortably enough from Germany. Ray Barbuti won his second gold medal in the longer relay.

Above: Only 19 years old, Percy Williams of Canada celebrates with delighted supporters after winning both the 100 metres and 200 metres in 1928.

Great Britain's 800-metres specialist Douglas Lowe, who repeated his 1924 win in 1928, becomes the first to win the event twice.

Amsterdam

The start of the 10,000 metres in 1928. Paavo Nurmi, the great Finnish runner, is on the extreme right. His rival and fellow-countryman, Ville Ritola, who finished second to him, is third from the left. Edwin Wide, who finished third, is third from the right.

Paavo Nurmi

Paavo Nurmi's world records have long since been surpassed, as is the fate of all records, but on the strength of his long career, his 22 world records, his nine Olympic gold medals, his four years of never losing a race and his manner of victory, he must be accounted the greatest runner of all time. He was born on 13 June 1897 at Turku, Finland, and did not really come to the fore as an athlete until he was a soldier in his early twenties. He was selected for Finland's squad for the 1920 Olympic Games and began his amazing Olympic career by winning the gold medal in the 10,000 metres, the silver in the 5,000 metres and the gold medals in the individual and team cross-country. He started breaking world records in June 1921 with a 10,000-metres time, breaking seven more before the 1924 Olympics, at distances of 1,500 metres, a mile, 2,000 metres, 3,000 metres, 3 miles and 5,000 metres. The 1924 Olympic Games in Paris was his peak, and 10 July perhaps his greatest day. Unbeaten for four years, he won the 1,500 metres and 5,000 metres gold medals with just over an hour's rest between them. He went on to win the cross-country event a couple of days later, winning the individual and team gold medals, and next day repeated the double in the 3,000 metres team race. He won all his heats in these events. He was not selected for the 10,000 metres, which he probably would also have won. Before the end of the year Nurmi had set new world records in the 10,000 metres and four and five miles. He went to the U.S.A. for five months, where he showed he was not infallible, losing two of his 70 races. The style of his running was remarkable. Before lap times were announced, he ran with a stop watch in his hand, constantly consulting it so that he ran at an even pace. Occasionally he would set his watch down carefully beside the track before running the last lap. He ran with his body upright, never seeming to tire. He became known as a mechanical man. Having recaptured or set new world records at 2,000 and 3,000 metres and in the 4 × 1,500-metres relay, he came to the 1928 Amsterdam Olympics to win more medals, taking the 10,000 metres gold but 'only' the silver behind Ritola in the 5,000 metres. He also tried the 3,000-metres steeplechase, and took another silver. As the 1932 Olympics approached he set more world records for the 3,000 metres, six miles, 15,000 metres, 10 miles, 1 hour and 20,000 metres. His distances were getting longer, and he trained for the marathon at the 1932 Olympics. Trials suggested he could win, but the I.A.A.F. decided he had infringed the amateur code with excessive expenses and although he travelled to Los Angeles he was not allowed to compete. The decision was rescinded for domestic competition in Finland, but it left him bitter. At the 1952 Olympic Games in Helsinki he carried the Olympic torch on its last stage, and he and his great inspiration, Hannes Kolehmainen, lit the flames in the stadium, outside which there is a bronze statue of him. He died on 2 October 1973 in Helsinki.

Ville Ritola of Finland, Paavo Nurmo of Finland and Edwin Wide of Sweden in the order in which they finished in the 5,000 metres in Amsterdam.

Below. The finish of the 110-metres hurdles, with South African Sydney Atkinson (dark vest) just beating Stephen Anderson of the U.S.A. (second) and John Collier of the U.S.A. (third).

For once the Finns misjudged the marathon. The favourite was Martti Marttelin, but he and two Japanese, Kanematsu Yamada and Selichiro Tsuda, and an American, Joie Ray, appeared to set too hot a pace. Marttelin held on for third, but was passed near the finish by a French Algerian, Boughera El Ouafi, who won the gold, and a Chilean, Miguel Plaza.

The U.S.A. recovered some lost prestige in the field events. Americans came first and second in the high jump (won by Robert King) and first and third in the long jump (Ed

Left: Lord Burghley (444), the British 400-metres hurdler, won the event in the 1928 Olympics.

Amsterdam

The winner of the marathon in 1928 was the Frenchman from Algeria, Boughera El Ouafi.

Right: The winner of the 1928 hammer final, Patrick O'Callaghan, was the fourth Irish-born winner, but was the first actually to represent Ireland. The others had represented the U.S.A.

Far right: The discus winner in 1928 was American Clarence Houser, who was repeating his 1924 victory.

Hamm took the gold). The only representative from Haiti, Silvio Cator, divided the Americans in the long jump. His silver is the only Olympic medal ever won by his country at athletics. The triple jump provided Japan with her first-ever gold medal, won by Mikio Oda, who was a member of the organizing committee in Tokyo in 1964.

For the second successive Games Americans took all three pole vault medals, the winner being Sabin Carr, with the 1924 winner Lee Barnes, now 21, dropping back to fifth.

In the throwing events, John Kuck (U.S.A.) won the shot, and Dr. Clarence Houser (also U.S.A.), who had won both shot and discus in 1924, repeated his discus win but only after qualifying for the final with his last throw. Ireland at last got her reward in the hammer, Dr. Pat O'Callaghan winning his country's first gold, after three Irish-born throwers had won previously for the U.S.A. O'Callaghan, an all-round athlete, had been throwing for only a year, but had been trained by John Flanagan, the great triple winner, who had returned to Ireland. A

Swede maintained the Scandinavian record of having always won the javelin, Erik Lundkvist taking the gold.

The decathlon was another victory for Finns, who took the first two places, with Paavo Yrjola taking the gold.

Canada dominated the new women's track and field events and was the only country to take two gold medals. Elisabeth Robinson (U.S.A.) won the 100 metres from two Canadian girls. A third Canadian, Myrtle Cook, was disqualified after two false starts and was inconsolable. Canada won the 4 × 100-metres relay comfortably. A German, Lina Radke, won the 800 metres, but so many girls collapsed in distress at the end of the race that there was much discussion about the suitability of such 'killer' events for women. It was to be 1960 before women again raced further than 200 metres in the Olympics. Another Canadian win came in the high jump, where Ethel Catherwood, much admired by the newspapers of the day for her beauty, jumped 1.59 metres for the gold. A Pole, Helena Konopacka, won the discus.

There was an entry of 33 competitors from 11 countries for the modern pentathlon, and for the first time Swedes did not take *all* the medals – a German took the bronze. Sweden's Sven Thofelt won the gold.

In the swimming pool Americans took 10 of the 15 medals, five in the men's events and five in the women's. Five swimmers or divers took two gold medals. The only competitor to do so in individual events was the American diver, Pete Desjardins, who had taken the silver in the 1924 springboard while still a 17-year-old student. Other individual gold winners who took another gold in the relays were the Americans, Johnny Weissmuller, George Kojac, Martha Norelius and Albina Osipowich, who was only 14 years old. Arne Borg of Sweden at last won a gold medal, beating Boy Charlton of Australia in the 1,500-metres freestyle, after getting a bronze in the 400-metres freestyle, where Charlton won another silver.

The boxing was marred once again by more incompetent decisions. In one case, after a Czechoslovakian was adjudged to have lost to an Italian, the spectators rioted and when

The high-jump victor, maintaining the American domination of the event, was Robert King.

the Czech, Jan Hermanck, tried to regain the ring, it provoked fighting between the police and the crowd. M. Paul Rousseau, the vice-president of the International Boxing Federation, said the whole tournament was nothing but a scandalous travesty, and an

Women ran an 800-metres race for the first time in 1928, but it was not run again until 1960. The winner was Lina Radke of Germany, seen finishing ahead of Kinuye Hitomi of Japan.

Below: Elizabeth Robinson of the U.S.A. (879) just beats Fanny Rosenfeld (left) and Ethel Smith (right), both of Canada, in the 100 metres final.

English official predicted it would be the end of Olympic boxing. The Italians won three gold medals and the Argentinians two.

Switzerland won five of the seven men's gymnastics events, Georges Miez winning the horizontal bar and the combined. For the first time there was a women's team event, won by Holland from Italy and Great Britain. It would be another 24 years before there would be individual events for women.

Gold medals in the seven rowing events were shared by six countries, the most notable performance coming from Paul Costello of the U.S.A., who, with a new partner, Charles McIlraine, won the double sculls for the third time. The equestrian events were also shared. The Dutch cheered an individual three-day event win by Lt. Charles F. Pahud de Mortanges riding Marcroix, who also helped Holland win a second consecutive team gold.

The soccer was again watched by huge crowds. Eighteen teams took part, but Great Britain, the founders of the modern game, refused to compete because of the sham amateurism of many of the other nations. Uruguay retained the title after a rough final with Argentina, which needed a replay. On the strength of their wins, Uruguay were awarded the first World Cup in 1930, which they won with many of the same players which recorded the Olympic victories.

England had won the previous field hockey tournaments in the Olympics, but India beat the favourites, Holland, before 50,000 people in the final, to begin a run of six consecutive wins. Dhyan Chand and Richard Allan were the stars of a wonderful team.

The U.S.A. won the most medals overall, led the track and field, but again Finland had proved best on the running track, and the Americans were most disappointed with their results. Unfortunately Major-General Douglas MacArthur, the President of the U.S. Olympic Committee, had expressed great confidence before the Games, saying that Americans could rest serene and assured. After the Games, he had the sportsmanship to say that it was 'a model for all future Olympics'. But Americans agonized over their poor effort in the athletics; their selection procedure and the long boat trip on the SS *President Roosevelt* were alternately blamed. Certainly it appears that the team over-ate, and perhaps an element of over-confidence was present.

British concern again centred on the abuse of the amateur concept. They condemned the European fashion for 'broken-time' payments to athletes, allowing them to train without losing salaries, as well as the American system of intensive subsidized training for college athletes. Great Britain had not sent a soccer team as a protest about amateurism, and indeed there were no shooting or tennis events in the Games because of similar controversies. While the British took the Games casually, as they thought amateurs should, the British public maintained a lack of interest in them, still preferring their own parochial sporting events. Because the British level of success was below what the public expected as their due, the public turned away.

The organization of the Games had been successful, there being few arguments, apart from the debacle of the boxing.

Coubertin had been absent due to illness but, as usual, was not short of high-flying sentiments, and his message before the Games hoped that the 'ninth Olympiad will be a noble and happy milestone on the path of chivalrous progress. May it be so. It is my wish and my conviction.' It was so, and from Lausanne he could view with pride the progress of his brain-child.

Ethel Catherwood of Canada was a popular winner of the women's high jump, written about as much for her charm as for her ability.

Johnny Weissmuller

Johnny Weissmuller is the most famous swimmer of all time, not only for his feats in the pool but because he became one of the cinema's favourite Tarzans. Born on 2 June 1904 in Windber, Pennsylvania, he began his swimming career by winning the U.S. A.A.U. Championships in 1921, and began breaking world records in 1922, becoming the first swimmer to break one minute for the 100 metres. He revolutionized the front-crawl stroke, riding high in the water and turning his head alternately from side to side to breathe. At the Olympic Games in 1924 he won gold medals in the 100-metres and 400-metres freestyle and in the 4 × 200-metres relay, and also took a bronze in the water polo. Between the 1924 and 1928 Olympics he broke several more world records, perhaps the most remarkable being his 51 seconds for the 100 yards, a record which stood for 17 years. In the 1928 Olympics he repeated his gold medal wins in the 100-metres freestyle and 4 × 200-metres relay. Having won 52 American titles, and set 28 world records at distances from 100 yards to 880 yards freestyle and for 150 yards backstroke, he turned professional in 1929. His prowess increased, and at 36 he swam the 100 yards in 48.5 seconds. Magnificently built, standing 1.90 metres (6 feet 3 inches), and with broad shoulders, he was chosen by M.G.M. to play *Tarzan the Ape Man* in 1932. He was the seventh man to play Tarzan in films, and easily the best-known before or since. But the years 1922 to 1929 formed the basis of his greatness where his Olympic gold medals were accompanied by so many long-standing records.

Lake Placid

The 1932 Winter Olympics was held at Lake Placid in the north of New York State, near the Canadian border. Only 568 metres (1,862 feet) high, it suffered from a lack of snow, much of which had to be brought from Canada by truck. The long distance from Europe meant that only 17 nations took part, entering 306 competitors.

The Nordic skiing was, as usual, a clean sweep for Scandinavians. Sven Utterstroem of Sweden won the 18-km cross-country from a fellow-Swede, and Veli Saarinen of Finland won the 50-km cross-country after a long and hard race with his fellow-Finn, Vaino Likkanen. Norwegians took all the ski-jump medals. Hans Beck led by 5.0 metres on the first jump, but the great jumper Birger Ruud jumped 5.5 metres further on the second jump and won the first of his gold medals in the event. His brother Sigmund had won silver in 1928. In the combined event based on the shorter cross-country and the jump, the Norwegians again took all the medals. The winner was Johan Grottumsbraaten, taking

part in his third and last Games. He won the gold in 1928 and the bronze in 1924. He also had gold, silver and bronze from the individual cross-country races in previous Olympics.

The figure skating was held indoors for the first time. The men's event was won by Karl Schaefer of Austria who beat Gillis Grafstroem of Sweden, the winner in the three previous Games, into second place. Grafstroem, however, had a knee injury following a collision on the ice with a photographer. It was his fourth and last Games: score, three gold and one silver. Sonja Henie, at the peak of her career, took her second women's figure-skating title easily, as expected. Fritzi Burger of Austria was second again. The pairs was won by Pierre and Andrèe Brunet, the 1928 winners, who had since married.

The speed-skating events were a fiasco for the Europeans. For the only time in an Olympic or world championship event, the international rule of skating in pairs was replaced by the American mass start. The

Admiral Byrd welcomes the contestants to the 1932 Winter Olympic Games at Lake Placid.

A German two-man bobsleigh at the Lake Placid Games. Both bobsleigh events were won by the U.S.A., who provided four of the six medal-winning crews.

The men's figure-skating champion of 1932 in practice. Karl Schaefer of Austria won and repeated his win in 1936.

Americans and Canadians, encouraged by the spectators, were much better at elbowing and pushing than the Europeans, for whom this form of racing was new. Clas Thunberg, the Swedish co-winner of the 500 metres in 1928, declined to race. Americans and Canadians took all the medals except for a silver apiece taken by Norway's Bernt Evensen and Ivar Ballangrud, both champions from 1928. Two Americans completed double victories, John Shea in the shorter races and Irving Jaffee in the longer. (In later world championships at Lake Placid under the normal rules, Ballangrud won three events and the Americans were well beaten.)

In the four-man bob, the U.S.A. took the gold. Bill Fiske was steering as he did in 1928. Crewman Clifford Gray also won his second gold. The two-man bob was a new event, and was won by the American brothers, Hubert and Curtis Stevens, who had been led, after the first run, by Reto Capadrutt and Oscar Geier from Switzerland, who took the silver.

The Canadians won the ice hockey, as usual, but surprisingly had to struggle to beat the U.S.A. Germany and Poland were the only other teams competing.

Los Angeles

Los Angeles had been agreed as the venue for the 1932 Olympic Games as early as 1923, application having been made in 1920 for the Games of 1924 or 1928. The applicant was William May Garland, who was elected to the I.O.C. and became the organizer of the Games.

The general prosperity of the early 1920s ended with the Wall Street crash of 1929, and the depression together with the cost of sending large teams to the U.S.A. from Europe, threatened the success of the Games. In the previous American Olympic Games in 1904, over 90 per cent of the competitors had come from North America.

In the event the enterprize and imagination of the organizers made the Games the most successful so far. The problem of entries was overcome by the arrangement of transport and accommodation subsidies. For the first time an Olympic village was built. Covering 250 acres on a hill near the main stadium, the village consisted of two-room cottages for the athletes with a variety of dining rooms for all tastes. All the local services (fire station, hospital, policing and post office), common to any 'normal' small township could be found. The village differed mainly in that it was fenced in for privacy. Only the men stayed there; the 130 or so women competitors were installed in a large hotel. The village was such a success that it has become part of most Olympics since.

The other arrangements for the Games reached the same high standard, from the organization in the stadium to the dissemination of results and information to the press and public. New innovations included the electric photo-timing of races and the victory podium with its accompanying anthems and flags for medal ceremonies (some regard this as a regrettable development).

The Los Angeles stadium, in which the athletics were held, was expanded to contain 105,000 spectators. The track itself was made of crushed peat, and was as fast as any in the world, which made for a series of world records.

Los Angeles was decorated for the Olympic Games of 1932. The Olympic motto and the Olympic symbol are incorporated in the device in the foreground.

1932

The opening ceremony was held on 30 July 1932, and 200 doves were released. The weather, as it was to be throughout the Games, was perfect for sport: warm sunshine but not oppressive. Coubertin was absent (he was approaching 70), but would have been impressed with the accompanying festival of arts, with competitions for writing, painting, music, and so on, which helped make the Olympiad something like his 19th century vision. He was still preaching the Greek ideal of physical and spiritual harmony.

Two who *were* there as spectators were two of the greatest athletes of all time: Paavo Nurmi, who had wanted to compete, and Jim Thorpe. Both had offended the amateur code, and Thorpe had had difficulty in getting into the stadium at all. It was said Thorpe wept in the press box while Nurmi sat miserably in the stands.

Americans led the way in track and field, and regained their supremacy in the sprints. The 100 metres was won by the short stocky Eddie Tolan, the first black man to win an Olympic sprint title. Wearing glasses taped to his head and chewing gum, he won by the narrowest margin from his great American rival Ralph Metcalfe, both equalling the world record. The photo-finish helped the judges decide the result. In the 200 metres Tolan won easily with Metcalfe third, American George Simpson dividing them. Arthur Jonath of Germany, third in the 100 metres, was the only European in either final. Tolan was the only dual winner in track and field.

The 400 metres was one of the best races of the Games. It was run between two more great American rivals, short dark-haired 'Wee Willie' Carr, and tall, blond 'Big Ben' Eastman, world record holder for the 440 yards. Eastman led, and the pair drew away from their opponents, but Carr's devastating sprint finish got him home in a new world record, with Eastman, a stride back, also inside the old record. Sadly, a few months later, Carr broke his legs in an automobile crash which ended his athletics career.

American running supremacy ended at 400 metres, and the 800 metres was won by a

Left: An innovation for the Olympic Games of 1932 was the first Olympic village. Rows of stucco cottages were built in the Los Angeles hills.

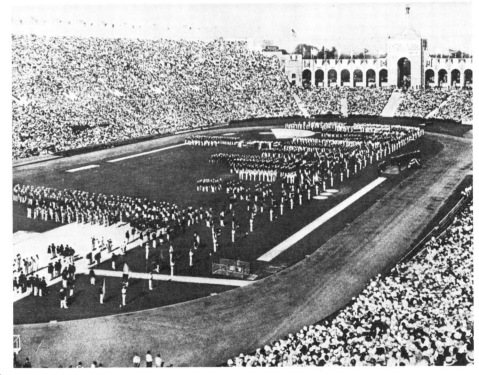

Above: The teams line up at the opening ceremony for the 1932 Olympics.

Eddie Tolan, nearest the camera, just wins the 100 metres from fellow-American Ralph Metcalfe, with Arthur Jonath of Germany finishing third.

Los Angeles

Right: The bespectacled Tommy Hampson of Great Britain wins the 800 metres from Alex Wilson of Canada in a new world record time.

Briton, Tommy Hampson, in another splendid race. A teacher, and be-spectacled, like Tolan, Hampson was not too well fancied, having world record-holder Sera Martin, Otto Peltzer and three highly favoured Americans to beat, but he came with a late challenge to beat two Canadians: Alex Wilson (third in the 400 metres) and Phil Edwards. Hampson was the first man to break 1 minute 50 seconds for the race, and set a new world record. It was the fourth successive win for Great Britain in the event.

Edwards also won bronze in the 1,500 metres, where the 1928 winner, Finland's Harri Larva, was well back. The surprise winner was an architect from Milan, Luigi Beccali, whose supporters chanted 'Luigi, Luigi' as he came home ahead of Great Britain's John Cornes.

Finnish distance running received some consolation in the 5,000 metres which was won in controversial fashion by Lauri Lehtinen, the world record-holder. For once an American was prominent in a distance race, and the unfancied Ralph Hill challenged in the final straight. Lehtinen swerved out and then back as Hill twice tried to pass, and just held on. The noisy displeasure of the crowd was silenced by the announcer, journalist Bill Henry, with the words 'Remember, please, these people are our guests'. There was no protest and the result stood. Another Finn, Lauri Virtanen, was third.

The Finns were beaten into second and third places in the 10,000 metres. This race gave Poland its first male track and field gold; Janusz Kusocinski won comfortably. The second man home, Volmari Iso-Hollo, won the 3,000-metres steeplechase for Finland, but only after running an extra lap due to an official's error. He won easily, but in the extra lap the silver and bronze medal positions altered when Great Britain's Tom Evenson passed American Joe McCluskey. When the error was revealed, Evenson tried to persuade McCluskey to accept the silver, but McCluskey insisted Evenson keep it.

Both the relays were won by the U.S.A. in world record times, the strength of American sprinters being such that the shorter relay was won without any individual medalists; the team was Robert Kiesel, Emmett Topino, Hector Dyer and Frank Wykoff. In the longer relay, Carr, the individual winner, won his second gold by anchoring the team.

The 110-metres hurdles was won by George Saling (U.S.A.), with Percy Beard (U.S.A.) second. Originally Jack Keller, also of the U.S.A., was placed third, but the film showed that Great Britain's Don Finlay was third, and the result was altered. Keller sportingly sought out Finlay to hand over the medal. George Saling was a second gold medalist to be involved shortly afterwards in an automobile accident; sadly, he was killed.

The 400-metres hurdles was another race in which Olympic sportsmanship was shown. The runners were excused the opening parade, because they raced on the first day, but Lord Burghley, the defending champion, hearing that his great rival, Morgan Taylor, of the U.S.A., was to carry the flag, insisted on taking part himself. In the event, Taylor finished third and Burghley fourth, there being a surprise winner from Ireland, Bob Tisdall, an all-round athlete who had led the decathlon field after the first day but had finished eighth. Tisdall beat the world record with a time of 51.7 seconds but knocked down the final hurdle, so could not claim the record under the rules then obtaining. Glenn Hardin (U.S.A.), who finished second, was given the world record at 51.9 seconds.

The marathon was the nearest to a 'blanket finish' so far, the first four all being in the stadium when the winner crossed the line. They were Juan Zabala of Argentina, Sam Ferris of Great Britain, Armas Toivonen of Finland, and Douglas Wright of Great Britain, in that order. Zabala was only 19 years old.

The 50-km walk was won easily by a 39-year-old British railwayman, Thomas Green, with Latvian Janis Dalinsh second and Ugo Frigerio, the Italian walker who had won in 1920 and 1924, third. The U.S.A. lost their monopoly of high-jump gold when a Canadian, Duncan McNaughton, won a four-way jump-off with two Americans, Robert van Odsel (who won silver) and Cornelius Johnson, and a man from the Philippines, Simeon Toribio, who took bronze.

The pole vault was again won by an American, Bill Miller, who broke the world record. A Japanese vaulter, Shuhei Nishida, was not far behind. The long jump also went

to an American, Edward Gordon, again with a Japanese jumper getting into the medals – Chuhei Nambu took the bronze. Nambu won the triple jump championship, the second successive win for Japan.

In the throwing events, the U.S. kept the discus; John Anderson beat three Frenchmen, two who won the minor medals, and a third,

Below: Volmari Iso-Hollo of Finland wins the first of his two 3,000-metres steeplechase titles in 1932.

Japanese supporters line the marathon route and watch the eventual winner, Juan Carlos Zabala of Argentina, sharing the lead with a Canadian who dropped out of the medal positions.

Los Angeles

Yoshiyuki Tsurata, the 200-metres breaststroke champion for the second time, was one of a brilliant team of Japanese swimmers who dominated the men's events in 1932.

Jules Noel, who was thought to have 'won' the event with a throw which was ordered to be retaken as officials were not ready for it. Leo Saxton won the shot for the U.S.A.; Pat O'Callaghan repeated his 1928 hammer victory for Ireland; and Matti Jarvinen led three Finns who took all the medals in the javelin.

James Bausch (U.S.A.) scored a world record points total in the decathlon, the previous record holder, Finland's Arkilles Jarvinen, having to be content with silver for the second time.

The United States took all but one of the gold medals in the women's events. The exception was the 100 metres which was won by Stanislawa Walasiewicz of Poland, who, however, had lived in the U.S.A. since she was two, and had won many U.S. sprint titles under the name Stella Walsh.

The star of the women's games was 18-year-old Mildred 'Babe' Didrikson, who took the 80-metres in the closest of finishes from Evelyn Hall (U.S.A.) and the javelin from two Germans. 'It just slipped', she said of her world record throw. In the high jump she was engaged in a jump-off with fellow-American Jean Shiley when she was disqualified for 'diving', the judges deciding that her feet did not clear the bar first. She was allowed the silver medal, however.

In the swimming pool, the Japanese men were a revelation, winning five of the six races, and combined with four silver and two bronze medals they took 11 of 16 possible medals. All their men raced in every final. Yoshiyuki Tsuruta retained his 200-metres breaststroke title and Kusuo Kitamura, the 1,500-metres freestyle winner, was only 14, the youngest man to win an Olympic title, and one of three Japanese teenage gold medalists. The break in Japanese domination came in the 400-metres freestyle which was won by American Clarence 'Buster' Crabbe, another swimming champion who became a film star. American athletes made a clean sweep of the men's diving.

The women's swimming and diving events were all won by Americans, except the 200-metres breaststroke, which went to Australia's Clare Dennis in a world record. The 400-metres freestyle also saw a world record set by Helene Madison (U.S.A.), who added two more golds in the 100-metres freestyle and the relay.

There was one of the few disagreements of the Games in the always controversial water polo. The Brazilians attacked the Hungarian referee after a defeat by Germany and were barred from the rest of the tournament. It made little difference. Hungary were so superior they scored 35 goals against two in taking the gold.

The boxing, for once, was relatively free of incident, except for the Argentinian boat trip home when a revolt broke out among the athletes which resulted in heavyweight champion Santiago Lovell being jailed on arrival home.

The leading gymnast of the Games was an Italian, Romeo Neri, who won three gold: combined, individual and team, and parallel bars. The wrestling was notable in that a Swede, Ivar Johansson, won the freestyle middleweight gold and then shed 5 kg (11 lb) to win the Greco-Roman welterweight. Another Swede, Carl Westergren, added the Greco-Roman heavyweight to the light-heavyweight gold he won in 1924 and the middleweight gold of 1920. He had been injured in 1928.

In the rowing, Henry Pearce of Australia retained his single sculls title, and 'Jumbo' Edwards of Great Britain won gold in both the coxless pairs and coxless fours. The U.S.A. again won the eights, the University of California crew beating Italy in a tremendous race.

France and Italy did well in cycling, equestrian and fencing events. India retained the hockey very easily. Johan Oxenstierna ensured that Sweden had won all the modern pentathlon gold medals to date (and all the silver for that matter).

That the Games was a huge success was agreed by all. Altogether 18 world records had been beaten or equalled. The average attendance at the stadium was 60,000, with a total of 1.25 million spectators overall. The organizers made one million dollars profit.

There was little controversy, and what there was was half-hearted, such as the speculation that the Japanese swimmers had taken oxygen.

Americans this time were very satisfied with their showing. With entries restricted to three per country per event, the U.S.A. competitors all reached the finals of the events in track and field except in the discus and 400-metres hurdles. The performances of the black sprinters, Tolan and Metcalfe, were noticed by the papers, and there were references to 'the physical prowess of the negro'. This theme was to be enlarged in 1936.

Mildred Didrikson

Born at Port Arthur, Texas, on 26 June 1914, Mildred 'Babe' Didrikson was an astonishing all-round sportswoman from an early age, throwing the javelin a world record distance as a 16-year-old schoolgirl. At the American women's championships two years later, she took part in eight events in 150 minutes, winning five, and won the 'team' championship on her own. Later in 1932 she entered the maximum (for women) of three events at the Olympic Games. She won the 80-metres hurdles and the javelin and finished second on a technicality in the high jump, when an official disqualified her over style. In each event she broke the world record. Babe Didrikson was three times in the All-American basketball team and also excelled at swimming, tennis, golf, diving, baseball and billiards. After the Olympics, she lost her amateur status by lending her name for advertising, and went 'on the halls', where she demonstrated athletics and acrobatics and played the mouth-organ. In 1934 she took up golf, and was reinstated as an amateur to begin a serious career in 1940. She won several Open tournaments before becoming U.S. Amateur Champion in 1946. In 1947 she won the British Ladies Championship and 17 consecutive tournaments before turning professional. She won the World Championship four times running from 1948 to 1951, and the U.S. Open in 1948, 1950 and 1954. In 1950 she set a record for a year's earnings with

One of the best all-round sportswomen of all time, Mildred 'Babe' Didrikson, wins her 80-metres hurdles title at the 1932 Olympics.

$14,800. Her last U.S. Open win came in the year following an operation for cancer, which, although she fought hard, was to overcome her in 1956. In 1938 she had married George Zaharias, a wrestler known as the 'crying Greek from Cripple Creek', and her golf successes were under her married name. She was voted by Americans 'Athlete of the Year' in 1932, 1945, 1946, 1947 and 1950, and in the 1950 poll for 'Athlete of the Half Century' she led the women's section. After a third cancer operation early in the year, she died in Galveston, Texas, on 27 September 1956, aged 42.

Opposite: Wrestling champions at the 1932 Olympic Games. From the left: heavyweight Carl Westergren (Sweden), light-heavyweight Rudolph Svensson (Sweden), welterweight Ivar Johansson (Sweden), lightweight Eric Malmberg (Sweden), featherweight Giovanni Gozzi (Italy) and bantamweight Jacob Brendel (Germany). Missing is middleweight V. Kokkinen (Finland).

Garmisch-Partenkirchen

Below: The poster advertising the Winter Olympic Games at Garmisch-Partenkirchen in 1936.

Below right: Karl Schaefer of Austria won his second men's figure skating title.

The 1936 Winter Olympics was held in the twin villages of Garmisch and Partenkirchen in Bavaria. The Games was the most popular yet in all respects. There were 755 competitors from 28 countries and over half a million spectators watched the 17 'official' and two demonstration events, with 150,000 watching the ski jump. The weather was perfect, a break in rain exactly coinciding with the duration of the Games. For the first time Alpine skiing was included in the programme. Coubertin did not attend, and Adolf Hitler, with his ministers Dr. Goebbels and General Goering in attendance, performed the opening ceremony. In the preparations there had been intimations of the racism of the summer Games. Despite there being a Jew in the German ice-hockey team,

signs on the toilets at first read: 'Dogs and Jews not allowed'. I.O.C. President Henri Baillet-Latour had to insist on their removal before the Games began.

Scandinavians took all the Nordic skiing medals. There were clean sweeps for the Swedes in the 50-km cross-country and for Norway in the Nordic combined, where no other country had yet won a medal in the four Games to date. The star of the Nordic events was Norwegian Birger Ruud, who kept his ski-jump title. Ruud also won the downhill race in the Alpine skiing, but this was not a separate event in 1936, and Ruud could finish

Left: Birger Ruud of Norway, one of the greatest of all ski-jumpers, won his second Olympic gold medal in 1936, and returned after the war to win a silver in 1948.

Below: Christel Cranz of Germany won the women's Alpine skiing combined event before there were separate races for Alpine skiers.

The Norwegian speed skater, Ivar Ballangrud, won three gold medals and a silver in 1936 to add to medals he had won in 1928 and 1932.

Below: The gold-medal performance of the German figure skaters, Maxi Herber and Ernst Baier, who won the pairs championship.

only fourth in the combined event behind Franz Pfnuer of Germany. Ruud and his two ski-jumping brothers were to be interned by the Germans in the Second World War. Germany's Christel Cranz won the gold in the women's Alpine combined.

Both figure-skating titles were retained by the 1932 winners: Karl Schaefer of Austria and Sonja Henie of Norway. But in taking her third gold Sonja Henie was hard-pressed by Great Britain's Cecilia Colledge, who was to be world champion the following year when Miss Henie had turned professional. Ernst Baier of Germany, second to Schaefer in the men's figure skating, won the pairs with Maxi Herber, whom he later married.

The star of the speed skating was the Norwegian Ivar Ballangrud, who amply

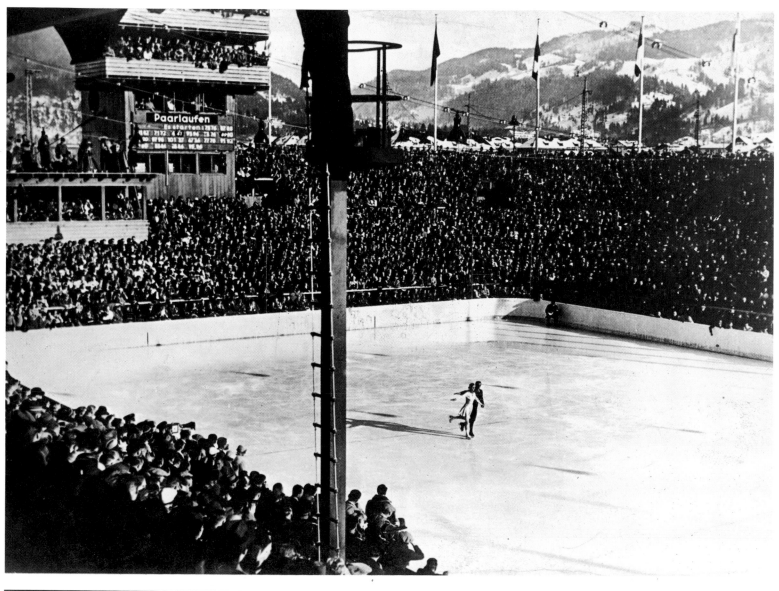

made up for his comparative failure in 1932 by winning the 500, 5,000 and 10,000 metres, finishing second to his countryman, Charles Mathiesen, in the 1,500 metres.

The U.S.A. won its only gold medal in the two-man bobsleigh through Ivan Brown and Alan Washbond. Switzerland finished second, but provided the first two crews in the four-man bob ahead of Great Britain.

The drama of the Games, and the big surprise, came in the ice hockey, previously a Canadian monopoly. Great Britain fielded a team which included a number of British-born Canadians including Jimmy Foster, a superb goal-minder. The Canadians objected to him, as he was under suspension in Canada, but the objection was over-ruled. The competition developed into a three-cornered fight between Great Britain, Canada and the U.S.A. Canada scored nearly three times as many goals as any other team, but lost 2–1 to Great Britain, whose only dropped points were draws with Germany and the U.S.A. The Americans lost 1–0 to Canada and 2–1 to Italy. So Great Britain scored the most surprising victory in the winter Olympics; their only other medal in the event was a bronze in 1924.

This Winter Olympics was highly successful and established itself as a major event in its own right, but it was to be 12 years to the next celebration in St. Moritz.

Sonja Henie

Born on 8 August 1912 in Oslo, Sonja Henie was Norway's best figure skater when only nine years old. She represented Norway at the first winter Olympics in 1924, but finished out of the first six. However, she won the women's gold medal in the Olympics of 1928, 1932 and 1936. Sonja Henie was very attractive, and brought a theatrical style and shorter skirts to figure skating. She won the world championship ten times in succession between 1927 and 1936 (equalling the record of Ulrich Salchow) and was European champion from 1931 to 1936. In March 1936 she gave her first professional exhibition and went to the United States. She rapidly became a film star (like Weissmuller, the Olympic swimming champion) and made films regularly till 1948, becoming one of the highest paid stars of the day. She built a fine modern art collection and donated it to an Oslo museum. She was on her way there when she died of leukemia on the airplane on 12 October 1969.

Sonja Henie, the Norwegian figure skater, at the height of her powers. She won three successive Olympic Games championships.

Berlin

A poster for the 1936 Olympic Games in Berlin.

The Berlin Olympic Games were held against a background of war. The Spanish Civil War was beginning, Italy and Japan were invading Abyssinia and Manchuria, and in Europe the Second World War was looming. Great Britain and the U.S.A. were experiencing severe unemployment. The Nazi regime in Germany was actively encouraging racial discrimination, particularly against Jews, and professing the superiority of the Aryan race.

The German Fuehrer, Adolf Hitler, used the Games as an opportunity for extreme political propaganda. That he was denied complete success, largely by the efforts of black American athletes led by Jesse Owens, is one of the legends of the Olympic Games. That blacks in the Southern States of the U.S.A. were themselves victims of a powerful colour prejudice is not so well remarked.

Many voices were heard in the United States and Great Britain advocating the removal of the Games from Berlin, or the boycotting of it. The I.O.C. President, Count Henri de Baillet-Latour, observed that he could transfer the Games if he felt that its spirit was threatened. All this made little

The German Fuehrer, Adolf Hitler, leads the parade of dignitaries at the Olympic Games of 1936, which he attempted to turn into a display of German mastery.

1936

difference to Hitler, and the Games was presented in a manner difficult to imagine today. Throughout Berlin there were thousands of swastikas, and martial music was played everywhere. The streets around the stadium were cleaned up and decorated with flags and garlands of flowers. On the day of the opening ceremony, thousands more than could get into the 100,000-capacity stadium thronged to Berlin and promenaded the streets, holding up the traffic. From all over Germany came thousands of members of the Strength through Joy organization. Wherever Hitler appeared crowds raised their arms in the Nazi salute, and 'Sieg Heil' was heard from loudspeakers on every side. Everything was ready for a display to the world of German efficiency and superiority.

The opening ceremony was held on 1 August 1936. The airship *Hindenburg* was overhead. Twenty thousand doves were released. A bell weighing over 14,000 kg (14 tons) was rung, 'Deutschland Uber Alles' and the Olympic hymn were sung, and Hitler received an olive branch from Spyridon Louis, the marathon winner of the first Games

The Olympic flame arrives in the stadium through masses of uniformed members of the Hitler Youth Movement backed by the huge swastika symbols of Nazi Germany.

Below: The man who did most to defeat the plans of Adolf Hitler, Jesse Owens, wins a heat of the 100 metres.

Berlin

Top: Archie Williams of the U.S.A. just beats Godfrey Brown of Great Britain (left) in the 400 metres, with James LuValle (right) of the U.S.A. third.

Above: Forrest Towns of the U.S.A. (second from right) on his way to a gold medal in the 110-metres hurdles.

40 years earlier, who was wearing Greek national dress. For the first time the Olympic torch was lit by the rays of the sun in Olympia, and it was carried in relay to the stadium by 3,000 athletes. The last stretch to the brazier was through ranks of thousands of uniformed members of the Hitler Youth Movement backed by huge swastika banners.

The salute to Hitler of the athletes during the parade varied greatly. The Americans did not salute at all, and were jeered, the British decided upon a mere 'eyes right' and were ignored, the Austrians gave the Nazi salute and the Rumanians goose-stepped, both being cheered, as were the French, whose Olympic salute was mistaken for the Nazi raised arm.

The arrangements for the events themselves were superb. The athletics stadium was that intended for the abortive 1916 Games, enlarged and improved, and surrounded by new stadia, a swimming pool to accommodate 18,000 spectators, gymnasia and excellent practice facilities. The latest technology for timing the events and communicating information was installed. Fourteen languages were used in the bulletins, for the benefit of the 3,000 journalists who were present, some of whose stories, it was suspected, were being noted by German 'journalists'. The 1936 Games was widely covered by television, with daily closed-circuit transmissions to 25 halls around Berlin.

The Olympic village was a larger and grander version of the 1932 village in Los Angeles, with well-built brick cottages and 38 dining halls to cater for all national requirements. The women were accommodated in the area around the stadium complex.

The track and field events provided the first big breakthrough for black athletes, who won all the running events up to 800 metres and the long jump and high jump. Three individual events were won by Jesse Owens. Usually a slow starter, Owens was away fast in the 100 metres and was never headed to win from another black American, Ralph Metcalfe, who was also second in 1932. In the 200 metres Owens won the final easily, again from black American Mack Robinson. Martinus Osendarp of Holland was third in both events.

Black athletes were first and third in the 400 metres. World record holder Archie Williams took the gold; Jim LuValle took the bronze; Great Britain's Godfrey Brown took the silver. The string of British wins in the 800 metres came to an end when John Woodruff, a young American, powered through from the back in unsophisticated fashion to win the gold. Canada's Phil Edwards, another black athlete, who finished third in the 1932 800 metres and 1,500 metres, completed a trio of bronze medals.

The United States took the 4 × 100-metres relay, where Owens took another gold. There was controversy in this race, because the Americans dropped Marty Glickman and Sam Stoller from the team and replaced them with Owens and Metcalfe. Glickman and Stoller were the two Jews of the American team, and this prompted a charge that German anti-Semitism was being appeased, but it is more probable that the Americans were determined to beat the powerful German team. American sprinting successes were finally halted in the 4 × 400 metres, which they had won in three previous Olympics, when the British team beat them by two seconds.

The 1,500 metres final was the great race of the Games. It was a golden age for the event and the first five men from 1932 were in the field, including Glenn Cunningham, the holder of the world mile record. Jack Lovelock, ninth in 1932, but who had recently beaten the 1,500 metres world record holder, was also in the final. The only absentee of the great runners was Britain's Sydney Wooderson, who had beaten Lovelock in the British championships, but who had been eliminated in the heats, suffering from a foot injury. Cunningham, Lovelock and the 1932 winner, Beccali of Italy, led down the back straight, but with 300 metres to go New Zealander Lovelock spurted ahead to win, he and Cunningham both being inside the world record, and the first five inside the Olympic record.

The 5,000 metres and 10,000 metres were both won by Finns. Gunnar Hoeckert won the 5,000 from the 1932 winner, Lauri Lehtinen, and Ilmari Salminen beat two more Finns in the 10,000 metres.

Third in the 10,000 metres was Volmari Iso-Hollo, who repeated his 1932 steeplechase win, finishing in front of another Finn. So in the three track distance events, Finns conceded only two bronze medals to athletes from other countries, equalling their performance of 1928 when Nurmi and Ritola were supreme.

Both hurdles races were won by Americans. The 110-metres hurdles was won by world record holder Forrest Towns from Great Britain's Don Finlay, the bronze medal winner in 1932 who was still good enough to win the British title in 1949. Black American Fritz Pollard led before finishing third. Glenn Hardin, the silver medalist in the 400-metres hurdles in 1932, went one better in 1936.

Great Britain's Harold Whitlock was a stylish winner of the 50-km walk in a world record time. In the marathon a sporting gesture might have cost his team-mate Ernie Harper the race. Harper warned the inexperienced Kitei Son, that the pace of the 1932 winner Zabala was too fast. Kitei Son slowed, Zabala burnt himself out as foretold but Kitei Son beat Harper for the gold in the last mile. Kitei Son represented Japan, as his native Korea was under Japanese rule.

Ernie Harper of Great Britain leads Kitei Son, a Korean representing Japan, in the marathon. Kitei Son won the race with Harper second.

Cornelius Johnson of the U.S.A., in the high jump, was the first black winner of the 1936 Games, and therefore the first to be ignored by Hitler.

Berlin

Top: Germans did well in the 1936 Olympics. Gerhard Stoeck won the javelin.

Above: The women's javelin was won by Germany's Tilly Fleischer, who broke the Olympic record.

The field events were dominated by Germany and the U.S.A.; only Naoto Tajima of Japan won from outside these countries when he registered the third successive win for his nation in the triple jump.

The high jump went to one of the band of black American athletes, who beat another into second place. Cornelius Johnson and Dave Albritton, joint world record-holders, finished first and second, with a third American, Delos Thurber, taking the bronze. Johnson arrived late for the competition, only entering when the bar was already at the Olympic record height.

Jesse Owens won the long jump after a good competition with the German, Luz Long. Owens was in danger of not qualifying through foul jumps but Long advised him to draw a take-off line a foot before the board on his third effort, and Owens qualified to go on and win. Long, who took silver, was sporting in defeat, and the two became friends. Sadly, Luz Long was killed in Sicily during the Second World War, his sportsmanship remembered as a gesture which contrasted with the German chauvinism inspired by Hitler.

The pole vault took ten hours to complete, ending under floodlights in a win for Earle Meadows of the U.S.A., who beat two Japanese competitors.

Germans took three of the four gold medals in the throwing events; Gerhard Stoeck beat two Finns to become the first non-Scandinavian winner of the javelin. Hans Woellke's victory in the shot, in which he beat the American world record holder, was Germany's first athletics Olympic gold medal. In the discus it was the turn of the German world record holder to be beaten, by Ken Carpenter of the U.S.A. The U.S.A. also won the decathlon; Glenn Morris broke the world record and was followed in the placings by two fellow-Americans.

In the women's events, Helen Stephens, an 18-year-old American, forced the holder Stanislawa Walasiewicz of Poland (Stella Walsh) into second place in the 100 metres, and took another gold when the U.S.A. won the 4 × 100-metres relay. In this event the favourites from Germany were winning easily until they dropped the baton. They wept bitterly. Italy won a gold when Trebisonda Valla won the 80-metres hurdles and set a new world record. Hungary's Ibolya Csak won a gold in the high jump in which she beat Great Britain's 16-year-old schoolgirl, Dorothy Odam, in a jump-off. German girls took the gold medals in the discus and javelin.

In the swimming pool the Japanese men continued where they had left off in 1932, winning 10 of a possible 17 swimming medals. Ferenc Czik of Hungary surprised them in the 100-metres freestyle, beating three Japanese from an outside lane, and Jack Medica of the U.S.A. relegated the Japanese to the minor medals in the 400-metres freestyle.

The swimming star was a Dutch girl, Hendrika Mastenbroek, who won golds in

the 100-metres and 400-metres freestyle and in the 4 × 100-metres relay, plus a silver behind team-mate Dina Senff in the 100-metres backstroke.

The Americans dominated the diving taking 10 of 12 medals. Dorothy Hill took a gold and a bronze, having, as Dorothy Poynton, won a gold in 1932 and a silver in 1928. A schoolgirl of 13 years and 9 months,

Marjorie Gestring, won the springboard diving to become the youngest gold medal winner until then in the modern Olympics. The water polo was again won by Hungary, with four of the team winning their second gold, including the one-legged Oliver Halassy.

The boxing was free of argument for once, although the use of two rings in the same hall

Above left: A spectacular shot of the men's highboard diving champion, Marshall Wayne of the U.S.A., performing one of his dives.

Above: Disappointment for the German runners in the women's 4 × 100-metres relay, when they dropped the baton on the last take-over when well ahead of the others.

Jesse Owens

Jesse Owens was born on 12 September 1913 in Danville, Alabama, and named James Cleveland Owens. His boyhood pronunciation of his name as 'J.C.' Owens sounded like 'Jesse' Owens, and the name stuck. One of eight children of a cotton-picker, he went to Ohio State University and was trained in athletics by Larry Snyder. In 1928 he met Charley Paddock, 'the world's fastest human', and determined to follow him as Olympic champion. He won the American long jump title in 1933, and on 25 May 1935 produced one of the great feats of athletics. Before 10,000 spectators at an inter-university meeting in Ann Arbor, Michigan, he set five world records and equalled another in four events in less than an hour. He had recently fallen downstairs and injured his back, but decided to compete anyway. He achieved the following: 9.4 seconds in the 100 yards (equalling the record), 26 feet $8\frac{1}{4}$ inches (8.13 metres) in the long jump (record),

20.3 seconds in the 220 yards (a record for this and the 200 metres) and 22.6 seconds in the straight 220-yard hurdles (a record for this and the 200-metres hurdles). His second great performance came in the 1936 Olympic Games. He won the 100 metres, the 200 metres and the long jump, and took a fourth gold in a world record 4 × 100-metres relay. Counting heats, he competed 12 times and finished first each time, beating the Olympic record time nine times and the world record time four times, although some were wind-assisted. As well as the world records mentioned above, Owens also set a 100-metre record in 1936. Owens turned professional a few months after the Games, ran against horses and cars, and helped support a home for abandoned children. In 1950, in an American poll, he was easily voted first as track and field athlete of the first half of the century, in front of Thorpe and Nurmi (Jim Thorpe was first as all-round sportsman). He died on 31 March 1980.

Berlin

Below: Sailing in the 6-metre class at Kiel in the 1936 Olympic Games.

Below right: The winners of the 2,000-metres tandem cycle race for Germany, Ernst Ihbe and Charley Lorenz.

caused some confusion. The medals were well spread. There was controversy, however, in the equestrian events, where Germans took all the gold medals. The other nations considered the three-day-event course to be too severe, and three horses were destroyed. The horse ridden by the individual gold winner, Captain Ludwig Stubbendorf, was called Nurmi.

Germany took five golds in the rowing, but could not beat either the U.S.A. in the eights (who recorded their fifth victory) or Great Britain's Jack Beresford and Leslie Southwood in the double sculls. It was Beresford's fifth Olympics – he had won a medal in each, three gold and two silver in four different events.

France did best in the cycling, but there seemed to be bias in the 1,000-metres scratch race, when a German was given the gold after some blatant obstruction. Two Germans, Alfred Schwarzmann and Konrad Frey, dominated the gymnastics, each winning three gold medals. Frey also won a silver and two bronze and Schwarzmann two bronze. Kristjan Palusalu of Estonia won the heavyweight class in both freestyle and Greco-Roman wrestling.

In the team games India once more showed how hockey should be played, scoring 39 goals against one in taking the gold, and Italy won the soccer after Peru had been disqualified for refusing to replay a match they had won against Austria when it was discovered they had illegally used a substitute.

The Games had been the most efficiently organized of all, but, particularly in the light of the Second World War which followed three years later, will always be remembered for Hitler's use of them to promote the superiority of the German race. To some extent Hitler might be said to have succeeded as Germans took the most medals, easily beating the U.S.A., but the outstanding efforts of Jesse Owens and his fellow black athletes on the track completely overshadowed German victories elsewhere. Much has been made of Hitler's 'refusal' to shake the hand of Jesse Owens, but the story has been

The three medalists in the women's highboard diving. From the left, Kaethe Koehler of Germany (third), Velma Dunn of the U.S.A. (second) and gold medalist Dorothy Hill who, as Dorothy Poynton, had also won in 1932.

Berlin

embroidered. Hitler had congratulated the first three winners including the Germans Tilly Fleischer, who won the women's javelin, and Hans Woellke, who won the shot, on the opening day. The first black winner was the high-jumper Cornelius Johnson. It was when he received his medal late in the day that Hitler left the stadium, according to a spokesman, 'to beat the crush'. Certainly Hitler ignored Owens, whose first gold

medal was won on the following day. But by then he had been told that his task was to preside over the opening and closing ceremonies only. Nevertheless much was made of Hitler's treatment of the black athletes and of Owens in particular, presumably because he was the most famous. Certainly the whole affair, whatever the motives, created bad and enduring publicity for Hitler.

The Americans had nearly boycotted the Games altogether. The principal advocate of a boycott had been American I.O.C. member Ernest Jahncke, who subsequently lost his position to Avery Brundage, who was the most powerful voice in favour of going. Brundage claimed that sport should not be influenced by politics, a position he held throughout his life. He did state that Americans would not permit the barring of Jews from the Olympics, and Hitler was forced to accept Jewish fencer Helena Mayer, the 1928 champion, and ice-hockey player Rudi Ball into the squad.

The German public seemed to take the Games at Hitler's valuation. The attendances were huge, and the excitement at home victories and dismay at home defeats more marked than usual. Hitler commissioned Leni Riefenstahl to make a film of the Games, and the two parts of 'Olympia' constitute a masterpiece, but do nothing to soften the propaganda of the strength of German youth. Hitler thought that Berlin would become the permanent home of the Games.

Opinion around the world was divided on whether or not Hitler's racist theories had gained or lost credence through the Games. Some held that he had demonstrated a resurgent Germany under a powerful leader, others that the athletes themselves had proved that a spirit of equality and friendship among various nations and creeds could triumph even in a chauvinistic atmosphere.

Hitler's crusade against Jews was soon to become one of the greatest tragedies of mankind. Brundage did not see it clearly in 1936, viewing the proposed boycott of the Games partly as a Jewish-inspired political move. Nor did the rest of the world who went to Berlin see it. Perhaps Captain Wolgang Fuerstner, the director of the Olympic village, did. Of Jewish descent

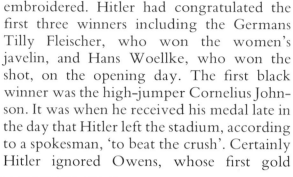

Some of the United States team for the Berlin Olympics pose by the swimming pool.

himself, Fuerstner was told that his army career would be terminated after the Games. He completed his duties, and after the closing ceremony committed suicide.

The black population was the other main recipient of Nazi hate. The newspaper of Dr. Goebbels, the German propaganda chief, referred to the black athletes as 'auxiliaries' of the American team and omitted their wins from the medal charts.

The ten black American athletes won six gold, three silver and two bronze medals, plus two more gold in relays, and won more medals in track and field than any single nation. A British newspaper article written by Bevil Rudd, the 400 metres gold medalist of 1920, wondered if black athletes held a physical superiority over white, and might not eventually have separate Games.

The question of sex tests for women was also mentioned during the Games, when there was a suggestion that unless something was done some countries might not send girls to compete against 'freaks'. The same British newspaper article mentioned above also advocated that women should be excluded from the Games for reasons of 'inferiority', seeing nothing to admire in the developed masculinity of women.

Coubertin was not at the Games, but appeared satisfied with them, writing to his friend Dr. Carl Diem, the inventor of the torch relay, that he, Coubertin, had not accomplished what he wanted and urged Diem to carry on. Coubertin died in 1937. Despite the horrors of 1936 his great movement was to continue and grow. But before the next Olympiad Hitler was to instigate a terrible war.

Jack Lovelock

Jack Lovelock was born on 5 January 1910 in Greymouth, New Zealand, and went to Oxford University as a Rhodes scholar in 1931 to study medicine. He ran in the 1,500 metres in the 1932 Olympics and finished ninth. In 1933 he went to the United States to represent Oxford and Cambridge against selected American universities. He won the mile and while there, he later set a world mile record of 4 minutes 7.6 seconds. In 1935 he won a 'Mile of the Century' in Los Angeles, and in 1936 won one of the greatest Olympic 1,500 metres of all time, setting a new world record. He then retired and qualified as a doctor at St. Mary's Hospital, London, where Sir Roger Bannister, the world's first four-minute miler, later studied. An accident to his head when falling from a horse in 1940 seriously injured his eyes. He went to work in a New York hospital, but he died when he fell under a subway car when returning home early from work after one of his frequent dizzy spells on 29 December 1949.

Jack Lovelock of New Zealand won a superb 1,500 metres in 1936. Glenn Cunningham of the U.S.A. finished second and Luigi Beccali of Italy, the 1932 winner, came third.

Gymnast Alfred Schwarzmann of Germany during the Olympic trials. He was to win three gold and two bronze medals in 1936.

St. Moritz

Tokyo/Helsinki 1940

The International Olympic Committee in 1936 awarded the 1940 Games to Tokyo and the winter Games to Sapporo, Japan, the first Games to be scheduled for Asia. Enthusiastic preparations were afoot when war between Japan and China began. I.O.C. member Avery Brundage again insisted that politics had nothing to do with the Olympics and pointed out that the venue could not be changed unless the host city withdrew. Tokyo withdrew on 16 July 1938. The I.O.C. immediately awarded the 1940 Games to Helsinki. The Winter Games was awarded to St. Moritz in Switzerland, but there was argument over amateurism. The Swiss would not support the I.O.C., who classified skiing instructors as professionals. In June 1939 the Winter Games was transferred to Garmisch-Partenkirchen, an extraordinary decision, as Germany had already invaded Austria.

On 1 September 1939 Germany invaded Poland, and on 3 September Great Britain and France declared war on Germany. Incredibly, preparations for the winter Games continued until 22 November 1939. In December 1939 Soviet troops invaded Finland. Naturally, preparations for the Helsinki Games stopped. However, an I.O.C. meeting in Paris in February 1940 was still making plans. The Finnish Olympic Committee finally announced in April 1940 that it could not host the Games, and in May the I.O.C. at last gave up all hopes.

London 1944

At the I.O.C. meeting in June 1939 the Games of the thirteenth Olympiad of 1944 were awarded to London in preference to Detroit, Lausanne and Rome. The Winter Games was to be held in Cortina d'Ampezzo in Italy. Both Games had to be cancelled because of war.

The President of the I.O.C., Count Henri de Baillet-Latour, died in January 1942. The Vice-president was J. Sigfrid Edstrom, who became President in 1946. In the interim Coubertin's friend, Dr. Carl Diem, on the strength of this friendship and letters from Coubertin tried to transfer the headquarters of the Olympic movement from Lausanne to Berlin, but his attempts in this direction were unsuccessful.

By this time Avery Brundage had become a power in the I.O.C. (When Edstrom became President in 1946 he nominated Brundage as his successor. Brundage took over in 1952.) Meanwhile Brundage, in 1944, had expressed the hope that Germany and Japan would be invited to the next Olympics, an extremely unpopular view which did not prevail. But Brundage, callous and pig-headed as he seemed, was consistent in his view that nothing should impede the Olympic movement and he and Edstrom did much to re-establish the Olympics after the war, whatever one might think of the appropriateness of International Games after the bloodshed of the previous years.

There were five new nations entered in the Winter Olympic Games of 1948, but the number of competitors was down on 1936; 636 men and 77 women represented 28 countries, excluding the defeated Germany and Japan; the Soviets did not enter. St. Moritz was chosen as the venue for its convenience, but training facilities were poor and most European countries and competitors suffered the additional drawback of a daily currency allowance of as little as five francs. The Americans, with no such restriction, lived at ease in contrast.

President Enrico Celio of Switzerland opened the Games, calling it a symbol of a 'new world of peace and goodwill'. It was, in relation to the war, but there were to be the usual quarrels. The weather was generally good, a partial thaw causing only a few postponements.

The main change in the programme was the advance of Alpine events. There were six Alpine skiing events compared to five Nordic, and 25 nations were represented in the Alpine events as against only ten in the Nordic.

The Nordic skiing was again dominated by the Scandinavian countries, Sweden, Finland

1948

and Norway taking all 15 medals. The 18-km cross-country was a clean sweep for Sweden; Martin Lundstroem won and took a second gold in the 4 × 10-km relay. Nils Karlsson won the 50-km cross-country, with another Swede second, but a Finn managed to win the bronze. The ski jumping was won by Petter Hugsted of Norway from Birger Ruud, also of Norway, who was competing in his last Olympics, aged 36, having won the gold in 1932 and 1936. Third was another Norwegian, but a Finn, Matti Pietikainen, who finished fourth, and an American, Gordon Wren, each jumped further than the winner,

but lost marks on style. The combined Nordic gold medal went to a Finn, Heikki Hasu, with his countryman, Martti Huhtala, second and Sfen Israelsson of Sweden, third.

The Alpine skiing medals went to Europe and the U.S.A. Henri Oreiller of France won a medal in all three events, taking gold in the downhill and combined and finishing third behind Edi Reinalter of Switzerland in the slalom. Hedy Schlunegger of Switzerland won the women's downhill, but the slalom provided a surprise win for 29-year-old American Gretchen Fraser, pigtails flying. Trudi Beiser of Austria, who finished second

France's Henri Oreiller won both the downhill and the combined in the Alpine skiing events of 1948, and he also took the bronze medal in the slalom.

St.Moritz

A leap by Dick Button of the U.S.A. on his way to his first gold medal in the men's figure skating at St. Moritz. He won again in 1952.

The U.S.A. No. 2 bob won the four-man event in the Olympics. Left to right are: William d'Amico, Patrick Martin, Francis Tyler (the pilot) and Edward Rimkus.

in the downhill, won the combined, with Miss Fraser finishing second.

The men's figure skating saw a new star, 18-year-old American Dick Button, who brought a new style of strength and athleticism to skating. He was the U.S.A.'s first male figure-skating medalist, winning easily from a Swiss and an Austrian. The women's figure-skating winner was also impressive, but Canadian Barbara Ann Scott had been allowed to compete only after that stern upholder of amateurism, Avery Brundage, had made her return a car given to her by her native city, Ottawa, the previous year. Belgium won a first figure-skating medal of any sort when Pierre Baugniet and Micheline Lannoy won the pairs from Hungarian and Canadian couples.

The speed-skating gold medals were all won by Scandinavians, after some nations had threatened to withdraw over a rules dispute. The star was the Swedish veteran, Ake Seyffarth, who won the 10,000 metres and took the silver in the 1,500 metres. Odd Lundberg of Norway was the other dual medalist, with one silver and one bronze.

Swiss crews took the first two places in the two-man bob, Felix Endrich and Fritz Waller in Switzerland II beating the Switzerland I crew. The U.S.A., third in the two-man, took the four-man bob, where U.S.A. II beat the Belgian crew. Before the bobsleigh races, the Americans protested that two of their sleds had been interfered with. There was also a skeleton tobogganing event, the second ever held in the Olympics. The first also had been on the St. Moritz Cresta Run 20 years before. Nino Bibbia of Italy won with John Heaton of the U.S.A. finishing second, as he had done behind his brother in 1928.

There was confusion in the ice hockey, causing embarrassment to the U.S.A. who sent two teams: one was sent by the Amateur Hockey Association, responsible for international events, the other by the United States Olympic Committee. The first took part and finished fourth, but was subsequently disqualified. There was a bad-tempered game between Canada and Sweden, ending in a free fight. Canada and Czechoslovakia fought for the gold, the goalless draw between them being the only point either dropped. Canada took the title on goal average. The Czech team included Jaroslav Drobny, six years later a bespectacled Wimbledon tennis champion.

Despite the meagre facilities, the numerous squabbles and the first mutterings about sham amateurs which were to grow and bedevil future Winter Olympics, the first post-war Games was held in a good spirit overall, and did its part in re-establishing the Olympics.

Far left: Nino Bibbia, an Italian who was born in St. Moritz, won the skeleton tobogganing event in the 1948 Olympic Games there.

Left: Nino Bibbia on his run in the skeleton tobogganing event.

London

The I.O.C. was anxious to stage the 1948 Games as soon as the Second World War was over, and in 1946 the Games was awarded to London, which had been scheduled to hold it in 1944.

Six years of war naturally meant that arrangements had to be austere. It was to be another two or three years before the British public was free from rationing, and there was a shortage of materials and supplies. There was no Olympic village, and athletes were housed in converted schools and military camps. No new stadia were built but Britain was well-equipped with venues. The stadium which had been built at Wembley for the 1924 British Empire Exhibition and which had staged the F.A. Cup Final since 1923 was used for the athletics; a temporary cinder track was laid where greyhounds usually raced. The nearby Empire Pool housed the swimming and the boxing, Harringay Arena in London the basketball, the track at Herne Hill the cycling events, and the Empress Hall

at Earls Court the gymnastics (the bad weather forced the gymnastics to be transfered from the main Wembley Stadium itself). Outside London, the rowing events were held at Henley, the home of the famous annual regatta, and the yachting at Torbay in Devon.

There were more competitors than ever before, over 4,000, a tenth of whom were women. Despite the absence of Germany and Japan, the defeated aggressors in the war, and of the U.S.S.R., newly affiliated to the I.O.C., but choosing not to take part, 59 countries sent competitors. The Victoria and Albert Museum was the home of the last of the Olympics arts competitions.

Television was in the early stages of its subsequent tremendous popularity. There were about 80,000 sets in Great Britain, on which over half a million viewers saw some of the Games. It was the first time the Games had been televised for the public at home.

The torch relay from Olympia in Greece, first seen at the 1936 Games, was continued, but it missed out the hostile Balkan countries of Albania, Bulgaria and Yugoslavia.

King George VI presided at the opening ceremony on 29 July 1948, when 83,000 spectators saw the usual release of the doves. Unfortunately, the greyness of post-war London was accompanied by rain throughout much of the Games, but the enthusiasm of the crowds and the athletes was maintained by some excellent performances from what was, by necessity, mostly a new group of sportsmen, different from those at Berlin 12 years before.

One of these excellent performances came in the 100 metres, where the United States was to retain its superiority of the years just before the war. The favourite was the world record holder for 100 yards, Mel Patton, a notoriously nervous performer. The American second string was Barney Ewell, and the third string was Harrison Dillard, who was the world record holder for 120-yards hurdles. He had failed to qualify for the American hurdles team, having hit a hurdle and fallen, but he had scraped into the trio for the 100

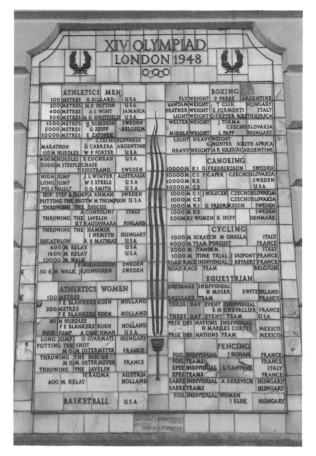

A plaque outside the entrance of Wembley Stadium, London, shows the names of some of the winners in the 1948 Olympic Games.

The athletes parade at the opening ceremony of the 1948 Games at Wembley before King George VI.

metres. All three were in the final, with two Britons, Emanuel McDonald Bailey and Alistair McCorquodale, and a Panamanian, Lloyd La Beach. In an exciting race Ewell just beat La Beach and thought he had won, but it was the hurdler, Harrison Dillard, who had got away fast in lane six, who had just broken the tape first.

Barney Ewell and Lloyd La Beach had to be content with silver and bronze in the 200 metres also, as Mel Patton regained his form in this race and just beat the two of them in another very close finish. Ewell got his gold in the 4 × 100-metres relay, and Dillard and Patton their second when they teamed up with Lorenzo Wright in the U.S.A. team. But they had to wait two days for them. The U.S.A. had finished comfortably ahead of Great Britain, but were disqualified for a foul baton change. It was only when a Jury of Appeal examined the film of the race two days afterwards that it was seen that the change-over between Ewell and Wright was

legal. It was with relief that the Britons, perhaps remembering 1908 and not wanting to win on a disqualification, handed over the medals. The Hungarians, originally placed third, had already gone home, and had to forward their bronze medals to the Italians.

The 400 metres was another splendid race. The favourite was the Jamaican Herb McKenley, a close fourth in the 200 metres and the world record holder for 400 metres. McKenley led for most of the race, but probably ran too fast in the conditions. Around the final turn his countryman, Arthur Wint, a 6-foot 4-inch (1.93 metres) runner with an enormous stride and beautiful flowing action, began to cut down the lead, and he just managed to get up to win near the line. American Mal Whitfield was third, well behind.

Whitfield, however, was an 800-metres specialist, and three days earlier he had won this race, beating Wint into second place. Whitfield won a second gold in the 4 × 400-

London

metres relay, but this was a fortunate win, as the hot favourites, Jamaica, with the first two in the individual event, retired when leading comfortably after Arthur Wint had collapsed with cramp in the third leg of the race.

One of the hottest favourites of the Games, Sweden's Lennart Strand, was beaten in the 1,500 metres, when his countryman, 29-year-old fireman Henry Eriksson, well used to finishing second to Strand, easily turned the tables on a very wet track.

The great Czech athlete, Emil Zatopek, made his first Olympic appearance in 1948 and ran away with the 10,000 metres on the first day. There was another beaten favourite in this race, Finnish Viljo Heino, who held the world record. He led for eight laps, but when Zatopek sprinted past, he was so disconcerted he retired. Zatopek ground on and on and won by nearly a lap from Alain Mimoun of France. Inexperience probably caused Zatopek a double in this Games. In a 5,000-metres heat, he and Eric Ahlden of Sweden had raced unnecessarily for the tape, despite being certain to quality. In the final he again set a fast pace, but although finally shaking off Ahlden, he appeared to have nothing left when Gaston Reiff of Belgium shot ahead followed by Willem Slijkhuis of Holland. At the bell, Zatopek was 20 yards behind Slijkhuis and fully 50 yards behind Reiff. He then got second wind and, in an astonishing last lap, passed Slijkhuis and only failed to catch Reiff by a couple of strides.

Left: The third lap of the 10-km walk, with John Mikaelsson of Sweden, the winner, already leading. He won again in 1952.

The 3,000-metres steeplechase was won by a Swede, Tore Sjostrand, who was followed home by two other Swedes. Sweden had a good Games in track and field, as Swedes also won both walking events: the 10-km walk was won by John Mikaelsson, and the 50-km walk by John Ljunggren.

The two hurdles races were won by Americans, the 110 metres being a clean sweep for the U.S.A. William Porter won the shorter race and Roy Cochran, a veteran who had been U.S. champion in 1939, won the 400-metres hurdles. Cochran won his second gold of the Games as a member of the American 4 × 400-metres team.

The marathon was, as always, a dramatic race, which those with long memories compared to the the London marathon of 1908. The favourite was Britain's 41-year-old Jack Holden, but he was forced to drop out after trying to keep pace with a 21-year-old Belgian paratrooper, Etienne Gailly. Gailly led up to 18 miles, but was five seconds behind Delfro Cabrera of Argentina with a mile to go. With a supreme effort, Gailly took the lead near the stadium, but entered it in a state of near exhaustion. On his lap of the track he was passed again by Cabrera, who took the gold, and then by Great Britain's other veteran, Tom Richards, who took the silver. The staggering Gailly took the bronze and, like Pietri 40 years earlier, the sympathetic cheers of the crowd.

The Americans did well in the field events,

winning four gold medals, but surprisingly could do no better than third in the high jump, which was won by Australian John Winter. The Australian long jumper, Tommy Bruce, however, was comfortably beaten into second place by American Willie Steele. The pole vault was held in a downpour, the competitors sheltering in a tunnel between jumps. American superiority was upheld by Guinn Smith. In the absence of the Japanese, the winners of the previous three Olympics triple jumps, Arne Ahman of Sweden just beat Australia's George Avery for the gold.

In the throwing events, Wilbur Thompson took the gold medal for the shot put with two fellow Americans behind and Adolfo Con-

The three United States medalists in the 110-metres hurdles take an obstacle almost level. From the left: Clyde Scott (second), William Porter (the winner) and Craig Dixon (third).

London

Above: Imre Nemeth of Hungary, the winner of the hammer. His son won the javelin 28 years later.

solini beat another Italian, Guiseppe Tosi, in the discus. The Finnish speciality, the javelin, provided that country with its only track and field gold medal of the Games through Tapio Rautavaara. In the hammer, Hungarian Imre Nemeth won Hungary's first track and field gold medal for 48 years.

The decathlon was the stage for a marvellous performance by a 17-year-old high-school boy from California, Bob Mathias, who was taking part in only his third decathlon. At the end of the first day, in which there were five events, he was third of the 28 competitors. He took the lead after the third event on the second day, when he threw the discus nearly three metres further than the second best. This day saw the worst of the weather, with a continuous downpour of rain, and when the last event, the 1,500 metres, began under floodlights after several gruelling hours of effort, Mathias led by a comfortable 261 points. Mathias was third slowest of the competitors, but although Ignace Heinrich of France halved his deficit to take the silver, Mathias had well won the gold.

If this was an exciting victory, the undoubted star of the 1948 Olympics was a 30-year-old mother-of-two, Fanny Blankers-Koen, who had competed in the 1936 Games. She was entered in four events, which, with heats, involved 12 races. She won them all. In the 100 metres, she won the final easily from

The only Australian winner of the Olympic high-jump title, John Winter, in action at Wembley in 1948.

The 17-year-old decathlon winner, Bob Mathias, throws the discus. His best event, it took him clear of the field on the second day.

Great Britain's Dorothy Manley and Australia's Shirley Strickland. The 200 metres, run for the first time by women in an Olympic Games, was another easy victory; she beat another British girl, Audrey Williamson, who came second and an American, Audrey Patterson, who came third. She had a hard race in the 4 × 100-metres relay, taking the anchor leg and having to overtake two rivals to beat Australia's Joyce King on the line with Canada third. Her hardest race came in the 80-metres hurdles, where another Briton, Maureen Gardner, led for most of the race. The two girls appeared to cross the line at the same time, but victory went to Fanny Blankers-Koen.

The high jump was won by the United States' black jumper Alice Coachman, who beat Great Britain's Dorothy Tyler after both had cleared 1.68 metres (5 feet 6¼ inches). Coachman won because she cleared the height at her first attempt, Tyler at her second. Dorothy Tyler was one of the unluckiest athletes in the history of the Games. In 1936, as 16-year-old Dorothy Odam, she had lost the gold in a jump-off. The rules for deciding ties were changed after the 1936 Games. Had the new rules been in operation then, she would have won the gold.

Ironically, had the old rules been in operation in 1948, Dorothy, now Mrs. Tyler and the mother of two children, would again have won the gold. Mrs. Tyler, who held the world record in 1939 and was possibly deprived of a gold medal because of the war, went on to compete in the 1952 and 1956 Olympics (aged 36 in 1956) and finished seventh and twelfth, a remarkable record.

In the other women's field events, the long jump was won by Olga Gyarmati of Hungary, with a jump well below Mrs. Blankers-Koen's best. The discus and shot provided a notable double for France's Micheline Ostermeyer, a shot putter who optimistically entered the discus, and surprised herself by winning. She also took a bronze in the high jump. Austria's Hermine Bauma changed her country's luck by taking Austria's first track and field gold in the javelin.

In an excellent swimming tournament, eight Olympic records and one world record were beaten. The events were dominated by the U.S.A. The world record went to the American 4 × 200-metres relay team of Walter Ris, Wallace Wolf, Jimmy McLane and Bill Smith. Ris also won the 100-metres freestyle, Smith the 400-metres freestyle and McLane the 1,500-metres freestyle as well as taking the silver in the 400 metres. The U.S.A. won all the men's swimming and diving events; American highboard diving champion, Dr. Sammy Lee, was only 5 feet 1 inch (1.55 metres) tall. It must be said though that the absent Japanese men, who had done so well in the last two pre-war Olympics, generally achieved better times in Japan's own national championships, held to coincide with the Olympics. The U.S.A. and Denmark did best in the women's swimming; American Ann Curtis won gold medals in the 400-metres freestyle and the 4 × 100-metres relay, and her colleague Victoria Draves took both diving titles. Italy won the water polo, but not without the usual bad feeling and arguments.

There was the largest entry yet in the boxing, and gold medals were won by boxers from five countries. Again there was criticism of some of the judging, however, and a terrible mix-up at the weigh-in when the Argentinian boxers, Arnoldo Pares and Pas-

The women's javelin event was won by Hermine Bauma, who became the first track and field gold medalist from Austria.

Left: Laszlo Papp of Hungary winning the first of his three boxing gold medals in 1948. He said Great Britain's John Wright gave him his hardest fight in the Olympics.

cual Perez, were confused. Perez eventually won the flyweight title and went on to become one of the best world professional champions. Two other future world champions were beaten at these Olympics. Vic Toweel, of the famous family of South African boxers, was beaten in the bantamweight class after winning 188 of 190 bouts, 160 inside the distance. He received a very unpopular decision, and immediately turned professional. He lost his world title to Australia's Jimmy Carruthers, who had been beaten by Perez in the Olympics. Another legendary boxer making his first appearance at the Games and taking the first of three gold medals was the Hungarian middleweight, Laszlo Papp.

France and Hungary each won three gold medals in the fencing. Ilona Elek retained her women's foil title, won 12 years earlier in Berlin. The runner-up, Karen Lachmann (Denmark), also competed in Berlin, while

the bronze medalist, Ellen Mueller-Preis, had won the gold in 1932 and bronze in 1936. A fencing competitor at the Games whose career was even longer was Denmark's Ivan Osieer, who had won a silver medal in 1912 and had appeared in the London Olympics in 1908.

The cycling road race was held over a course of approximately 7¼ miles (11.67 km) in Windsor Great Park. About 1,000 metres from the finish the winner, José Beyaert of France, had opened a gap.

France and Mexico each won two equestrian events, but France was awarded the gold in team dressage only after finishing a distant second to Sweden. A year after the event the Swedes were disqualified when it was discovered that one member of the team, Gehnall Persson, was not an officer, a requirement at the time.

The most notable shooting gold medalist was the Hungarian, Karoly Takacs, who had lost his right shooting hand in 1938 and had taught himself to shoot left-handed.

The modern pentathlon returned to Sweden, after the hiccup of 1936, when William Grut won.

The weightlifting was contested by 120 competitors from 30 countries; the U.S.A. and Egypt shared the gold medals. The most impressive winners were the huge heavyweight, John Davis, a garage mechanic from Brooklyn, and Joseph de Pietro, only 4 feet 8 inches (1.42 metres) tall, who won the new bantamweight class.

Turkey won six of the wrestling gold medals, and Sweden five.

Finland, overshadowed for once on the track, took six gold medals in gymnastics, three of them in the pommel horse, where the three Finnish competitors tied for first place.

There were surprises in the cycling, but the traditionally strong nations of France, Italy and Belgium shared the gold medals. The programme ran so late that it was almost dark when the last event was decided.

The rowing and canoeing events were held at Henley and provided Great Britain with two rare wins at the London Games. Herbert Bushnell and Richard Burnell won the double sculls, and John Wilson and Stanley Laurie, back in the country after ten years in the Sudan, won the coxless pairs. Mervyn Wood of Australia took the gold in the single sculls, and American Jack Kelly, Jr., the son of the 1920 winner, just missed a bronze. The U.S.A. maintained its fine record in the eights, beating Great Britain and Norway.

In the canoeing, the victories were shared by Sweden (four), Czechoslovakia (three) and the U.S.A. (one). Sweden's Gert Fredriksson won both kayak singles – he was to take the gold in the next three Olympics. A great Danish yachtsman, Paul Elvstrom, also won his first gold medal in 1948, taking the Firefly class – he, too, was to win gold medals in the following three Olympics.

Of the team games, the soccer, contested by 17 countries, was won by Sweden who beat Yugoslavia 3–1 in the final. They scored an odd goal in the semi-final against Denmark, when Gunnar Nordahl, who was sheltering in the net to avoid being offside, caught the ball as it was headed in by Henry Carlsson. Gunnar Nordahl was the best of three Swedish brothers in the winning team, the others being Bertil and Knud. All played for Norrkoping, all were consecutively elected Swedish footballer of the year and each later played in the Italian league.

The basketball, held for the second time, was won again by the U.S.A., who won all eight matches, although it won the first by only two points against Argentina.

The Games, despite Great Britain's slow recovery from a crippling war, was as successful as anybody could have wished. Although the poor weather and the lack of opportunity for practice by most athletes meant that few records were broken, more nations than ever had reason to be satisfied with at least one performer: 42 countries placed a competitor in the first six of an event. The track and field gold medals were shared by athletes from ten countries, the most yet.

Gert Fredriksson of Sweden won six Olympic gold medals in canoeing events. Here he wins a heat in the 1,000 metres kayak singles at Henley-on-Thames.

The United States took most gold medals overall, 35, including 11 in track and field. For once the Finns were overshadowed on the track, no doubt partly due to the war. For the first time since 1908 no Finnish runner won a gold medal. However, another Scandinavian country, Sweden, maintained a good Olympic record, taking five gold medals in the all-important athletics.

The British had good reason to be proud of the organization of the Games, which even showed a small profit, but the performance of British athletes had reached its lowest. There was not too much recrimination. The generation which might have provided medal winners had, after all, spent six years in more serious combat. Where criticism was voiced, it concentrated on the lack of facilities and dedication to training, and comparisons were drawn to American University coaching.

The triumph belonged perhaps to the shade of Coubertin. The Olympic spirit had survived the war and was in good condition to advance to Helsinki.

Fanny Blankers-Koen

Francina Koen was born in Amsterdam on 26 April 1918. She did well at several sports as a girl, and at 18 took part in the 1936 Olympics, sharing sixth place with another girl in the high jump and finishing fifth in the 4 × 100-metres relay. In 1938 she equalled the world record for 100 yards and in 1940 married athlete and coach Jan Blankers. She continued throughout the war years to equal or beat world records, and by the time the 1948 Olympics arrived had achieved world's best in the following: 80 metres hurdles (1942), high jump (1943), long jump (1943), 100 yards (1944), 4 × 110-yards relay (1944), 4 × 200-metres relay (1944), 100 metres (1948), 80-metres hurdles (1948) and 4 × 110-yards relay (1948). By the time of the 1948 Olympics she was a 30-year-old housewife with two children, and according to her husband, 'too old'. She was limited to three individual events, and chose 80-metres hurdles and 100 and 200 metres. She won all three, and collected her fourth gold of the Games, a record for a woman, in the 4 × 100-metres relay.

In the middle of the Games she had contemplated going home, as she missed her children. Had she been allowed to take part in the jumps, she would almost certainly have won the long jump, fatigue permitting, and possibly the high jump, too. She took part in the European games of 1946 and 1950 and won eight medals, five of them gold. After the 1948 Olympics, she continued her record-breaking with a world record in the 220 yards (with a bend) in 1950 and in 1951 she set a world record in the pentathlon. She competed in the 1952 Olympics, aged 34, but a blood infection destroyed her form and she did not win another medal. She retired, but remained in athletics as an administrator, generally acknowledged as the greatest of all women athletes.

Perhaps the greatest woman all-round track and field performer, Fanny Blankers-Koen of Holland, wins one of her four gold medals at Wembley. This is the 100 metres, with Dorothy Manley of Great Britain, second, and Shirley Strickland of Australia, third.

Oslo

The 1952 Winter Olympics was the first to be held in a capital city, Oslo. A record number of nations took part, 30, including Germany and Japan, making their post-war winter reappearances. New Zealand and Portugal took part for the first time. Just over 700 competitors, 108 women, competed in 22 events.

The Olympic flame was brought from a house in southern Norway where Sondre Norheim, the 19th century 'father of skiing', had been born. The Games began on 14 February 1952, and Princess Rahnhild declared it open after two minutes silence had been observed for King George VI of Great Britain, who had recently died.

The Nordic skiing events were a triumph for the Norwegians and Finns, who this time managed to limit the Swedes to a few minor medals. Hallgeir Brenden of Norway won the 18-km cross-country, beating two Finns, and Veikko Hakulinen, the 50-km cross-country, from a Finn, Eero Kolchmainen, and a Norwegian. Finland won the 4 × 10-km relay from Norway, for whom Brenden won a silver to add to his gold. The Swedes took the bronze. Simon Slattvik of Norway won the combined, beating a Finn and a Norwegian. Heikki Hasu of Finland won the silver to add to a gold won in the relay.

The ski jump at Holmenkollen was watched by 130,000 excited spectators, who

The opening ceremony of the 1952 Olympic Games in Oslo. The Games was the biggest winter celebration so far, with Germany and Japan back after the war.

1952

saw Norway's Arnfinn Bergmann win from a countryman and a Swede. There was a 10-km cross-country event for women and Finns took all three medals; the winner was Lydia Wideman.

The Alpine downhill skiing was won by Zeno Colo of Italy, with two Austrians taking the minor medals; one of the Austrians, Othmark Schneider, who took the downhill silver, won the slalom. Norwegians took the minor places in the slalom, and the silver medalist, Stein Eriksen, amid the great enthusiasm of the Norwegian spectators, went one better in the giant slalom and took the gold. It seemed Norway's early opposition to Alpine skiing was premature, but Alpine medals of any sort were to be rare for Scandinavians in the years to come. The second man, Christian Pravda of Austria, had finished third in the downhill.

The women's downhill was won by Trude Jochum-Beiser of Austria, but both slaloms were won by a girl from the U.S.A., Andrea Mead-Lawrence. As 15-year-old Andrea Mead she had competed in St. Moritz in 1948, finishing 35th and eighth in the downhill and slalom, but with more experience and a husband, skier Dave Lawrence, she won the giant slalom from Austria's Dagmar Rom and then the slalom from Germany's Ossi Reichert, after a fall in the first leg. She fell in the downhill. Germany's Annemarie Buchner got a silver and two bronze medals in the three races.

Dick Button of the U.S.A. performed the first triple-rotation jump in the men's figure skating, and won the gold medal even more easily than he had in 1948. The women's title went to Great Britain's Jeanette Altwegg, third in 1948, who won from Tenley Albright, a 16-year-old American, who was to win in 1956. Miss Altwegg retired to help run the Pestalozzi Children's Village in Switzerland. The pairs title was won by Paul and Ria Falk from Germany, a husband and wife team who beat Michael and Karol Kennedy of the U.S.A. and Laszlo and Marianna Nagy of Hungary.

An American, Ken Henry, won the 500-

Above: The Olympic arena at Bislett, Oslo, where the speed-skating events were held.

Left: Zeno Colo of Italy who won the downhill event in 1952.

Below: Stein Eriksen wins the giant slalom at the 1952 Olympic Games.

Oslo

Right: The medalists in the women's figure skating: Jeanette Altwegg of Great Britain won the gold, Tenley Albright of the U.S.A. (left), the silver (she won the gold in 1956), and Jacqueline du Bief of France, the bronze.

Below: Kenneth Henry of the U.S.A. in the 500-metres speed skating, in which he took the gold medal.

metres speed skating from his colleague Donald McDermott, but the three longer races were all won by the star of the Games, Norways' Hjalmar Andersen. He won his three gold medals on consecutive days; Kees Broekman of Holland was the runner-up in the two longer races.

German crews won both bobsled events from the U.S.A. and Switzerland, Andreas Ostler and Lorenz Nieberl winning two gold medals each, but the German crews were so heavy that the International Bobsleigh Federation had to introduce a weight limit for sleds and riders into its rules to make competition fairer.

The ice-hockey title was retained by Canada, whose only dropped point was in a draw with the U.S.A., the silver medalists, whose tactics were considered somewhat rough.

The organization of the Games was faultless, and a triumph in every respect for the Norwegians, who headed the medal count easily. There was a little criticism of the difficulties of transport to reach the various venues, but the knowledge and hospitality of the Norwegian officials and spectators were well received.

Dick Button

Richard Button was one of the great figure skaters, and he performed the first triple loop in a major championship in the 1952 Olympics. He was born on 18 July 1929 in Eaglewood, New Jersey, and won his first U.S. title in 1946 and held it until 1952. He was European champion (then an Open championship) in 1948 and world champion from 1948 to 1952. He easily won the Olympic gold medals in 1948 and 1952. His only defeat after 1943 was in the 1947 world championship, when he was beaten by Hans Gerschwiler of Switzerland. He was a dynamic free-skater, who did much to popularize the sport in the U.S.A. He turned professional in 1952, becoming a television commentator and a member of the Ice Capades, and graduated from Harvard Law School.

Above: The speed-skating star of 1952 was Hjalmar Andersen of Norway, seen during his victorious 10,000-metres race. He had already won the 1,500 and 5,000 metres.

Both bobsleigh events in 1952 were won by Germany. Andreas Ostler (left) and Lorenz Nieberl (right) won two gold medals each.

Helsinki

The sky is filled with pigeons at the opening ceremony of the 1952 Olympics in Helsinki.

Helsinki had been chosen for the Olympic Games of 1940, when Tokyo was forced to relinquish it because of the war. In turn, Helsinki also had to forego the honour. However, on 17 June 1947, Helsinki was awarded the Games for 1952.

Right: The athletes of the day broke ranks to see the legendary Paavo Nurmi carry the torch into the stadium and light the sacred Olympic flame.

Preparations were enthusiastic. Everything was done to make this the best Games so far. Nearly 5,000 sportsmen and women from 59 nations took part, and the rivalry between the U.S.A. and the U.S.S.R. and exciting performances from outstanding personalities ensured a success. The rain which began at the opening ceremony was the only mild blemish. Germany and Japan were back and the Soviets sent a squad for the first time in 40 years. There were omissions: East Germany was not granted Olympic recognition, and when Red China was accepted, Nationalist China withdrew. In the event Red China did not appear.

The Soviets proved awkward, not permitting the Olympic torch relay on Soviet territory, and then refusing to allow their athletes to live in the Olympic village. At first the Soviets intended to fly their athletes in for their events, but then a special village for the Eastern Communist countries was built at Otaniemi, 5 miles (8 km) outside Helsinki. This flouting of the Olympic spirit was, surprisingly, sanctioned by the I.O.C., and it is a measure of the friendliness of the Games that as events progressed, fraternization between Eastern and Western athletes increased. New blocks of flats were built for the main men's village at Kapyla, 1½ miles (2.4 km) from the stadium, while the women's village was in a nurses' training college half a mile from the stadium.

The opening ceremony witnessed an amusing intervention by a large lady in white, who managed half a lap of the track before being allowed onto the rostrum to begin a speech. She was bustled off and identified as a young German peace zealot.

Not only the Finnish spectators were moved when it was seen that the Olympic torch was being carried into the stadium by none other than a nearly bald 55-year-old Paavo Nurmi. After lighting the Olympic flame he handed the torch over to 62-year-old Hannes Kolehmainen, who lit a second flame on top of the stadium tower, precisely 72.71 metres high, the distance of the winning javelin throw by Matti Jarvinen in 1932.

On the track, the 100 metres was an extremely close race. Lindy Remigino of the U.S.A. led from the start, followed closely by E. McDonald Bailey of Great Britain and Dean Smith of the U.S.A. Herb McKenley of Jamaica finished fastest so that these four crossed the line almost together and all four were given the same time. Only two metres separated the first six runners. Opinion as to the winner was divided between Remigino and McKenley. The official photograph was studied, and Remigino was given the gold, although many, McKenley included, could not separate the first two, and if ever a race could have been called a dead-heat, it was this one.

Andy Stanfield of the U.S.A., perhaps the fastest sprinter at the Games, decided to concentrate on the 200 metres, and he duly took the race comparatively comfortably from fellow Americans Thane Baker and James Gathers.

Herb McKenley of Jamaica, the unlucky 100-metres second, was also in the 400-metres final, the event in which he had been favourite in 1948, but had lost to another Jamaican, Wint. In 1952 he again found a compatriot too good, losing by inches to George Rhoden. As in the 100 metres he was given the same time as the winner, a new Olympic record, but on this occasion was clearly, if very narrowly, beaten.

The United States took the 4 × 100-metres relay in which Remigino and Stanfield won their second gold. Harrison Dillard also won a second gold when he later won the hurdles. Dean Smith was the fourth member of that team which beat the U.S.S.R. and Hungary. Everybody was pleased when Jamaica took the 4 × 400-metres relay. It made up for the disappointment in 1948, when the team was leading until Wint suffered cramp, and it finally provided McKenley with his gold medal. Wint and Rhoden were also in the team, with Leslie Laing. McKenley made up yards to pass the U.S. runner on the third leg and Rhoden came home in a new world record, with the Americans, just behind, also inside the old record.

Left: The photo-finish in the 100 metres. The athletes, from the top, are Vladimir Soukharev of the U.S.S.R., Herb McKenley of Jamaica (second), Lindy Remigino of the U.S.A. (first), Dean Smith of the U.S.A., Emmanuel McDonald Bailey of Great Britain (third) and Jack Treloar of Australia.

A member of the defeated American relay team was Mal Whitfield, sixth in the individual 400 metres, and holder of the Olympic 800-metre title. He retained his title by repeating his record time of 1948, with Arthur Wint once again a couple of strides back.

The 1,500-metres field included Great Britain's Roger Bannister, who two years later became the first man to run a mile in

The U.S.A. took all the medals in the 200 metres. Andy Stanfield (983) is shown winning, Thane Baker (984) was second and James Gathers (985) was third. McDonald Bailey of Great Britain (166) was fourth.

Helsinki

Mal Whitfield

Mal Whitfield was a good runner at distances from 100 yards to a mile, but was best at 800 metres and 880 yards. He was born on 11 October 1924 in Bay City, Texas, and came to the fore at the London Olympics of 1948 in which he won the 800 metres, took a gold in the 4 × 400-metres relay, and a bronze in the 400 metres. Between June 1948 and June 1954 he was beaten only twice at his specialist distances. He returned to the Olympics in 1952 and again won the 800 metres, finished sixth in the 400 metres and won a silver medal in the 4 × 400-metres relay. A powerful competitor, Whitfield usually made his winning effort going into the back straight on the second lap of his two-lap races. He equalled the 880-yard world record in 1950 and broke it in 1953, when he also broke the 1,000-m world record. He was in the U.S. teams which broke world records for 4 × 400-m and 4 × 800-m relays in 1952.

Above: The last bend of the 1,500 metres. Josef Barthel of Luxembourg (406) won; Bob McMillen of U.S.A., running third, finished second; and Werner Lueg of Germany (739) was third. Great Britain's Roger Bannister, running eighth, was fourth.

under four minutes. He was a warm favourite, with Germany's Werner Lueg and Frenchman Patrick El Mabrouk regarded as the danger men. The field was so large an extra heat had to be run, which told against Bannister, never a robust runner. The pace in the final was fast, but Bannister's customary back-straight sprint failed to shake off the field, and two outsiders shot through to contest the gold. Luxembourg's Josef Barthel won his country's only gold medal in an Olympic record, 5.3 seconds faster than he had ever run before, and American Bob McMillen, a failure in the steeplechase in 1948, was just two metres behind. Lueg was third and Bannister fourth.

The 5,000 metres was won by the undoubted star of the Games, Emil Zatopek, the silver medalist of 1948. Zatopek was a showman who grimaced in apparent agony throughout most of his races. In a heat of the 5,000 metres he had finished third after practically stopping in a successful effort to encourage a Soviet, Aleksander Anufriev, to win. The final was an exciting race, with four runners entering the back straight together: Great Britain's Chris Chataway leading from Germany's Herbert Schade, France's Allain Mimoun and Czechoslovakia's Zatopek. As Schade went to pass Chataway, Chataway tripped on the curb and fell, probably due to exhaustion more than anything else. Zatopek and Mimoun also shot past, and finished first and second, with Schade third. It was one of the closest races in Zatopek's medal-winning career.

The 10,000 metres was quite different. Zatopek was the holder and after seven laps he sprinted into a lead. Only Mimoun and Great Britain's Gordon Pirie tried to stay with him, but Zatopek's technique of putting in sudden spurts killed them off, and he won by half a lap, knocking no less than 42.6 seconds from his Olympic record. Mimoun, as in 1948, held on for second, like Edwin Wide in the era of Nurmi, being unfortunate to be a contemporary of one of the world's best ever.

To complete a triumphant Games, Zatopek ran in his first-ever marathon, shattering the favourite and world-record holder Jim Peters of Great Britain, who was leading, by asking if they were going fast enough. Peters collapsed with cramp, Zatopek took the lead soon after halfway and won by 2½ minutes from Reinaldo Gorno of Argentina and Gustaf Jansson of Sweden, the half-way leader.

Harrison Dillard, the hurdler who had won the 100 metres in 1948, took the 110-metres

Harrison Dillard

Harrison Dillard was born on 8 July 1923 in Cleveland, Ohio, and was inspired by Jesse Owens, who presented him with his 1936 Games running spikes, to become a great athlete. He specialized in the high hurdles, and in June 1948 was unbeaten in 82 consecutive hurdles races and holder of the world records at 120- and 220-yards hurdles. In the U.S. Olympic trials he hit a hurdle and failed to finish, and was thus omitted from the team for the 1948 London Olympics. He qualified as only third string for the 100 metres, but the story has a romantic end; he won the event, equalling Owens' time, and established a joint Olympic record. He also won a gold medal in the 4 × 100-metres relay. In the 1952 Olympics, he was entered in his favourite 110-metres hurdles. Short for a high hurdler at 5 feet 10 inches (1.78 metres), he had great speed between the hurdles, and he won in Olympic record time. Later he won his fourth Olympic gold medal in the 4 × 100-metres relay.

Above: The famous incident when Chris Chataway of Great Britain fell in the final of the 5,000 metres. Emil Zatopek of Czechoslovakia leads, Allain Mimoun of France is second, and Herbert Schade of Germany is third – the order in which they finished.

Opposite top: The 800 metres. Arthur Wint of Jamaica, who is leading, finished second; Heinz Ulzheimer of Germany, just behind, was third; and Mal Whitfield (986) of the U.S.A. came through to win the event for the second time.

Harrison Dillard of the U.S.A. (1002), the 100-metres winner in 1948, takes the final hurdle to win his specialist event, the 110-metres hurdles, in 1952.

Helsinki

Right: Jerome Biffle of the U.S.A., an army private, wins the long jump. He was making a comeback to competition after a two-year absence.

Far right: Celebrating the leap which brought him his first gold medal in the pole vault is Bob Richards of the U.S.A., sometimes known as the 'Vaulting Vicar'.

hurdles, winning from two other Americans, Jack Davis and Arthur Barnard.

The U.S.A. also won the 400-metres hurdles, when Charles Moore justified his selection as favourite with an easy win over Yuriy Lituyev of the U.S.S.R. There was another American victory over the U.S.S.R. in the steeplechase, but this time Vladimir Kazantsev from Kiev was a firm favourite. He led in the last lap, but slipped at the water jump. Horace Ashenfelter, an F.B.I. agent, shot past to win, and Kazantsev only just held off Great Britain's John Disley for the silver.

In the walks, John Mikaelsson of Sweden repeated his 1948 win in the 10 km and Italy's Guiseppe Dordoni won the 50 km.

American high-jump victor, Walter Davis, had suffered from polio as a boy and had taken to jumping to strengthen his legs. He won from another American, Ken Wiesner. The U.S.A. also took the first two places in the long jump (Jerome Biffle won the gold) and the first two in the pole vault (the winner was preacher Bob Richards, who had been third in 1948 and was to win again in 1956).

The triple jump was also won by an athlete who repeated his win in 1956. Brazil's Adhemar Ferreira da Silva broke his own world record four times.

The shot was a clean sweep for the U.S.A., and was won by 20-year-old Parry O'Brien, who developed the current style of shot-putting. This was the first of four Olympics for O'Brien; his personal best shot put would occur 14 years in the future. Sam Iness won the discus for the U.S.A., beating the 1948 winner, Adolfo Consolini of Italy, into second place. Hungary's Josef Csermak won the hammer, with his countryman, Imre Nemeth, the 1948 champion, third; Karl Storch of Germany separated them.

The javelin, a Finnish speciality, was a disappointment for the spectators, as the leading Finn, Toivo Hyytiainen, could finish only third behind two Americans; the giant Cy Young took the gold.

The decathlon was a repeat victory for American Bob Mathias, who had said after winning in 1948 that he would not compete in the decathlon again. However, he set a world record in 1950, and, bigger and stronger in 1952, he retained his title easily with another world record, the only dual Olympic decathlon winner.

In the women's events there was a superb Australian sprinter, Marjorie Jackson, who easily won both the 100 metres and the 200 metres, equalling the world record in the

Far left: A great triple-jump specialist, Adhemar Ferreira da Silva of Brazil, sets a world record in winning his first Olympic gold medal.

Left: There was another world record in the javelin and the only American men's victory in this event to date, when Cy Young took the gold.

former. Between 1950 and 1954 Marjorie Jackson won nine gold medals in major Games and beat or equalled six world records. Her only major defeat was in the 4 × 100-metres relay in the 1952 Olympics, when the baton was knocked from her hand on the last take-over, with Australia leading. The U.S.A. won in a world record time from Germany and Great Britain.

There was another impressive Australian in the 80-metres hurdles; Shirley Strickland also broke the world record when she won the gold.

A South African, Esther Brand, won the high jump from Great Britain's Sheila Lerwill, and Yvette Williams of New Zealand the long jump from U.S.S.R.'s Alexandra Chudina, who was third in the high jump, and Great Britain's Shirley Cawley. The shot and discus were won by Soviets, Galina Zybina winning the former and Nina Romashkova the latter. The javelin was won by Dana Zatopkova of Czechoslovakia, Emil's wife, who won the same day that her husband took the 5,000 metres.

The swimming pool saw a wide spread of medals although the American men and the Hungarian women dominated. The Japanese men were disappointing, managing only

Left: Hungary retained the Olympic championship in the hammer through the victory of Josef Csermak.

Helsinki

silver medals. The victory of Jean Boiteux of France in the 400-metres freestyle was followed by his father diving fully clothed into the pool in celebration. American Army Major Sammy Lee retained his highboard diving title.

In the women's events, Hungarian women won three of the four individual races, and broke the world record in the 4 × 100-metres freestyle relay, in which Katalin Szoke won her second gold medal, having already won a close 100 metres. Eva Novak of the relay team had already won two individual silvers. Mrs. Pat McCormick of the U.S.A. took both women's diving titles.

Of the ten boxing titles, the U.S.A. won five. Floyd Patterson won the middleweight title, and was later to be world professional heavyweight champion, losing and regaining this title in fights with Sweden's Ingemar Johansson. Johansson was disgraced in the Olympic heavyweight final, when he was disqualified for not trying against Ed Sanders of the U.S.A., thus forfeiting even a silver medal. Sanders also turned professional but died of a brain injury received in the ring. Laszlo Papp, the middleweight champion of 1948, won the new light-middleweight category in 1952. Had he fought Patterson in the

middleweight class, he would probably have won. In a preliminary round he knocked out Ellsworth 'Spider' Webb, an outstanding future professional.

The U.S.S.R. made a big haul of medals in the gymnastics, eight of the 22 being gold (including the two team competitions). Viktor Chukarin won four gold and two silver medals.

Great Britain's lone gold medal came in the equestrian events, when the British team won the team medal in the show jumping, the last event of the Games. André Jousseaume of France won the bronze in the dressage, his fifth medal in his fourth Olympics.

Six countries supplied the six gold medalists in the shooting, Karoly Takacs of Hungary winning his second gold medal in the rapid-fire pistol. The modern pentathlon winner was Lars Hall, who won the seventh gold medal for Sweden in this event in eight Olympic Games, but surprisingly Sweden was beaten by Hungary in the new team event.

France, Italy and Hungary shared the fencing gold medals, as in 1948. No other country had supplied a gold medal winner since 1932. The great Hungarian fencer, Ilona Elek, now 45 years old, having won the

The finish of the women's 200 metres, and a victory for Australia's great sprinter Marjorie Jackson. She is hiding Bertha Brouwer of Holland who came second. Nadyezhda Khnykina of the U.S.S.R. (third) is on the left.

The first Olympic gold medal for the U.S.S.R. after an absence of 40 years from Olympic competition was won by Nina Romashkova in the discus. She won again in 1960 as Nina Ponomaryeva.

individual foil in 1936 and 1948, lost the gold after a tie with Irene Camber of Italy, whom she had already beaten twice in the competition.

Russell Mockridge of Australia won two cycling gold medals. John Davis of the U.S.A. retained his heavyweight title in the weightlifting, in which Americans and Soviets divided the gold medals 4–3. In the wrestling Axel Groenberg of Sweden was the only 1948 winner to repeat his win, in the Greco-Roman middleweight class.

On the water, Sweden's Gert Fredriksson continued collecting Olympic medals when he took his third gold and second silver in the canoeing, and Denmark's Paul Elvstrom took

his second gold in the yachting. There was a young winner in the coxed pairs rowing event; Bernard Malivoire, who coxed France's Raymond Salles and Gaston Mercier to a gold, was only 12 years old.

In the team games, India won the field hockey for the fifth successive time, the U.S.A. the basketball for the third successive time (with Bob Kurland winning a second gold medal), and Hungary won the association football for the first time with one of the finest sides ever seen, including such players as Bozsik, Kocsis, Puskas and Hidegkuti. This side, in the following year, became the first foreign side ever to beat England on an English pitch.

Bob Mathias

Bob Mathias, born on 17 November 1930 in Tulare, California, was thin and anaemic as a child, but by the time he reached high school had developed a muscular frame and shown ability as an all-round sportsman. Persuaded to take up the decathlon, he qualified for the U.S. Olympic squad only 16 days after his first trial. Still three months short of his 18th birthday he surprised everybody by winning this most exhausting event in the 1948 Olympics. 'Never again,' he said, but in 1950 he won the U.S. championship and set a world record at his home town of Tulare. He retained this title in 1951 and 1952 and attempted to become the only athlete to retain a decathlon championship at the 1952 Olympics in Helsinki. He won easily by 912 points and set yet another new world record with the following performances: 10.9 seconds in 100 metres, 6.98 metres (22 feet 11 inches) in the long jump, 15.30 metres (50 feet 2½ inches) in the shot, 1.90 metres (6 feet 3 inches) in the high jump, 50.2 seconds in the 400 metres, 14.7 seconds in the 110-metres hurdles, 46.89 metres (153 feet 9¾ inches) in the discus, 4.00 metres (13 feet 1½ inches) in the pole vault, 59.21 metres (194 feet 2½ inches) in the javelin and 4 minutes 50.8 seconds in the 1,500 metres. Mathias at his peak was 6 feet 3 inches (1.90 metres) tall and weighed 217 lb (98.43 kg). He was never beaten in a decathlon. In 1953 he lost his amateur status by appearing in a film about his career. He took up politics and was a member of the House of Representatives.

Above: Pat McCormick of the U.S.A. had an impressive Olympic record, winning both the highboard and springboard titles at two Olympic Games, 1952 and 1956.

Bob Mathias in the high jump. He is the only man to date to win two Olympic decathlon titles.

When the Games had ended it was generally agreed that this had been the finest yet. There were no controversies, only outstanding personalities and performances. The crowds had been enthusiastic, and while there were no Finnish track and field gold medals, the Finns could rejoice that the star of the Games, Emil Zatopek, was a worthy successor to their great athletes, Kolehmainen and Nurmi.

The behaviour of the Soviets, returning to the Olympics after 40 years, was a pointer to Communist attitudes of the future. They had only competed when assured of doing well, and had remained aloof and apart in their own quarters. Before the Games they had stated that sport was a weapon in the fight for peace and the promotion of friendship among peoples, a sentiment with which Coubertin would have entirely agreed, but coming from the U.S.S.R. it had the chilly air of meaning something quite different.

The propaganda did not go well for the Soviets. They erected a huge scoreboard in their village to show the unofficial points totals of competing nations. After the gymnastics and wrestling events, the board showed them with a big lead, which continued up until the last day. When the Americans came with a late rush of medals including five boxing gold, the Soviets hastily removed all the points from their board. The final 'score' was U.S.A. 614, U.S.S.R. $553\frac{1}{2}$.

Sigfrid Edstrom retired and Avery Brundage became President of the International Olympic Committee. He was satisfied with the Games, saying that international friendship and fair play had been brought closer, but warning that the spirit of the Olympics would be destroyed if it became a giant contest between two great nations. He was to have his problems in the future, but meanwhile, as the *New York Times* said: 'The dream does not wholly die'.

Emil Zatopek

Emil Zatopek was one of the best and most popular distance runners, whose front-running style combined even-paced running with devastating sprints to kill off his rivals. With his habit of rolling his head and grimacing as if each breath were his last he was cheered by spectators wherever he went. He was born on 19 September 1922 in Koprivnice, Moravia, soon after the state of Czechoslovakia was founded. He worked in a shoe factory, and did not discover his great talent until he was 18 years old. At 22 he was breaking Czech records at distances up to 5,000 metres, and he ran in the European Championships of 1946, finishing fifth. At the 1948 Olympics he ran away from the field in the 10,000 metres, and produced an amazing last lap in the 5,000 metres, just failing to win after apparently having given up with a lap to go. In 1949 he began breaking world records, twice reducing the 10,000-metres time in the European Championships of 1950. He came to the 1952 Helsinki Olympics at his best. He won the 10,000 metres, again with ease, took the 5,000 metres with another devastating last lap and then entered his first marathon. He came into the stadium a full $2\frac{1}{2}$ minutes ahead of the field. He was then 30, but set about breaking world records at new distances. In all, between 1949 and 1955, he set 18 world records, at all distances between 5,000 metres and 30,000 metres. At the 1954 European Championships, while he and Chris Chataway were watching each other closely in the 5,000 metres, Vladimir Kuts beat both by using Zatopek's method of running in quick bursts – he never came back to the field. Zatopek, however, won the 10,000 metres. In 1956 he ran in his last Olympics, finishing sixth behind his old adversary, Alain Mimoun, in the marathon. His wife Dana was also a world record holder in the javelin, an event she won at the 1952 Olympics and 1954 European Championships on the days that Emil also won gold medals. Zatopek supported Premier Dubcek in the Prague revolution of Spring 1968 and lost his Communist party membership, his rank of Colonel in the Czech army and his sports coaching position. What he will never lose is the affection of his followers, inspired by his efforts and his sportsmanship.

Cortina d'Ampezzo

The 1956 Winter Olympics began at the end of January at Cortina d'Ampezzo in Italy. Snow arrived just before the Games started, after three weeks without, just in time to prevent the organizers from needing to fetch it from the Alps. Superb venues had been subsidized by money from the state-owned Italian football pools, *Totocalcio*. This was the first Winter Olympics to be televised in other countries, and the carnival atmosphere came over well. The 800 competitors were the most yet, although they came from only 24 nations. The Soviets competed for the first time and surprisingly took most medals, although the star of the Games was an Austrian, Toni Sailer.

The Games were opened by President Giovanni Gronchi, and there was an amusing incident when Guido Caroli, the speed skater, tripped over a microphone wire while carrying the torch, brought from the Temple at Jupiter in Rome, around the arena. Luckily only the dignity of the occasion was injured.

The Scandinavian monopoly of Nordic skiing events was at last broken when the U.S.S.R. won the 4 × 10-km relay. Scandinavians held on to the individual events in the men's competitons; Hallgeir Brenden of Norway repeated his 1952 victory in the 15-km (until this Games the distance had been

Above: Sixten Jernberg of Sweden in the 1956 Olympics. He won a gold, two silver and a bronze in Nordic skiing events, and added three more gold and another bronze in 1960 and 1964.

Toni Sailer of Austria wins the giant slalom. By winning all three Alpine skiing events he established himself as the greatest Alpine skier in Olympic history.

Hayes Jenkins of the U.S.A. won the men's figure skating event. His brother, David, who was to win in 1960, came third.

18-km) cross-country, and Veikko Hakulinen of Finland won the new 30 km race, having won the 50 km in 1952. Sixten Jernberg of Sweden won the 50 km, finishing second in the other two cross-country races.

The ski jumping for the first time was *not* won by a Norwegian – the nearest Norwegian was ninth. Finns, holding their arms back in the new style, took the first two places, Antti Hyvarinen winning. It was the end of Norwegian domination. Sverre Stenersen, however, won the Nordic combined for Norway. A Soviet, Ljubox Kozyreva, won the women's 10-km cross-country, while Finland took the 3 × 5-km relay.

The Alpine skiing was a triumph for Austria's Toni Sailer. He first won the giant slalom by more than six seconds from Anderl Molterer who, like him, came from Kitz-

buhel. He then took the special slalom by four seconds from Chiharu Igaya, who won Japan's first winter Games medal, although he was living in the U.S.A. He finished by taking the downhill by $3\frac{1}{2}$ seconds from Raymond Fellay of Switzerland, on a difficult course in which three quarters of the skiers fell.

Swiss girls won two of the women's Alpine events. Madeleine Berthod won the downhill as impressively as Sailer, finishing with a margin of nearly five seconds over Frieda Daenzer of Switzerland. Berthod was fifth in the slalom; Renne Colliard won the gold for Switzerland. Ossi Reichert of Germany won the giant slalom, having been second in the slalom in 1952.

American skaters, inspired by Dick Button, took all three medals in the men's figure skating. Hayes Jenkins, the world champion,

Cortina d'Ampezzo

won, but a brilliant free-skating display by Ronald Robertson almost caught him. The judges took two hours to decide the placings. Jenkins' younger brother, David, took the bronze.

The ladies' figure skating title was won by Tenley Albright (U.S.A.), the silver medalist of 1952, from Carol Heiss, also of the U.S.A. Albright skated with an injured ankle, having cut it with a skate in practice. The pairs title marginally went to Kurt Oppelt and Eliza-

The winner of the women's figure skating title, Tenley Albright of the U.S.A., in the compulsory figures.

beth Schwarz of Austria, but the judges were pelted with oranges after their markings of some of the lower-placed competitors.

The Soviets came to the Games expecting to win some speed-skating titles, and they were not disappointed. Yevgeniy Grischin won the 500 metres in a world record time, and then broke the world 1,500-metres record in tying with another Soviet, Jurij Mikailov. Both were awarded the gold. Boris Schilkov won the 5,000 metres, and a Swede, Sigvard Ericsson, won the 10,000 metres to prevent a clean sweep of gold for the U.S.S.R. Grischin had competed in the 1952 Games as a cyclist.

Italy's only gold medal came in the two-man bob, and Switzerland won the four-man, Franz Kapus, at 46 becoming the oldest gold medal winner in the Winter Olympics. The great Italian bobsledder, Eugenio Monti, was in the crews which finished second in each race.

The Soviets won the ice hockey, beating both Canada and the U.S.A., and the Canadians' defeat by the Americans relegated them to third place, their worst result till then.

The Games was a great success for the U.S.S.R., who headed the unofficial medals table, and hinted at expected Soviet prominence in the Summer Olympics to come. The biggest winner was probably the winter holiday industry as the widely televised Games had been seen by millions.

Toni Sailer

Toni (short for Anton) Sailer has claims to being the greatest Alpine skier of all. He was born on 19 November 1935 in Kitzbuhel, Austria, and had his first big success in the Lauberhorn Cup in 1955. In the Olympic Games of 1956 he won all three Alpine skiing medals (only Killy has since emulated him). The manner and margin of his wins set him apart from other skiers. He used an exciting hip-swinging *wedeln* style. The Games made the handsome plumber an overnight celebrity, and he appeared in a number of films. They also made him world champion, a title he retained in 1958, but he was criticized for making money from the sport and retired at 23 to train the Austrian ski team.

The Soviet speed skater, Yevgeniy Grischin, won both the 500 metres and the 1,500 metres in both 1956 and 1960, and won a silver medal at his third Olympics in 1964.

Below left: Toni Sailer, whose performances in the Alpine skiing in 1956 made him an Austrian idol.

Below: A general scene of the speed skating at Cortina in 1956. The skater passing the finishing line is Boris Schilkov of the U.S.S.R., the winner of the 5,000 metres.

Melbourne

The Duke of Edinburgh takes the salute at the opening of the 1956 Olympic Games in Melbourne, the first Games held in the southern hemisphere. On the left is the President of the International Olympic Committee, Avery Brundage.

Bobby Morrow

Bobby Morrow was born on 15 October 1935 in Harlingen, Texas. He studied at Abilene Christian College, and chose to concentrate on athletics rather than football, excelling at both. He was selected for the 1956 Olympic sprints and emulated Owens when he won gold medals in the 100 and 200 metres and the relay, not being beaten in any of his races, and when he set a world record in the 4 × 100-metres relay. He was beaten only once in a major race in three years. In 1956 and 1957 he equalled the world record at 100 yards and 100 and 200 metres. A powerful man at 6 feet 1½ inches (1.87 metres) he was an elegant, relaxed runner, who just missed selection for the 1960 Olympics.

Bobby Morrow of the U.S.A. wins the 100 metres in Melbourne. He was the first male sprinter since Jesse Owens to complete the sprint double.

For the first time the Olympic Games was held in the southern hemisphere, and thus came late in the year, running from 22 November to 8 December 1956.

The world was once more in conflict. Shortly before the Games came the Hungarian uprising and its brutal crushing by the Soviet Union. Thus the news from Hungary preceded the Olympic news from Melbourne in the world's newspapers. In addition British, French and Israeli troops had been engaged against Egypt over the Suez Canal.

There were withdrawals and talk of cancellation. The Dutch withdrew over the Soviet violence in Hungary, followed by Spain and Switzerland. Egypt withdrew, after demanding the disqualification of their 'aggressors', and were joined by Iraq and the Lebanon.

The Hungarians themselves took part. Some had been on their way to Australia before the U.S.S.R. had sent in its tanks and others had been awaiting a plane in Prague. Fierce fighting began while they were there but as they had been unable to return to Budapest, they had proceeded, fearing for their families, to Melbourne. They were greeted at Essendon Airport by earlier refugees, by Australian well-wishers and by the press, and wept as they were presented with flowers and sympathy. They sang 'God Bless Hungary' around crepe-draped flags.

Avery Brundage insisted the Games would *not* be cancelled. 'We will not let any country use the Olympics for political purposes' he said. There was a rumour that the rules prevented warring nations taking part, but this was squashed.

There were the more usual worries about the preparations. The Australians experienced such delays in building the venues that Brundage was forced to make an inspection trip. The Olympic village training track was still unready when the Games began. The village itself was excellent, and the hospitality of the Australians of the highest order. The Hungarians tore down the Communist flag over their quarters, and raised the flag of Free Hungary. There was trouble when, by mistake, the flag of Communist China was raised over the quarters of the Republic of China. Red China again did not take part, as they did not recognize the Republic.

Eventually over 3,000 athletes were ready for the Games to begin. This was the smallest number since 1932, but 71 nations were represented. Ethiopia, Kenya and Malaya appeared for the first time, and East and West Germany sent a joint team.

The Duke of Edinburgh opened the Games at the Melbourne Cricket Ground, where a new track had been laid. The weather was extremely hot, and several athletes fainted at the opening ceremony, among them Galina Zybina, the powerful women's shot-put champion. The Olympic flame was lit by the junior world mile record holder, Ron Clarke, soon to be one of the world's great athletes, who burnt his arm doing it. There was tremendous applause during the parade for the Hungarian team, not all in uniform because of the chaos of their arrival. Eleven American warships and U.S. Air Force planes were to have visited Melbourne for the Games, but were absent because of 'the current world situation'.

The equestrian events were not held in Melbourne because of Australia's quarantine regulations, but had been held earlier in Stockholm.

Spectators at the track and field events witnessed some superb performances. The U.S.A. had one of its best sprinters in 21-year-old Bobby Morrow. He came from behind smoothly to win the 100 metres from another American, Thane Baker, and an Australian, Hector Hogan, who had led. He won the 200 metres even more easily, beating Andy Stanfield, the 1952 winner, and Thane Baker who came third. Morrow and Baker joined Ira Murchison and Leamon King to take the 4 × 100-metres relay. Morrow was first to the tape in all his races, heats and finals. He won three gold medals. Baker's gold accompanied two silver and a bronze, won in individual events in 1952 and 1956. The fastest man in the relay squad might have been Leamon King, joint 100 metres world record holder, who had finished fourth in the U.S. trials.

America had a surprise winner in the 400 metres when Charles Jenkins beat his team-mate, world record holder Lou Jones, who ran out of stamina and finished fifth after starting too fast in the outside lane. There was a tie for the bronze medal, the only one ever on the track.

The 800-metres final was one of the closest and best races of the Games. American Tom Courtney, a big powerful runner, took the lead 80 metres from the tape and sprinted for the line only to be overtaken by Great Britain's Derek Johnson, a much smaller man. Straining every sinew, Courtney rallied, and the two broke the tape almost together. Courtney collapsed and needed medical treatment. Half expecting he had lost, he was told he had won the gold by inches.

The 1,500 metres provided a rare and surprising gold medal for Ireland. The crowd hoped John Landy, Bannister's great rival, who had taken the Olympic oath on behalf of the athletes, could win, but he had suffered leg trouble and could finish only third. Ireland's Ron Delany had recently lost twice to Great Britain's Brian Hewson, who was first to sprint for the tape, but Delany finished strongest to win from Klaus Richtzenhain of Germany.

The 10,000 metres was run on the first day, as usual, and was a dramatic race. The U.S.S.R.'s Vladimir Kuts and Great Britain's Gordon Pirie, who had been swopping world records, were the principals. Kuts started at suicidal pace, and only Pirie kept with him.

The finish of the 800 metres. Tom Courtney of the U.S.A. (153) just beats Derek Johnson of Great Britain (137) on the line.

Kuts then began a series of sprints, passing 5,000 metres in a time faster than Zatopek's Olympic record. Still Pirie kept with him, 100 metres ahead of the rest. At 8,000 metres Kuts slowed, forcing Pirie to lead, and then burst past with another sprint. Pirie was beaten at last and eventually dropped back to eighth, but undoubtedly was the second best man in the field. Hungarian Jozsef Kovacs finished second, but refused to shake hands with Kuts. Pirie declared himself 'murdered' and never forgot the race.

In the 5,000 metres five days later, Kuts again led throughout. Great Britain had a trio of great middle-distance runners in the race: Chris Chataway, Derek Ibbotson and, of course, Pirie. Pirie at the time held the world record, Chataway had held it in the past and

The strength of Vladimir Kuts' leg muscles are suggested in this photograph of him as he nears the end of the 5,000 metres, in which he won his second gold medal.

Christopher Brasher of Great Britain takes the water jump on his way to a surprise victory in the 3,000-metres steeplechase. Controversy followed his win.

had beaten Kuts in a dramatic race in London, and Ibbotson was to break the mile world record next year. They followed Kuts at a respectful distance. Pirie this time did not attempt to stay with him, and won the silver medal he deserved; Ibbotson took the bronze. Hungary, too, had some excellent middle-distance runners at this time, notably Laszlo Tabori, Istvan Rozsavolgyi and Sandor Iharos, who had held the 5,000 and 10,000 metres world records. Not surprisingly they could not do themselves justice at the Games.

The 3,000-metres steeplechase was a surprise win for Great Britain's Chris Brasher, who had paced Bannister to the first four-minute mile, but who was very much Britain's third string behind John Disley and Eric Shirley. Brasher, an ungainly runner, who relied on guts rather than style, won fairly easily after a bumpy race, only to be disqualified for an alleged foul on Norway's Ernst Larsen. Hungary's Sandor Rozsnyoi, the second man home, was awarded the race. There was an appeal, and all three medal winners sportingly spoke up for Brasher. Three hours after the event Brasher was reinstated as the deserving winner.

There was a popular victory in the marathon when 36-year-old Alain Mimoun of France, the man who had three times followed Zatopek home in Olympic events, won by $1\frac{1}{2}$ minutes. Zatopek was also in the race, making his Olympic farewell, and finished sixth. Mimoun, waving aside photographers, patiently waited for Zatopek to finish, and the two friends congratulated each other on splendid careers.

The 4 × 400-metres relay and the two hurdles races were triumphs for the United States. Jenkins and Courtney won their second gold medals in the relay and Americans won all the medals in the hurdles: Lee Calhoun just beat Jack Davis in the shorter race; Davis earned his second silver in close finishes in this event; and Glenn Davis won the longer race.

Leonid Spirin won the Soviet Union's third gold medal in men's track and field in the 20-km walk, three more than the U.S.S.R. had won in 1948, and a New Zealander, Norman Read, lead throughout to win the longer walk.

The U.S.A., as usual, dominated the field events. Charles Dumas, the first man to jump 7 feet (2.13 metres), was considered a certainty for the high jump, but only just beat Charles Porter, an Australian. Bob Richards, too, was a hot favourite for the pole vault, but he twice failed to clear 3.40 metres (11 feet 1¾ inches), well below his best. However, he succeeded with his third try and won at 4.56 metres (14 feet 11½ inches). The long jump also went to an American, Gregory Bell. The triple jump was a repeat win by the great Brazilian specialist, Adhemar Ferreira da Silva, with Vilhjalmur Einarsson finishing second and winning Iceland's first medal.

The shot put was won by Parry O'Brien of the U.S.A., winning his second gold at the event, and the discus was won by Al Oerter, the first of an astonishing sequence of four. The run of American victories was stopped by Egil Danielsen of Norway in the javelin. On his fourth throw he threw 85.71 metres (281 feet 2 inches), over 10 metres better than the Olympic record, and 5.73 metres better than the second man.

A big story of the Games featured the hammer winner, American Hal Connolly.

On his fifth throw he overtook Mikhail Krivonosov, from whom he had just taken the world record. Connolly's hammer win was the more remarkable because he was born with a withered left arm. During the Games Connolly had been attracted by the Czech discus thrower, Olga Fikotova, whom he had watched practise. He began to escort her in the village, and the two fell in love. After the Games they corresponded, and then Connolly went to Czechoslovakia seeking permission to marry her. He was at first refused by the authorities, but later was granted permission after the U.S. Department of State intervened. They married in Prague on 27 March 1957. Emil Zatopek was best man and

Top: Hal Connolly, the American hammer thrower. He won in Melbourne, but it was his romance with Czech Olga Fikotova which captured the headlines.

Above: Mrs. Hal Connolly, who as Olga Fikotova of Czechoslovakia won the discus in 1956.

Al Oerter won his first discus gold medal in 1956, and by winning the event on three more occasions set a record for a current Olympic event.

Melbourne

Above: Betty Cuthbert of Australia wins the 100 metres from Christa Stubnick of Germany, on the right, and Marlene Mathews of Australia (470). These runners filled the same positions in the 200 metres.

Dawn Fraser of Australia (left) with Grant of Canada after a 100-metres freestyle heat. Fraser won this event in three Olympic Games.

Lorraine Crapp, another Australian record-breaking swimmer, won the 400-metres freestyle.

marriage of East and West was not for ever, and the couple divorced in 1974.

The decathlon finished at 7 p.m. on its third day, and was won by Milton Campbell of the U.S.A., who was exhausted after setting a personal best in the last event, the 1,500 metres, to beat world record holder Rafer Johnson (U.S.A.) and Vasiliy Kuznetsov (U.S.S.R.).

Australia was without a gold medal in the men's athletics, but the stars of the women's events were both Australian. Betty Cuthbert, an 18-year-old who had bought tickets to watch the Games before being selected for the Australian team, won both sprints, with Christa Stubnick of Germany and Marlene Mathews of Australia following her home in both races. The 80-metres hurdles was won in impressive manner by Shirley de la Hunty of Australia, who as Shirley Strickland had won the event in 1952. Again a German and an Australian took the minor places. The two girls teamed up in the 4 × 100-metres relay to win their third Olympic gold medal each, from Great Britain and the U.S.A. It was Shirley de la Hunty's third Games – she also won a silver and three bronze medals.

The high jump was won and a world record set by Mildred McDaniel of the U.S.A., with Thelma Hopkins (Great Britain) and Maria Pisaryeva (U.S.S.R.) tying for the silver. Elzbieta Krzesinska equalled her world record in taking the long jump. Tamara Tyshkyevich, a 238 lb (108 kg) Soviet athlete, took the shot with the holder, Galina Zybina, just behind. Another Soviet, Inese Jaunzeme, won the javelin.

The swimming events were a triumph for Australia who had so expected to do well that all seats in the pool were sold long before the Games, and were fetching three times their face value when the swimming started.

Australia won all the freestyle events. The men's 100 metres finished with John Henricks, John Devitt and Gary Chapman, all Australian, in the first three places. The 400 metres and 1,500 metres were both won by Murray Rose, who had emigrated to Australia from Scotland when a boy. In each race, Tsuyoshi Yamanaka (Japan) and George Breen (U.S.A.) followed him home. Australia also took the 4 × 200-metres relay,

Dana Zatopkova was the matron of honour. As Olga had won the women's discus, the four principals were all gold medal holders. The Connollys had four children, and as Mr. and Mrs. Connolly they represented the U.S.A. in three further Olympics, without gaining more medals, although Hal Connolly held the world record till 1965. Sadly, the

when Rose and Henricks joined Devitt and Kevin O'Halloran to add to their gold medals. David Theile continued Australia's run with a world-record win in the 100-metres backstroke, but Japan and the U.S.A. won a gold medal each when Masaru Furukawa won the 200-metres breaststroke and Bill Yorzyk the 200-metres butterfly. The U.S.A. and Mexico won the diving titles through Robert Clotworthy and Joaquim Capilla Perez, who progressed from bronze in 1948 and silver in 1952. But the popular Mexican's victory was bitterly disputed, as the American coach, Karl Michael, alleged that the Soviet and Hungarian judges had deliberately marked down the American diver, Gary Tobian, who was very narrowly beaten.

Australians also did well in the women's swimming. Dawn Fraser, aged 19, won the first of her Olympic gold medals in the 100-metres freestyle, with Lorraine Crapp second; the result was reversed in the 400-metres freestyle. The two swimmers took their second golds in the 4 × 400-metres relay. The breaststroke, butterfly and backstroke titles went to Ursula Happe of Germany, Shelley Mann of the U.S.A. and Judy Grinham, who won Great Britain's first swimming gold medal since 1924. Pat McCormick of the U.S.A. won both diving titles as she had done in 1952, the only diver, to date, to score two doubles.

Hungary met the Soviet Union in the semi-finals of the water polo, always a rough sport, and there were numerous fouls, as the Hungarians released their animosity towards their country's invaders. Finally, a Hungarian was butted, and blood poured from above his eye. The referee blew for time, although it was not quite time, and the Soviets fled to safety. Hungary won 4–0, and later won the gold by beating Yugoslavia.

The U.S.S.R. won three boxing championships, and the U.S.A. and Great Britain two each. The outstanding performance was by Hungary's Laszlo Papp, who won his third boxing gold medal, aged 30. In the final, he beat Jose Torres who was to become the world light-heavyweight champion. Pete Rademacher won the heavyweight title, and turned professional to challenge Floyd Pat-

terson for the world professional championship, but was outclassed. Great Britain's two winners, Terry Spinks and Dick McTaggart, were both skilful rather than tough boxers, and McTaggart won the Val Barker trophy as the best stylist of the Games.

In the gymnastics, shooting and wrestling events the Soviets began to overhaul the Americans in the unofficial points table. Viktor Chukarin won three gold medals in gymnastics to add to the four from 1952 – his haul also included three silver and a bronze. An outstanding woman gymnast, Larissa Latynina, won four gold medals, while Agnes Keleti of Hungary won three. The Soviets took three gold medals in the shooting, but the most noteworthy performance was by Canadian Gerald Quellette in small bore rifle, prone position. He hit the bull with all 60 shots, but was disallowed a record because the range was found to be 1.5 metres short. Soviet athletes won six of 16 wrestling titles. (A British loser, Ken Richmond, became the man who struck the gong in J. Arthur Rank films.)

Lars Hall of Sweden repeated his 1952 win in the modern pentathlon, but the U.S.S.R. won the team event.

Viktor Ivanov of the U.S.S.R., after he had thrown his silver medal into the air and lost it in Lake Windouree. He was given another.

In the rowing events, John B. Kelly Jr. was third in the single sculls and Bernard Costello Jr. second in the double sculls – their fathers had won the double sculls together in 1920 and 1924. The single sculls winner was 18-year-old Vyacheslav Ivanov of the U.S.S.R., who recorded the first of three wins. A fellow-Russian, Viktor Ivanov, second in the coxless pairs, threw his medal up in the air in delight and dropped it in the lake. He was given a replacement. The Yale crew won the eights for the U.S.A., but had finished third in their first race, and only continued in the competition through a repechage.

The cycling meant medals as usual for France and Italy, with Leandro Faggin of Italy winning two gold. But Ian Browne and Anthony Marchant of Australia won the 2,000-metres tandem.

France, Italy and Hungary again shared the fencing medals, with Christian d'Oriola of France retaining his foil title. There was a surprise in the women's foil, when Gillian Sheen won a first fencing gold medal for Great Britain.

The U.S.A. won four weightlifting titles to the Soviet Union's three, just as in 1952. Paul Anderson of the U.S.A. won the heavy-weight title from Humberto Selvetti on body weight, after both had lifted 500 kg.

The Stockholm equestrian events were won by Sweden, Germany and Great Britain, with Hans Winkler of Germany winning gold medals in individual and team show jumping, and Henri St. Cyr of Sweden winning gold medals in the individual and team dressage, as he had in 1952.

In the field hockey India won for the sixth consecutive time, but now had Pakistan as a serious rival. India beat Pakistan 1–0. The U.S.A. took the basketball for the fourth time, with the Soviet Union again second.

The U.S.S.R. won the soccer from Yugo-slavia.

At the closing ceremony of the Games, the athletes broke ranks and marched and danced with each other around the stadium in a spontaneous display of friendship for peoples of other nations. The Australian public enjoyed the Games and had been generous and efficient hosts.

The Olympic scoreboard emphasized that classification of nations on a points basis was not recognized, and Avery Brundage said beforehand that 'the nation by nation scor-ing system and designations such as the

The equestrian events of the 1956 Games were held in Stockholm. The Olympic torch is carried into the arena.

Vladimir Kuts

Vladimir Kuts was a tough marine in the Soviet navy, who discovered his talent for distance running by accident after being a boxer. He was born in Aleksino in the Ukraine on 7 February 1927, and did not begin to run seriously until 1951, coming to prominence in the European Cham-pionships of 1954. Everybody expected Emil Zatopek, the world record holder, and Chris Chataway to fight out the 5,000 metres, but while they watched each other Kuts sped away and won easily, breaking the world record. Six weeks later Kuts faced Chataway again, and this time Chataway stayed with him throughout the race and beat him at the tape in yet another world record, Kuts having taken the three-mile record on the way. Ten days later Kuts regained his world record when he beat Zatopek again. At the 1956 Olympics Gordon Pirie held the 5,000-metres world record, but Kuts beat him into second place. Kuts himself was by now the 10,000-metres world record holder, and he beat Pirie in this race, too, after a tremendously exciting battle. After the Olympics, Kuts regained his world 5,000-metres record, the eighth and last world record of his career. Kuts was an extremely strong runner who lacked a sprint finish, but won his races instead by a series of powerful surges, often beginning on the first lap, which left his rivals gasping and de-moralized. He was described as an iron man, and Roger Bannister called him 'Nature's attempt at an engine in boots'. Sadly ill-health conquered the iron man. He died of a heart attack in 1975, aged 48.

"Russian team" and "United States team" are strictly unofficial'. Nevertheless, scores were kept, and for the first time the U.S.A. was surpassed by the U.S.S.R., despite the fact that the Soviets won only five track and field gold medals.

Of the Hungarian athletes, some did not return to Hungary. The gold medal water-polo team tried to remain together as a touring side, and appeared in a carnival for Hungarian relief. Some athletes with families in Hungary were forced to return, although, as freedom fighters, they risked death. In a way, politics had been kept out of the Olympics, but these sportsmen were victims of politics, and their departure was in contrast to the overall happiness of the Games.

Hans Winkler of Germany on Halla in the show jumping. Winkler won the individual event despite suffering an injury in the first round. Winkler won five gold medals and a bronze in five Olympics beginning in 1956.

The medalists in the show jumping. From the left: Raimondo d'Inzeo of Italy (silver), Hans Winkler (gold) and Piero d'Inzeo of Italy (bronze).

Laszlo Papp

Laszlo Papp came from Hungary, a country which does not recognize professional boxing. Otherwise he would almost certainly have become world professional champion. Instead he won boxing immortality in the Olympic Games. He was born on 25 March 1926 in Budapest and won the Olympic middleweight championship in 1948, when he beat Johnny Wright of Great Britain, who, he claimed, gave him his hardest fight. With the introduction of a light-middleweight class at the Olympics of 1952, Papp won that title, beating on the way America's Ellsworth 'Spider' Webb, who was to beat three world champions in a good professional career. In 1956 Papp retained this title, beating in the final Jose Torres of the U.S.A., who was to become world professional light-heavyweight champion. He could, perhaps, have won two more Olympic titles, but in 1957 the Hungarian government allowed him to become the first professional boxer from a Communist country. A skilful southpaw with a powerful punch, he was unbeaten in 29 professional bouts, winning and six times defending the European middle-weight championship. In 1965 he was refused permission to fight for the world title and retired to become a coach.

Squaw Valley

The most surprising thing about the Squaw Valley Winter Olympics was that it was held at Squaw Valley at all. Before the Games, which began on 18 February 1960, all the resort boasted was a tourist hotel. The nearest city was Reno, the gambling centre, in the Nevada desert. The land was owned by Alex Cushing, who promised the I.O.C. a Californian grant to build facilities. Squaw Valley won the vote by 32 to 30 over Innsbruck in Austria. The facilities for the Games were purpose-built, which proved a great advantage, cutting down travelling between events. There were drawbacks: artificial obstacles were built for the downhill skiing which was against the rules, and the bobsleigh events were not held, as there were only nine entries and the organizers refused to build a run.

Walt Disney, the film cartoon king and inventor of Disneyland, was put in charge of the 'effects', and did the expected good job. Rain and heavy snow threatened to spoil the whole extravaganza, and indeed caused a postponement of the men's downhill, but the weather relented as if by magic for the opening ceremony, although it made Vice-President Richard Nixon, who officiated, 15 minutes late.

There were some difficulties in organization and five inexperienced American speed-skating officials had to be replaced, but the Games proceeded in an informal, happy atmosphere.

The competitors numbered 521 men and 144 women, a drop on the four previous Games, but 30 countries sent competitors, two more than in 1936 and 1948.

Germany took two medals in the Nordic skiing, the others being shared by Finland, Sweden and Norway, who complained that the altitude was too high for cross-country skiing. Sixten Jernberg of Sweden and 35-year-old Veikko Hakulinen of Finland were the most impressive skiers and added to their collections of medals. George Thoma, a postman from Germany, became the first non-Scandinavian to win the Nordic combined gold medal, and his countryman, Helmut Recknagel, the first to take a ski-jumping gold. The combined German team used Beethoven's Ninth Symphony, with special words added, as their 'anthem'.

There was a new event, the biathlon, a combination of a cross-country race with shooting exercises at four points, and it was won by Klas Lestander of Sweden.

The six Alpine skiing gold medals went to skiers from five different countries. Jean Vuarnet of France, an all-round sportsman, won the men's downhill; Ernst Hinterseer of Austria, the country of Toni Sailer who won all the events in 1956, regained some prestige for his country by winning the slalom from his team-mate Matthias Lietner; and Roger Staub of Switzerland took the giant slalom.

Heidi Biebl of Germany won the women's downhill from the favourite, Penny Pitou of the U.S.A., and Anne Heggtveit of Canada broke the European monopoly by winning the slalom, after Marianne Jahn of Austria hit a pole when challenging hard. Yvonne Ruegg of Switzerland won the giant slalom to give her country a second gold, with Penny Pitou getting her second silver.

David Jenkins of the U.S.A. did a brilliant freestyle phase to overhaul Jarol Divin of Czechoslovakia in the men's figure skating. He had been third to his brother in 1956. Carol Heiss, runner-up in 1956, beat Holland's Sjoukje Dijkstra to win the women's figure skating. She later married Hayes Alan Jenkins, the 1956 men's cham-

Andrea Lawrence-Mead of the U.S.A., the slalom winner in 1952, arrives with the Olympic flame at the stadium at Squaw Valley for the 1960 Winter Olympics.

Far left: David Jenkins of the U.S.A. followed his brother in winning the men's figure skating title.

Left: Carol Heiss made it a figure skating double for the U.S.A. when she took the women's gold medal.

pion. A Canadian pair, Robert Paul and Barbara Wagner, won the pairs event.

The U.S.S.R. and Norway shared the men's speed-skating titles; Soviet star, Yevgenyi Grischin, retained his 500-metres title by equalling his own world record and shared the 1,500 metres with Roald Aas of Norway. He had also shared the title in 1956. Second in the 500 metres was an American called W. Disney – William, not Walt. Soviet Viktor Kositschkin easily beat Norway's Knut Johannesen in the 5,000 metres, but the positions were reversed in the 10,000 metres, when the first five men, including Great Britain's Terence Monaghan, got inside the world record.

For the first time there were women's speed-skating events. Soviet women won three events and a German the other. Lidia Skoblikova of the Soviet Union won the two longer races and set a world record in the 1,500 metres.

In the ice hockey, the Americans sprang a surprise by beating the favourites, the Canadians, 2–1, only their third victory over them since 1920, thanks mainly to a brilliant display by John McCartan in goal. They then registered their first victory over the Soviets, coming from behind to win 3–2. Needing to beat Czechoslovakia to win the title, they

Heidi Biebl of Germany, the winner of the women's downhill race in the 1960 Alpine skiing events.

trailed 3–4 at the end of the second period, and were then advised by the Soviet captain to inhale oxygen. Most did, and they won 9–4 for a famous triumph, with Canada second and the U.S.S.R. third.

The comradeship of the Soviets was reflected further in the closing ceremony, when all the competitors mingled casually in friendship. It was a fitting end to a strange and happy Games, conducted just as Coubertin would have wished.

Rome

Below top: This stadium was built by Mussolini.

Bottom: The blanket finish of the 100 metres. From the left: Armin Hary of Germany (the winner), Peter Radford of Great Britain (third), Enrique Figuerola of Cuba (fourth), Ray Norton of the U.S.A. (sixth), Frank Budd of the U.S.A. (fifth) and Dave Sime of the U.S.A. (second).

Rome should have staged the Games of 1908 – the 'cancellation' meant a wait of 52 years for the Romans. They made up for it by presenting the 1960 Games superbly. Over 5,000 athletes took part, of which a tenth were women, from 83 countries. It was to be the last Games for South Africa, whose *apartheid* policy was contrary to I.O.C. regulations. The Chinese problem was removed, if not settled, when Communist China withdrew from I.O.C. membership, and nationalist China competed under the name of Formosa.

The Germans again sent a joint East/West team.

A feature of the Games was the merging of ancient and modern in Rome. The wrestling was held in the ancient Basilica of Maxientius, and the gymnastics in the Terme di Caracalla, while the marathon was run from the Capitol. The wartime dictator, Mussolini, had built marble stadia for an anticipated (by him) Games in 1944. There were magnificient new arenas, notably the Sports Palace for boxing, and the Velodrome for cycling. Much of the money came from the state football pool, *Totocalcio*, as it had for the Cortina Winter Games. There was an exhibition of sport in art and history, which would have pleased Coubertin had he been alive.

Avery Brundage opened the Games on 25 August 1960, the day after the Pope had welcomed the athletes to the city, and the opening ceremony was a colourful pageant with the terraces packed with bright clothes and flags in the brilliant Roman light. It was to be scorchingly hot throughout the Games, which caused distress for the distance runners and resulted in small crowds for the early heats and events as even the Romans found the city uncomfortable.

For the first time since 1928 Americans were beaten in the sprints, although Ray Norton started favourite. In the 100 metres, Armin Hary of Germany exploded from the blocks and held off Dave Sime of the U.S.A.

A sequence showing Livio Berutti of Italy winning the 200 metres, while the silver medalist, Lester Carney of the U.S.A., sprawls on the track, attempting to gain the victory.

with the slow-starting Peter Radford of Great Britain also closing fast in third place. Hary was the master of the fast start, and indeed had one false start in the final. Scientific tests were later to show that he reacted to the starting pistol much quicker than the 'normal' athlete. He won Germany's first male track gold medal.

In the 200 metres came the most popular victory of the Games for the always-partisan Italian crowd. Livio Berutti, who always ran in dark glasses, equalled the world record in both semi-final and final, and beat American Lester Carney. Torches made from newspapers were lit by the spectators. Germany won the gold medal in the 4 × 100-metres

relay. Hary won his second gold, the U.S.S.R. finished second and Great Britain came third, but only after the U.S.A., who had finished first in world record time, had been disqualified for a faulty baton change. Germany had equalled the world record. The faulty take-over was between Frank Budd and Ray Norton, who took the baton a metre outside the zone. It was a disastrous Games for Norton, who finished last in both individual sprint finals; he had been confidently tipped to win three gold medals.

When Americans are disappointed in the sprints, they often find a surprise winner elsewhere, and in 1960 it was Otis Davis, a 28-year-old veteran who had tried his hand at a

Karl Kaufmann of Germany throws himself at the line in the 400-metres final. It earned him a joint world record, but the gold medal went to Otis Davis of the U.S.A. Malcolm Spence of South Africa (109) was third.

Rome

Far right: Herb Elliott on his way to the 1,500 metres title. Istvan Rozsavolgyi of Hungary, half-hidden, finished third, and Michel Jazy of France (470) finished second.

Below: A desperate finish in the 110-metres hurdles. Lee Calhoun of the U.S.A. (farthest from camera) won from Willie May of the U.S.A. with Hayes Jones of the U.S.A. (nearest camera), third. The fourth man is Germany's Martin Lauer.

number of events, and had just scraped into the 400-metres squad. He steadily improved throughout his heats, and in the final had set up a big lead with 100 metres to go. Then a German, Karl Kaufmann, chased him hard and threw himself over the line to sprawl on the track just as Davis reached it. The photograph gave the gold to Davis, though both were given the same world record time.

Davis won a second gold in another world record when he anchored the American team to victory in the 4 × 400-metres relay. Again Kaufmann finished second. Also taking his second gold of the Games in the winning relay team was Glenn Davis, who earlier had

Right: Peter Snell of New Zealand wins his first Olympic gold medal in the 800 metres. Roger Moens of Belgium is a close second.

retained his championship in the 400-metres hurdles. Both hurdles races for the second consecutive Games resulted in clean sweeps for the U.S.A.; Lee Calhoun also repeated his 1956 win in the 110-metres hurdles.

A new Olympics star announced himself in the 800 metres. Peter Snell, a 21-year-old from New Zealand, was drawn in the outside lane of a strong field in the final which included Belgian world record holder Roger Moens. Moens took the lead in the back straight, and appeared to have the race won from the final bend. He looked right to check on his main rival, George Kerr of Jamaica, when the big, powerful, relaxed Snell surged through on his inside to win with something in hand.

The greatest performance of the Games was in the 1,500 metres. Herb Elliott, the 22-year-old Australian, was expected to win, as two years earlier he had beaten the world record for both 1,500 metres and mile, but there was a strong field and a close race was expected. It was close only until 600 metres from the tape, when Elliott began a finishing sprint that took him clear. He did not falter, and won by 20 metres from Michel Jazy of France and Istvan Rozsavolgyi of Hungary. The first six were inside the Olympic record,

and Elliott, out on his own, beat his own world record.

The 5,000 metres was another interesting race, and had a popular winner in New Zealand's Murray Halberg. Halberg was a 27-year-old school teacher who at 17 had suffered a near-fatal accident at rugby. His left arm was so badly crushed and so withered that he had difficulty keeping his running vest on his shoulder. He turned to athletics, finishing eleventh in the 1,500 metres at the 1956 Olympics, and winning the Commonwealth Games three miles in 1958.

In the 5,000 metres final, run in great heat, he stayed last of 12 for the first 1,000 metres, then gradually worked his way to the front. With three laps to go he put in a lap of 61.8 seconds, taking him 20 metres clear. Although he wilted and his last lap of 73 seconds was his slowest of the race, the chasing pack was just unable to catch him and he won by eight metres from Hans Grodotzki of Germany and Kazimierz Zimny of Poland. With three laps to go he put in a lap of 61.8 Halberg collapsed at the tape. He went on to set three world records in 1961, in the two miles, three miles, and 4 × one-mile relay, and retained his Commonwealth gold medal in 1962. In the 1960 Olympics, the 10,000

Herb Elliott

Elliott was perhaps the most outstanding runner of all time at the classic racing distance of a mile, or its metric equivalent, 1,500 metres. He was born on 25 February 1938 in Subiaco near Perth, Australia. In 1954, when he was 16, he began his serious track career, running a first lap in a mile race quicker than Bannister's first lap in the first four-minute mile the same year. At 18, he set a world junior record, and at 19 he was under four minutes for the first time. He was trained by Percy Cerutty, who looked after every detail of his development, even to his food, and strengthened him by having him run up and down the sand hills at Portsea where Cerutty lived. At the 1958 Commonwealth Games, when he was 20, Elliott won the mile and 880 yards. Shortly afterwards he set a world mile record of 3 minutes 54.5 seconds at Dublin, beating the old record by 2.7 seconds, and a world 1,500-metres record of 3 minutes 36 seconds at Gothenburg, beating the previous holder, Stanislav Jungwirth, and reducing the record time by 2.1 seconds. In 1959 he was in the team which broke the world 4 × one-mile relay world record. His greatest race was the Olympic Games 1,500 metres in 1960, when his winning margin of 2.8 seconds has only once been bettered, by Keino's 2.9 seconds in 1968. Elliott set a new world record at 3 minutes 35.6 seconds, which stood for four years. Elliott retired two years later in 1962, only 24. From the time an older boy beat him in 1952 when he was 14, he was never beaten in a race over a mile or 1,500 metres.

Far left: Murray Halberg of New Zealand wins the 5,000 metres. Hans Grodotzki of Germany is finishing second and Kazimierz Zimny of Poland, third.

Although Herb Elliott of Australia won only one Olympic medal, he is one of the greatest Olympic champions. He is about to step on to the rostrum for the 1,500-metres ceremony. Michel Jazy of France is on the left and Istvan Rozsavolgyi of Hungary on the right.

Rome

Above: The first four in the 10,000 metres. Hans Grodotzki of Germany, who leads, finished second; Pyotr Bolotnikov of the U.S.S.R. won; Desiatchkov of the U.S.S.R. was fourth; and Dave Power of Australia finished third.

One of the greatest walkers, Vladimir Golubnichiy of the U.S.S.R., seen winning the 20-km walk in 1968, first won the event in 1960. He competed in four Olympics, winning two gold, a silver and a bronze.

metres, until then usually run at the beginning, was run six days after the 5,000 metres, and Halberg was the firm favourite, but he could not repeat his supreme effort. An Australian, Dave Power, who had run prominently in the 5,000 metres, attempted the Halberg tactics with a fast lap after 6,000 metres, but could not shake off two Soviets and the German, Grodotzki, the 5,000-metres silver medalist. Just before the bell, the 30-year-old Soviet, Pyotr Bolotnikov, a disciple of Kuts, surged ahead to win, with Grodotzki again second and Power third.

A Pole, Zdszilaw Krzyszkowiak, won the steeplechase from two Soviets; the 20-km walk went to Vladimir Golubnichiy who beat an Australian, Noel Freeman, and a Briton, Stan Vickers; Great Britain's Don Thompson won the 50-km walk beating John Ljunggren of Sweden and Abdon Pamich of Italy. Bespectacled Thompson trained for Rome's heat in the steam of his bathroom.

The marathon was won by a remarkable runner, Abebe Bikila, a member of Emperor Haile Selassie's household guard in Ethiopia, who ran in bare feet. He got away from the Moroccan, Rhadi Ben Abdesselem, in the last mile to win without apparent effort. Barry Magee of New Zealand was third. It was the first athletics gold medal for a black African, for a man whose country had been conquered by Italy 25 years before when Bikila was a toddler. Bikila was quite unknown to the massed sports journalists in Rome.

There were some stirring battles in the field events. The high jump provided a surprise for world record holder John Thomas of the U.S.A. He jumped only 2.14 metres (7 feet $\frac{1}{4}$ inch), 8 cm below his record, and finished third to two Soviets, Robert Shavlakadze and Valeriy Brumel, who each jumped 2.16 metres (7 feet 1 inch). Ralph Boston of the U.S.A. had to beat Jesse Owens' 24-year-old Olympic record to win the long jump by 1 cm from Irvin Robertson, also from the U.S.A. Two Americans were also beyond the Olympic pole vault record, Don Bragg winning from Ron Morris. The dual triple jump champion, Ferreira da Silva, could finish only 14th in his fourth Olympic Games; a Pole, Jozef Schmidt, took the first of his two gold medals in the event.

There was known to be little love lost between the Americans Parry O'Brien, twice shot put champion, and his two main rivals, Bill Nieder and Dallas Long. Nieder got into the squad as a late replacement for Dave Davis, and on his fifth throw he passed O'Brien's leading put by 0.57 metres (nearly two feet) to win; O'Brien and Long took the silver and the bronze respectively.

The world record holder and Olympic champion, Hal Connolly, was well below form in the hammer, and Communist athletes took the medals, Vasiliy Rudenkov of the U.S.S.R. coming out on top. The javelin winner of 1956, Egil Danielsen of Norway, could not even reach the final rounds, and saw Viktor Tsibulenko of the Soviet Union take his title with a throw shorter than his own winning throw of four years earlier. Tsibulenko had been fourth in 1952 and third in 1956.

The decathlon was one of the most exciting ever seen, a battle between Rafer Johnson of

In winning the long jump, Ralph Boston of the U.S.A. finally beat Jesse Owens' Olympic record which had stood since 1936.

Far left: Great Britain's Don Thompson, who won the 50-km walk, had prepared thoroughly for the steamy heat of Rome.

Left: One of the big surprises of the Games was the convincing marathon victory of Abebe Bikila of Ethiopia who, in bare feet, ran away from the rest of the field.

Rome

Don Bragg of the U.S.A. sails over the bar to win a gold medal in the pole vault.

The graceful American sprinter, Wilma Rudolph, wins the 100 metres on the way to the sprint double. Great Britain's Dorothy Hyman is finishing second. She took the bronze in the 200 metres.

the U.S.A., second in 1956, and Yang Chuan-Kwang of Formosa. The two trained together in the U.S.A. and were friends. The three decathlon throwing events, in which Johnson had easily beaten Yang, gave him a 67-point lead as the last event, the 1,500 metres, began. Yang had beaten Johnson in all the running and jumping events, and had to beat him by about 10 seconds to win the championship. Johnson managed to stick right behind Yang until just before the tape; he lost the race but won the gold medal by 58 points.

The star of the women's athletics was the tall American sprinter, Wilma Rudolph. She ran away with the 100 metres from Great Britain's Dorothy Hyman and Italy's Giuseppina Leone, in a world record time which was not allowed because of wind assistance. She took the 200 metres just as easily, from Jutta Heine of Germany and Hyman again, and

won her third gold medal when making up ground in the 4 × 100-metres relay.

Apart from the high jump, Soviet women won all the other events. Irina Press won the 80-metres hurdles from Great Britain's Carole Quinton, and her elder sister, the powerful Tamara Press, won the shot and finished second in the discus. The discus was won by Nina Ponomaryeva, regaining the title she held as Nina Romashkova in 1952, having been third in 1956. She was to finish 11th in 1964, but is most famous in Britain for being charged with stealing three hats from an Oxford Street shop in 1956 before a contest between Great Britain and the Soviet Union. The Soviets cancelled the contest. Ponomaryeva was found guilty and discharged.

The high jump was won by the long-legged 6 foot 1 inch (1.86 metres) Rumanian Iolanda Balas. Great Britain's Dorothy Shirley and Poland's Jaroslawa Jozwiakowska tied for the silver. It was the fifth Olympics in succession that a British girl had finished second in the high jump.

The gold medals in the swimming and diving events all went to Australia and the United States, with the exceptions of the women's 200-metres breaststroke, which was won by Great Britain's Anita Lonsborough, and the two women's diving events, both won by Germany's Ingrid Kraemer.

In the men's events, Murray Rose of Australia repeated his 1956 400-metres freestyle victory but lost his 1,500-metres title to his countryman Jon Konrads, whose sister Ilsa won a silver in the relay team. David Theile of Australia retained the 100-metres backstroke title. There was controversy in the 100-metres freestyle when John Devitt was awarded the gold on the strength of two of three first-place judges placing him first. Although two of the second-place judges had placed him second and the electronic timing devices and slow-motion television replay seemed to confirm that American Lance Larson should have had the gold, Devitt kept his medal. Jeff Farrell of the U.S.A. had been the favourite before an appendectomy, but he was confined to relays where he (and his team) won two gold medals.

Dawn Fraser of Australia won her second 100-metres freestyle from Christine von Saltza of the U.S.A. and Natalie Steward of Great Britain. Sixteen-year-old von Saltza won the 400 metres and American teammates, 17-year-olds Carolyn Schuler and Lynn Burke, also won gold medals. They all won two more gold medals in the relays.

The light-heavyweight boxing championship was won by an 18-year-old American who made himself the best-known athlete in the village, Cassius Clay, later to become the

best-known sportsman in the world, heavyweight champion Muhammad Ali. Another outstanding gold medalist at the Games was Italy's Nino Benvenuti, later the world middleweight champion, but perhaps the most popular winner was Italy's heavyweight Franco de Piccoli, who knocked out the European champion, Andrei Abramov of the Soviet Union, in the first of his matches. There was one controversial decision; American Eddie Crook's victory over Tadeusz Walasek of Poland was booed for several minutes.

In the rowing events at Lake Albano, a German eight using a new type of oar and a new technique, broke the 40-year American domination of the eights by winning from

Above left: Ingrid Kraemer of Germany in the highboard diving. She won the gold medal in both diving events.

Above: The finish of the 800 metres, a race which was reinstated after the doubts following the 1928 event. Ludmila Shevtsova of the U.S.S.R. won from Brenda Jones of Australia.

Left: The young Australian world record-holder, Jon Konrads, winning the 1,500-metres freestyle.

Rome

Wearing the gold medal won in the light-heavyweight boxing division, Cassius Clay arrives back at Louisville, U.S.A., to be greeted by his brother (right) and other young fans.

Below: Boris Shakhlin of the U.S.S.R. wins the pommel-horse gold medal in 1960. In three Olympics he won seven gold medals, four silver and two bronze in gymnastics.

Canada and Czechoslovakia. Vyacheslav Ivanov of the U.S.S.R. won his second single sculls.

Gert Fredriksson of Sweden won his last Olympic conoeing medals in 1960, winning the 1,000-metres kayak pairs and taking the bronze in the singles. From 1948, when he was already 29 years old, he won six gold medals, one silver and one bronze in four Olympics.

The Bay of Naples was the venue for the yachting, and Paul Elvstrom of Denmark won a gold medal for the fourth consecutive Games. He also won 11 world championships.

The gymnastics events were again dominated by the Soviet athletes. Boris Shakhlin added to his collection of medals with four gold, two silver and a bronze, and Larissa Latynina did the same with three gold, two silver and a bronze. Japan, however, won the men's team title.

Italy's main successes came in the cycling events, where all 12 of the squad won medals, and only the Soviet victory in the road race

Far left: Larissa Latynina of the U.S.S.R., a superb gymnast, who, not counting Ray Ewry's medals in the 1906 Interim Games, has a record haul of nine gold, five silver and four bronze medals.

Left: An Italian idol, Sante Gaiardoni, wins the 1,000-metres cycling sprint race before his home crowd.

Below: Rudolf Karpati of Hungary (left), who won six sabre gold medals in four Olympics, is congratulated after a semi-final victory in 1960.

prevented a clean sweep of gold. Sante Gaiardoni was the most successful cyclist with gold medals in the 1,000-metres sprint and 1,000-metres time trial. In the road race a Danish rider, Knud Jensen, died. There were many retirements because of the fierce sun, but Jensen was possibly also a victim of drugs.

The Soviet Union won three gold medals in fencing, and Italy and Hungary took two each – for once the French failed. Two fine Olympic records ended. Aladar Gerevich, aged 50, of Hungary won his sixth successive gold medal in the team sabre event; his first medal was won in Los Angeles 28 years earlier. He also won the individual gold in 1948, a silver in 1952 and a bronze in 1936, and a team foil bronze in 1952. Edoardo Mangiarotti of Italy, a mere 41, did slightly better from 1936 to 1960, winning, in foil and epee, one gold, one silver and two bronze medals in individual events and five gold and four silver in team events.

The modern pentathlon was won by Ferenc Nemeth, who also helped Hungary take the team gold medal.

Rome

Soviet heavyweight lifter Yuriy Vlassov set a world record in winning his gold medal in 1960.

American weightlifters won only one gold medal, as the Soviets began to dominate, but Americans won three wrestling gold medals, their first since 1952. Turkey won seven gold medals. There seemed to be collusion in the Greco-Roman lightweight battle, where a Bulgarian appeared to lose deliberately to a Soviet, Avtandil Koridze, to allow him to win the gold rather than the Yugoslav, Branislav Martinovic, who won the silver. The Bulgarian, Dmitri Stoyanov, was disqualified.

In the three-day equestrian event, Lawrie Morgan of Australia won gold medals in the individual and team championships.

India at last lost the field hockey championship, after six successive wins, to Pakistan, but the U.S.A. kept up its score in

Raimondo d'Inzeo of Italy won the show-jumping event in 1960 after finishing second in 1956.

basketball, with a fifth successive win. Communist countries had a third successive win in the soccer; this time it was the turn of Yugoslavia, who won with a 3–1 final victory over Denmark.

The Games had been friendly, and no major conflicts had erupted anywhere in the world. The Soviets displayed much more friendship and sportsmanship than usual. Perhaps they could afford to, as it was clear that the United States had been surpassed in overall performance. Although Americans still led in track and field, they did not dominate as once they had, and more nations were now supplying athletes to contest the medals. The first two places in the marathon suggested that African runners might soon be a force.

There were 100,000 at the magnificent closing ceremony. As the light went out in the stadium, thousands of newspaper torches were lit on the terraces making a spectacular display, and a battery of artillery on the slopes overlooking the arena fired a salute. A fireworks display was too enthusiastic perhaps, as a number of cars, a wood and private gardens were set ablaze by falling rockets. The Games was memorable to the end.

Wilma Rudolph overcame severe handicaps to win three gold medals in the sprint events in the 1960 Olympics. She beat the paralysis of her left leg so well that she was called 'the Black Gazelle' by the Italian sports writers.

Wilma Rudolph

Wilma Rudolph's career was a triumph over handicaps. She was the 17th of 19 children (her father married twice) and weighed only $4\frac{1}{2}$ lb (2.04 kg) when she was born on 23 June 1940 in Clarksville, Tennessee. It was a poor family and Wilma claimed she was fast because she had to move quickly when dinner was served. At the age of four double pneumonia and scarlet fever nearly killed her and her left leg was paralyzed. She only walked again when she was seven, and wore an orthopaedic shoe until she was eleven. She then took up basketball and was spotted by an athletics coach and trained as a sprinter. At 16 she competed in the Melbourne Olympics, being eliminated in a 200 metres heat, but winning a bronze medal in the relay. At the 1960 Olympics in Rome, she was supreme, winning the 100 metres, where she equalled the world record of 11.3 seconds in a heat, and then clocked an astonishing 11.0 seconds in the final, wind–assisted. She then won the 200 metres, for which she held the world record, and took her third gold medal in the 4 × 100-metres relay. By now she was tall at 6 feet (1.83 metres), and ran with a grace that caused the Romans to call her 'La Gazzella Nera', or 'the Black Gazelle'. She later set further world records for the 100 metres and 4 × 100-metres relay (twice). She retired after marital troubles in 1961, still only 21, and a film was later made of her life.

Innsbruck

The 1964 Winter Olympics coincided with Innsbruck's mildest February in living memory. Thousands of cubic metres of snow were brought down from the mountains by the Austrian army to enable the Games to proceed. In contrast to Squaw Valley in 1960, the venues were scattered, involving much travelling for journalists. The Games was reported and televised in detail, journalists outnumbering competitors, but the number of competitors, 1,186, and participating nations, 36, were easily the highest yet. For the first time computers were installed, a boon in the figure skating, the results of which had sometimes taken hours to work out.

In practice for the Games there were two fatalities. Ross Milne, an Australian skier, crashed into a tree at speed while navigating the course which ran through a narrow wooded glade, and Kay Skrzypecki, a Polish-born tobogganist representing Great Britain, was also killed in an accident.

The opening ceremony, attended by 60,000, was held in the bowl at the base of the ski jump. The Games was well attended throughout – nearly a million spectators watched the competitions.

Scandinavians retained their hold on the Nordic skiing events, allowing only one gold medal to escape, to Soviet Vladimir Melanin

Below: The Olympic flame bursts into life at the opening ceremony, held at the foot of the ski jump, of the 1964 Innsbruck Games.

Below right: The winner of the giant slalom, François Bonlieu of France.

A new event in 1964 was an 80-metres ski jump. It was won by the Norwegian Toralf Engan.

in the biathlon. Eero Mantyranta of Finland won both the shorter cross-country races. Veikko Kankkonen of Finland won the 70-metres ski jump with the last jump of the competition from Norway's Toralf Engan. The positions were reversed in the 90-metres jump.

The star of the Nordic skiing was Sweden's 35-year-old veteran Sixten Jernberg, who won the 50-km cross-country and a second gold in the 4 × 10-km relay. He ended an Olympic career in which in three Games he won four gold, three silver and two bronze medals, a record for a skier. Soviets took all three women's Nordic skiing gold medals; Klaudia Boyarskikh won the individual events and also was in the winning relay team.

In the Alpine skiing events, the stars were the French sisters, Marielle and Christine Goitschel, who were first and second in the giant slalom and slalom, each sister winning a gold and silver. Austrian girls took all three medals in the downhill, Christl Haas winning.

The men's Alpine skiing gold medals were also shared by Austria and France. The giant slalom went to François Bonlieu of France with Austria's Karl Schranz finishing second. Jean-Claude Killy, who was to make a mark in 1968, was sixth. The bronze medalist, Josef Stiegler of Austria, won the slalom, the only man to win two Alpine skiing medals in 1964. Two Americans finished in the minor places, the U.S.A.'s first medals in Alpine skiing. Egon Zimmermann of Austria won the downhill, less than two seconds separating him from Karl Schranz, who was seventh.

For the first time since 1936 there were no Americans among the figure-skating gold medalists. The men's event was won by Manfred Schnelldorfer of Germany. Alain

Calmat of France fell twice before taking the silver, and Scott Allen of the U.S.A., the bronze medalist, might have forfeited his chance of a silver by ostentatiously waving to the crowd, a gesture for which artistic merit marks might have been deducted. Sjoukje Dijkstra of Holland, the silver medalist of 1960, won the women's figure skating and incidentally, her country's first Olympic gold medal since 1952. The pairs were won by the popular Oleg Protopopov and Ludmilla Belousova, the Soviet Union's husband and wife team.

Top: The Goitschel sisters of France, who filled the first two places in both the slalom and giant slalom, each winning a gold and silver: Marielle (left) and Christine (right).

Above: The men's downhill winner, Egon Zimmermann of Austria.

Left: The winner of the men's figure skating, Manfred Schnelldorfer of Germany.

Innsbruck

Above: The women's figure-skating event was won by the runner-up of 1960, Holland's Sjoukje Dijkstra.

Right: The Norwegian speed skater, Knut Johannesen, won the 5,000 metres and finished third in the 10,000 metres.

The men's speed-skating events were won by skaters from four different countries. Knut Johannesen of Sweden was the most successful skater, setting a world record in taking the 5,000 metres, and getting a bronze in the 10,000 metres. Richard McDermott was the U.S.A.'s only winner of the Games when he took the 500 metres. Three skaters tied for second place: the winner at the two previous Games, Yevgeniy Grischin (U.S.S.R.), Vladimir Orlov (U.S.S.R.) and Alv Gjestvang (Norway).

Like the Nordic skiing, the women's speed-skating events were all won by the Soviet Union, and in this case by the same girl, Lidia Skoblikova, who had won the two longer races in 1960. She was the first woman to win four individual gold medals at one Winter Olympics.

Tony Nash and Robin Dixon won the two-man bobsleigh for Great Britain, where Italy's Eugenio Monti showed true Olympic spirit in giving Nash and Dixon an axle bolt from his own sled after theirs had broken.

Monti finished third, and also took a bronze in the four-man bob, won by Canada. Thus both bobsleigh events were won by countries without a bobsleigh course between them, although both winning crews had devoted years of hard practice to winning.

For the first time in the Olympics there were tobogganing events. The men's single-seater event provided Germans with all three medals, and Austrian crews took first and second places in the two-seater event. The women's event medals were shared by competitors from Germany and Austria, these two countries and Italy being the main homes of the sport.

The ice hockey title depended on the match between the unbeaten Soviets and the Canadians, who had lost narrowly to Czechoslovakia. The U.S.S.R. won 3–2, thus relegating Canada to fourth place, behind Sweden and Czechoslovakia.

The Games was a great success for the Soviets, who took 11 gold, eight silver and six bronze medals, more than twice as many as the next country, the hosts Austria. No newspapers compiled a points total by nations, a departure from recent practice which might have had as much to do with the Soviet Union's obvious overwhelming superiority as anything else. Coubertin would have approved.

Once again the Games had been impeccably organized, but Brundage, no great lover of the Winter Olympics, remarked on the commercialism, a factor which was to be a continuing controversy. With so many countries showing televised events, and newspaper photographs being carried all over the world, the practice of skiers displaying brand names of skis in pictures caused objections. The Olympics brings publicity and subsequent big increases in custom to those countries with heavy investments in winter holiday trade, but the prospect of individual competitors benefitting was considered un-Olympic, and raised doubts over their amateurism.

Lidia Skoblikova of the U.S.S.R. won all four women's speed-skating races, taking her tally of Olympic gold medals to six.

Below: Great Britain's only gold medalists in the bobsleigh events, Tony Nash and Robin Dixon, winning the two-man.

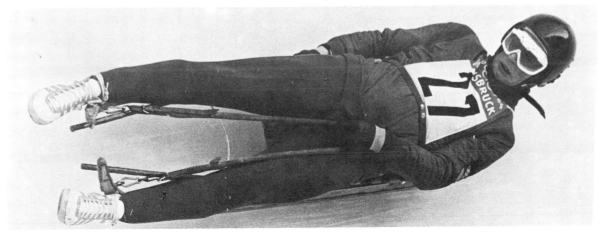

Left: Thomas Koehler of Germany was the men's single-seater winner in the new tobogganing events in 1964.

Tokyo

The world experienced some tragedies between the 1960 Olympics and the celebrations in Tokyo in 1964. The greatest single shock was the assassination of President Kennedy in 1963. A traumatic experience not only for the local combatants but for young Americans at home was the war in Vietnam, which began in 1964. A still surviving monument to the cold war was the building of the Berlin Wall to separate East and West in 1961. Technology advanced, the Soviets put a cosmonaut in space, and the Chinese exploded a nuclear device.

During these times of turmoil the people of Tokyo, the world's largest city, were preparing for the Olympic Games. They had been awarded the Games in 1959, and were determined to show that the Japanese people could be kind and friendly hosts. They succeeded. Calculations of the money spent in preparing the magnificent new stadia and accompanying facilities were staggering. All the competitors, officials and the journalists were impressed by the hospitality offered, and the Games was called the 'happy' Games.

The events were watched by the largest audience ever, millions receiving televised pictures through the new satellite Telstar.

There were, of course, the usual political hiccups. Indonesia had been suspended by the

I.O.C. for barring competitors to the 1962 Asian Games, and held its own GANEFO Games in 1963. These were the Games of the New Emerging Forces, to which Communist China was invited, and the I.O.C. decreed that any nations taking part were ineligible for the Olympics. Nevertheless Indonesians and North Koreans travelled to Tokyo, and those who had not competed in the GANEFO Games were invited to compete. However, both squads, numbering nearly 300, returned home, and a situation which had threatened to provoke boycotts and sabotage the Games was resolved.

The Games was held late in the year, between 10 and 24 October 1964. The torch from Olympia was relayed to Tokyo, and the last lap to light the flame was run by 19-year-old Yoshinoro Saki, a young athlete born in Hiroshima on the day of the atomic bomb. Ten thousand pigeons of peace were released,

Below: The torch at the opening of the 1964 Olympic Games in Tokyo was carried by a university student, born on the day of the Hiroshima atom-bomb blast 19 years before.

Below right: The torch being carried between the 'flame drums' at the national stadium.

Bob Hayes of the U.S.A., the winner of the 100 metres, clocked a fantastic 9.9 seconds in a wind-assisted semi-final.

Henry Carr of the U.S.A. was a stylish winner of the 200 metres from Paul Drayton of the U.S.A. and Edwin Roberts of Trinidad.

and the stadium was packed with eager Japanese spectators anxious to take part in the festivities. The enthusiastic large crowds, often sitting in the rain, were a feature of the Games. The number of competitors, just over 5,000, was slightly down on 1960 because of greater travelling costs for many countries, but the total of 94 nations present was a new record.

The sprint titles, all of which had escaped Americans in 1960, triumphantly returned to the United States. The 100 metres was a victory for a man who, when in full stride, was one of the fastest ever seen. Bob Hayes, not quite 22 years old, was not always the fastest starter, and he had a rolling, pigeon-toed ungainly gait, but he was very strong and when flat out, powered his way along the track. In a wind-assisted semi-final, he recorded what would have been a world record 9.9 seconds, and he equalled the world record

Tokyo

in winning the final in 10 seconds. Enrique Figuerola of Cuba and Harry Jerome of Canada were well beaten. Hayes won his second gold medal in the 4 × 100-metres, bringing home the U.S.A. team by three metres in a new world record time. The 200 metres was a triumph for style. Henry Carr improved his times with each succeeding heat and smoothly eased his way to the gold medal in the final, leaving Paul Drayton, also of the U.S.A., and Edwin Roberts of Trinidad, vainly chasing.

Mike Larrabee, a 30-year-old teacher from California, won the 400 metres, and teamed up with Carr, Ollan Cassell and Ulis Williams to take the 4 × 400-metres relay for the U.S.A. The British team captain, Robbie Brightwell, a disappointing fourth in the 400 metres, produced a fast final lap to move Great Britain into second place with Trinidad and Tobago third. All three teams were inside the world record.

The 800 metres was won by the outstanding athlete of the Games. Peter Snell of New

Peter Snell's second 800-metres victory, followed by a 1,500-metres win, made him the outstanding runner of the Games.

Mike Larrabee of the U.S.A. (709) in the semi-final of the 400 metres. A 30-year-old high-school teacher, he won the final impressively.

Zealand, the defending champion, had decided to concentrate on the 1,500 metres in Tokyo. Only when at Tokyo did he revise his plans and add the 800 metres to his programme. He conserved his energy in the heat and semi-final, still finishing first, however. In the final he dropped back and then made his bid approaching the final bend. He passed George Kerr, bronze medalist in Rome, and Wilson Kiprugut of Kenya, and sprinted on to win. Canada's Bill Crothers came with a late burst to deprive Kiprugut of second place.

The next day Snell began his 1,500-metres campaign by finishing fourth in the slowest heat, doing just enough to qualify. In the semi-final, still taking it easy, he won in the faster time of the two winners. The final was something of a formality, Snell beginning a sprint with 200 metres to go and rounding the last bend with the race won. Josef Odlozil of Czechoslovakia was second and John Davies of New Zealand, third. Snell was the last athlete to perform this double; only Great Britain's Albert Hill in 1920 had managed it since the First World War.

The track distance races were a tragedy for Australia's Ron Clarke, who was confidently expected to win one or both. The 10,000 metres was switched back to its old position of being run on the first day of the Games. Clarke was the world record holder at this event and at six miles. There were 38 runners, too large a field. After 1964 there were heats. Clarke led as usual, but Mohamed Gammoudi of Tunisia and an unknown American, Billy Mills, managed to stay with him. Murray Halberg and Pyotr Bolotnikov, the 5,000 and 10,000-metres champions, were dropped with two laps to go, and then Gammoudi sprinted into what looked like a winning lead, brushing Clarke and Mills as he went. The home stretch was full of straggling lapped runners. Suddenly Mills began a tremendous sprint which took him through the stragglers and past Gammoudi to win; Clarke was third. The unknown Mills soon slipped back into obscurity, but on his one day of fame he was tremendous, the first American to win a long-distance Olympic gold medal.

The 5,000 metres was a sad affair for the demoralized Clarke, who again led but without convincing the spectators that he could leave the field for dead as he so often did. Michel Jazy of France, second to Elliott in the 1960 1,500 metres, was clear round the final bend, but on the muddy track the home straight proved too much. He faded to fourth as American Bob Schul powered past to win, with Harald Norpoth of Germany and Bill Dellinger of the U.S.A. also passing him for the minor medals. Schul's victory was a shock to all but the Americans who had seen him set a world two-mile record just before the Games. The victories of Mills and Schul suggested a breakthrough for American athletics in the longer races, but the effort has not quite been maintained.

The 3,000-metres steeplechase provided a popular Olympic medal for Belgium's ever-

green Gaston Roelants, who was fourth in 1960 and seventh in 1968. He was a great performer in distance events and cross-country, in which he was three times international champion, all through the 1960s. Great Britain's Maurice Herriott and the

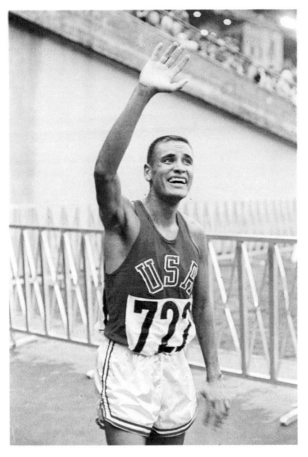

A big surprise was the victory in the 10,000 metres of American Billy Mills who was part Sioux Indian and a United States Marine.

Ron Clarke of Australia (centre) was a disappointing third in the 1964 10,000 metres, one of the best athletes never to win an Olympic gold. Kip Keino of Kenya (left) was to win two, in 1968 and 1972, and Gaston Roelants of Belgium (right) won the 1964 steeplechase.

Tokyo

Above: One of the best performances from an American in 1964 was the victory of Bob Schul in the 5,000 metres. Harald Norpoth of Germany (209) was second and William Dellinger of the U.S.A. (right) was third.

Above right: Thirty-year-old Ken Matthews of Great Britain was an easy winner of the 20-km walk.

Soviet Union's Ivan Belyayev chased him home.

The two hurdles races again went to Americans. In the 110-metres hurdles Hayes Jones stepped up on his 1960 bronze to win from fellow-American Blaine Lindgren, and Warren Cawley won the 400-metres hurdles from Great Britain's John Cooper.

Perhaps the greatest performance of the Games, on a par with Snell's, was that of Ethiopia's marathon man, Abebe Bikila. Bikila had a handicap that even Snell could not have overcome. Five weeks before the Games he had his appendix removed. It was astonishing that he could even run a marathon at all. But the barefoot Rome victor appeared, this time wearing spotless white shoes. With half a million lining the route and Japanese television showing the whole race, he jogged effortlessly into the stadium over four minutes ahead of the next man, Kokichi Tsuburaya of Japan, who, to the despair of the Japanese fans, was passed in the stadium itself by Great Britain's Basil Heatley, who took the silver medal. Bikila, meanwhile, had not only beaten the world record by nearly two minutes but had performed a series of physical exercises while waiting for the next man – perhaps as part of his convalescence.

Britons did best in the walks. The workmates of Ken Matthews, a 30-year-old fitter

at a power station near Birmingham, had a whip round so that his wife could fly to Tokyo with him. Nobody was disappointed as Matthews won the 20-km walk easily, beating the Soviet Union's Vladimir Golubnichiy, the winner in 1960 and again in 1968, into third place. Italy's Abdon Pamich, bronze medalist in 1960, won the 50-km walk with Great Britain's Paul Nihill pressing him all the way.

The high jump was won by world record holder Valery Brumel of the U.S.S.R., but American John Thomas, less fancied than in Rome, lost only on the countback of misses.

There was a proud moment for Great Britain in the long jump. No British athlete had won a gold medal in a field event since Tim Ahearne won the triple jump in 1908. Welshman Lynn Davies, later known as 'Lynn the Leap', was facing joint world record holders Ralph Boston of the U.S.A., the current Olympic champion, and Igor Ter-Ovanesyan of the U.S.S.R., but in a competition held in driving rain and with a strong cold wind against the jumpers, he handled the conditions best, and his fifth jump relegated the record holders to the minor positions.

The pole vault was won by Fred Hansen of the U.S.A. from two Germans. The new glass-fibre poles enabled nine men to beat the Olympic record, with Hansen 40 cm (1 foot 3¾ inches) higher than Don Bragg in 1960. Jozef Schmidt of Poland retained his title in the triple jump, beating two Soviets, only two months after a knee operation.

Dallas Long, third in 1960, won the shot put for the United States. Parry O'Brien, the winner in 1952 and 1956 and silver medalist in 1960, finished fourth. The discus constituted a third win for Al Oerter, who beat the man who had just taken his world record, Ludvik Danek of Czechoslovakia, into second place. Oerter had damaged his ribs in practice, and threw the discus with heavy strapping and a pain-killing injection. He was the first man to

A first long-jump gold medal for Great Britain came when Lynn Davies coped best with the difficult conditions to win with his fifth leap.

Betty Cuthbert

Betty Cuthbert was a golden girl of Australian athletics, who had a remarkable record in the Olympics. She was born a twin on 20 April 1938 in Merrylands near Sydney, Australia, and reached the top in 1956 when the Olympics were held in her native Australia. Only 18, she streaked to victory in the 100 metres, 200 metres and 4 × 100-metres relay. The relay team set a world record. Later in December she set more world records in relays: the 4 × 100-metres, 110 yards, 200 metres, and 220 yards. The ballyhoo attending her affected her performances for a while, and she failed in the 1958 Commonwealth Games, al-

though she set more records between 1958 and 1960: 60 metres, 100 yards, 200 metres, 220 yards (three times) and 440 yards (twice). A hamstring injury prevented her appearance at the 1960 Olympics, when races with Wilma Rudolph might have proved highlights of the Games, and retired for a spell in 1961. She ran again in 1962 however, although not shining in the Commonwealth Games, and in 1963 twice lowered the 440-yards world-record mark. The 400 metres was a new event for women in the 1964 Olympics, and Betty Cuthbert was the first winner. It was her fourth gold medal in four attempts, equalling Fanny Blankers-Koen's record of four golds in four events in 1948.

The first Olympic 400 metres for women was won by Betty Cuthbert of Australia, the dual sprint champion of 1956, who just beat Great Britain's Ann Packer (left) with Judith Amoore of Australia, third.

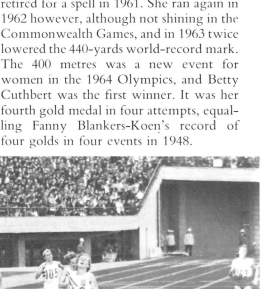

Tokyo

Wyomia Tyus of the U.S.A. (217) wins the first of her 100-metres titles from her compatriot Edith Maguire (216), with Poland's Ewa Kobukowska (right), third.

Right: A happy Ann Packer of Great Britain ran away from the field in the home straight to win the 800 metres in a world record time.

Far right: Another world record and a notable long jump double for Great Britain came when Mary Rand easily won the gold medal.

win three gold medals in a single athletics event since Ray Ewry and John Flanagan in 1900, 1904 and 1908, and Martin Sheridan, who was helped by the Interim Games of 1906.

The hammer throw was won by Romuald Klim of the Soviet Union, and the javelin gold medal was taken back to Finland after a break of 16 years by Pauli Nevala.

The string of American victories in the decathlon, which had started in 1932, was halted in 1964. For the first time there was not even an American medalist (not counting 1912 when Jim Thorpe was disqualified). Only 240 points separated the first six; Willi

Holdorf of Germany pushed himself to exhaustion to win by a mere 45 points.

No single girl dominated the women's events in 1964, although there were some excellent performances. Wyomia Tyus of the United States donned the mantle of Wilma Rudolph and won the 100 metres impressively from her team-mate, Edith Maguire, who took the 200 metres from a Polish girl with a big future, Irena Kirszenstein (later Szewinska). These were the only two track and field gold medals for American girls. Poland won the 4 × 100-metres relay in a world record time from the U.S.A. and Great Britain, the anchor leg being run by the

100-metres bronze medalist, Ewa Ko-bukowska. She was later to fail a sex test, and was deprived of the world record, but was allowed to keep her Olympic medals. Irena Kirszenstein won her first gold medal.

The 400 metres for women was a new event, and it was won by Betty Cuthbert of Australia, who beat the favourite, Great Britain's Ann Packer, into second place. Cuthbert had won both sprints in 1956, and had missed the 1960 Games through injury. There was more than adequate compensation for Ann Packer in the 800 metres, which she entered more in hope than expectation. She ran a relaxed race and challenged round the final bend, passing several girls to win in a new world record time. She said she was inspired by the disappointment of her fiancé, British team captain Robbie Brightwell, who was justed edged out of a medal in the 400 metres.

The 80-metres hurdles went to Karin Balzer of Germany, and Iolanda Balas of Rumania easily retained her high-jump title.

The long jump was a splendid victory for Mary Rand, which gave Great Britain a remarkable long-jump double. Blonde Mary Rand was the golden girl of the Games. As Mary Bignal, only 20 years old, she had been disappointed in Rome, finishing 9th in the

Peter Snell

Peter Snell was born on 17 December 1938 in Opunake, New Zealand. As a youngster he was a good tennis and rugby player. He took up running seriously only at 18. His physique was unusual for a middle distance runner. He stood 5 feet 10½ inches (1.79 metres) and weighed 171 lb (77.56 kg), and had muscular legs and a broad chest. He was coached by Arthur Lydiard, and was unknown outside New Zealand when he came to Rome for the 1960 Olympics. He won the 800 metres impressively. In 1961 he helped a New Zealand squad set a world record for the 4 × 1 mile relay, and in 1962 set world records at 800 metres, 880 yards and mile in the Commonwealth Games. At the Tokyo Olympics in 1964 he decided to attempt both the 800 metres and 1,500 metres, which meant racing six times. He planned his tactics carefully, and there was no doubt from a long way out in the 1,500 metres final that he would be dual champion, the only man to achieve this feat since 1920. Later in 1964 he set a world record for 1,000 metres and lowered his mile time. On tour in Europe and in North America in 1965 he was not at his best and decided to retire. He was voted Track Athlete of the Decade at the end of the 1960s.

The long-legged Iolanda Balas of Rumania out-jumped her rivals in the high jump to win by 14 centimetres (over 5 inches).

Tokyo

Tamara Press of the U.S.S.R. won the discus and shot in 1964. She also won the shot in 1960, when her sister, Irina, won the 80-metres hurdles.

Don Schollander of the U.S.A. (who won five swimming gold medals, four in 1964) after his win in the 100-metres freestyle. Bobby McGregor of Great Britain (left) won the silver and Hans-Joachim Klein of Germany (right), the bronze.

Larissa Latynina

Larissa Latynina was a brilliant gymnast for whom technique was everything. She was born on 27 December 1934 in Kherson in the Ukraine and took part in the Olympics of 1956 where she won four gold medals. In 1958 she won five gold medals in the world championships in Moscow, and at the Rome Olympics she took three more gold medals. She then began to be challenged by Vera Caslavska of Czechoslovakia. In the Tokyo Olympics of 1964, her last, she took two more gold medals, to end an Olympic career with nine gold medals, five silver and four bronze. She coached the Soviet team and was largely responsible for the continuing prominence of Soviet women in gymnastics.

long jump but a surprising fourth in the hurdles. Marriage to Sydney Rand, an Olympic sculler, and the birth of a daughter did no harm to her athletics ability, and in 1964 she took a silver medal in the pentathlon and a bronze in the relay as well as making six inspired jumps, each of which would have won at least the silver medal. Poland's Irena Kirszenstein won her second silver medal of the Games. Mary Rand later remarried, her husband being American Bill Toomey, the decathlon winner in 1968.

The women's pentathlon, the first of the Olympic Games, was won by the U.S.S.R.'s Irina Press, the 80-metres hurdles winner at Rome. Her sister, Tamara Press, was the only dual gold medal winner in women's athletics, winning the shot and discus to add to the gold and silver she won in 1960. The javelin was, surprisingly, won by Mihaela Penes of Rumania, who at 17 years 2 months became the youngest athletics gold medal winner.

Young Americans dominated the swimming pool. A squad of which the oldest member was 23 years old won 16 of 22 events. An 18 year old from California, Don Schol-

146

lander, became the first swimmer to win four swimming gold medals at the same Games. Schollander shaved his body and head for streamlining, and won the 100 and 400-metres freestyle and anchored two freestyle relay teams. Except in the 100 metres he set world records in them all. The medley relay, in which Schollander might have had another gold had he swum, was another world record for the Americans, as were the 200-metres backstroke (Jed Graef) and 400-metres individual relay (Richard Roth). Australians were not out of it, however, and Bob Windle won the 1,500-metres freestyle, and Ian O'Brien and Kevin Berry the breaststroke and butterfly, both in world records.

Dawn Fraser won the women's 100-metres freestyle for Australia, the first woman to win three successive Olympic gold medals in the same event. Otherwise young Americans dominated, world records being set by Cathy Ferguson (backstroke) and Sharon Stouder (butterfly) and by both relay teams. Sharon Stouder was in both relays, thus winning three gold medals in three world records. Ingrid Kraemer, now Ingrid Engel, of Germany, retained her springboard diving title but was second in platform diving to Lesley Bush (U.S.A.).

The boxing was notable for the heavyweight victory of Joe Frazier, later to be world professional champion. Frazier's gold was the only medal won by Americans in boxing, wrestling and weightlifting, the strong-man sports in which they usually did well. The boxing was marred by disputed decisions; there were two suspensions for boxers attempting to assault referees, the one who succeeded in his attempt being suspended for life. A boxer from South Korea sat down in the ring for nearly an hour in protest at a decision. The U.S.S.R. generally did best in the muscular sports, but Japan picked up plenty of gold medals in the lighter weights at both weightlifting and wrestling. Hungary's Imre Polyak won the Greco-Roman wrestling featherweight title after being second in the three previous Games.

Judo was introduced as an Olympic sport, and Japan took three of the four gold medals, but the Japanese suffered when their hero, Akio Kaminaga, lost in the open final to

Above: Judo was introduced into the Olympic programme in 1964 and Japan won three of the four classes. Isao Inokuma beat A. H. Douglas Rogers of Canada for the heavyweight gold.

The judo champion in the open category was the huge Antonius Geesink of Holland.

Anton Geesink, a huge Dutchman.

Another new Olympic sport was volleyball. The Soviet Union won the men's title, but the women's final was more exciting, an electric confrontation between the U.S.S.R. and Japan which the much smaller Japanese girls won, displaying extraordinary athleticism.

Tokyo

The gold medal on the beam was one of three won by the brilliant Czechoslovakian gymnast, Vera Caslavska.

Below: After a long series of American wins in the eights had been interrupted in 1960 by a crack German crew, the Vesper club of Philadelphia regained the Olympic title for the U.S.A. in 1964.

The host nation also did well in the gymnastics, winning five of the eight men's titles. The star was Yukio Endo who won three gold medals. The U.S.S.R.'s Boris Shakhlin won on the horizontal bar, and ended his Olympic career with no less than seven gold medals, four silver and two bronze, over three Olympics. The women's events were divided between the Soviet Union and Czechoslovakia. Vera Caslavska of Czechoslovakia won three individual titles, including the combined. The U.S.S.R.'s Larissa Latynina won a gold, three silver and a bronze plus a team gold. She ended her Olympic career with nine gold medals, five silver and four bronze.

The rowing events saw Soviet Vyacheslav Ivanov win his third successive gold medal in the single sculls, and the U.S.A. regain the eights title. The Vesper club of Philadelphia, after losing its first race to Germany and qualifying on a repechage, beat the champions, the Ratzeburg crew of Germany.

Italians won three cycling titles. In the road team trial three brothers from Sweden, Erik, Gosta and Sture Pettersson, took bronze medals behind Holland. Italy, however, was shut out of the fencing gold, as was France. The Soviets, with three gold medals, continued their improvement and were Hungary's chief rivals. Hungarians won four gold medals.

A third competitor won his third successive gold medal at the 1964 Olympics. He was Hans Winkler in the show-jumping team event, won by Germany. Pierre d'Oriola of France regained the individual title, having won it in 1952, 12 years earlier. France, like

Great Britain in 1952, thus won her only gold medal in the last event of the Games.

India regained the field hockey title, beating Pakistan 1–0 in a noisy, bad-tempered, partisan final. For the fourth successive time the Soviet Union reached the basketball final to challenge the United States, but once again the Americans won easily. Hungary won the soccer, beating Czechoslovakia 2–1 in the final.

The 'happy' Games came to an end with a happy closing ceremony, at which the New Zealanders began the informal atmosphere by dancing round the stadium. The United States for the first time since 1952 won most gold medals, 35 to the U.S.S.R.'s 30. But the Soviets again won most medals overall, 96 to 90. Thirty-seven of the American medals came in swimming. However, as the U.S.A. had won 14 track and field events to the Soviet Union's five, the Americans had most cause for satisfaction. There were so many track and field successes for the U.S.A. that a shortened version of the 'Star-spangled Banner' was played – an American trumpet player insisted on finishing off the anthem on his own.

Avery Brundage was most impressed with the Games, calling it a triumph for Japan and the Olympic movement, and a phenomenal success.

Abebe Bikila of Ethiopia wins his second marathon gold medal in 1964 in a world record. One of the most popular of all Olympic winners, he died following a car crash a few years later.

Abebe Bikila

Abebe Bikila was an astonishing marathon runner, who, despite his incredible feats, did not, perhaps because of injury, show the world his best. He was born on 7 August 1932 on the outskirts of Addis Ababa, Ethiopia. When he approached the Arch of Constantine in Rome in 1960, winning the Olympic Games marathon in a time better than Zatopek's, the world's journalists did not know if his name was Abebe Bikila or Bikila Abebe: it was only his third marathon, he was the first athletics gold medal winner from black Africa . . . and he was running in bare feet. Later he was identified as a corporal in the Household Guard of the Emperor. At Rome, in 1964, he ran in shoes. He had done nothing extraordinary in athletics since 1960, and had had his appendix removed five weeks before the Olympics. It seemed like a

sentimental trip. But Bikila won again, in a world's best time and by the biggest margin ever, 4 minutes 8 seconds. He then delighted the crowd with a series of calisthenics in the centre of the arena, possibly to prevent cramp. He was promoted to lieutenant. Bikila stood 5 feet 10 inches (1.78 metres) but weighed only 137 lb (57.61 kg). His economical lope took nothing out of him, and in the sweltering Rome marathon he lost only 7 lb (3.17 kg). He ran in the 1968 marathon, but had suffered a severe leg injury the year before which caused him to retire at 10 miles. He hoped to run in Munich in 1972 but in 1969 received spinal injuries in a car crash which confined him to a wheelchair for life. He was treated at Stoke Mandeville hospital in England and took up paraplegic sports, especially archery. He died of a cerebral haemorrhage on 25 October 1973, aged 41.

Grenoble

The tenth Winter Olympics, held at Grenoble, France, between 6 and 18 February, had its disputes both before and during competition. One of the more enduring concerned commercialism. A lot of money was spent on the Games, but half of it was for permanent facilities such as roads, not strictly in the Olympic spirit. A more damaging problem, and one which bothered Avery Brundage, was the advertising of trade names on skis and other equipment, and the associ-

In the Winter Olympics of 1968, East and West Germany competed as separate nations for the first time. Franz Keller of West Germany won the Nordic combined gold medal.

The Swedish skier, Toini Gustafsson, won both the women's Nordic skiing cross-country races and added a silver medal in the relay.

ation of leading skiers with the equipment companies. Skiers and many national associations were sponsored by the manufacturers, and the fabric of the sport would have undergone a change had an I.O.C. ban on markings been allowed to stand. Finally, after much argument, a compromise was reached, and skiers were required to remove equipment for photographs or television interviews.

The I.O.C. also had to rule on the case of Ralph Poehland, an East German skier, who defected to the West a month before the Games began. He was not allowed to compete. East and West Germany competed separately for the first time in the Olympics.

President de Gaulle declared the Games open before 60,000 spectators in a stadium built solely for the ceremony – it was dismantled afterwards. Artificial roses were dropped from helicopters, and the Olympic flags fluttered from parachutes in an impressive display. The events were again held at widely dispersed venues, involving difficult journeys of up to 40 km for journalists and spectators. The unseasonable weather, with plenty of fog, wind and rain as well as snow, did not help the organizers or competitors, who exceeded 1,300 from a record 37 nations.

The Nordic skiing was not the usual Scandinavian benefit. Although Norway won five gold medals, and Sweden two, there were wins for Italy, West Germany, Czechoslovakia and the U.S.S.R. The Italian win, by Franco Nones in the 30-km cross-country, was the first Nordic cross-country medal for any competitor outside the Scandinavian countries and the U.S.S.R. Norway took the other three men's races, including the relay, which enabled Harald Gronningen and Olle Ellefsaeter to win a second gold medal each. There were further shocks for the Scandinavians when Jiri Raska of Czechoslovakia won the 70-metres ski jump from two Austrians, and finished second to Vladimir Beloussov of the Soviet Union in the 90-metres jump, and Franz Keller of West Germany came out top in the Nordic combined, from a Swiss and an East German.

Jean-Claude Killy of France became the second man to win all three Alpine skiing events in 1968, but his slalom win was tinged with controversy.

A little-fancied Norwegian policeman, Magnar Solberg, won the biathlon, but the U.S.S.R. beat Norway in the biathlon relay.

An outstanding skier from Sweden, Toini Gustafsson, won both the women's Nordic races, the 10-km by over a minute, but she took only silver in the relay in which Norway beat Sweden.

The star of the Games was the Alpine skier, Jean-Claude Killy of France. On a downhill course that dropped more than 760 metres (2,500 feet) in 2,750 metres (3,000 yards), he sped down to beat Guy Perillat, also of France, albeit by only 0.08 of a second. A giant slalom win was easier, and then came the slalom, in which he hoped to emulate Toni Sailer's clean sweep of 1956. There was a row before the event. Because of the large number of competitors, it was proposed to hold an eliminating race, which would serve to decide the skiing order for the following day. The top skiers, led by Killy, objected, claiming that the points scored by each skier in the season should decide both questions. This would have favoured the regular skiers,

of course, those that the I.O.C. thought of as partly professional. In the end, fog cancelled the eliminator, and all went in the 'final', in conditions perhaps even poorer. Killy led on the first run, but his two-run time was vulnerable, and was beaten by Haakon Mjoen of Norway and the veteran Karl Schranz of Austria. Mjoen was disqualified for missing two gates. The position of Schranz caused much bitter argument. Schranz pulled up on his second run at Gate 22, claiming a course policeman had crossed the track, a fact verified by witnesses. Schranz was given a second run, and beat Killy's time. In his first run, however, Schranz had missed Gates 17 and 18, and the French protested that he should have been disqualified anyway. The jury had to decide if the obstruction further down could have caused Schranz to miss these gates, as he claimed, and after three hours decided for Killy.

The women's Alpine events were less controversial. Olga Pall of Austria won the downhill and Marielle Goitschel the slalom from Nancy Greene of Canada. Goitschel was

Grenoble

Above: Nancy Greene of Canada on her way to a popular win in the giant slalom.

Above right: The men's figure skating champion, Wolfgang Schwarz of Austria.

Right: The medalists in the women's figure skating. From left: Gabrielle Seyfert of East Germany (silver), Peggy Fleming of the U.S.A. (gold) and Hana Maskova of Czechoslovakia (bronze).

the first Alpine skier to win gold medals in separate Games. The most clear-cut win, and one of the most popular, was that of Nancy Greene in the giant slalom. She finished with over $2\frac{1}{2}$ seconds in hand.

Austria's Wolfgang Schwarz was a surprise winner of the men's figure skating, but Peggy Fleming of the U.S.A. in the women's and Oleg Protopopov and Ludmila Belousova of

the U.S.S.R. in the pairs dazzled, each getting several marks of 5.9 from the judges. The veteran Protopopovs, at 35 and 32, were retaining their title after long careers.

Three speed-skating gold medals went to Dutch skaters, the most impressive being Kees Verkerk in the 1,500 metres. He beat the world record and finished second to Anton Maier, who also beat the world record, in the 5,000 metres. An odd occurrence was the triple tie of the three American girls in the 500 metres behind the Soviet Union's only speed skating medalist, Ludmila Titova.

The bobsleigh events were both won by Italy, and the great Eugenio Monti took two gold medals, to popular satisfaction. He had won two silver and two bronze since 1956, but he was nine times world champion, and he retired at 40 after his Olympic successes.

The men's tobogganing events went to Austria and East Germany. In the women's event the East Germans were disqualified for heating their runners, in what they called a 'capitalist conspiracy', but it was a Pole who ruled them out. The coaches of seven teams threatened to walk out if the whole East Germany team was not disqualified, but as the Olympics are for individuals, the right decision was taken, and East German men won. Erica Lechner won the women's event for Italy, breaking the Austrian/German monopoly of gold.

The U.S.S.R. won the ice hockey, but was beaten 5–4 by Czechoslovakia, and needed Sweden to draw 2–2 with Czechoslovakia in order to finish first.

After the overwhelming Soviet successes in the 1964 Games, the gold medals were more evenly shared in 1968, and indeed Norway, with a population of only four million, took

six gold medals to the U.S.S.R.'s five.

The arguments which broke out at various stages of the Games continued to the end when the I.O.C. announced the re-admittance of South Africa, who promised the team for Mexico would not be picked on *apartheid* principles. It was understood to be a close vote, but its repercussions were to be wide. So the quarrelsome Games ended, with the Japanese providing the happy touch by distributing flags and artificial perfumed roses as an invitation to Sapporo in 1972.

Below left: Cornelis Verkerk of Holland winning the 1,500-metres speed-skating.

Below top: The 1964 figure-skating pairs champions retained their title. Ludmila Belousova and Oleg Protopopov of the U.S.S.R.

Bottom: Jean-Claude Killy with Herbert Huber (left) and Alfred Matt, both of Austria, the slalom medalists.

Jean-Claude Killy

Skier Jean Claude Killy was sixth in the giant slalom in the 1964 Olympics; in 1966 he was world champion; and in 1967 and 1968 he won the first two World Cups. But his greatest feat was to win all three Alpine skiing events in the 1968 Olympics, a feat only performed once before by Toni Sailer. Killy was born on 30 August 1943 in Saint-Cloud, France, and trained at Val d'Isère. His Olympic triumph was not without controversy, particularly over the disqualification of Karl Schranz in the slalom. He immediately turned professional, perhaps influenced by the I.O.C. concern over professionalism among the top skiers, and made a lucrative career from endorsements. His name comes from the Irish Kellys of the Napoleonic wars. He was world professional champion in 1973.

Mexico City

Below top: Spectators sitting on the 'Mexico 68' symbol to get a view of the proceedings.

Bottom: The 10,000-metres race, which answered the questions regarding the dangers of distance running at altitude. The winner, Naftali Temu (575) of Kenya, is lying fourth. The silver medalist, Mamo Wolde (329), is second; and the bronze medalist, Mohamed Gammoudi, is sixth. Also in the picture are Kip Keino and Ron Clarke.

As in 1956, the 1968 Olympic Games was held in the shadow of Communist aggression; Soviet tanks had been used in the summer to crush the liberal regime of Premier Dubcek in Czechoslovakia. Furthermore, the Games itself was held with troops in attendance as a student protest against the Mexican government had been halted by troops and police only ten days before the Games began. In a fierce battle in the Square of the Three Cultures, hundreds of demonstrators were killed, injured or imprisoned.

Mexico City had been awarded the Games in 1963, despite many protests. There was widespread medical concern about the thin air of Mexico City, nearly 2,500 metres (7,400 feet) above sea level. It was thought that a lack of oxygen might even cause deaths among the distance runners, and some countries built high-altitude sports centres to test the effects of altitude on athletes.

A dispute about the eligibility of South Africa threatened to reduce drastically the number of competing nations. In February the I.O.C. decided to re-admit South African athletes. There were immediate protests. Black African nations, the U.S.S.R. and militant black athletes in the U.S. squad all threatened to withdraw, and were backed by the Mexican organizers, who feared for the status of their Games. The I.O.C., to the dismay of Avery Brundage who saw the whole episode as politics interfering with sport, was forced to reverse its decision.

As in the earlier winter Games, East and West Germany competed as separate nations.

The organization for the Games was not of the best. Communications, traffic and accommodation for those who went to Mexico City were poor, and rain storms made conditions dismal.

The 1968 Games was opened on 12 October and, for the first time, a woman lit the Olympic flame: Enriqueta Basilio, a Mexican runner in the 400 metres. The number of countries participating, 112, was the highest yet, and of over 6,000 competitors, nearly 800 were women.

The fears about the altitude were soon put to the test, as the 10,000 metres was held on the first day. After an initial slow pace, seven men broke away, four of whom were born at high altitude and two of whom had lived for a long period at altitude. Ron Clarke, the world record holder, was the other. Clarke was the first to drop out with fatigue that blurred his vision. He finished, collapsed, and was revived with oxygen. With two laps to go the three medalists had broken away, with the finishing speed of Naftali Temu of Kenya winning him the gold medal from Mamo Wolde of Ethiopia and Mohamed Gammoudi of Tunisia, who had been second in 1964. The time was 1 minute and 48 seconds

outside Ron Clarke's world record. A Mexican was fourth. Great Britain's Ron Hill, who finished seventh, claimed to have won the race for 'sea level' athletes. The distressed athletes soon recovered, dispelling some of the medical fears, but the altitude had had a decisive effect on the result.

In the more explosive events the altitude helped the athletes, and many world records were set. Jim Hines of the U.S.A. equalled the world record in the 100 metres, and anchored the American 4 × 100-metres relay team to a new world record. This team was without the services of Tommie Smith and John Carlos, first and third in the 200 metres, because of what happened at the medal ceremony.

Both Smith and Carlos had threatened to boycott the Games over the South African controversy and related Black Power aims (about which more later). In the event itself, their performances were admirable, particularly in the final when both were suffering from injury, Smith to his leg, Carlos to his back. Carlos led but Smith came through elegantly to win in world record time. An Australian, Peter Norman, finished fast to deprive Carlos of the silver medal. At the medal ceremony, each appeared with identifiable track shoes in one hand (there was

Balloons float into the air during the opening ceremony for the 1968 Mexico Olympics.

Tommie Smith of the U.S.A. wins the 200 metres. Partly hidden is John Carlos of the U.S.A. who finished third. Their antics on the rostrum caused them to be sent home.

Mexico City

Tommie Smith still giving a Black Power salute after receiving his gold medal for his 200-metres win.

John Carlos and his wife surrounded by newsmen as they leave the Olympic village after being ordered out of the country by the U.S. Olympic Committee.

Below: The finish of the 400 metres. Lee Evans (270) is the winner, Larry James (280) was second and Ron Freeman (273) third, to give the U.S.A. a clean sweep.

much I.O.C. heartsearching about athletes being bribed to wear particular brands), a human rights badge on their tracksuits, which were rolled up to reveal black socks, and black gloves on one hand. When the anthem was played they raised their gloved fists in the air in a Black Power salute and bowed their heads. Two days later they were expelled from the U.S. squad and sent home.

The day of the 'disgrace' of Smith and Carlos was the day on which Lee Evans, another black American athlete, won the 400 metres in another world record. Evans, another militant, had spoken with Carlos and Smith on the morning of the race. He was in tears as he considered whether or not he should run. Evans, who also wore black socks, beat two other black American athletes, Lawrence James and Ronald Freeman, which gave the U.S.A. a clean sweep of the medals. At the victory ceremony they wore black berets, but removed them for the anthem. They waved fists to the crowd, but their actions were not considered punishable. The three teamed up with a fourth black American to win the 4 × 400-metres relay in another world record, and again black berets and clenched fists were seen on the podium.

The 800 metres was won by an Australian,

Kip Keino of Kenya has no rival in the picture as he wins the 1,500 metres by the widest margin so far in the Olympics.

Below: A heat of the 800 metres. Ralph Doubell of Australia (105), the eventual gold medalist, trails H. Szordykowski of Poland and R. Ouko of Kenya.

Ralph Doubell, who equalled the world record of Peter Snell but only just beat Kenya's Wilson Kiprugut, who had been third to Snell in 1964.

The 1,500 metres was another race in which the high-altitude athletes held an advantage. Jim Ryun, the American world record holder, was the favourite, but he was an unlucky runner and had been ill. Kenya's Ben Jipcho set a fast pace, but his countryman Kip Keino took the lead at halfway and opened a big gap. There was no way he could be caught, and he won in the second fastest time ever, beating the fast-finishing Jim Ryun by 2.9 seconds, the widest margin in any Olympic 1,500 metres.

Keino had set himself the impossible task of trying to win the 1,500, 5,000 and 10,000 metres. He had been forced to retire in the longest race, but in the 5,000 he and Temu, the 10,000 winner, moved up menacingly to challenge the leader Mohamed Gammoudi of Tunisia, third in the 10,000. Gammoudi managed to fight off Keino, and won from the two Kenyans, with the Mexican, Juan Martinez, who was fourth in the 10,000, finishing fourth again. It was the slowest final since 1952, and once more the altitude runners had prevailed.

Left: Mohamed Gammoudi of Tunisia wins a well-deserved gold medal by taking the 5,000 metres, beating Kip Keino, the 1,500 metres winner.

Mexico City

Right: Mamo Wolde of Ethiopia, the winner of the marathon in succession to his countryman Abebe Bikila.

It was the same story in the 3,000 metres steeplechase and the marathon. The steeplechase was won by a 19-year-old Kenyan, Amos Biwott, who ran with natural exuberance, giving nothing to technique or tactics. He was 30 metres down at the bell and in a hopeless position, but he produced a tearaway last lap to win comfortably from his fellow-Kenyan, Benjamin Kogo.

An injured Abebe Bikila ran in the marathon, but could manage only about 17 km (10 miles). His countryman, Mamo Wolde, second in the 10,000 metres, took up the running with 10 km (6 miles) to go, and won by over three minutes from Kenji Kimihara of Japan and Michael Ryan of New Zealand.

Willie Davenport of the United States beat his countryman, Irvin Hall, to win the 110-metres hurdles, and David Hemery of Great Britain impressively beat an excellent field to win the 400-metres hurdles in world record time. His winning margin of nearly a second was the largest so far in this race. Fellow-Briton, John Sherwood, took the bronze; his wife Sheila took the silver in the women's long jump.

Vladimir Golubnichiy regained the 20-km walk title he had won in 1960 and lost in 1964, and in the 50-km walk Christoph Hoehne won East Germany's first track gold medal – by a margin of 10 minutes. Following Golubnichiy home was José Pedraza who only just failed to become Mexico's first athletics champion.

Above: Willie Davenport of the U.S.A. takes a hurdle on his way to victory in the 110-metres hurdles.

David Hemery of Great Britain in his impressive 400-metres hurdles win in world record time. His team-mate, John Sherwood (422), finished third.

The field events again provided a rich harvest of gold medals for the U.S.A. Nobody caused as much comment as 20-year-old Dick Fosbury in the high jump. He had perfected a new technique, taking off on his outside foot and going over the bar head first, his body facing upwards. He just beat Ed Caruthers of the U.S.A., and the 'Fosbury Flop' is now used by most leading jumpers.

The long jump, however, was the most extraordinary event of the Games, producing perhaps the greatest single feat in athletics history. On the fourth jump of the final, the first three competitors having fouled, Bob Beamon of the U.S.A. jumped an amazing 8.90 metres (29 feet 2½ inches). This was 55 cm (1 foot 9¾ inches) beyond the world record. Nobody had even approached 28 feet (8.53 metres) before, and Beamon went past 29 feet. The competition was effectively over. Neither of the previous joint record-holders, Ralph Boston or Igor Ter-Ovanesyan, nor Olympic champion Lynn Davies, could approach that distance, although Boston finished third. Klaus Beer of East Germany took the silver, but he was more than two feet behind. Beamon bothered to jump only once more – there was no point in further effort.

The triple jump was also remarkable for the battering taken by the old world record.

Above left: Christoph Hoehne of West Germany on his way to victory in the 50-km walk.

Above: This superb leap of Bob Beamon of the U.S.A. advanced the world long jump record by a prodigious 55 cm (nearly 22 inches).

Left: A new high-jump technique won a gold medal for Dick Fosbury of the U.S.A.

Mexico City

Nine times it was beaten, and the mark improved five times during competition. Twice it was raised by Giuseppe Gentile of Italy who took only the bronze medal for his efforts, once by Nelson Prudencio of Brazil who led but took silver, and twice by Viktor Saneyev of the U.S.S.R. whose last jump won him the gold medal.

An American and two Germans fought out a long pole-vault competition. It was won by Bob Seagren of the U.S.A., who successfully gambled on passing his turn at a late height – he won by virtue of fewer failures; the minor medalists, Claus Schiprowski of West Germany and Wolfgang Nordwig of East Germany, both achieved the same height as the winner.

The great American discus thrower, Al Oerter, earned a unique place in Olympic history by winning his fourth successive gold medal, never before achieved in track and field. It was a triumph for character and competitiveness, as Oerter, suffering from a torn calf muscle, beat the world record holder, American Jay Silvester, into fifth place.

Hal Connolly, the American hammer champion of 1956, was also taking part in his fourth Olympics. He failed to qualify for the final throws but his wife, the 1956 discus champion, finished sixth in her event. The hammer title went to Hungary's Gyula Zsivotzky, twice before silver medalist, who reversed the 1964 placings with the Soviet Union's Romuald Klim. Janis Lusis of the U.S.S.R. stepped up two places from 1964 to win the javelin, and Randy Matson beat fellow-American George Woods in the shot.

Bill Toomey of the U.S.A. held a useful halfway lead in the decathlon, and held off the second-day rush of Hans-Joachim Walde of West Germany to win the gold medal.

World records were broken in the women's sprints. Wyomia Tyus of the U.S.A. won the 100 metres in 11.0 seconds and became the first athlete to win a sprint title at successive Games. Barbara Ferrell of the U.S.A. was second and Poland's Irena Szewinska (nee Kirszenstein) third. Mrs. Szewinska broke her own world record in the 200 metres, winning from two Australians, Raelene Boyle and Jennifer Lamy. The American team won the relay, with Tyus taking her third Olympic gold medal, in a new world record, from Cuba and the U.S.S.R.

The 400 metres was a surprise result, as Great Britain's 19-year-old Lillian Board was a warm favourite. She led into the straight, but the altitude tired her, and she was beaten by a little-known French girl, Colette Besson. The following year Board won the European

Colette Besson of France (117) wins the 400 metres from Great Britain's Lillian Board on the right. Unplaced were Helga Henning (5) of West Germany and Aurelia Penton (69) of Cuba.

Bob Beamon

Never has an athletics record been shattered so completely as the long jump record was on 18 October 1968. The man who did it was Bob Beamon, and his jump has been called the most outstanding athletics feat of all time, and it is claimed that the record will last 100 years. Beamon was born on 29 August 1946 in Jamaica, New York. He was a fast sprinter (9.5 seconds for 100 yards), and a potentially brilliant jumper, who lacked technique and was consequently erratic, but who could occasionally produce a big jump. His biggest before the 1968 Olympics was 8.33 metres (27 feet 4 inches), just two centimetres behind the world record. He was one of the three or four men fancied for the title, but only qualified for the final with his last jump, 8.19 metres (26 feet 10½ inches). In the final rounds he was fourth to jump and propelled his long lanky frame (6 feet 3 inches, 165 lb or 1.90 metres, 74.84 kg) at speed down the runway, jumped high with his legs and arms spreadeagled and nearly reached the end of the pit. It took some time to measure the distance: 8.90 metres (29 feet 2½ inches). To realize the enormity of the performance: the long jump record had climbed from just 25 feet at the turn of the century, through 26 and 27 feet to 27 feet 4¾ inches, and Beamon had gone straight past 29 feet. He had increased the world record by 55 cm (1 foot 9¾ inches), the previous 55 cm improvement having taken 44 years. There were, of course, rare helpful conditions. The altitude of Mexico City reduced resistance through the air; the following wind was at about the maximum allowable for a record; the new Tartan surface for the run-up was extremely fast; and, most important, the uninhibited Beamon got everything right for once, hitting the take-off board perfectly.

Beamon had not had a happy childhood, having lost his mother when young and generally wasting his schooldays in clowning. He went to the University of Texas and returned there after the Olympics, but had difficulty in recovering psychologically from his great feat. He never again jumped further than 8.20 metres (26 feet 11 inches). He obtained a diploma in sociology in 1972, failed to make the Munich Olympic team, turned professional for a while and in 1974 went to New York to look after abandoned children. He had been expelled from university in 1969, divorced, and gone on a spending spree which put him in debt. He was an ordinary man who could not at first handle his international fame, and who went back to his roots to re-establish himself.

Mexico City

Right: Madeline Manning of the U.S.A., the 800-metres winner, leads in one of the heats.

Far right: The colourful medal ceremony for the women's shot put. Margit Gummel of East Germany set a new world record in winning.

championship 800 metres, and overtook Besson to win the 4 × 400-metres relay for Britain in a world record time, but she was to die of cancer just after her 22nd birthday, having that year gained her fourth world record.

The 800 metres was too much for world record holder Vera Nikolic of Yugoslavia, who overdid her training and retired distressed in the semi-final. It was said that immediately afterwards she had to be restrained from jumping off a bridge just outside the stadium. The final was won impressively by American Madeline Manning.

The world record holder in the 80-metres hurdles, Soviet Vera Korsakova, also failed to reach the final, and 17-year-old Maureen Caird of Australia equalled the world record to win from her more-fancied teammate, Pam Kilborn, thus becoming the youngest Olympic track gold medalist.

There was also a young winner in the high jump, Czechoslovakia's 18-year-old Miroslava Rezkova. Behind on the countback, she cleared 1.82 metres (5 feet 11½ inches) on her last attempt to beat two Soviets, a result cheered by the crowd in view of the U.S.S.R.'s forceful intervention in Czechoslovakia. Rumania's Viorica Viscopoleanu beat Great Britain's Sheila Sherwood in the long jump, with a world record, set, like Beamon's, on her first jump. Another Rumanian, Lia Manoliu, although below her world record, won the discus in her fifth Olympics, having won bronze medals in the previous two. East Germany's Margit Gummel set a world record to win the shot, and

Angela Nemeth of Hungary beat the holder, Mihaela Penes of Rumania, to take the javelin. Ingrid Becker of West Germany took the pentathlon gold medal by overtaking Austria's Liese Prokop in the last event.

The altitude and stomach indispositions upset many of the competitors in the swimming pool. The events were dominated by the United States even more than in Tokyo – they won 21 of 29 events and over half the medals overall. Only three new world records were set in individual events. Australia's Mike Wenden set a new record in the 100-metres freestyle, as did American Kaye Hall in the women's 100-metres backstroke, and East Germany's Roland Matthes improved the world 100-metres backstroke time in the medley relay team which finished second to the United States. Matthes was one of the dual gold-medal winners in the men's individual events, winning both backstroke titles. Wenden took both 100- and 200-metres freestyle, American Charles Hickcox the 200 and 400-metres individual medleys, and his countryman, Mike Burton, the 400 and 1,500-metres freestyle.

The most individual gold medals, however, went to American Debbie Meyer. The 200 and 800-metres freestyle were new events for women and Meyer won both of these and the 400 metres. Claudia Kolb of the U.S.A. won two individual gold medals in the two individual medleys.

Don Schollander added a silver and a relay gold to the four gold medals he won in 1964, and Mark Spitz, a pre-Games favourite in many events, won a silver, a bronze and two relay gold medals to begin his Olympic career. The platform diving provided a first gold medal for Italy's outstanding Klaus Dibiasi, and in the women's event another victory for a Czech over a Soviet, Milena Duchkova winning.

The gymnastics events included some strange marking, with protests from the spectators and interventions by the technical committee. After at least one such disagreement a mark was changed. The star was the Czech Vera Caslavska, who won four gold and two silver medals. The Japanese won over half of the men's medals: Akinori Nakayama

A victory in the final event allowed Ingrid Becker of West Germany, seen long jumping, to win the pentathlon.

Far left: Heavyweight boxing champion George Foreman of the U.S.A. waves a small American flag after his gold medal victory. In the main, the American boxers did not support the Black Power demonstrations.

Left: Roland Matthes of East Germany won four backstroke swimming medals in 1968 and 1972. At the 200-metres backstroke ceremony he watches Americans Mitchell Ivey (left), the silver medalist, and Jack Horsley, the bronze medalist, congratulate each other.

won four gold medals, Sawao Kato three. In both men's and women's events the challengers were the Soviets.

The boxing had some of its periodic troubles with the officials – five referees were withdrawn. The winner who gained most renown later was heavyweight champion George Foreman of the U.S.A., who waved a tiny American flag at the medal ceremony in contrast to the Black Power salutes of some of the other athletes. Foreman later won the world professional championship, knocking out previous Olympic champion, Joe Frazier. Another winner to turn professional was Great Britain's Chris Finnegan, the middleweight champion, who was later European light-heavyweight champion and lost a hard fight to Bob Foster for the world title. It

took several hours and many pints of beer before the colourful Finnegan could pass the urine test.

The U.S.S.R. and Japan each won five gold medals in weightlifting and wrestling. Several weightlifters and wrestlers retained their titles, the most notable perhaps being the Soviet Union's heavyweight lifter, Leonid Zhabotinsky, known as Zhabo.

Bob Braithwaite won a gold medal for Great Britain in the shooting events, the first since 1924, and Gary Anderson (U.S.A.) retained his free rifle title. Daniel Morelon and Pierre Trentin each won two cycling gold medals for France. West Germany was disqualified in the final of the pursuit race when one of the team was helped; Denmark took the gold. The three Pettersson brothers

Mexico City

A rare gold medal for Great Britain in shooting was won by Bob Braithwaite in the trap-shooting event.

Bill Steinkraus of the U.S.A. won the show-jumping gold medal, America's first individual gold in the event. The horse is Stroller, runner-up for Great Britain with Marian Coakes.

from Sweden, who had won bronze medals in the road team time-trial in 1964, were joined by a fourth, Tomas, in 1968 and won the silver behind Holland.

Bill Steinkraus won the U.S.A.'s first show-jumping gold medal, beating two Britons, Marian Coakes and David Broome. Steinkraus was 43, and had won bronze and silver team medals in 1952 and 1960. An even older British veteran, 54-year-old Derek Allhusen who had competed in 1948, won the silver medal in the three-day event and, with Richard Meade and Ben Jones, took the team gold. Rodney Pattisson of Great Britain, crewed by Iain MacDonald-Smith, won the first of his yachting gold medals in the Flying Dutchman class, and in the rowing Aleksandr Timoshinin, with Anatoli Sass, won his first double sculls gold medal for the U.S.S.R. West Germany regained the eights title.

It was thought that the United States players were at last vulnerable in the basketball, but they beat Yugoslavia comfortably enough in the final, after Yugoslavia had surprisingly beaten the Soviet Union 63–62. There was no such happy outcome for India in the field hockey, beaten 2–1 by Australia in the semi-final and being forced to take bronze, their worst result since 1928. Pakistan beat Australia 2–1 to win the gold medals. The Hungarians retained the soccer title, beating the Bulgarians 4–1 in a bad-tempered match in which they had three men sent off – Bulgaria had one. Yugoslavia, after many

Al Oerter

Despite his four world records, Al Oerter will be remembered as the man who was the ultimate competitor. In four successive Olympic Games he won the discus, sometimes fighting both pain and men with better records, and his feat is unique in Olympic history. He was born on 19 September 1936 in Astoria, New York, and was American high-school discus record holder in 1954. In 1956, at 20, he was a surprise winner of the Olympic gold medal with a personal best throw; the world record holder, Fortune Gordien, was second. In 1960 he again won with another personal best, again beating the world record holder, Richard Babka, into second place. Oerter broke the world record himself in 1962 (twice) and again in 1963 and 1964, but by the time of the Olympics in 1964 his Czech rival, Ludvik Danek, held the record. Oerter threw with surgical tape round his ribs to protect torn cartilages and a brace round his neck to ease the pain of a cervical disc. On his fifth throw he overtook Danek and for the third time relegated the world record holder to second place. Oerter trained hard for the 1968 Olympics, but was again handicapped by neck pain and a torn thigh muscle. Danek was again in the field, as was Jay Silvester, awaiting ratification of a new world record over five metres better than Oerter's best-ever throw. Oerter produced another personal best, Danek and Silvester finished third and fifth. Oerter kept in trim and could still throw over 62 metres (203 feet 5 inches) in the late 1970s, and was hoping to compete in the 1980 Moscow Olympics when the Americans withdrew.

Far left: The winning West German dressage team. From the left: Josef Neckermann on Mariane, Liselott Linsenhoff on Piaff and Reiner Klimke on Dux.

Left: The Flying Dutchman class yacht, *Superdocious*, in which Rodney Pattisson and Iain MacDonald-Smith of Great Britain won the gold medal on Acapulco Bay.

near misses, at last won the water polo, and the Japanese women could not repeat their 1964 virtuosity in the volleyball, being runners-up to the Soviet Union, as were their men.

The talking points of the Games, outside the performances themselves, were the first Olympic sex tests for women, strict testing for drugs, the reputedly huge sums given to some top American athletes by two competing track shoe companies for the favour of using their shoes, and the Black Power demonstrations. No women were disqualified, possibly because of similar tests at the European championships earlier; there were no drugs scandals; and the I.O.C. did not search too hard for proof of the shoe money handouts. The stories had started when an American athlete cashed a cheque made out to him by a sports goods company.

The Black Power display had been brewing for some time. It arose from a proposed black American boycott of the Games to highlight the injustices which many blacks felt they suffered in the U.S.A. The idea grew with the proposed invitation to South Africa for the Olympics. The reversal of the I.O.C.'s decision took the impetus from the boycott, and most athletes who had previously decided not to take part, including gold medal winner Tommie Smith, changed their minds.

Smith and Carlos then made their gesture on the podium: 'a victory for black people everywhere' said Tommie Smith. They were backed in various degrees by other black athletes. Several had said that they did not want medals presented to them by Avery Brundage in protest against his views on the South African question. Lee Evans wore the black socks, one of the symbols of the revolt,

and more muted gestures followed the dismissal of Smith and Carlos in the form of black berets and raised, if ungloved, fists. Beamon wore black socks for his medal ceremony, Boston was barefooted. Most of the black athletes supported the Black Power line; for example Wyomia Tyus acknowledged Smith and Carlos after the relay win. Some however, did not, notably George Foreman who waved his little flag.

The atmosphere of the Games, then, was not always happy. The Mexicans themselves had their troubles, and could not afford the lavish spending which had made the Tokyo Games so colourful. They did their best, and the achievements of so many great athletes have lasted longer in memory than the politics and squabbles.

Vera Caslavska

Vera Caslavska was the second female gymnast to make a big impression in the Olympics, and her medals haul eventually approached Latynina's. She was born on 3 May 1943 in Prague, Czechoslovakia, and took a silver medal in the team event in the 1960 Olympics. In 1964 she began her reign as the world's best, taking three gold and a silver medal at Tokyo, and in 1968 she was supreme, with four gold and two silver. She delighted the Mexican spectators with her victories over the Soviets and with her floor exercises to the tune of the 'Mexican Hat Dance'. She retired after the 1968 Olympics, marrying Josef Odlozil (who was beaten by Snell in the 1964 1,500-metres race) in the cathedral in Mexico City before returning home. As well as her Olympic medals, she won four gold medals in world championships and 11 in European championships.

Vera Caslavska

Sapporo

The 1972 Winter Olympics, beginning on 3 February, was held at Sapporo on Hokkaido, the northernmost island of Japan, where changeable weather caused one or two problems. It was the first Winter Games to be held in Asia. Immediately after the Games gales marooned many competitors who were unable to take off at the airport.

There was a major controversy on the eve of the Games when the I.O.C. decided to ban Austria's famous skier, Karl Schranz, for cashing in on his fame. Schranz was picked as the most blatant example of a professional – Brundage claimed to have 40 names on a blacklist – and he was expelled by 28 votes to 14. Several countries threatened to withdraw in protest. Austria did, but re-entered at the request of Schranz himself. Schranz went home to a hero's welcome, waving to 100,000 Austrians from the chancellery in Vienna.

Enormous expense went into the Games, designed partly as publicity for the city of Sapporo as the ski-centre for wealthy Japanese. The media men outnumbered the 1,128 competitors by over two to one. Emperor Hirohito declared the Games open in a colourful opening ceremony at which 18,000 balloons were released.

The scene at the opening ceremony of the 1972 Sapporo Winter Olympics as the balloons are released.

Erhard Keller of West Germany winning the 500 metres speed skating to retain the title won in 1968.

Far right: Soviet skier Galina Kulakova who won three gold medals in the Nordic skiing cross-country races.

The 12 Nordic skiing events were shared by skiers from six countries, but the Soviet Union claimed six gold medals, including those for the three women's events. The most popular result was in the 70-metres ski jump, where Yukio Kasaya of Japan won from two of his countrymen. The 90-metres jump, however, just went to Poland's Wojciech Fortuna, after a huge first jump. An East German, Ulrich Wehling, won the combined. A Norwegian and a Swede won two of the cross-country events, but a Soviet, Vyacheslav Vedenin, won the other, and collected another gold in the relay. Magnar Solberg of Norway retained his biathlon title, but the U.S.S.R. again took the relay. In the women's events, Galina Kulakova (U.S.S.R.) won both individual titles and a third gold in the relay.

Half the Alpine skiing medals went to Switzerland, thanks largely to Marie-Therese Nadig, who beat Annemarie Proell, the favourite from Austria, into second place in both the downhill and giant slalom. Barbara Cochran of the U.S.A. just beat Danielle Debernard of France in the slalom, the first Alpine gold for the U.S.A. for 20 years. In the men's events, Gustavo Thoeni of Italy, the World Cup holder, won the giant slalom, and he and his brother Rolando finished second and third behind a surprise winner from Spain, Francisco Fernandez-Ochoa, in the slalom – the first winter gold medalist from Spain. Bernhard Russi won from another Swiss skier, Roland Collombin, in the downhill.

The men's figure skating was won for the first time by a Czech, Ondrej Nepela, who won despite a fall, and Austrian Beatrix Schuba, who won the women's, was only the second winner from that country. She won on her compulsory figures. Janet Lynn of the U.S.A. gave a brilliant freestyle display, marred by an elementary sit-down, which did not prevent her scoring a six for artistic expression, and taking the bronze. With the retirement of the Protopopovs, two more Soviet teams fought for the pairs title. The winners were Alexei Ulanov and Irina Rodnina. There was romance afoot here, for

Marie-Therese Nadig of Switzerland was the leading Alpine skier of 1972, winning both the downhill and the giant slalom.

Sapporo

Gustavo Thoeni of Italy won the giant slalom and finished second in the slalom in Sapporo.

Ulanov later married Ludmila Smirnova, the silver medalist, and made her his skating partner, but it was Rodnina who went on to the greater triumphs.

The star of the Games was a strong blond Dutchman, Ard Schenk, who won the three longer speed-skating titles, after falling in the 500 metres. In view of arguments over professionalism, it was instructive to discover him immediately seeking a sponsor for a round-the-world public relations trip. Two of the four women's speed-skating titles were won by Americans, Anne Henning and Dianne Holum, who remarkably both came from Northbrook, Illinois.

The two-man bob resulted in two West German crews finishing first and second, and Switzerland won the four-man. East Germans dominated the luge tobogganing, finishing in the first three places in the men's single-seater, taking the tied first place and a third in the two-seater, and taking all three medals in the women's. Thus they claimed eight of the nine medals possible.

The U.S.S.R. won the ice hockey, the team's only hiccup coming with a 3–3 draw with Sweden. The U.S.A. finished second, having surprisingly beaten Czechoslovakia. The once supreme Canadians did not take part, dropping out of amateur hockey, but in the summer, the Soviet gold medalists played the Canadian professionals in an eight-game challenge series; the Canadians won the series 4–3 with one game drawn.

Nearly half the medals at the 1972 Winter Games were shared by four countries: the U.S.S.R., East Germany, Norway and Finland. The progress made by the East Germans suggested what was to come in the summer and in succeeding Games.

The main topic for discussion of the Games, though, was professionalism, still a dominant and unresolved problem of the Winter Olympics.

Above: The men's downhill Alpine skiing event was won by the Swiss skier, Bernhard Russi, who takes to the air as he flashes down.

Left: The Swiss No. 1 four-man bobsleigh team, driven by Jean Wicki, shoots past the photographers on the way to winning the gold medal.

Munich

The Games of the twentieth Olympiad, held in Munich from 26 August to 11 September 1972, was the scene of enormous tragedy which so overshadowed the sport that it came near to being abandoned in mid-flow.

In their plans for the Games, the Germans intended and were determined to make the 1972 Olympics the biggest, most expensive sporting display ever seen, and the spread of television meant that for two weeks the attention of most of the civilized world was to be concentrated on Munich.

Television fees contributed handsomely to the cost of staging the bonanza, and an enthusiastic programme of fund-raising, which included the promotion of lotteries, realized some of the remainder of the expenses, which totalled around the equivalent of £300 million or nearly $1,000 million.

A sporting complex just outside Munich was built, which included blocks of luxury flats for the athletes around the various stadia. The main feature was the enormous roof of steel and acrylic glass which was built to undulate over part of the main stadium, the sports hall and swimming pool. Brundage was concerned with the expense, which suggested an element of competition which would reduce still further the possible venues for future Games. The Games provided a huge pay day for German industry and technology, and, of course, the simultaneous photographing and timing of the races was of the highest standard.

Over 7,000 competitors were present from a record 122 nations, with almost as many representatives of the communications industry. With a television audience of about a thousand million, the Games was ideal for the ruthless exploitation which was to follow.

The main political controversy before the Games, which was to have an echo in the later tragedy, centred around the consent of the I.O.C. in 1971 to allow participation by Rhodesia, based on the status of Rhodesia as a British colony, which the Rhodesians had unilaterally abandoned in 1965. African nations had agreed to Rhodesians competing

Sadly the 1972 Olympic Games will be remembered for the act of terrorism which resulted in the killing of hostages from the Israeli team. A terrorist (right) discusses terms in the Olympic village with Herr Hans-Dietrich Genscher (centre), the West German Minister of the Interior, and other officials.

The memorial service for the slain Israeli athletes at the magnificent new stadium in Munich.

as British subjects under the colonial flag, and a team of 46 Rhodesian athletes duly arrived in Munich. However, the African national Olympic committees then announced that the Games organizers had failed to justify legally the nationality of the Rhodesians, and that the Rhodesians were exploiting their participation for political purposes. Thirty-two African nations threatened to withdraw if Rhodesia competed, and the I.O.C. was forced into an emergency meeting, which voted 36–31, with three abstentions, to rescind its previous decision. In practice, whatever the merits of the case, the I.O.C. had capitulated to pressure and Avery Brundage, in his last few days as President, was furious.

The events which shocked the world began on the morning of 5 September, when a squad of eight Arab terrorists representing the Black September movement avoided security guards and entered the building on Connollystrasse (named in honour of Hal and Olga Connolly) which housed the Israeli athletes. They had machine guns and rounded up nine Israeli competitors, whom they held as hostages. Some team members narrowly escaped; two were killed in the initial re-

sistance. The terrorists demanded the release of 200 Palestinian terrorists held in prisons in Israel, and their own safe passage to freedom.

As deadlines were made and extended, and negotiations and offers were rejected by the terrorists, the television crews and pressmen present for the Games relayed the story in detail around the world. At first the Games continued, but later in the day all events were suspended.

Eventually it was agreed that the terrorists and the hostages would be transported by two helicopters to Fuerstenfeldbrueck, a military airfield, and flown out of Germany from there. The plan was that police marksmen would pick off the terrorists between the helicopters and the plane.

The plan misfired, as the terrorists did not show themselves together. Only three were shot immediately, and the remainder fought back, shooting the hostages and eventually destroying a helicopter with a hand grenade. At the end, the nine hostages and a policeman were dead, together with five terrorists. The other three were captured. Despite the presence of the media in force, the first report claimed that the hostages had been saved; the full horrible story followed.

The dual sprint champion, Valeri Borsov of the U.S.S.R. (932), on his way to the 200-metres gold medal. Larry Black of the U.S.A. (973) was second and Pietro Mennea of Italy (528) was third.

Munich

Top: Vincent Matthews and Wayne Collett of the U.S.A. first and second in the 400 metres refuse to stand to attention and face the flag at the medal ceremony.

Above: Soviet Yevgeni Arzhanov stumbles on the line and is just beaten in the 800 metres by Dave Wottle of the U.S.A. Mike Boit of Kenya was third.

There was an immediate call to abandon the Olympics, and Willi Daume, the Chairman of the Organizing Committee, agreed that it would be difficult to continue. But the I.O.C. would not concede victory to terrorism and decreed the Games would be finished, after a memorial ceremony, which was held the following morning.

Unfortunately, the memorial ceremony itself was widely criticized. Willi Daume made the opening speech, and the Israeli team manager, Schmeul Lalkin, thanked the I.O.C. for the mark of respect and the German security forces for their efforts. But

Avery Brundage in his speech talked of the Games having been 'subjected to two savage attacks'. He referred to the stand over the Rhodesian inclusion as naked political blackmail, and his coupling of this controversy with the slaughter of the hostages angered the African countries and seemed totally inappropriate to most of the watching world.

On the track, some new names announced themselves as world stars. For the first time the Soviets had a world-class sprinter, Valeri Borsov, and he very smoothly achieved the sprint double, only the second since Jesse Owens. There was an American mix-up over the 100-metres quarter-final starting times, and two of their runners were eliminated in their absence, which took some of the gloss from Borsov's win, but Borsov won the 200 metres equally impressively. Borsov won a silver medal in the 4 × 100-metres relay, which was won by the American team.

Vince Matthews and Wayne Collett, two black Americans, finished first and second in the 400 metres, and enacted a protest display on the podium, chatting and laughing with their backs to the flag as the anthem was played. As they walked off, one gave a Black Power salute. Both were banned from further competition and sent home. Their actions were less blatant than those of the 1968 protestors, but as they came two days after the Israeli massacre they were badly received by officials and spectators.

Matthews and Collett were due to run in the 4 × 400-metres relay, and the Americans decided against replacing them and scratched. Kenya won the race from Great Britain, and Julius Sang, who, as bronze medal winner, had stood at attention on the podium throughout the antics of Matthews and Collett, won a gold medal.

The 800 metres was a victory for one of the characters of the Games, American Dave Wottle, who ran in a golf cap and always left his sprint finish as late as possible. In the final, he was almost too late, looking well beaten as the Soviet Union's Yevgeni Arzhanov approached the line, but Arzhanov stumbled with exhaustion two metres out and Wottle won by inches. Wottle, who was on his honeymoon, off-handedly remarked that he was just trying to catch up.

Vincent Matthews of the U.S.A. raises his arms as he wins the 400-metres final. Wayne Collett of the U.S.A. is finishing second and Julius Sang of Kenya, third.

Below: Kip Keino of Kenya leads in the 1,500 metres but was beaten into second place by Pekka Vasala (226) of Finland. No. 284 is Great Britain's Brendan Foster.

The 110-metres hurdles was won by Rod Milburn (U.S.A.), who beat Guy Drut of France, and the 400-metres hurdles was a brilliant win by an unknown Ugandan, John Akii-Bua, one of 43 children of a father with eight wives. He was a brilliant all-round athlete who held the African decathlon record. His Olympic hurdles win was in a world record time, the previous record-holder and Olympic champion, David Hemery, finishing third. As Hemery won a silver in the relay, he had a complete set of Olympic medals.

Kenya's Kip Keino attempted to retain his Olympic championship in the 1,500 metres, but after moving from the back to lead with two laps to go, he was passed on the final bend by Pekka Vasala of Finland, who drew away to win, with New Zealand's Rod Dixon winning the bronze. American Jim Ryun was again unlucky, being bumped off his feet in a heat, and not able to get back in contention.

The 10,000 metres was also won by a Finn, Lasse Viren, with an extraordinary performance. There were several more fancied runners, and when Viren fell just before halfway, bringing down Mohamed Gammoudi, he appeared to have lost his chance. However, he fought his way back to the leaders, and began a long run a lap and a half from the finish which brought him home over a second ahead of Emiel Puttemans of Belgium, with Miruts Yifter of Ethiopia

Munich

Right: The unlucky Jim Ryun of the U.S.A. falling in his 1,500-metres heat. Billy Fordjour of Ghana also fell while Vitus Ashaba of Uganda avoided the trip.

Above: The 10,000-metres final. Lasse Viren of Finland, the winner, is leading. The silver medalist, Emiel Puttemans of Belgium, is running fourth; and the bronze medalist, Miruts Yifter of Ethiopia, is second.

Right: The marathon winner, the first for the U.S.A. since 1908, Frank Shorter.

his hand at the steeplechase. Clumsy at the hurdles, he waited at the back for most of the race, and then used his speed at the end to win from fellow-Kenyan Ben Jipcho and Tapio Kantanen of Finland.

A 24-year-old American who had been born in Munich, Frank Shorter, won the marathon; Mamo Wolde, the title-holder, was third. A 22-year-old student, Norbert Sudhaus, tarnished the immediate glory a little by running only the last mile and entering the stadium as the 'winner' just before Shorter.

The two Germanys provided the winners of the walks, East Germany's Peter Frenkel (20 km) and West Germany's Bernd Kannenberg (50 km). Vladimir Golubnichiy of the U.S.S.R. finished second in the 20-km, to add a silver to his two gold and one bronze in the event.

Americans experienced their poorest Games so far as the field events were concerned; Randy Williams was the only American winner. With an injured leg, he went all out in his first long-jump effort, and achieved enough to win. Only once before had an American not won the pole vault – in the 1906 Interim Games – but in Munich the

third. Furthermore, the time was inside Ron Clarke's world record, which had stood for over seven years. Viren later ran in the 5,000 metres and completed a double win (a feat achieved by Kolehmainen, Zatopek and Kuts) when he kicked entering the final straight and won comfortably from Mohamed Gammoudi of Tunisia and Ian Stewart of Great Britain. Gammoudi thus won a gold, two silver and a bronze in distance events in three Olympics.

Because the 1,500- and 5,000-metres finals were scheduled to be run within an hour of each other, Kip Keino, who did not want to come from Nairobi for just one event, tried

champion, Bob Seagren, was pushed into second place by East Germany's Wolfgang Nordwig, who had placed third in 1968. Seagren was not allowed to use his catapult glass-fibre pole, with which he had set the world record.

The high jump went to a Soviet, Yuri Tarmak, who beat Stefan Junge of East Germany and the U.S.A.'s Dwight Stones. Viktor Saneyev of the U.S.S.R., in taking the triple jump, was the only track and field athlete to retain his title.

Wladyslaw Komar of Poland beat American George Woods in the shot, ending a run of six American victories. Ludvik Danek of Czechoslovakia at last won the discus, with his last throw, after finishing second and third to Al Oerter in previous confrontations. American Jay Silvester, again the favourite,

was second. Anatoli Bondarchuk (U.S.S.R.) won the hammer, and a West German, Klaus Wolfermann, beat the holder of the javelin title, Janis Lusis (U.S.S.R.), by just two centimetres. One of the best athletes of the Games was a 24-year-old Soviet citizen, Nikolai Avilov, who broke the world record for the decathlon to win easily.

The women's track and field was dominated by East Germany, whose athletes won six events, while West Germans won four. The powerfully built Renate Stecher of East Germany was the star, winning both the sprints, equalling the world record in the 200

Below top: Kip Keino of Kenya, the 1,500-metres winner in Mexico, flies high over the water jump on the way to a gold medal in the 3,000-metres steeplechase.

Bottom: The West German walker, Bernd Kannenberg, seen here in second place in the 50-km walk. He went on to win the gold medal.

Kip Keino

Kip Keino was not a compiler of a long unbeaten record he ran too often for that – nor a regular world record collector. He ran mainly because he liked it, and on the big occasions he was superb. He was the first of the great African track athletes, and he inspired many others to follow. Kipchoge Keino was born on 17 January 1940 in Kipsano, Kenya, became a policeman, and started running competitively in 1962. At the 1964 Olympics in Tokyo he entered the 1,500 metres and 5,000 metres, finishing fifth in the latter. In 1965 he set his two world records, at 3,000 and 5,000 metres. He won the mile and three miles at the Commonwealth Games of 1966 and in the 1968 Olympics, where he was able to run at an altitude which suited him, he entered three events: the 10,000 metres, from which he dropped out; the 5,000 metres, in which he finished second; and the 1,500 metres, which he won by the largest margin for the event in the Olympics. He contested the 1,500 and 5,000 metres in the Commonwealth Games of 1970, finishing first and third respectively, then went to Munich for his third Olympics. He had lost a little of his powerful finish, and was second to Vasala in the 1,500 metres, but he entered the 3,000-metres steeplechase and won. He went to the United States in 1973 to join a short-lived professional squad.

munich

Right: A spectacular shot of Wolfgang Nordwig of East Germany attempting 5.56 metres in the pole vault. He won the event at 5.50 metres.

Far right: Hildegard Falck of West Germany (159) in the final of the 800 metres, where she took the gold medal.

Above: Yuri Tarmak of the U.S.S.R. clears the bar in the high jump. He went on to win the competition.

Right: A delighted Klaus Wolfermann of West Germany, the winner of the javelin. On the right is silver medalist, Janis Lusis of the U.S.S.R., the defending champion, and on the left, William Schmidt of the U.S.A.

metres. Raelene Boyle of Australia was second in each case, bringing her collection of silver medals to three. The West Germans, however, beat East Germany in the relay, again equalling the world record. In the 200 metres Irena Szewinska of Poland added a bronze medal to her Olympic collection. Monika Zehrt of East Germany won the 400 metres, and ran in the victorious 4 × 400-metres relay team. This was a new Olympic event for women. The 800 metres was won by Hildegard Falck of West Germany.

Another new event for women was the 1,500 metres, and it was won easily by Ludmila Bragina of the Soviet Union in a world record time. There was a change, too, in the hurdles race, which for the first time was run over 100 metres instead of 80 metres. It was won by East Germany's Annelie Ehrhardt, who beat Valeria Bufanu (Rumania) and Karin Balzer (East Germany). Balzer came third in this Olympics after winning the 80-metres hurdles in 1964 and having slumped to fifth in 1968.

Ulrike Meyfarth of West Germany was a popular high-jump winner. A 16-year-old schoolgirl, she improved her best performance by almost 8 cm (3 inches) to clear 1.92 metres (6 feet 3½ inches) – still short, however, of her height: she stood 6 feet 4 inches (1.93 metres). The long jump was won by West Germany's golden girl and world record holder, Heide Rosendahl.

Soviets won the shot and discus. Nadyezhda Chizhova improved on her third in the 1968 shot, and set a new world record, and Faina Melnik, who during her career broke the discus world record 11 times, won with a mere Olympic record. Ruth Fuchs of East Germany won the first of her javelin titles.

The pentathlon was an exciting and memorable dual between the West German idol, Heide Rosendahl, who had already won gold in the long jump and shortly won another in the 4 × 100-metres relay, and Britain's Mary Peters, a 33-year-old track and field veteran who lived in Belfast, Northern Ireland. At the end of the first day Mary Peters, with a record first-day score, led from the world record holder Burglinde Pollak of East Germany, by just 76 points with Heide Rosendahl fifth, but with her best events to come. Rosendahl easily won the long jump, with a leap further than her gold medal effort in the individual event, and won the last event, the 200 metres, where both she and Peters achieved their individual bests. Rosendahl beat Peters by 1.18 seconds, but Peters had won the gold by a mere ten points with Pollak third. Such was Mary Peters' engaging personality that even the disappointed German crowd cheered her win.

The swimming events in 1972 will always be remembered for the performances of Mark Spitz, of whom so much had been expected in 1968. He made good with a vengeance, winning a record seven gold medals at one Games. He took the 100 and 200 metres in both freestyle and butterfly, all in world record times, and won three more gold medals and set three more world records in the relay teams. The star of the women's events was Australia's 15-year-old Shane Gould, who won two gold, a silver and a bronze in the individual freestyle races and a gold in the individual medley – she set world records in all her wins. Other impressive performances came from East Germany's Roland Matthes, who retained his two backstroke titles, and Klaus Dibiasi of Italy, who retained his highboard diving title.

The unluckiest loser in the pool was American Rick Demont, who 'won' the 400-metres freestyle, and then failed the drug test. He had taken a drug containing ephedrine, which was banned. Demont took it for asthma, and had said so on his entry form,

Above left: Ludmila Bragina of the U.S.S.R. wins the first 1,500 metres for women in the Olympic Games.

Above: Renata Stecher of East Germany won both sprints in 1972. In the 200-metres final, Raelene Boyle of Australia is a close second and the defending champion, Irena Szewinska of Poland, third.

Left: The tall 16-year-old West German girl, Ulrike Meyfarth, wins the women's high jump.

Munich

Right: Faina Melnik of the U.S.S.R., the 1972 women's discus champion.

Far right: The first of two javelin wins came in 1972 for Ruth Fuchs of East Germany.

Below: The climax of a brilliant pentathlon. Heide Rosendahl of West Germany wins the 200 metres but is unable to overhaul the points total of Mary Peters of Great Britain (111) who is finishing fourth. Burglinde Pollak of East Germany (143) won the bronze medal.

but nobody had pointed out to him it was banned. Officialdom's mistake cost him his gold medal, and the chance to win another in the victorious relay team.

The best boxer on view was Cuba's heavyweight, Teofilio Stevenson, who destroyed the American favourite Duane Bobick on his way to his first Olympic title.

He refused a lucrative professional career. A beaten semi-finalist was Great Britain's Alan Minter, later world professional middleweight champion, and the light-heavyweight champion, Mate Parlov of Yugoslavia, also became a professional champion. There was one bad decision when American Reggie Jones was adjudged to have lost to a Soviet, which held up the programme for 15 minutes while spectators booed.

The Olympic competitor who made most impact on television viewers around the world was a 17-year-old girl from the Soviet Union, Olga Korbut, who won three gold medals, including a team gold, in gymnastics. A late substitute in the team, she was only seventh in the combined exercises behind Ludmila Tourischeva, also from the U.S.S.R., but her gamin charm (4 feet 11 inches and 88 lb or 1.50 metres and 39.92 kg) captivated all who saw her. Sawao Kato and Akinori Nakayama each took their gold medal tally to six in ensuring Japanese mastery in the men's events.

Great Britain retained the equestrian three-day event team title, and Richard Meade won

Far left: Mark Spitz of the U.S.A. was the outstanding figure of the 1972 Olympics in terms of statistics – he won seven gold medals.

Left: Gunnar Larssen of Sweden won the 400 metres individual medley by two-thousandths of a second: 4 min 31.981 sec to 4 min 31.983 sec.

Below: The leading woman swimmer in 1972 was Shane Gould of Australia.

Bottom: The victorious West German team who won the 4 × 100-metres relay: Annegret Richter, Christine Krause, Heide Rosendahl and Ingrid Mickler.

the individual gold medal, to capture three gold medals in this event. Graziano Mancinelli of Italy won the show jumping from Great Britain's Ann Moore and American Neil Shapiro. Alexandr Medved (U.S.S.R.) won the freestyle super-heavyweight wrestling gold medal – his third gold medal in successive Games, having moved up a weight each Olympiad. Another super-heavyweight who caught the eye was the Soviet weight-lifter, Vassili Alexeyev, who won his first gold medal.

A North Korean, Ho Jun Li, scored 599 points out of 600 in the small-bore rifle, prone, and confided that he had imagined he was shooting his country's enemies, as the Prime Minister had suggested. There was shooting of a more sporting nature from 18-year-old American army private John Williams, who easily won the gold medal for men's archery, an event which was staging a comeback as an Olympic sport after 52 years.

Japan won only the lighter weights in the judo. A Dutchman, Willem Ruska, won the heavyweight and open categories, while Great Britain surprisingly won a silver and two bronze through Dave Starbrook, Brian Jacks and Angelo Parisi. Japan at last won the men's volleyball, but the women again finished second to the Soviets.

The yachting competition was superbly organized, and Rodney Pattison of Great

Munich

Olga Korbut, the Soviet gymnast, captured the imagination of the Munich public and the television audiences round the world.

Ludmila Tourischeva of the U.S.S.R. was the most successful woman gymnast, winning the combined exercises individual medal.

Valeri Borsov

Borsov is the only outstanding sprinter so far to have come from the Soviet Union. He was born on 20 October 1949 near Lvov, and was selected by a group of physiologists as a potential sprinter and trained accordingly. In 1971 he won both the 100 and 200 metres in the European Championships, and did the same in the Munich Olympics a year later. He was unable to race against two of the top American sprinters in the 100 metres because they missed their heats, but the relaxed manner of his running and the ease with which he won suggested he was a worthy champion, and the best white sprinter since Bobby Morrow. He suffered a reaction after his Olympic successes, but retained his European 100-metres title in 1974, and after injury finished third in the 100 metres in the 1976 Olympics, the first male 100-metres winner to win a second medal in the event (not counting Archie Haan in the Interim Games of 1906). He won another bronze in the sprint relay.

Britain retained his Flying Dutchman championship, this time with Chris Davies. East Germans did well in the rowing, although the powerful New Zealand crew which won the eights took most plaudits, when they beat the Americans and Germans, who had enjoyed a string of successes. The Soviets won all but one of the canoeing gold medals.

There were new champions in field hockey; West Germany eliminated Pakistan and India to the minor placings. The Pakistani players were disgusted with the refereeing in their 1–0 defeat by West Germany, demonstrated at the medal ceremony and were suspended from future Olympic competition. Yugoslavia won the first handball

competition (there had been an outdoor handball event in 1936) and the state-sponsored Communist teams dominated the soccer, Poland beating Hungary 2–1 in the final, with such World Cup stars as Deyna and Lubanski in the side.

The basketball final was sensational. The Americans, who had never lost a basketball game in the Olympics, were under attack from the Soviet team who led by eight points with only six minutes left. With three seconds to play, Doug Collins of the U.S.A. was fouled. He converted his shots to give U.S.A. a 50–49 lead, there was a further stoppage with one second to play, and then the Americans began to celebrate their win. But an official decided that there had been three seconds to play, not one, so the clock was reset, and a throw the length of the court found Alexander Belov, who scored the winning points to give the U.S.S.R. victory – 51–50. There was a great deal of dispute relating to the original decision to play three more seconds and the alleged impossibility, given the play, of the score being made in

Left: Akinori Nakayama of Japan won his last gymnastic medals in 1972, bringing his total to six gold, two silver and two bronze. He won the gold medal on the rings in 1972.

Below left: Hans Winkler of West Germany competed in his fifth and last Olympic Games in 1972. His overall medal tally was five gold and a bronze.

Below: Richard Meade of Great Britain in the show-jumping stage of the three-day event, in which he won the individual gold medal and his second team gold medal.

three seconds anyway. The American team refused the silver medals in protest.

In the arena, the Games had been a success for East Germany in particular, whose competitors had won 20 gold medals, compared to the U.S.S.R.'s 50 and the U.S.A.'s 33. The total medals won by East and West Germany together exceeded that of either the U.S.A. or U.S.S.R. For the first time since 1960 the Soviet Union topped the gold medal list.

Avery Brundage retired as President of the I.O.C. after the Games and Lord Killanin,

born in London in 1914 but living in Dublin, took over. In interviews, he deplored the commercialization and nationalism of the Games, and criticized the view that gold medals proved either that the American or Soviet way of life was best. He professed to dislike the flags and the national anthems, and he wanted the Games to be on a smaller scale.

The lavish, mammoth Games of Munich had left their mark, but sadly it was the violence and deaths that will be most remembered.

The Soviet weightlifter, Vassili Alexeyev, won the new super-heavyweight class, a win he was to repeat in 1976.

Far left: Archery was restored to the Olympic Games in 1972 and the men's winner was John Williams of the U.S.A.

Left: The basketball final between the U.S.A. and the U.S.S.R. in the 1972 Olympics ended in bitter controversy when 'extra' time was played allowing the Soviets to win.

Mark Spitz

Mark Spitz was a brilliant if temperamental swimmer whose career included some lows as well as the tremendous high of the 1972 Olympic Games. He was born on 10 February 1950 in Modesto, California, and came to the 1968 Olympics as the new wonder-boy of swimming, expecting to win six gold medals. He won two, in relays, and an individual silver and bronze. He was not only extremely disappointing, he was arrogant and unpopular with most of his colleagues. He was kicked out of the famous Santa Clara Swim Club and had a lot of ground to make up at the 1972 Olympics. He started by winning the 200-metres butterfly in a world record (he had finished last in the 1968 final) and anchored the 400-metres freestyle relay team to another world record. Next day he won the 200-metres freestyle in a world record, beating colleague Steve Genter who had recently undergone surgery for a collapsed lung. Genter badly wanted to beat Spitz. Two days later came two more gold medals and two more world records in the 100-metres butterfly and the 800-metres freestyle relay. A victory in the 100-metres freestyle – again in a world record – gave him his sixth gold medal at one Games, itself a record, and he added a seventh in the 400-metres relay, his final world record. Spitz's last win came just before the seizure of the Israeli hostages, and Spitz, being Jewish, was taken to a Munich hotel for safety and then flown home. Spitz was a handsome 6 feet 3 inches (1.90 metres) and weighed 160 lb (72.56 kg). He was studying dentistry, but gave it up after Munich to make a fortune in endorsements. In his career, beginning in 1967, he set 27 new world records and equalled many others.

Innsbruck

The 1976 winter Games returned to the small Tyrolean city of Innsbruck in Austria, which had staged events so well in 1964, and after the troubles of Sapporo in 1972 the Games were a great relief. Thirty-six countries sent 1,368 competitors, the highest number yet. The existing 1964 facilities were used again, and the opening ceremony was again held in the bowl of the ski jump, where 60,000 watched. Because it was Innsbruck's second Games two Olympic flames were lit.

The U.S.S.R. won the shorter cross-country events, but Ivar Formo of Norway maintained the Scandinavian monopoly in the 50 km, winning in a snow storm, and the Finns won the relay. Karl Schnabl of Austria took the gold in the 90-metres ski jump and a bronze behind Hans-George Aschenbach of East Germany in the 70-metres jump. Another East German, Ulrich Wehling, took his second combined title. Nikolai Kruglov of the U.S.S.R. won the biathlon, and took a second gold in the team relay. The women's cross-country events were shared by Helena Takalo of Finland and Raisa Smetanina of the U.S.S.R., a gold and silver each. Smetanina won a second gold, and Takalo a second silver, in the relay.

Above: Franz Klammer won the downhill skiing gold medal in Innsbruck in 1976 to the delight of the Austrian spectators.

For the first time an Austrian won a ski-jump gold medal in 1976. Karl Schnabl took the 90-metres jump.

Rosi Mittermaier of West Germany nearly became the first woman to make a clean sweep of the Alpine skiing events. She won two and finished second in the other.

The big excitement for the home spectators was the victory of Franz Klammer in the Alpine downhill, where he beat the Swiss veteran and 1972 champion, Bernhard Russi, into second place. Swiss competitors finished first and second in the giant slalom, Heini Hemmi winning from Ernst Good. The great Swedish skier, Ingemar Stenmark, finished third. It was an Italian 1–2 in the slalom, Piero Gros beating the 1972 silver medalist, Gustavo Thoeni.

In the women's Alpine events there was nearly a first 'grand slam'. Rosi Mittermaier of West Germany won the downhill, her first-ever victory in a downhill, and the slalom, where Lise-Marie Morerud, the fancied Swiss skier, fell. But Rosi, who was the star of the Games, just failed to take all three events when Kathie Kreiner of Canada beat her in the giant slalom, winning Canada's first winter gold medal since 1968. Marie-Therese Nadig, the dual winner of 1972, was below her best because of influenza which spread in the village.

There was a new star in the figure skating, where Great Britain's John Curry brought a touch of ballet to the leaps and turns and easily won the gold medal. The women's winner was hardly less impressive. The U.S.A.'s graceful Dorothy Hamill maintained her country's good showing in this event, and Irina Rodnina (and the U.S.S.R.) retained her pairs title, this time with her new partner, Aleksander Zaitsev.

The men's speed skating medals were well shared. Sten Stensen of Norway and Piet Kleine of Holland ably contested the two longer races and won one each, and American Peter Mueller won the new 1,000-metres event. A Soviet and a Norwegian took the other races. Soviet contestants won three of the four women's events; Tatyana Averina won two gold medals and two bronze. The other race was won by American Sheila Young, a former world champion cyclist, who also won a silver and a bronze.

East Germany, West Germany and Switzerland crews filled the first three places in

Innsbruck

both bobsled events; the East Germans, driven by Mainhard Nehmer, won each time. All three luge tobogganing titles went to East Germany.

The ice-hockey title was won for the fourth successive time by the Soviets who, in the deciding match, scored twice in the last five minutes to beat Czechoslovakia 4–3.

Two competitors at the Games, a Soviet skier and a Czech ice-hockey player, failed drug tests, but these were mistakes over a nasal spray and an antibiotic used to combat the 'flu, and there were no unpleasant incidents anywhere. Because of the small budget, the Games was called the 'simple' Games, but it was most successful, and in view of the troubles of the Montreal summer Games which followed, perhaps a pointer to the future.

Above: The pairs figure skating champions performing at Innsbruck, Irina Rodnina and Aleksander Zaitsev of the U.S.S.R.

Right: The elegant winner of the women's figure skating title, Dorothy Hamill of the United States.

Far right: The former world cycling champion, Sheila Young of the U.S.A., won three speed skating gold medals, including the gold in the 500 metres.

John Curry performs his free-style routine in the 1976 Olympics, where he became the first winner from Great Britain of the men's figure skating event.

John Curry

John Curry had a slow rise to the top in figure skating, became a legend in a matter of months and, as is the way with modern skaters, immediately turned professional. He was born on 9 September 1949 in Birmingham, took up skating early, and developed a style which drew heavily from ballet, combining brilliant choreography with the athleticism of the triple jumps and spins. He perhaps suffered as innovator at first, in 1972 finishing fifth in the European championships, ninth in the world championships and eleventh in the Olympics. The following year he went to the United States to train under the Italian coach, Carlo Fossi, and gradually improved his rankings till in 1975 he was second in Europe and third in the world. Then came his complete triumph in 1976, when he took the European, Olympic and world titles. He then gave up amateur skating and formed an ice-ballet company.

Montreal

The events of Munich were in the minds of all during the preparations for the 1976 Olympics, and the Games took place under intense police security. The huge cost of this was only a small part of the tremendous expense of the Games, which was estimated at above $1.5 billion. Much of this expense was born by the local people, whose bill for two weeks of entertainment was likely to take them perhaps 25 years to pay in increased rates and taxes. Part of the reason was that the building of the stadia and other facilities was delayed by industrial action and costs escalated in a desperate attempt to catch up with the schedule. The whole operation was almost out of control, and the experience probably ended the concept of 'ever-more-gigantic'

The finish of the 100 metres in Montreal in 1976. Hasely Crawford of Trinidad just beat Don Quarrie of Jamaica with the champion, Valeri Borsov, third.

Below: The parade of athletes at the opening ceremony in Montreal.

Games, which had taken a big step forward at Munich. Certainly no other city in the world is likely to want to compete with Montreal over the manner of the staging of the 1976 Olympics.

The facilities, when in use, were excellent. Only the Olympic Stadium itself was criticized by some athletes for creating wind pockets – the other venues were magnificent. The main stadium showed instant action replays on a large screen to spectators.

There were the usual last-minute political problems before the Games began. The Canadians recognized mainland Communist China, mainly because they exported millions of bushels of wheat there, and would not invite the 'Republic of China' except under the name of Taiwan. Taiwan did not compete. A late letter signed by 16 African nations demanded the expulsion of New Zealand because of a New Zealand rugby union tour of South Africa. New Zealand was not barred, and 22 nations withdrew. Not all withdrawals were over New Zealand – some African countries just could not afford the trip. There was little sympathy for the African attitude, as it was felt New Zealand was being singled out from many other countries with South African sporting links, but there was much sympathy for the actual African athletes who were forced to return home, particularly for those such as Filbert Bayi, who had a genuine chance of winning a gold medal. Finally, 95 nations were represented, a drop of 27 on 1972, and just over 6,000 athletes competed, a drop of over 1,000.

For the first time since 1928, there was not a single American medalist in the 100 metres. Hasely Crawford, a tall powerful sprinter from Trinidad, won all his heats and stormed home in the final to win his country's first-ever gold medal. He and Don Quarrie of Jamaica, who finished second, had lost their chances through injury in 1972. Valeri Borsov, the champion, finished third. Quarrie won the 200 metres in determined fashion, but this time two Americans did win medals, Millard Hampton and Dwayne Evans finish-

John Walker of New Zealand throws his arms in the air after winning the 1,500 metres in 1976. Following him home are Ivo Van Damme of Belgium (second), Paul-Heinz Wellmann of West Germany (third), Eamonn Coghlan of Ireland (514) (fourth) and Frank Clement of Great Britain (fifth).

Below: Don Quarrie of Jamaica wins the 200-metres final from Millard Hampton of the U.S.A.

ing second and third. Crawford pulled up with a muscle injury, and Borsov did not run owing to a thigh injury. Borsov ran in the 4 × 100-metres relay, however, winning a bronze, and the United States redeemed its reputation by winning the race from East Germany.

A 400-metres specialist, Alberto Juantorena of Cuba, ran first in the 800 metres, in which he had run only three previous races. He was fastest in the heats and semi-finals, and after his customary slow start powered through to win the final from Ivo Van Damme of Belgium, who was killed in a car crash later in the year when only 23 years old. The novice Juantorena had broken the world record. Naturally he was a hot favourite for the 400 metres. He won neither of his heats, but took the semi-final, and after a slow start in the final treated the race as a long sprint and won easily from Fred Newhouse and Herman Frazier of the U.S.A. Juantorena was nick-named 'White Lightning', and he is the only runner to achieve the double of 400 and 800 metres, except for Paul Pilgrim in the 1906 Interim Games. He ran again in the 4 × 400-metres relay, but was left with too much to do in the final, and the race was won by the American squad.

Montreal

Above: For only the third time the 110-metres hurdles was not won by an athlete from the U.S.A. The winner was Guy Drut of France, taking the hurdle just in front.

The 1,500 metres suffered from the absence of the world record-holder Filbert Bayi. After some fast heats, the final itself was slow, with no runner wishing to set the pace. New Zealand's John Walker took the lead at the bell and held off all challenges to win in a slow time, with Ivo Van Damme again second. Walker followed Snell and Lovelock as New Zealand winners of the 1,500 metres.

The 10,000 metres, held early in the Games, was another slow race till halfway, when Portugal's Carlos Lopes took up the challenge. Gradually all the fancied runners dropped back except the champion, Lasse Viren of Finland, who sprinted away just before the bell to win from Lopes, with Great Britain's Brendan Foster and Tony Simmons leading the rest. Viren then attempted to become the first man ever to achieve the 5,000 and 10,000 metres double twice. He qualified for the final by finishing fourth in his heat. In the final Viren led a bunch of five runners at the bell, and his strength from the final bend got him home in front of Dick Quax of New Zealand, who had just recovered from in-

The only track success for the U.S.A. came in the 400-metres hurdles, where Ed Moses was an impressive winner.

The 3,000-metres steeplechase. The leader, Bronislaw Malinowski of Poland, eventually took the silver medal. The winner was Sweden's Anders Garderud (812). Frank Baumgartl of East Germany, half-hidden by Malinowski, finished third after falling at the last hurdle.

Below: Daniel Bautista of Mexico, all in red, winning the 20-km walk to get a first-ever track and field gold medal for Mexico.

fluenza, and West Germany's Klaus-Peter Hildenbrand, who threw himself over the line to snatch the bronze from Rod Dixon of New Zealand. Brendan Foster, who had set a new Olympic record in the heat, could not reproduce the time and finished fifth.

The 110-metres hurdles had been won by black Americans since 1932, but a Frenchman, Guy Drut, was confident he could win, and in the final he led from the second hurdle and just beat Alejandra Casanas of Cuba, to become France's first male track gold medalist since 1920. The veteran 33-year-old Willie Davenport of the U.S.A. finished third in his fourth Olympics – he had won in 1968. The African withdrawal robbed the 400-metres hurdles of the champion and world record holder John Akii-Bua as well as Bill Koskei of Kenya, but the race contained another great champion in 20-year-old Ed Moses of the United States, who beat second man Mike Shine, also from the U.S.A., by just over a second, the biggest winning margin in the event. It was a new world record, the previous two having also come in Olympic finals. Moses' win was the only American track success.

Montreal

Jacek Wszola of Poland wins the high jump in 1976, when he beat the local jumper, Greg Joy.

Below: The decathlon winner in 1976, Bruce Jenner, leading in the 1,500 metres. The silver medalist, Guido Kratschmer of West Germany, is No. 428.

The steeplechase was an exciting race between the world record holder, Anders Garderud of Sweden, the European champion, Bronislaw Malinowski of Poland, and East Germany's Frank Baumgartl. At the final hurdle Baumgartl, challenging Garderud, caught his heel and fell, Malinowski just avoided him, and Garderud was clear to win in a new world record time. Baumgartl got up to take the bronze.

Lasse Viren was a runner in the marathon, attempting a superman task, but was dropped from the leading group after halfway. An impressive East German, Waldemar Cierpinski, finally got away from the 1972 champion, Frank Shorter, to win, running an unnecessary extra lap at the end because there was a 'I' on the lap counter. Shorter and Karel Lismont of Belgium, the first two in 1972, were second and third, and the amazing Lasse Viren was fifth, just over three minutes behind the winner.

Mexico's first Olympic athletics gold medal came in the 20-km walk, Daniel Bautista, a 23-year-old policeman, managing what Jose Pedraza just failed to do before his own people in 1968. The East Germans, Hans Reimann and Peter Frenkel, added a silver and a bronze to their bronze and gold of 1972, and 40-year-old Soviet Vladimir Golubnichiy finished seventh: his positions in five Olympics being first, third, first, second, seventh.

American high-jump world record holder Dwight Stones was booed by the crowd for criticizing the Games organization, and during the competition was warned of a threat against his life. More to the point, his fast run up was handicapped by the pouring rain, which he mopped up between jumps. He could finish only third to a 19-year-old Pole, Jacek Wszola. There was great excitement as the main challenger was a little-known Canadian, Greg Joy, but he had to accept the silver.

The American defeat in the pole vault in 1972 was repeated in 1976, where the leading American, world record holder Dave Roberts, could finish only third behind a Pole and a Finn. Arnie Robinson was an impressive long jump winner for the U.S.A., however, emulating Beamon in Mexico by winning with his first jump in the final, but unlike Beamon he then added two more jumps further than the silver medalist, Randy Williams. Robinson had been third in 1972.

Viktor Saneyev of the U.S.S.R. won the triple jump for the third successive time and then looked to Moscow in 1980 when he hoped to emulate Al Oerter's record of four wins in one event. Amazingly, since 1952, only three triple jump champions had shared the seven gold medals.

There were three new medalists in the shot. Udo Beyer of East Germany beat two Soviets, Evgeniy Mironov (silver) and Aleksandr Baryshnikov, the new world record holder, who was third. Personal rivalry among the U.S.A. discus throwers equalled that between the shot putters of the previous generation, and the world record holder Mac Wilkins, who took the gold medal, did not seem too disappointed when Wolfgang Schmidt of East Germany deprived previous world record holder John Powell of the silver. Yuri Sedykh (U.S.S.R.), coached by the 1972 winner Anatoli Bondarchuk, won the hammer, Bondarchuk finishing third, and the javelin was won by Miklos Nemeth of Hungary with a world record on his first throw. Nemeth was the son of Imre Nemeth, the hammer winner in London in 1948, and this was the first father/son gold

medal double in Olympic track and field.

American Bruce Jenner set a world record in the decathlon to win comfortably from Guido Kratschmer of West Germany and the champion Nikolai Avilov (U.S.S.R.), who made a disastrous beginning with two false starts in the 100 metres. Jenner, a fine all-round sportsman, had been tenth in 1972, and had quit his job to train for 1976.

East Germans dominated the women's track and field, but it was a West German girl, Annegret Richter, who set a new world

Above: Rosemarie Ackermann of East Germany winning the high jump from a strong field.

record in her 100-metres semi-final, and went on to take the gold from the reigning champion, Renate Stecher, with another West German, Inge Helten, third. Raelene Boyle of Australia was fourth. Richter was just beaten in the 200 metres by Barbel Eckert of East Germany, with Stecher third. Boyle was disqualified after two false starts in her semi-final, somewhat controversially for moving her shoulders. The 4 × 100-metres relay was an excellent race, with East Germany just beating West Germany.

The 400 metres was a case of Irena Szewinska first and the rest nowhere. The 30-year-old Polish mother was the world record holder at 200 and 400 metres, and opted for the longer race in the Olympics, leading throughout to win easily in a new world record time. Poland did not enter a team in the 4 × 400-metres relay, and the powerful

Left: Annegret Richter of West Germany, the winner of the 100 metres and runner-up in the 200 metres.

Montreal

Right: Sigrun Siegl of East Germany long jumping in the pentathlon competition in which she took the gold medal.

Far right: The tall American, Jim Montgomery, won three gold medals in 1976 including the 100-metres freestyle in world record time.

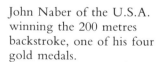

John Naber of the U.S.A. winning the 200 metres backstroke, one of his four gold medals.

East German girls smashed their own world record to win easily from the U.S.A., who were also inside the old record.

The world record took a hammering in the 800-metres final, where four girls finished inside it. Tatyana Kazankina (U.S.S.R.) was the strongest, and sprinted late for a convincing win. She was the world record holder for the 1,500 metres, and duly won in a slow time well outside the Olympic record of Ludmila Bragina (U.S.S.R.), who was fifth.

The champion and world record holder in the 100-metres hurdles, Annelie Ehrhardt, who was injured, was eliminated in the semi-finals, leaving the way clear for a surprise winner, Johanna Schaller of East Germany.

There were bigger surprises in the high jump, where several fancied competitors were eliminated early, including the champion, Ulrike Meyfarth, now 20 years old. Rosemarie Ackermann, the world record holder from East Germany, seventh in 1972, won, and the following year became the first woman to clear two metres. East German successes continued in the long jump, where again many girls were below form. Angela Voigt won, with a little-known American, 18-year-old Kathy McMillan, battling away for silver.

World records were not threatened in the throwing events. Faina Melnik, the discus record holder and defending champion, could finish only fourth, although a throw which put her second was disqualified after the event because she had twice moved out of the circle in preparation. A Polish girl, Danuta Rosani, was disqualified from the final for failing the anabolic steroid test, the first in Olympic history. It all added up to another gold medal for East Germany, won by Evelin Schlaak.

The defending Soviet shot-put champion, Nadyezhda Chizhova, was beaten into second place by Ivanka Khristova, a 34-year-old Bulgarian competing in her fourth Olympics – she had been third in 1972, and had broken the world record earlier in 1976. Ruth Fuchs of East Germany became the first woman to retain a javelin title.

The pentathlon was the most exciting ever, with five points between the first three, all East Germans. Sigrun Siegl beat Christine Laser only because she beat her in three events to two; they had the same points total. Burglinde Pollak was again third, five points behind. Siegl owed her win to a tremendous last race, the 200 metres, where she moved up from seventh place. In fact the first five girls were in reverse order before the final event.

In the swimming pool, only four world records and one Olympic record survived the onslaught of the American men and the East German women. American men won 12 of 13 events, the East German women 11 of 13. And no East German girl had won an Olympic swimming gold before!

While nobody dominated like Spitz in 1972, there were several stars. Among the men, 20-year-old John Naber, a popular psychology student, perhaps did best, winning four gold medals and a silver. In 1974 he had been the first man for seven years to beat Roland Matthes in a backstroke event, and he took Matthes' two backstroke titles at Montreal. In doing so, he reduced the 200-metres backstroke world record to below that of the 200-metres butterfly for the first time, an amazing achievement. Jim Montgomery, a 22-year-old giant of 6 feet 5 inches (1.96 metres) and 187 lb (85 kg), won three gold and a bronze, the first swimmer to beat 50 seconds for the 100-metres freestyle.

Among the women, Kornelia Ender, not quite 18 years old, was the queen. She took up swimming as therapy for a deviated hip bone, and swam in the Munich Olympics when 13, collecting three silver medals, two in relays. In Montreal she won four gold medals and a silver, like Naber, and by the time of her 18th birthday had collected 23 world records. Shirley Babashoff, aged 19, swam in six events, winning a gold medal in a relay and four silver medals.

The only two swimming winners from outside the U.S.A. or East Germany were David Wilkie of Great Britain in the 200-metres breaststroke (he also took the silver in the 100 metres) and Marina Koshevaia of the Soviet Union in the women's 200-metres breaststroke.

A great performer in the highboard diving, Klaus Dibiasi of Italy won his third successive Olympic gold medal, and registered the first Olympic maximum of 10 points for a dive.

David Wilkie of Great Britain became the only male gold medalist in the swimming pool not to come from the United States when he won the 200-metres breaststroke.

Montreal

Above: Leon Spinks of the U.S.A., on the right, winning the light-heavyweight title from Sixto Soria of Cuba. Both Spinks and his brother won gold medals and became professional champions.

'Sugar' Ray Leonard of the U.S.A. (left), who became a great professional champion, winning the light-welterweight final from Andres Aldama of Cuba.

The boxing saw the advance of Teofilio Stevenson of Cuba, who knocked out American John Tate in the first round of the semi-final. Tate later was to hold a version of the world professional title. Stevenson, of course, took the gold. Another future heavyweight champion, Leon Spinks of the United States, won the light-heavyweight gold medal, while his brother, Michael, won the middleweight. The light-welterweight champion was 'Sugar' Ray Leonard, later to be a brilliant world champion.

The performer who became most famous in the Games was a 14-year-old Rumanian gymnast, Nadia Comaneci. Never before at the Olympics had a perfect mark of 10 points been awarded for an exercise: Miss Comaneci recorded six during the week. Television viewers around the world watched in fascination as she balanced and swung her way to three gold medals, a silver and a bronze. She was not without strong competition. The Soviet girls won the team event, helping Nelli Kim, their best performer, to three gold medals and a silver. She, too, recorded two perfect marks of 10. Ludmila Tourischeva finished third in the combined, and won the team gold and two silver, while Olga Korbut managed just one silver with her team gold.

In the men's gymnastics, the Soviets strongly challenged the Japanese. Nikolai Andrianov (U.S.S.R.) won the combined title, with three other gold, two silver and a bronze, but Japan just won the team title. Sawao Kato was still there at 29, finishing second in the combined and also collecting two gold medals. His final career tally was eight gold, three silver and a bronze in three Olympics.

The modern pentathlon was remarkable for the wrong reason. A British competitor, Adrian Parker, was certain he had not been hit when losing in the fencing to Boris Onischenko of the U.S.S.R. His team-mate, Jim Fox, deliberately invited a hit but avoided it. Onischenko's light went on, Fox challenged, and Onischenko's épée was examined and found to be wired illegally. He was disqualified. Fox was shattered and unable to produce his form for a while, but rallied in time for Great Britain to take the team gold medal. Danny Nightingale was the third member. Janusz Pyciak-Peciak of Poland was the individual winner.

Princess Anne represented Great Britain in the equestrian three-day event, but American Ted Coffin won. The U.S.A. also took the team gold. Alwin Schockemoehle of West Germany won the show jumping with a double clear round.

Soviets won five of the nine weightlifting gold medals, the impressive super-heavyweight Vassili Alexeyev being the only lifter to retain his title, but Norair Nurikyan of Bulgaria won his second gold medal by dropping down a weight category. Soviet

Irena Szewinska

Irena Kirszenstein was born on 24 May 1946 in a refugee camp in Leningrad, U.S.S.R. She was to become one of the best sprinters in the world over a period of 16 years, appearing for Poland in no less than five Olympic Games. In 1964 at Tokyo, when only 18, she won silver medals in the 200 metres and long jump, and won a gold medal in the 4 × 100-metres relay. In 1965 she set world records for the 100 metres and 200 metres, and in the 1966 European Championships won gold medals in the 200 metres, long jump and 4 × 100-metres relay, and silver in the 100 metres. In 1968 she married former athlete and news photographer Janusz Szewinska, and ran under her new name in the Mexico Olympics, winning a bronze medal in the 100 metres and a gold in the 200 metres in a new world record time. She surprisingly failed in the long jump, and dropped the baton in the relay. She had a son, Andrei, born in 1970, and in the 1971 European Championships collected only a bronze medal in the 200 metres, a feat she repeated in the 1972 Olympic Games. She was back in business in 1974. She became the first woman to run 400 metres in less than 50 seconds, and she also ran the 200 metres in another world record time, but this was not recognized because of timing problems. In the 1974 European Championships, she decided to run in the 100 metres and 200 metres, and beat the reigning dual Olym-

pic champion, Renate Stecher, in both events. She also took a bronze in the relay. At the 1976 Olympic Games in Montreal, she won the 400 metres in a dazzling world record performance. She then broke the 440 yards world record, and decided to ease off her athletics career to look after her son. She was then 30. Incredibly it was not the end, because she appeared at the 1980 Moscow Olympics, aged 34, and reached the semi-final of the 400 metres, but injury prevented her going further. Her Olympic medal tally is three gold, two silver and two bronze.

Above left: The Great Britain team which won the modern pentathlon. From left: Jim Fox, Adrian Parker and Bob Nightingale.

Above: The fencing match which caused the disqualification of Boris Onischenko of the U.S.S.R., left, with Fox right.

Below: Irena Szewinska winning the 1976 400 metres.

Above: Alwin Schockemoehle of West Germany on Warwick Rex set an Olympic record in the show jumping by winning the gold medal with two clear rounds.

Right: Lasse Viren of Finland retains his 5,000-metres title, winning from Dick Quax of New Zealand. It was Viren's fourth gold medal in 10,000 and 5,000 metres races.

Lasse Viren

Finns dominated distance running in the Olympics between the wars, and before the Second World War had won five of the six 10,000-metres races, and two thirds of all the medals available, as well as over half the medals awarded for the 5,000 metres and steeplechase. After the Second World War, a bronze in the marathon was all that was achieved before 1972. The wispy-bearded Lasse Viren changed all that. Born on 22 July 1949 in Myrskyla, he became a village policeman, took up running and lined up for the 10,000 metres at the Munich Olympics in 1972. He fell soon after halfway, but got up, chased the leaders, and won, surpassing the world record in the process. He then ran in the 5,000 metres and won again, later setting a new world record for this event. His double had been achieved before by Kolehmainen, Zatopek and Kuts. He did little else before the Olympics of 1976, but trained hard to repeat his double, and did so, becoming the first man to win four gold medals in these events, beating the three of Nurmi and Zatopek. He then tried the marathon, finishing a creditable fifth. Such was his supremacy at Olympics that it was suggested he was having special blood transfusions, but his great rival, Brendan Foster, discounted this; he merely trained to reach a peak for the Olympics. Tall and spare, his physique was ideal for distance running. Viren ran in the 10,000 metres in the 1980 Olympics, finishing fifth, and then failed to finish in the marathon. He revived Finnish distance running, and it will take a new Nurmi or Zatopek (or Viren) to challenge his record.

competitors also picked up 12 gold medals in wrestling, three winning their second gold: Levan Tediashvili, Ivan Yarygin and Valeri Rezantsev.

Japanese competitors maintained their edge in judo, and at last had the open champion, Haruki Uemura. They also regained the women's volleyball title, but the Poles won an exciting men's final by outlasting the Soviet team, who had not previously dropped a game.

East Germans dominated the rowing events, winning five of the eight men's events including the eights, where they beat Great Britain and the champions New Zealand, who took the minor medals. There was another silver for Great Britain in the double sculls. Rowing events for women were introduced into the Olympics in 1976, and East Germans won four of the races, including the eights, finishing second to Bulgaria, who also did well, in the other two.

The single sculls winner in 1976, Pertti Karppinen of Finland. Karppinen retained his title in 1980.

In the yachting events, Rodney Pattison of Great Britain, with a third partner, Julian Brooke Houghton, just failed to register a hat-trick of Flying Dutchman successes, finishing second to the West German brothers Jorg and Eckart Diesch. There was a British win, however, in the new Tornado class, for Reg White and John Osborn.

The United States regained its basketball championship, but did not have the chance to avenge its controversial defeat of 1972 by the Soviet Union, who were surprisingly beaten by Yugoslavia in the semi-final. The U.S.A. beat Yugoslavia 95–74 in the final. For the first time there was a women's competition, in which the U.S.S.R. beat the U.S.A. Americans retained both archery titles, Darrell Pace and Luann Ryon taking the gold medals.

There was a major surprise in the field hockey, where Pakistan took the bronze and India finished seventh. The final between New Zealand and Australia was won by New Zealand 1–0. The tournament was played on artificial turf, which might or might not have affected the results.

The largest crowd of the Olympic Games watched the soccer final, despite a persistent downpour. It was again a Communist monopoly, but with a surprising result: East Germany beat Poland 3–1. Both teams were packed with World Cup 'amateurs'.

The Games were a trifle disappointing for the Americans, who, despite their swimming successes, found themselves passed in the medals lists by East Germany as well as the Soviet Union. The American men still led in track and field with six gold medals, but the East Germans led overall in track and field, thanks to the eight gold medals won by their women. There were heartening signs that the medals were being more widely spread.

Despite the romantic intrigue introduced when a 17-year-old Soviet diver disappeared, apparently out of love for an American heiress, causing Soviet officials to threaten to withdraw unless the poor 'abducted' boy was returned, and the light relief of a streaker at the closing ceremony, allegations of corruption in building preparations and the commercialization of everything in sight cast a shadow on the Olympic ideal. There were many former believers who felt that the Games had now outlived the spirit of their conception. The Canadians had every reason to feel disappointed: they did not win a gold medal; the African boycott had marred their Games; and, of course, they still had the enormous bills to pay. On the credit side, there were some great performers: Lasse Viren, Alberto Juantorena, John Naber, Kornelia Ender and Nadia Comaneci will be remembered when the rest has been forgotten.

Alberto Juantorena of Cuba, dubbed White Lightning, won the 800 metres and the 400 metres in Montreal. This race is a 400-metres heat, with C. Joseph of Trinidad and Tobago chasing.

Alberto Juantorena

A few athletes had attempted the 400 metres and 800 metres double in the Olympics before Juantorena. Paul Pilgrim did it in the 'unofficial' Interim Games of 1906, Bevil Rudd was first and third in 1920, Arthur Wint was first and second in 1948, and Mal Whitfield was first and third in the same year. Rudolf Harbig might have done it had there been a 1940 Games, as he held the world record for both distances, but the only man who did achieve it was Alberto Juantorena in 1976. He was born on 3 December 1951 in Orente, Cuba, and was a basketball player, switching to running when 19, and just missing selection for the 1972 Olympics. He won the World Student Games 400 metres in 1973. He was then injured, but at the 1976 Olympics powered round the track in the 800 metres, a relatively new event for him, and set a world record in winning. He made a slow start in the 400-metres final, but when in full stride he was an awesome sight and looked unbeatable as he sped through to win. He stood a muscular 6 feet 2 inches (1.88 metres), weighed 184 lb (83.46 kg), and had a long powerful stride. In the white vest and long white socks of Cuba he was dubbed 'White Lightning'. Suffering from minor injuries, he attempted the 400 metres at the Moscow Olympics in 1980, but finished only fourth.

Klaus Dibiasi

Klaus Dibiasi was born on 6 October 1947 at Solbad Hall in Austria, but his parents were Italian. His father, Carlo, was an Italian diving champion and later national coach. When Klaus was a boy they all went to live in Bolzano in Italy. At the 1964 Olympics as an unknown 17-year-old, he led in the highboard diving with two dives to go, and finished with the silver medal. In winter he had to make a 60-mile round-trip journey in order to train so the people of Bolzano covered their outdoor pool and provided him with training facilities. In 1966 he won the European high diving gold medal, and in the 1968 Olympics won a gold in the high diving and a silver in the springboard. In the European Champion-ships in 1970 he won two silver medals, his highboard defeat being his only one in championships after 1964. He retained his highboard title in the 1972 Olympics and in 1973 won a gold in the highboard and a silver in the springboard in the World Championships. In the European Championships of 1974 he won both gold medals, and then took gold and silver again at the 1975 World Championships. At Montreal in 1976, he was led by the brilliant American, Greg Louganis, after the compulsory figures, but fought back in the freestyle to win his third Olympic high-diving gold medal, a unique feat. He was the world's leading diver for ten years, and in 1976 succeeded his father as Italian coach.

Kornelia Ender

Women swimmers have short competitive lives and Kornelia Ender was at the top for about three years. She was born on 25 October 1958 in Plauen, East Germany, and took up swimming at ten on her doctor's advice as therapy for a deviated hip bone. When not quite 14 she swam in the 1972 Olympic Games and won three silver medals, two in relays. In 1973 she began breaking world records, and took four more gold medals in the 1974 European Championships, and four more plus a silver in the 1975 World Championships. Then came Montreal, and she scored her almost customary four gold medals and a silver. Two events, the 200-metres freestyle and 100-metres butterfly, were held within 25 minutes of each other – she set a world record in one and equalled it in the other. By this time she had set 23 world records, in all strokes except the backstroke. She was powerfully built and was called a swimming machine, but she had plenty of other interests, and retired just after her 18th birthday to continue studying.

Above: Kornelia Ender of East Germany, the leading woman swimmer at Montreal, where she won four gold medals.

Nadia Comaneci

Nadia Comaneci brought perfection to gymnastics in the Montreal Olympics. Never before in Olympic history had a gymnast been given a perfect score of 10, but Comaneci recorded six such scores during the competition. She was born on 12 December 1961 in Gheorghiu-Dej, Rumania, and was 'discovered' as a gymnast at the age of seven, coached expertly, and was Rumanian champion when 12, going on to win four gold medals in the European Championships. Only 14 at the 1976 Olympic Games, she won the asymmetrical bars with a perfect score of 20, won the beam, finished third in the floor exercises and fourth in the vault. She helped Rumania to the silver in the team competition. She was superb in the combined exercises, dropping no more than 0.25 points on any of the four exercises, and winning easily. At the world championships in 1978 she had grown 4 inches (10 cm) and was 20 lb (9 kg) heavier, and won only a gold and a silver, plus a team silver. The results caused her team officials to protest at her markings, but the truth is that nowadays a gymnast's life is short at the top. She competed in the 1980 Olympics, winning two gold and two silver medals, but it is the 'perfect' week at Montreal for which she will be remembered.

Breathless performances at Montreal earned Nadia Comaneci a string of unprecedented maximum scores of 10.

Lake Placid

The colourful opening ceremony at the 1980 Winter Olympics at Lake Placid.

As in 1976, the winter Olympics was held for a second time at a previous venue, Lake Placid having presented the 1932 Games. As in 1976, the decision was a success, both for the Games itself, which proceeded without hitch, and for the American public, who had two great moments in the ice hockey. The Games began on 12 February 1980, and 37 nations participated, which equalled the highest number at Grenoble in 1968.

The Nordic skiing saw the continued progress of the Soviets, who won six events, and the improvement of the East Germans, who won four, leaving just two gold medals for the once unbeatable Scandinavians, one for Sweden and one for Finland, while an Austrian won the last medal. For the first time ever, there was not a single gold medal for a Norwegian.

Nikolai Zimjatov of the U.S.S.R. won the 30-km and 50-km events, and won a third gold medal in the relay, the first cross-country skier to win three gold at one Games. Thomas Wassberg of Sweden won the other race in the closest possible finish, by a hundredth of a second from Juha Mieto of Finland, who also won silver in the 50 km and a bronze in the relay. In the women's races, Raisa Smetanina of the U.S.S.R. won the 5 km having won the 10 km and been second in the 5 km in 1976. Barbara Petzold of East Germany won the 10 km. The runner-up in each case was Finland's Hilkka Riihivouri. Petzold won another gold in the relay in which Galina Kulakova of the U.S.S.R. won

Right: Raisa Smetanina, the Soviet Nordic skier, in the 4 × 5-km relay, where she won a silver medal, having taken gold in the 5-km individual event.

Far right: Frank Ullrich of East Germany won the 10-km biathlon and took the silver medal in the 20-km event.

The Swedish specialist in the slalom, Ingemar Stenmark, won both slalom gold medals in 1980.

Below: Hanni Wenzel of Liechtenstein, like Stenmark, won both slaloms and also took a silver medal in the downhill, equalling Rosi Mittermaier's feat of the previous Games.

a silver medal: in four Games she won four gold, two silver and two bronze medals.

Toni Innauer of Austria won the 70-metres ski jump, after finishing second on the 90-metres jump. The Nordic combined title was won by the champion, Ulrich Wehling, whose third consecutive win in the event is a skiing record.

For the first time there were two biathlon events. The new 10-km event was won by East Germany's Frank Ullrich, who finished second in the 20 km. The 20 km was won by A. Aljabiev (U.S.S.R.), who took a second gold in the relay.

In the Alpine skiing events, the leading Swedish slalom expert, Ingemar Stenmark, who does not compete in downhill events, won both the slalom and giant slalom, having previously won only a bronze in 1976. In both events Stenmark won with his customary devastating second run, having been behind on the first. Phil Mahre of the U.S.A. and Andreas Wenzel of Liechtenstein were the silver medalists. The downhill was a surprise victory for Austria's Leonhard Stock, a late and controversial choice for the Austrian team. Stock has had difficulty winning another race since. Peter Wirnsberger of Austria and Steve Podborski of Canada were second and third.

In the women's events Hanni Wenzel of Liechtenstein, brother of the men's giant slalom silver medalist, won both slaloms and a

Lake Placid

Above: Annemarie Moser-Proell of Austria won the downhill in a great comeback after disappointments in 1972.

Robin Cousins, who kept in Great Britain the men's figure skating title won by John Curry in 1976.

Great Britain had a worthy ice-skating successor to John Curry in Robin Cousins, a 22-year-old from Bristol, who had been 10th in 1976. He just beat Jan Hoffman of East Germany with a brilliant free-skating performance, but Hoffman later turned the tables in the world championships to deprive Cousins of the great treble achieved by Curry. Charles Tickner of the United States was third. There was disappointment for the U.S.A. in the women's events when the 19-year-old world champion, Anett Poetzsch of East Germany, defeated Linda Fratianne who was much fancied. There was further disappointment when the American pair, Randy Gardner and Tai Babilonia, were prevented by injury from contesting the pairs title. It was retained by the Soviet pair, Aleksander Zaitsev and Irina Rodnina, Rodnina's third victory in the event at 30. The ice-dance championship was won by Gennadi Karponosov and Natalia Linichuk of the Soviet Union. Great Britain's young Christopher Dean and Jayne Torvill, later to win the World Championship, were fifth.

The speed-skating performances of Ard Shenk in 1972 were utterly eclipsed by American Eric Heiden in 1980. The standard in all the races was exceptional: the first six men home in each race beat the Olympic record, no fewer than 16 and 17 doing so in the 1,000 and 1,500 metres. Heiden won all five races to become the first competitor to win five gold medals at one winter Olympics. Two Norwegians managed a pair of minor medals. In all his races except one (Stensen having retired) Heiden beat the 1976 champion, two of them, Evgeni Kulikov in the 500 metres and Piet Kleine in the 10,000 metres, finishing second. Like many great speed skaters, Heiden was also a top-class cyclist. The women's races were won by skaters from the Soviet Union, East Germany, Holland and Norway, Norway's only gold medal of the Games.

The bobsleigh races provided two more battles between crews driven by Meinhard Nehmer of East Germany, the dual winner in 1976, and the Swiss veteran Erich Schaerer, second and third in 1976. This time Schaerer won the two-man, partnered again by Josef Benz, and added a silver in the four-man.

silver in the downhill, to equal the performance of Rosi Mittermaier in 1976. The downhill was won by the Austrian veteran, Annemarie Moser, who as Annemarie Proell had been a hot favourite for all events in 1972, but won only two silver medals. Annemarie won five successive World Cups, but retired in 1975, thus missing the 1976 Games, before making a return to the sport.

Nehmer won the four-man and added a bronze in the two-man. East Germans again won the men's luge tobogganing titles, Hans Rinn and Norbert Hahn repeating their two-seater win and Bernhard Glass winning the single-seater, but a Soviet competitor took the women's championship to prevent another East German clean sweep.

The ice hockey provided the great shock of the Games, and a tremendous thrill for the American spectators. By beating Czechoslovakia and earning a draw with Sweden, the U.S.A. qualified for the final pool, but were given no chance against the favourites, the U.S.S.R., the winners of the previous four Olympic tournaments. In a frenetic match with great audience participation, the U.S.A. won 4–3. A further stirring performance to come from behind to beat Finland and another 2–2 draw with Sweden was enough to give the U.S.A. its second ice hockey championship. Part of the excitement may have arisen from the Americans seeing the victory as a satisfying revenge for the controversial basketball defeat of 1972. It concluded another excellent Games; the Winter Olympics, after the disputes of the 1960s and early 1970s, had settled down into a sporting festival.

Above: The United States speed skater, Eric Heiden, won all five events in 1980. Never before had anybody won five gold medals at one Winter Games.

The excitement of the United States ice hockey team at their defeat of the U.S.S.R. and their subsequent winning of the gold medal was shared by the spectators.

Moscow

Politics in one form or another have interfered with the Olympic Games since the beginning, most tragically in 1968 and 1972. The Games of 1976 was boycotted by African nations, but the Olympics of 1980 suffered most from the absence of the largest number of potential medal winners. The problem was the Soviet invasion of Afghanistan just prior to the Games. Many countries tried to organize a Western boycott of the Moscow Games in protest. In the event many nations did not go, the absence of the U.S.A., West Germany and Japan probably making the most difference to the eventual results.

It was an emotional argument between those who thought sport, and a nation's sportsmen, could not ignore atrocities and accept the hospitality of the perpetrators, and those who still held, possibly naively, possibly selfishly, that on no account should politics be allowed to interfere with the Olympics, the Olympic movement supposedly having no national allegiances. Almost certainly Brundage, now dead, and probably Coubertin, would have taken the latter view, as did Killanin.

There was fierce debate in Great Britain, where governments still have difficulty in interfering with the liberties of individuals, and while the government encouraged athletes not to go and authorities made absences from work difficult for public employees, the matter was left to the individual consciences of competitors. Most went, some did not, but the decision was undoubtedly the most democratic one, and while there must be sympathy with the boycott view, the countries who agreed to boycott the Games and forbade their athletes to attend can reflect that a government restriction on the activities of athletes is a weapon that the Soviet Union might be expected to use in similar circumstances. There was a strong feeling among sportsmen and women that while trade and diplomatic relations continued, they should not be chosen as sufferers merely because a boycott was a convenient gesture and would not interfere too much with the business of the day.

In the end, 81 nations were represented at Moscow, a drop of only 14 on 1976 when the Africans did not compete, but a drop of 41 on the highest total, 122 in 1972. Some nations were competing for the first time. The major absentees were the U.S.A., Canada, West Germany, Japan, Kenya, Norway, Israel and Turkey.

The British Olympic Association made its protest over Afghanistan. The general

Below and bottom: Two of the impressive displays mounted by thousands of Soviets at the opening ceremony of the 1980 Olympics in Moscow.

The most anticipated event of the 1980 Games, the 1,500 metres. The winner, Sebastian Coe, leads his great rival Steve Ovett, who finished third, his first defeat in 45 races over 1,500 metres or a mile.

Below: Allan Wells of Great Britain, nearest the camera, just wins the 100 metres from Silvio Leonard of Cuba on the far side.

secretary alone marched in the parade, carrying the Olympic flag, and the Olympic flag and hymn replaced the Union Jack and national anthem at the medal ceremonies. Other countries did the same, and there were ceremonies where three Olympic flags were raised.

The arrangements at Moscow were superb, with only the expected over-enthusiastic security providing problems; most security measures proved intensely irritating but others were so silly as to be amusing. The displays of dancing and gymnastics were breathtaking, and the mosaics formed by the spectators with boards impressive for those who had not seen it before.

The 100 metres was the narrowest of wins for Great Britain's Allan Wells who beat Silvio Leonard of Cuba in the last stride; both were given the same time. Wells was not so lucky in the 200 metres, where Pietro Mennea of Italy came through late to beat him on the dip. The 1976 winner, Don Quarrie of Jamaica, was third.

The 400 metres was won by 23-year-old Viktor Markin of the U.S.S.R. and both the

relays were won by the Soviet teams, where Markin won his second gold medal.

The 800 metres and 1,500 metres were the most eagerly awaited events in the Games, with the showdown between the Britons, Seb Coe and Steve Ovett, the two outstanding runners in the world, who had not met for two years. Coe was favoured to win the 800 metres, but he ran a bad race tactically, leaving his final effort far too late. His great

rival, Ovett, was clear to win the gold medal
and Coe had to settle for the silver. This made
Ovett, unbeaten in 45 races over a mile and
1,500 metres, a firm favourite for the 1,500.
The East German, Jurgen Straub, set the pace,
but this time Coe was the more aware, getting
first run and streaking away up the straight.
Ovett gave up the chase, and even allowed
Straub the silver. So the honours finished
even in the clash of the giants, Coe, perhaps,
feeling more satisfied because of his comeback
and of his having won the 'Blue Riband' of
the Games.

The 5,000 and 10,000 metres was a brilliant
double by Miruts Yifter of Ethiopia, the sixth
such double of the Olympics. The previous
double champion, Lasse Viren, finished fifth
in the longer race. It would have been a great
race between the two had Yifter been at

Montreal. He had won a bronze at Munich in
1972, and though his age was between 33 and
40 and he had eight children, his
repsonsiblities had not affected his carefree
attitude to running or his ability to sprint
whenever he felt like it.

The two hurdles winners, Thomas
Munkelt and Volker Beck of East Germany,
would have been unlikely to beat Renaldo
Nehemiah and Ed Moses of the U.S.A. had
they been present, but Bronislaw Malinowski
of Poland, who sadly was to lose his life later
in an accident, was a worthy steeplechase
winner. Filbert Bayi of Tanzania, one-time
world record holder for 1,500 metres,
finished second. His best chance of gold
would have been in 1976, when he was called
home.

The marathon provided a second gold
medal for the East German, Waldemar
Cierpinski, who threatened to out-do the
great Bikila by winning a third at Los Angeles
in 1984.

The field events were dominated by the
Soviets and the East Germans. One of the best
performances came from Gerd Wessig of East
Germany in the high jump, where he set a
new world record to beat the 1972 champion,
Jacek Wszola of Poland. Another East
German, Lutz Dombrowski, jumped 8.54
metres (28 feet), still a long way behind

Far left: The marathon was won for the second time by East Germany's Waldemar Cierpinski, who equalled Abebe Bikila's double.

Left: Gerd Wessig of East Germany celebrates a gold medal and a world record in the high jump.

Viktor Saneyev of the U.S.S.R. attempts a fourth win in the triple jump in Moscow. He was beaten into second place by a fellow-Soviet, Jaak Uudmae.

Viktor Saneyev

Viktor Saneyev could not quite match Al Oerter's record by winning his event at four separate Olympics. Saneyev was a triple jump specialist, whose ankles, it was said, must have been like iron to withstand the strain he put on them over a long career. He was born on 10 March 1945 in Soukhoumi, U.S.S.R., and developed into a muscular 6 foot 2 inch (1.88 metres), 182 lb (82.55 kg) athlete. He had his first international win in the triple jump in 1967, and was only beaten once in his prime, by Joerg Drehmel of East Germany in 1971. In 1968 he broke the world record in taking his first Olympic title. He won the European Championship in 1969 and then retained his Olympic title in 1972, shortly afterwards regaining the world record he had lost to Pedro Perez. He was European champion in 1974, but lost his world record in 1975 to João de Oliveira, who raised it by over a foot in the high altitude of Mexico City. Saneyev defeated de Oliveira, however, in the 1976 Olympic Games, winning his third gold medal. In Moscow in 1980, aged 35, Saneyev tried to equal the record of four Olympic wins, but while he again beat de Oliveira, who won the bronze medal, Saneyev had to make do with silver, his last jump not reaching that of his countryman, Jaak Uudmae.

Moscow

Right: The long jump was won by 21-year-old Lutz Dombrowski of East Germany, who set a 'sea level' record, but was still a long way behind Beamon.

Far right: The Olympic flame and a world record pole vault. Wladyslaw Kozakiewicz of Poland wins the gold medal.

Marita Koch of East Germany, who won the gold medal in the 400 metres, running in the 4 × 400 metres relay, in which she had to be content with a silver.

Beamon, but the second best ever in the long jump. Wladyslaw Kozakiewicz of Poland set a world record in the pole vault, and Yuri Sedykh of the U.S.S.R. retained his hammer title with a new world record. Viktor Saneyev of the U.S.S.R. just failed in his attempt to equal Al Oerter's record of four gold medals in one event when he was beaten in the triple jump by his countryman Jaak Uudmae. The decathlon was won by Britain's Daley Thompson, who led throughout.

The women's track events were notable for wins by Marita Koch of East Germany who won the 400 metres, Nadyezhda Olizarenko of the Soviet Union who set a world record in winning the 800 metres, and Tatyana Kazankina of the U.S.S.R. who retained her 1,500 metres title and won her third Olympic gold medal. In the field events, Sara Simeoni of Italy won the high jump (the holder, Rosemarie Ackermann, finished only fourth), and Ilona Slupianek of East Germany set a world record in winning the shot. There was also a world record in the pentathlon, won by Nadyezhda Tkachenko of the Soviet Union. Ironically both Slupianek and Tkachenko had been suspended for using anabolic steroids two years earlier.

Events in the swimming pool were most affected by the absence of the American men, but there were excellent performances. In the men's swimming and diving, Soviet competitors won eight events, Sweden two, East Germany two and Great Britain, Hungary and Australia one each. The best performance was by Soviet Vladimir Salnikov, who beat the world record in the 1,500-metres freestyle and won two more gold medals in the 400-metres freestyle and the freestyle relay. Great Britain's gold medal came in the 100-metres breaststroke for the shaven-headed Duncan Goodhew, who also won bronze in the 4 × 100-metres medley relay, won by Australia.

The division of the women's gold medals was 12 to East Germany, two to the Soviet Union and one to Australia. The best performers were: Barbara Krause, who set a world record in a heat of the 100-metres freestyle and won three gold medals; Petra Schneider, who set a world record in the 400-

Ilona Slupianek of East Germany wins the shot in a world record. She had once been suspended for using anabolic steroids, but was reinstated by the I.A.A.F.

Daley Thompson

The best all-round athlete in the world was the claim made for Daley Thompson in 1982. Born on 30 July 1958 in London, of a Nigerian father and Scottish mother, his all-round ability was apparent when he was only 16, when he scored remarkably well in his first-ever decathlon in the Welsh Open. At 18 he took part in the Montreal Olympics, finishing 18th and impressing Bruce Jenner, the winner. In 1978 he won the Commonwealth Games gold medal and the European championships silver. In 1980 he beat Guido Kratschmer of West Germany, the silver medalist in the 1976 Olympics, and who would have been his chief rival in the Olympics had West Germany participated. In doing so, he set his first world record. He duly won the decathlon gold medal at the Olympics in 1980, and later regained the world record which Kratschmer had won back. Thompson lost his world record to West German Jurgen Hingsen, who was not at Moscow, but Thompson beat him in the European championships of 1982 and established himself as the world's No. 1 all-round athlete.

Daley Thompson of Great Britain putting the shot in the decathlon, in which he won the gold medal.

Moscow

Top: The most impressive male swimmer in this Olympics was Vladimir Salnikov of the U.S.S.R.

Above: Great Britain's swimming gold medalist in 1980, Duncan Goodhew (bareheaded), in the 100-metres breaststroke.

Alexandr Dityatin of the U.S.S.R. won eight medals at the 1980 Olympics including the gold medal in the combined exercises.

Both team titles in the gymnastics were won by the Soviet Union. Nikolai Andrianov was deprived of the men's combined gold medal by a brilliant Alexandr Dityatin, who won a record eight medals at one Games, three gold, four silver and a bronze. Nadia Comaneci and Nelli Kim were joint first in the women's floor exercise, and each won a second gold, Comaneci in the beam and Kim in the team event. The combined winner, however, was Ylena Davydova of the Soviet Union, with Comaneci sharing the silver with Maxi Gnauck of East Germany. Many of Comaneci's marks were questioned, a common occurrence since Montreal.

France regained the position of 'leading nation' in fencing, but the Soviets took a share of medals, as they did in cycling. An 18-year-old Finnish man, Toni Poikolainen, and a Soviet woman took the archery gold medals, previously held by the Americans. Communist countries won the weightlifting titles, with the Soviet Union taking half, although Vassili Alexeyev, after injury, was

metres individual medley, where she beat Great Britain's Sharron Davies into second place; and Rica Reinisch, who broke the world record in the 200-metres backstroke, and won three golds. Australian Michelle Ford won the 800-metres freestyle.

The American championships, held just after the Olympics, suggested Americans could have taken a share of the gold medals.

Cubans won six of the boxing titles, no other country getting even two, and Teofilio Stevenson won his third heavyweight title and became the newest challenger to Al Oerter's four-timer.

eliminated in his event. The Soviets took more than half the gold medals in the wrestling. The judo medals, in the absence of the Japanese, were well spread, with two winners from France and the U.S.S.R. and one each from Italy, Switzerland, Belgium and East Germany. A French winner was Angelo Parisi, a bronze medalist for Great Britain in 1972. Great Britain's Nick Adams won a silver and Arthur Mapp a bronze in the Open category.

In the equestrian events, Soviet challengers took all the team gold medals, but the individual events went to Italy, Poland and Austria. The Soviets also took three of the seven shooting gold medals, and the team and individual events in the modern pentathlon.

On the water, the Soviets were expected to win most of the canoeing medals, considering their successes at Montreal and Munich, and

their tally of only four gold and three minor medals was disappointing for them, especially as one man, Vladimir Parfenovich, had a hand in three of the gold medals. East Germany took three gold medals, including the women's events. In the rowing, the East Germans were supreme, winning seven of eight men's events and four of six women's. There were several gold medals for the champions of Montreal, principally for Pertti Karppinen of Finland in the single sculls, for East Germany's Jorg and Bernd Landvoigt in the coxless pairs and Harald Jahrling and Friedrich Ulrich with cox Georg Spohr in the coxed pairs. The East Germans retained their eights title, but a Great Britain eight pushed them close. Brazilians won gold medals in the Tornado and 470 classes in the yachting. No other nation won two yachting events, and Denmark's Paul Jensen, Vald Bandolowski,

The Cuban heavyweight boxer, Teofilio Stevenson, won his third gold medal in 1980, beating Zaev of the U.S.S.R. in the final.

Teofilio Stevenson

A powerful right hand helped Teofilio Stevenson to over 100 victories by a knock-out in a long amateur career which saw him win three Olympic gold medals. He was born on 29 March 1952 in Oriente, Cuba, and grew into a huge, muscled heavyweight, who at his peak stood 6 feet 6 inches (1.98 metres) and weighed 204 lb (92.53 kg). He fought in the Olympics at Munich when 20, and destroyed the U.S.A.'s 'white hope' Duane Bobick, on the way to an impressive gold medal, for which he fought only 7½ minutes. None of his opponents lasted the distance, and one declined to fight in the final through injury. He had many offers to turn professional, but fought again in the 1976 Olympics, where he beat John Tate of the U.S.A., who later temporarily held a version of the world professional title. Stevenson knocked him out in one round, and retained the gold without effort. He might have become world champion had he wished to leave Cuba, but he preferred to be a hero in his own country. He won his third Olympic gold in Moscow in 1980, but was forced to travel the distance in two fights. He thus equalled Laszlo Papp's record of three boxing gold medals and, as he will be only 32 in 1984, he might yet achieve another gold.

Moscow

Angelo Parisi winning a
gold medal in the
heavyweight category in
judo. He represented France,
after having won a bronze
medal for Great Britain in
1972.

and Erik Hansen were the only yachtsmen to
retain a championship by winning the Soling
class.

In the absence of the Japanese, the Soviets
won both volleyball titles, but failed to take
advantage of the Americans' absence in the
basketball, finishing only third as Yugoslavia
defeated Italy 86–77 for the gold medals. East
Germany beat the Soviet Union 23–22 in the
handball final to take their first medals of any
sort in the men's event, but the Soviets kept
the women's title. India won the hockey for
the first time in four Olympics. Spain was
beaten 4–3 in the final, but added a silver
medal to the bronze won in 1960. Zimbabwe
won the first women's hockey tournament.
Czechoslovakia beat holders East Germany
1–0 in the soccer final.

The Games was the least interesting for
many years for most of the spectators
watching on television around the world,
although the Soviet crowds at the events
themselves were enthusiastic enough. For
non-partisans it was a glum exercise watching
the efficiency of the super-drilled sportsmen
and women of the U.S.S.R. and East
Germany defeat the rest, particularly in the
technical and team sports. At least Wells,
Mennea, Coe, Ovett and Yifter could keep
them at bay on the track. The Soviets won 80
gold medals, a record for one country in any
one Games, and the East Germans were well
in front of the rest with 47.

No Games, of course, could be
representative of world sport without the
Americans. The 1980 Olympics were always
going to be a makeshift affair from the time
the American government decided on a
boycott. To the Olympic medal winners,
though, a medal is a medal, whoever
happened to be or not to be competing. The
Games is already history, and the boycott will
be a progressively smaller detail of that
history as time passes.

People in the West will never agree on
whether the Games should have been
boycotted or not. Sport is in the political
arena, as everything in life is. Coubertin
himself acknowledged that sport could be
used to consolidate peace or prepare for war.
Long before the first modern Olympics he
said 'The rebirth of sport will perhaps assure it
of an international role which no one can yet
fully envisage'. The time for the test might be
near. Let us hope the athletes of the world
meet in Los Angeles in 1984 in an Olympic
spirit of friendship for all.

The final of the Olympic
soccer tournament between
East Germany and
Czechoslovakia, who won
1–0. The state teams of
Eastern Europe, whose
players are, in effect,
professionals, have
dominated Olympic soccer
since 1952.

Sebastian Coe

Seb Coe was born on 29 September 1956 in London, but his family went to live in Yorkshire, where he won schools and youth championships in 1972 and 1973 before receiving a stress fracture in 1974. He came back and just missed selection for the 1976 Olympic Games. An achilles tendon injury further hampered his progress, and he took only a bronze medal in the European championships 800 metres in 1978. In 1979 he had a brilliant spell, in six weeks breaking the world records for 800 metres, 1,500 metres and the mile, to become the first athlete to hold these three records simultaneously. In 1980 he broke the 1,000-metres world record to hold four, then reduced his 800-metres time. He won the 1,500 metres in the 1980 Olympics, and took a silver in the 800 metres behind Ovett. After injury, there was another brilliant spell in 1981, in which he swopped world records with Steve Ovett. He again reduced his 800-metres time on 10 June and his 1,000-metres time on 11 July; he regained his lost mile record from Ovett on 19 August, lost it again on 26 August and finally took it back from Ovett on 28 August. A proposed series of 'super-matches' between Coe and Ovett in 1982 did not materialize as both were injured. Coe stands 5 feet 9¼ inches (1.76 metres) and weighs only 128 lb (58 kg). It is the high power-weight ratio and his elegant style and acceleration which make him one of the most exciting of all runners.

Steve Ovett

The rivalry of the British middle-distance runners Seb Coe and Steve Ovett was one of the highlights of athletics in the late 1970s and early 1980s. Steve Ovett was born on 9 October 1955 in Brighton, and is thus nearly a year older than Coe. He began by winning the English Schools under-15 400-metres title in 1970, and throughout the 1970s contested and won races up to distances of a half-marathon. Having won the European Cup 800 metres in 1975, he ran in the 800 metres and 1,500 metres in the 1976 Olympics, finishing fifth in the shorter race and being eliminated in the semi-final of the longer. In 1977 he lost

The 800-metres medal ceremony. Steve Ovett of Great Britain (centre) was the winner; Sebastian Coe of Great Britain (left) the 1,500-metres champion, finished second; and Nikolai Kirov of the U.S.S.R. was third.

his first important race over 1,500 metres to Steve Scott of the U.S.A., but was subsequently unbeaten over 1,500 metres or a mile until the Olympic final of 1980. In 1977 he won the European Cup and World Cup 1,500 metres. He was surprisingly beaten by Olaf Beyer in the European Championships 800 metres in 1978 but won the 1,500 metres, and then broke the world two-miles best time. His best times were just behind Coe's in 1979, but in 1980 he broke the world mile record and equalled Coe's world 1,500-metres record, although slower on the hundredths of seconds. He won the Olympic 800 metres in 1980, but, possibly suffering reaction, was beaten by Coe in the 1,500 metres where he took the bronze medal. He then set a new world record in the 1,500 metres. In 1981 he lost his world mile record to Coe, regained it and lost it again, all in nine days. A bad leg injury in 1982, caused when he ran into a railing, curtailed his activities and prevented further competition with Coe that year.

Los Angeles

The Summer Games of the twenty-third Olympiad will be held at Los Angeles from 28 July to 12 August 1984. Los Angeles was the host to the Olympic Games of 1932, and thus becomes the third city in which the Games has been held twice, not counting Athens, which held an Interim Games in 1906. Paris, in 1900 and 1924, and London in 1908 and 1948, were the previous cities to host the Olympics twice.

The Games of 1932 was the best organized to that time and the meticulous arrangements set standards which have been followed by subsequent Games. The biggest innovation was the Olympic village in the Los Angeles hills which provided living accommodation for the athletes and every facility to be found in a 'normal' village. The Olympic village has been a feature of succeeding Games, helping to foster the spirit of friendship which has become part of the Olympic ideal.

Because of travelling expenses, the number of athletes at the Games of 1932 was the smallest since 1904, but the stature of the Olympics is such now that only a political upheaval (perhaps not be discounted in Orwell's 1984?) is likely to affect the numbers this time. What can be relied upon with confidence is the weather, which in 1932 helped athletes to break several records.

Another auspicious pointer to the Games of 1984 is the fact that the 1932 Games was so organized as to finish showing a profit. The enormous costs of the Munich Olympics in 1972 and those of Montreal in 1976, the last two Games to he held in the West, caused misgivings among supporters of the Olympic movement. At the time of the Montreal Games, sports officials and administrators at Munich, where the Games were the most expensive till then, drew up a balance sheet to show that the burden of costs had been worthwhile. It was based on the fact that the sports and recreation centres were being put to good use and that the improved roads and other communications were drawing visitors to sports and many cultural and commercial events. However, many apartments in the Olympic village remained empty and some of the stadia remained almost unused.

The Los Angeles Olympic Organizing Committee is tackling the arrangements for the 1984 Games so that there will be a surplus of revenue over expenditure. If they are successful, they will once again set a new standard which will become the norm for following Games. Funds will come from three major sources: the sale of sponsorships, television rights and tickets. Lotteries, used to raise funds for some previous Olympics, are illegal in California.

A great advantage which Los Angeles enjoys is the existence of stadia and facilities. New building is being kept to a minimum.

There will be no costs borne by the city of Los Angeles itself, and indeed taxpayers will benefit by the provision of new facilities. These include archery ranges, new synthetic tracks, the improvement of existing amenities, a new Velodrome and swimming pool, a new dining hall at the University of Southern California and a new administration building and sports medicine laboratory at the University of California, Los Angeles. The creation of new jobs and the involvement of youth are other benefits which the city will enjoy.

Sponsorship agreements, by which major corporations support the Games with money and materials for the right to use the Games in marketing their products, form a major part of the plans to raise funds. There are also licensing agreements and official suppliers. The Organizing Committee is carefully keeping the number of sponsors down to less than 50, and many agreements have already been signed. Despite these sponsorships, the Committee intends the Games to be less commercial than their predecessors.

The financial concept of the Games might become its most important aspect if the Games can be shown to be profitable, or at worst not prohibitively expensive, and of real value to the local people. The organization of future Games would be brought within the scope of many more cities of the world, and the movement started by Coubertin could advance more satisfactorily.

Los Angeles was awarded the Games on 20

October 1978, when the contract between the city and the I.O.C. was signed in the White House. The United States Olympic Committee had approved the Los Angeles candidature on 25 September 1977, and when applications closed on 31 October 1977, Los Angeles was the sole bidder. Soon after the signing of the contract, the city passed an amendment which prohibited any capital expenditure by the city that would not be paid back. Early in 1979 the Board of Directors of the Los Angeles Olympic Organizing Committee was named, and work began on planning the arrangements and negotiating all the necessary agreements with the television companies, the sponsors and the various venue proprietors. Finalizing all the arrangements would occupy the Committee for a large part of the six years remaining before the opening by President Reagan on 28 July 1984.

Among the facilities to be provided is the Olympic village. In 1984 athletes will be housed at two main sites: the student residences at the University of California, Los Angeles, and the University of Southern California. There will also be satellite housing for the rowers and canoeists who will compete at Lake Casitas. Housing problems do not end there, for accommodation is also needed for the 'Olympic Family', consisting of officials, committees, federations and representatives of the media and sponsors. It is estimated that this will amount to about 20,000 hotel rooms, and by October 1982 about 19,000 of these had already been booked in 72 'accredited official hotels' in Southern California.

There is a programme of commemorative coins planned for the Games, consisting of three coins: two silver dollars and a gold $10 piece, which will be the first gold coinage struck in the United States since 1933. This continues a tradition of Olympic commemorative coins, which were first struck by Finland for the 1952 Games, and which each host nation has followed since 1964. There will also be issues of Olympic Games stamps, and there will be an exposition of previous Olympic stamps at the Games.

Although medals for cultural events have not been awarded since the London Olympics of 1948, Los Angeles plans a three-day multi-arts festival and there will also be programmes of music, dance, visual arts, theatre and film, including a retrospective of official Olympic films and a 50-hour marathon of films which have used sports as a theme.

Major departures from recent Games are the expected return to competition of the Chinese, the I.O.C. ruling in 1981 that both Taiwan and the People's Republic might take part, and an expansion of events for women. There will be 75 women's events at the 1984 Games, 13 of them added since 1980.

The most popular is likely to be the marathon. Events like the New York and London marathons in recent years have proved that women are well able to excel in the race. It is appropriate that Los Angeles is to hold a marathon, because in the 1932 Games held there, 800 metres was considered too far for women to race, as so many runners had been distressed at the distance in 1928. There will also be a 400-metres hurdles and a 3,000 metres on the track, and the pentathlon will become a more testing heptathlon.

Two new Olympic events for women only will be synchronized swimming and rhythmic gymnastics. Two other sports in which there will be women-only events for the first time in the Olympics are cycling and shooting, and there will be additions in swimming and canoeing.

Twenty-one sports will be represented at the Games: archery at the El Dorado Park; athletics at the Los Angeles Memorial Coliseum; basketball at the Forum; boxing at the Los Angeles Memorial Sports Arena; canoeing at Lake Casitas; cycling at a new Velodrome at California State, Dominguez Hills; equestrian events at Santa Anita Park; fencing at Long Beach Convention Center Exhibition Hall; association football at the Rose Bowl, Pasadena; gymnastics at Pauley Pavilion, University of California, Los Angeles; handball at California Polytechnic, Pomona, and California State, Fullerton;

hockey at East Los Angles College; judo at California State University, Los Angeles; the modern pentathlon at Coto de Caza; rowing at Lake Casitas; shooting at a venue to be decided; swimming at the University of Southern California; volleyball at Long Beach Arena; water polo at Pepperdine University; weightlifting at Loyola Marymount University; wrestling at the Anaheim Convention Center; and yachting at Long Beach Marina and Harbor. There will also be two demonstration sports: baseball at the Dodger Stadium and tennis. Tennis was an Olympic sport until 1924.

The names of some of the venues illustrate the attraction of Los Angeles as a host city. The Rose Bowl is the famous home of the most important New Year's Day inter-collegiate American football game. Long Beach has been made famous by numerous feature films, and Hollywood itself is in the hills to the northwest of the city. Disneyland is within reach, and Walt Disney Productions are planning the opening and closing ceremonies, as they did for the Winter Games at Squaw Valley in 1960.

The ultimate responsibility for the Olympic Games is held by the International Olympic Committee, who pass on the task of organizing each Games to either the appropriate National Olympic Committee or a committee formed specially for the purpose, which is the case with Los Angeles.

Candidates for organizing the Games can only be cities, a decision of Coubertin's to prevent the possibility of government interference. Thus each Games is awarded to a city, not a country. Should more than one city from one country wish to apply for the Games, that country's National Olympic Committee must choose between them. Governments are involved, because the government of the candidate city must guarantee in writing its agreement with the I.O.C.'s rules, which is how the I.O.C. ensures there will be no discrimination against competitors, officials or journalists, and that none will be refused admittance.

The I.O.C. must also approve the organizing committee, and insists that the I.O.C. member of the country concerned and a majority of N.O.C. members have voting powers. The candidate city must also satisfy the I.O.C. regarding the programme and the facilities.

The planning of the Games thus starts with the I.O.C., who selects from the candidates for the Games the city to hold it, usually about six years in advance. It is then the task of the organizing committee to make all the necessary arrangements, which, as outlined above, can be considerable: extensive building for the various stadia and training facilities; arrangements for worldwide media coverage; the accommodation of the athletes, officials and press; proper medical facilities; and, sadly very necessary these days, the co-operation of the military and police authorities for an efficient security system.

The status, objects and powers of the I.O.C. are set out in the necessarily long Olympic Rules and Regulations. Basically, the I.O.C. is responsible for the control and development of the Games, and profit is not one of its objects. The four main aims are: (i) the regular celebration of the Games; (ii) making the Games ever more worthy of their history and ideals; (iii) encouraging the development of amateur sport; and (iv) inspiring and leading sport within the Olympic ideal, thereby promoting and strengthening friendship between the sportsmen of all countries.

It was stated above that the Los Angeles Games of 1984 is expected to show a profit. The L.A.O.O.C. has decided that this profit will be distributed in the following way: 40 per cent to the U.S. Olympic Committee, 40 per cent for amateur sports in the Southern California area and 20 per cent to the U.S.O.C. for distribution to the national governing bodies for sports in the Pan-American and Olympic Games. This satisfies the I.O.C. rule which states that a surplus from the Games must be applied to the Olympic movement or to the development of amateur sport. The I.O.C. gets its own resources from subscriptions by members, gifts and funds from approved sources, and a sum from cities entrusted with the Games.

Presidents of the I.O.C. are elected by secret ballot of the members, and a President is elected for an eight-year term, with the possibility of re-election each four years thereafter. Only eight men have served as President: Demetrius Vikelas (Greece) 1894–1896; Baron Pierre de Coubertin (France) 1896–1916; Baron Godefroy de Blonay (Switzerland) 1916–1919; Baron Pierre de Coubertin, for a second term, 1919–1925; Henri de Baillet-Latour (Belgium) 1925–1942; J. Sigfrid Edstrom (Sweden) 1946–1952; Avery Brundage (U.S.A.) 1952–1972; Lord Killanin (Ireland) 1972–1980; and Juan Antonio Samaranch (Spain) from 1980.

It is laid down in the rules of the I.O.C. that the mayor of the city holding the Games must keep the official flag of the I.O.C. in the principal municipal building until it is handed over to the mayor of the next Olympic city at the official opening ceremony.

The continuity of the Games has always been regarded as important, and the handing over of the flag is one convention designed to promote this continuity. The flag itself is one of many Olympic symbols. It has a plain white background without border in which are the five interlocking rings, the best-known Olympic device. The rings are coloured – from the left, blue, yellow, black, green and red – and symbolize the union of the five continents and the meeting of athletes in friendship and fair competition. At least one of the six colours in the flag is found in the flag of each nation of the world. The flag was presented to the I.O.C. Congress by Coubertin himself in 1914, a year after he found the emblem at Delphi.

There is also an Olympic motto, '*Citius, altius, fortius*' (faster, higher, stronger), which was invented by a Dominican monk, Father Henri Didon, and first used at the Paris Games of 1924. A secondary, better-known 'motto', has the words: 'The most important thing in the Olympic Games is not to win but to take part'. These (or similar) words were used by the Bishop of Pennsylvania at a service in St. Paul's Cathedral for the fourth Olympic Games in London in 1908, and impressed Coubertin, who adopted them. They have often been used in wider contexts than the Olympics and have become part of the concept of sportsmanship itself.

A special hymn was composed by the Greek musician, Spyros Samaras, with words by the national poet, Costis Palamas, for the opening ceremony of the first modern Olympics in Athens in 1896. Although a new hymn was composed by a Pole, Michel Spisak, in 1950, the old hymn was officially adopted as the Olympic hymn in 1957, and used at each celebration since.

The Olympic flame first burned at the Games of 1928. The idea of the torch relay was proposed by German I.O.C. member, Theodor Lewald, and introduced into Olympic protocol in 1934. It was agreed that a torch should be brought by a relay of runners from Olympia, and that the last runner was to circle the track and light the Olympic flame which should not be extinguished until the close of the Games. The first relay brought the torch to the Berlin Olympics of 1936, when 3,000 runners carried it from Olympia. The torch acknowledges the ancient origins of the Games and symbolizes the continuing burning of the ancient Olympic spirit.

The most prized possession of thousands of sportsmen and women the world over is an Olympic medal, of comparatively small commercial value but a symbol of ultimate sporting achievement. At the first modern Games in 1896, the winners were presented with a silver medal and the runners–up with a bronze. The first gold medals for winners were awarded in 1908. The medals are not, in fact, gold, but silver heavily gilded with gold. Currently, the first three in each event receive a medal: the first, a 'gold' medal; the second, silver; and third, bronze. As well as the place and year of the Games, each medal bears the name of the relevant sport, and is attached to a chain or ribbon. Winners have the additional honour of having their names inscribed on the walls of the stadium. The first eight in each event receive a diploma, and there are commemorative medals and diplomas for each competitor and official.

The release of doves or pigeons at the opening ceremony has been an official part of Olympic symbolism since the Antwerp Games of 1920, but the ceremony for the very first modern Games at Athens in 1896 included a flight of doves. The opening ceremony itself has its protocol, although the organizing committee has plenty of scope for spectacular display. The teams parade, with Greece leading in honour of its special place in Olympic history, and with the host nation bringing up the rear. Each team is led by a flag-bearer, who is usually one of its most respected athletes. The president of the organizing committee then introduces the President of the I.O.C., who asks the Head of State to open the Games. The Olympic flag is then raised, and the mayor of the host city receives a second flag from the mayor or representatives of the previous host city, which he must keep for passing on in turn. A three-gun salute and the release of the doves then precedes the arrival of the torch and the lighting of the Olympic flame. The flag bearers of each nation move to the rostrum and an Olympic oath is taken on behalf of all the competitors by a member of the team from the country in which the Games are being held. He holds a corner of his national flag and raises his right hand.

The Olympic oath was first taken at the Antwerp Games of 1920 by Victor Boin, a fencing competitor. It is: 'In the name of all the competitors I promise that we shall take part in these Olympic Games, respecting and abiding by the rules which govern them, in the true spirit of sportsmanship, for the glory of sport and the honour of our teams.'

The rules which govern the Games have been subjected to a great deal of discussion and change, particularly in the area which relates to eligibility and amateurism. The first definition of an amateur was in the first I.O.C. bulletin in 1894. The questions of expenses, payments for lost salary, whether a professional in one sport might be considered an amateur in another, sponsorships, advertising, 'athletics scholarships', equipment contracts, prizes, media interviews and the writing of books or articles have exercised the I.O.C. before and will continue to do so.

The parade of teams at the opening ceremony and the use of the word 'teams' in the oath are indicative of another conflict. The Games are meant for individuals, but they incorporate relays and sports like soccer and basketball, in which teams are necessary. And the Games themselves could not be organized without the help of national committees and some sort of national selection system, which itself leads to national 'teams'. However, the extensions of this, such as the traditions of raising national flags and playing national anthems at winning ceremonies, cause offence to many, who would like to see one or both dropped. It is a constant debate.

The requirements of the press, radio and particularly television are major considerations for the organizers of recent Olympic Games. It was estimated that over 1,000 million saw the televised opening ceremony of the 1972 Olympics in Munich, and the L.A.O.O.C. has estimated the television audience for the 1984 Games will have risen to 2,500 million, which is more than half the world's population. The American Broadcasting Company have bought television rights for $225 million, and plan about 207 hours of coverage.

The triumphs and tragedies of sportsmen and women unknown to the world before August 1984 will be seen by millions and become the topics of conversations all around the world. Already famous athletes will have their reputations confirmed or will have their myths shattered. It is notoriously dangerous to try to predict Olympic medal winners, particularly in athletics. The great men sprinters from the United States rise rapidly and seldom remain invincible for long: none has yet repeated an Olympic victory at 100 or 200 metres. The swimming events are even more difficult, as no doubt some of the 1984 winners will be barely out of school.

Should they compete, there will be at least two men seeking proud records. Teofilio Stevenson of Cuba in the heavyweight boxing tournament could equal Al Oerter's unique feat of winning the gold medal in the same event at four Olympiads, and Waldemar Cierpinski of East Germany could win his third successive marathon and surpass the record of the legendary Abebe Bikila. But mention of Bikila emphasizes the perils of forecasting. When he approached the stadium barefooted at the end of the marathon in Rome in 1960 a very solitary few of the thousands of professional sports journalists present had heard of him, and many were convinced that somewhere an error had crept into the proceedings.

That there will be a new hero or heroine at Los Angeles is certain. Each Games discloses a new star to the world. In Montreal there was Nadia Comaneci, Kornelia Ender and Alberto Juantorena; in Munich Mark Spitz, Valeri Borsov, Lasse Viren and Olga Korbut; in Mexico Bob Beamon. But there are fascinating questions to be answered. Will the super-efficient well-drilled squads of women swimmers, runners and throwers from the Soviet Union and East Germany carry all before them, or will there be a new Fanny Blankers-Koen to out run them or Dawn Fraser to out-swim them? Will the Finns produce another Kolehmainen or Nurmi or Viren to astonish track distance runners? Will Australia or New Zealand find another Jack Lovelock, Herb Elliott or Peter Snell to win

the 1,500 metres, or will Great Britain's Sebastian Coe or Steve Ovett be fit enough to put the seal on a fantastic career? Will black athletes dominate the men's sprints, as Jesse Owens, Bob Hayes and Tommie Smith did, or will there be a new Bobby Morrow or Borsov? Will there be an outstanding effort like Beamon's long jump, a new technique like Dick Fosbury's 'flop', the sad failure of a great athlete like Ron Clarke, the emergence of a personality like Emil Zatopek?

Whatever the answers, let us hope that politics do not intrude, and that the Games are 'ever more worthy of their glorious history and of the high ideals which inspired their revival by Baron Pierre de Coubertin and his associates', as article 11 of the rules of the International Olympic Committee states.

The Los Angeles Memorial Coliseum, which was used for the Olympic Games of 1932, will again be the venue for the athletics events in 1984.

Olympic Games Results

1896 ATHENS

ATHLETICS

100 metres
T. Burke USA
(12.0 sec)
F. Hofmann GER
A. Szokolyi HUN
400 metres
T. Burke USA
(54.2 sec)
H. Jamison USA
F. Hofmann GER
800 metres
E. Flack AUS
(2 min 11.0 sec)
N. Dani HUN
D. Golemis GRE
1,500 metres
E. Flack AUS
(4 min 33.2 sec)
A. Blake USA
A. Lermusiaux FRA
Marathon
S. Louis GRE
(2 hr 58 min 50.0 sec)
C. Vasilakos GRE
G. Kellner HUN
100-metres hurdles
T. Curtis USA
(17.6 sec)
G. Goulding GBR
(two finalists)
High jump
E. Clark USA
(1.81 m)
J. Connolly USA
R. Garrett USA
Pole vault
W. Hoyt USA
(3.30 m)
A. Tyler USA
E. Damaskos GRE
Long jump
E. Clark USA
(6.35 m)
R. Garrett USA
J. Connolly USA
Triple jump
J. Connolly USA
(13.71 m)
A. Tuffère FRA
I. Persakis GRE
Shot
R. Garrett USA
(11.22 m)
M. Gouscos GRE
G. Papasideris GRE
Discus
R. Garrett USA
(29.15 m)
P. Paraskevopoulos GRE
S. Versis GRE

CYCLING

2,000 metres
P. Masson FRA
(4 min 56.0 sec)
S. Nikolopoulos GRE
L. Flameng FRA

10,000 metres
P. Masson FRA
(17 min 54.2 sec)
L. Flameng FRA
A. Schmal AUT
100 kilometres
L. Flameng FRA
(3 hr 08 min 19.2 sec)
G. Kolettis GRE
12 hour
A. Schmal AUT
(314.997 km)
F. Keeping GBR
G. Paraskevopoulos GRE
Road race (87 km)
A. Konstantinidis GRE
(3 hr 22 min 31.0 sec)
A. Goedrich GER
F. Battel GBR
Team
SWE GBR USA

FENCING

Foil
E. Gravelotte FRA
(4 wins)
H. Callot FRA
P. Mavromichalis GRE
Foil for fencing masters
L. Pyrgos GRE
M. Perronnet FRA
K. Miliotis-Komninos GRE
Sabre
J. Georgiadis GRE
(4 wins)
T. Karakolos GRE
H. Neilsen DEN

GYMNASTICS

Parallel bars
A. Flatow GER
J. Zutter SUI
H. Weingaertner GER
Team
GER GRE GRF
Horizontal bar
H. Weingaertner GER
A. Flatow GER
Team
GER
Pommelled horse
J. Zutter SUI
H. Weingaertner GER
Long horse
C. Schuhmann GER
J. Zutter SUI
Rings
I. Mitropoulos GRE
H. Weingaertner GER
P. Persakis GRE
Rope climbing
N. Andriakopoulos GRE
(23.4 sec)
T. Xenakis GRE

LAWN TENNIS

Men's singles
P. Boland GBR

D. Kasdaglis GRE
Men's doubles
P. Boland GBR &
F. Thraun GER
D. Kasdaglis &
D. Petrokokkinos GRE

SHOOTING

Pistol (25 m)
J. Phrangoudis GRE
(344 pts)
G. Orphanidis GRE
H. Nielsen DEN
Military revolver (25 m)
J. Paine USA
(442 pts)
S. Paine USA
N. Morakis GRE
Military revolver (30 m)
S. Paine USA
(442 pts)
V. Jensen DEN
H. Nielsen DEN
Free rifle (200 m)
P. Karasseudas GRE
(2,320 pts)
P. Pavlidis GRE
N. Tricoupes GRE
Free rifle (300 m)
G. Orphanidis GRE
(1,583 pts)
J. Phrangoudis GRE
V. Jensen DEN

SWIMMING

100-metres freestyle
A. Hajos (Guttmann) HUN
(1 min 22.2 sec)
E. Choraphas GRE
O. Herschmann AUT
500-metres freestyle
P. Neumann AUT
(8 min 12.6 sec)
A. Pepanos GRE
E. Choraphas GRE
1,200-metres freestyle
A. Hajos (Guttmann) HUN
(18 min 22.2 sec)
I. Andreou GRE
E. Choraphas GRE
100-metres freestyle for sailors
J. Malokinis GRE
(2 min 20.4 sec)
S. Chasapis GRE
D. Drivas GRE

WEIGHTLIFTING

One hand
L. Elliott GBR
(71.0 kg)
V. Jensen DEN
A. Nikopoulos GRE
Two hand
V. Jensen DEN
(111.5 kg)

L. Elliott GBR
S. Versis GRE

WRESTLING

Greco-Roman Open
C. Schuhmann GER
G. Tsitas GRE
S. Christopoulos GRE

1900 PARIS

ATHLETICS

60 metres
A. Kraenzlein USA
(7.0 sec)
J. W. Tewksbury USA
S. Rowley AUS
100 metres
F. Jarvis USA
(11.0 sec)
J. W. Tewksbury USA
S. Rowley AUS
200 metres
J. W. Tewksbury USA
(22.2 sec)
N. Pritchard IND
S. Rowley AUS
400 metres
M. Long USA
(49.4 sec)
W. Holland USA
E. Schultz DEN
800 metres
A. Tysoe GBR
(2 min 01.2 sec)
J. Cregan USA
D. Hall USA
1,500 metres
C. Bennett GBR
(4 min 06.2 sec)
H. Deloge FRA
J. Bray USA
Marathon
M. Theato FRA
(2 hr 59 min 45.0 sec)
E. Champion FRA
E. Fast SWE
5,000-metres team
GBR FRA
2,500-metres steeplechase
G. Orton USA
(7 min 34.4 sec)
S. Robinson GBR
J. Chastanié FRA
4,000-metres steeplechase
J. Rimmer GBR
(12 min 58.4 sec)
C. Bennett GBR
S. Robinson GBR
110-metres hurdles
A. Kraenzlein USA
(15.4 sec)
J. McLean USA
F. Moloney USA
200-metres hurdles
A. Kraenzlein USA
(25.4 sec)

N. Pritchard IND
J. W. Tewksbury USA
400-metres hurdles
J. W. Tewksbury USA
(57.6 sec)
H. Tausin FRA
G. Orton CAN
High jump
I. Baxter USA
(1.90 m)
P. Leahy GBR
L. Gonczy HUN
Pole vault
I. Baxter USA
(3.30 m)
M. Colkett USA
C. Anderson NOR
Long jump
A. Kraenzlein USA
(7.185 m)

M. Prinstein USA
P. Leahy GBR
Triple jump
M. Prinstein USA
(14.47 m)
J. Connolly USA
L. Sheldon USA
Standing high jump
R. Ewry USA
(1.65 m)
I. Baxter USA
L. P. Sheldon USA
Standing long jump
R. Ewry USA
(3.21 m)
I. Baxter USA
E. Torcheboeuf FRA
Standing triple jump
R. Ewry USA
(10.58 m)
I. Baxter USA
R. Garrett USA
Shot
R. Sheldon USA
(14.10 m)
J. McCracken USA
R. Garrett USA
Discus
R. Bauer HUN
(36.04 m)
F. Janda-Suk BOH
R. Sheldon USA
Hammer
J. Flanagan USA
(49.73 m)

T. Hare USA
J. McCracken USA
Tug-of-war
DEN/SWE USA/FRA

CRICKET

FRA GBR

CROQUET

FRA FRA FRA

CYCLING

2,000-metres sprint
G. Taillandier FRA
(2 min 52.0 sec)
F. Sanz FRA
Lake USA

EQUESTRIAN

Show jumping
A. Haegeman BEL
(2 min 16.0 sec)
G. van der Poele BEL
de Champsavin FRA
High jump
D. M. Gardères FRA
(1.85 m)
G. G. Trissino ITA
A. Moreau FRA
Long jump
C. van Langhendonck BEL
(6.10 m)
G. G. Trissino ITA
de Prunelle FRA

FENCING

Foil
E. Coste FRA
(6 wins)
H. Masson FRA
J. Boulenger FRA
Foil for masters
L. Mérignac FRA
(6 wins)
A. Kirchhoffer FRA
J. B. Mimiague FRA
Epée
R. Fonst CUB
L. Perrée FRA
L. Sée FRA
Epée for masters
A. Ayat FRA
E. Bougnoi FRA
H. Laurent FRA
Epée for amateurs and masters
A. Ayat FRA
R. Fonst CUB
L. Sée FRA
Sabre
G. de la Falaise FRA
L. Thiébaut FRA
S. Flesch AUT

222

Sabre for masters
A. Conte *ITA*
I. Santelli *ITA*
M. Neralic *AUT*

GOLF

Men
C. Sands *USA*
W. Rutherford *GBR*
D. Robertson *GBR*
Women
A. Abbot *USA*
P. Whittier *SUI*
H. Pratt *USA*

GYMNASTICS

Combined exercises
G. Sandras *FRA*
N. Bas *FRA*
L. Démanet *FRA*

LAWN TENNIS

Men's singles
H. L. Doherty *GBR*
H. S. Mahony *GBR*
R. F. Doherty *GBR* &
A. B. J. Norris *GBR*
Women's singles
C. Cooper *GBR*
H. Prevost *FRA*
M. Jones *USA* &
H. Rosenbaumova *BOH*
Men's doubles
R. F. & H. L. Doherty *GBR*
S. de Garmendia *USA* &
M. Decugis *FRA*
A. Prevost & G. de la Chapelle *FRA* and
H. Mahony & A. B. J. Norris *GBR*
Mixed doubles
C. Cooper &
R. F. Doherty *GBR*
H. Prevost *FRA* &
H. S. Mahony *GBR*
H. Rosenbaumova *BOH* & A. A. Warder *GBR*
and M. Jones *USA* &
H. L. Doherty *GBR*

POLO

GBR GBR FRA

RUGBY

FRA GER GBR

ROWING

Single sculls
H. Barrelet *FRA*
(7 min 35.6 sec)
A. Gaudin *FRA*
St. George Ashe *GBR*
Coxless pairs
BEL BEL FRA
(7 min 49.6 sec)
Coxed pairs
HOL FRA FRA
(7 min 34.2 sec)
Coxed fours (1)
FRA FRA GER
(7 min 11.0 sec)
Coxed fours (2)
GER HOL GER
(5 min 59.0 sec)
Eights
USA BEL HOL
(6 min 09.8 sec)

SHOOTING

Free pistol
K. Roederer *SUI*
(503 pts)
A. Paroche *FRA*
K. Staeheli *SUI*
Rapid-fire pistol
M. Larrouy *FRA*
(58 pts)
L. Moreaux *FRA*
E. Balme *FRA*
Military revolver team
SUI FRA HOL
(2,271 pts)
Military rifle, prone
A. Paroche *FRA*
(332 pts)
A. P. Nielsen *DEN*
O. Ostmo *NOR*
Military rifle, kneeling
K. Staeheli *SUI*
(324 pts)
E. Kellenberger *SUI*
A. P. Nielsen *DEN*
Military rifle, standing
L. J. Madson *DEN*
(305 pts)
O. Ostmo *NOR*
C. P. du Verger *BEL*
Military rifle, three positions
E. Kallenberger *SUI*
(930 pts)
A. P. Nielsen *DEN*
O. Ostmo *NOR*
Military rifle, team
SUI NOR FRA
(4,399 pts)
Trap shooting
R. de Barbarin *FRA*
(17 pts)
R. Guyot *FRA*
J. de Clary *FRA*
Live pigeon
L. de Lunden *BEL*
(21 pts)
M. Faure *FRA*
D. MacIntosh *AUS*

SWIMMING

200-metres freestyle
F. Lane *AUS*
(2 min 25.2 sec)
Z. von Halmay *HUN*
K. Ruberl *AUT*
1,000-metres freestyle
J. Jarvis *GBR*
(13 min 40.0 sec)
O. Wahle *AUT*
Z. von Halmay *HUN*
4,000-metres freestyle
J. Jarvis *GBR*
(58 min 24.0 sec)
Z. von Halmay *HUN*
L. Martin *FRA*
200-metres team
GER FRA FRA
(32 pts)
200-metres backstroke
E. Hoppenberg *GER*
(2 min 47.0 sec)
K. Ruberl *AUT*
J. Drost *HOL*
Underwater
C. de Vaudeville *FRA*
(188.4 pts)
A. Six *FRA*
P. Lykkeberg *DEN*

200-metres obstacle
F. Lane *AUS*
(2 min 38.4 sec)
O. Wahle *AUT*
P. Kemp *GBR*
Water polo
GBR BEL FRA

YACHTING

Open
GBR GER FRA
0.5 ton
FRA FRA FRA
0.5–1 ton
GBR FRA FRA
1–2 ton
GER SUI FRA
2–3 ton
GBR FRA FRA
3–10 ton
USA FRA FRA
10–20 ton
FRA FRA GBR

1904 ST. LOUIS

ATHLETICS

60 metres
A. Hahn *USA*
(7.0 sec)
W. Hogenson *USA*
F. Moulton *USA*
100 metres
A. Hahn *USA*
(11.0 sec)
N. Cartmell *USA*
W. Hogenson *USA*
200 metres
A. Hahn *USA*
(21.6 sec)
N. Cartmell *USA*
W. Hogenson *USA*
400 metres
H. Hillman *USA*
(49.2 sec)
F. Waller *USA*
H. Groman *USA*
800 metres
J. Lightbody *USA*
(1 min 56.0 sec)
H. Valentine *USA*
E. Breitkreutz *USA*
1,500 metres
J. Lightbody *USA*
(4 min 05.4 sec)
F. Verner *USA*
L. Hearn *USA*
Marathon
T. Hicks *USA*
A. Corey *USA*
A. Newton *USA*
Cross-country (6,437 m)
USA USA
2,500-metres steeplechase
J. Lightbody *USA*
(7 min 39.6 sec)
J. Daley *GBR*
A. Newton *USA*
110-metres hurdles
F. Schule *USA*
(16.0 sec)
T. Shideler *USA*
L. Ashburner *USA*
200-metres hurdles
H. Hillman *USA*
(24.6 sec)
F. Castleman *USA*
G. Poage *USA*
400-metres hurdles
H. Hillman *USA*
(53.0 sec)

F. Waller *USA*
G. Poage *USA*
High jump
S. Jones *USA*
(1.80 m)
G. Serviss *USA*
P. Weinstein *GER*
Pole vault
C. Dvorak *USA*
(3.50 m)
L. Samse *USA*
L. Wilkins *USA*
Long jump
M. Prinstein *USA*
(7.34 m)
D. Frank *USA*
R. Stangland *USA*
Triple jump
M. Prinstein *USA*
(14.35 m)
F. Engelhardt *USA*
R. Stangland *USA*
Standing high jump
R. Ewry *USA*
(1.50 m)
J. Stadler *USA*
L. Robertson *USA*
Standing long jump
R. Ewry *USA*
(3.48 m)
C. King *USA*
J. Biller *USA*
Standing triple jump
R. Ewry *USA*
(10.55 m)
C. King *USA*
J. Stadler *USA*
Shot
R. Rose *USA*
(14.81 m)
W. Coe *USA*
L. Feuerbach *USA*
Discus
M. Sheridan *USA*
(39.28 m)
R. Rose *USA*
N. Georgantos *GRE*
Hammer
J. Flanagan *USA*
(51.23 m)
J. DeWitt *USA*
R. Rose *USA*
56-lb weight
E. Desmarteau *CAN*
(10.46 m)
J. Flanagan *USA*
J. Mitchel *USA*
Triathlon
(100 yds, long jump, shot)
M. Emmerich *USA*
J. Grieb *USA*
W. Merz *USA*
Decathlon
T. Kiely *GBR*
Tug-of-war
USA USA USA

ARCHERY

Men
Double York round
P. Bryant *USA*
(820 pts)
L. Ashburner *USA*
R. Williams *USA*
W. H. Thompson *USA*
Double American round
P. Bryant *USA*
(1,048 pts)
R. Williams *USA*
W. H. Thompson *USA*

Team
USA USA USA
(1,344 pts)
Women
Double Columbia round
M. C. Howell *USA*
(867 pts)
E. C. Cooke *USA*
H. C. Pollock *USA*
Double national round
M. C. Howell *USA*
(620 pts)
H. C. Pollock *USA*
E. C. Cooke *USA*
Team
USA USA
(506 pts)

BOXING

Flyweight
G. Finnegan *USA*
M. Burke *USA*
Bantamweight
O. L. Kirk *USA*
G. Finnegan *USA*
Featherweight
O. L. Kirk *USA*
F. Haller *USA*
Lightweight
H. Spanger *USA*
J. Eagan *USA*
R. Van Horn *USA*
Welterweight
A. Young *USA*
H. Spanger *USA*
J. Lydon *USA*
Middleweight
C. Mayer *USA*
B. Spradley *USA*
L. Feuerbach *USA*
Heavyweight
S. Berger *USA*
C. Mayer *USA*

FENCING

Foil
R. Fonst *CUB*
A. Van Zo Post *CUB*
C. Tatham *CUB*
Epée
R. Fonst *CUB*
C. Tatham *CUB*
A. Van Zo Post *CUB*
Sabre
M. De Diaz *CUB*
W. Grebe *USA*
A. Van Zo Post *CUB*
Single sticks
A. Van Zo Post *CUB*
W. Grebe *USA*
W. S. O'Connor *USA*

GOLF

G. S. Lyon *CAN*
C. C. Egan *USA*
B. McKinnie *USA*
Team
USA USA

GYMNASTICS

Combined exercises
J. Lenhart *AUT*
(69.80 pts)
W. Weber *GER*
A. Spinnier *SUI*
Team
USA USA USA

Combined, nine events
A. Spinnier *SUI*
(43.49 pts)
J. Lenhart *AUT*
W. Weber *GER*
Combined, seven events
A. Heida *USA*
(161 pts)
G. Eyser *USA*
W. Merz *USA*
Horizontal bar
A. Heida *USA* &
E. Hennig *USA*
(40 pts)
G. Eyser *USA*
Parallel bars
G. Eyser *USA*
(44 pts)
A. Heida *USA*
J. Duha *USA*
Pommelled horse
A. Heida *USA*
(42 pts)
G. Eyser *USA*
W. Merz *USA*
Long horse
A. Heida *USA* &
G. Eyser *USA*
(36 pts)
W. Merz *USA*
Rings
H. Glass *USA*
(45 pts)
W. Merz *USA*
E. Voigt *USA*
Rope climbing
G. Eyser *USA*
(7.0 sec)
C. Krause *USA*
E. Voigt *USA*
Club swinging
E. Hennig *USA*
(13 pts)
E. Voigt *USA*
R. Wilson *USA*

LACROSSE

CAN USA

LAWN TENNIS

Men's singles
B. C. Wright *USA*
R. LeRoy *USA*
Men's doubles
E. W. Leonard &
B. C. Wright *USA*
A. L. Bell &
R. LeRoy *USA*

ROQUE

C. Jacobus *USA*
S. O. Streeter *USA*
D. C. Brown *USA*

ROWING

Single sculls
F. Greer *USA*
(10 min 08.5 sec)
J. Juvenal *USA*
C. Titus *USA*
Double sculls
USA USA USA
(10 min 03.2 sec)
Coxless pairs
USA USA USA
(10 min 57.0 sec)
Coxless fours
USA USA
(9 min 53.8 sec)

Eights
USA CAN
(7 min 50.0 sec)

SWIMMING

50-yards freestyle
Z. von Halmay *HUN*
(28.0 sec)
J. S. Leary *USA*
C. Daniels *USA*
100-yards freestyle
Z. von Halmay *HUN*
(1 min 02.8 sec)
C. Daniels *USA*
J. S. Leary *USA*
220-yards freestyle
C. Daniels *USA*
(2 min 44.2 sec)
F. Gailey *USA*
E. Rausch *GER*
440-yards freestyle
C. Daniels *USA*
(6 min 16.2 sec)
F. Gailey *USA*
O. Wahle *AUT*
880-yards freestyle
E. Rausch *GER*
(13 min 11.4 sec)
F. Gailey *USA*
G. Kiss *HUN*
1-mile freestyle
E. Rausch *GER*
(27 min 18.2 sec)
G. Kiss *HUN*
F. Gailey *USA*
4 x 50-yards relay
USA USA USA
(2 min 04.6 sec)
100-yards backstroke
W. Brack *GER*
(1 min 16.8 sec)
G. Hoffmann *GER*
G. Zacharias *GER*
440-yards breaststroke
G. Zacharias *GER*
(7 min 23.6 sec)
W. Brack *GER*
H. J. Handy *USA*
Highboard diving
G. Sheldon *USA*
(12.66 pts)
G. Hoffmann *GER*
F. Kehoe *USA* &
A. Braunschweiger *GER*
Plunge for distance
W. E. Dickey *USA*
(19.05 m)
E. Adams *USA*
L. Goodwin *USA*

WEIGHTLIFTING

Super-heavyweight
One hand
O. P. Osthoff *USA*
(48 pts)
F. Winters *USA*
F. Kungler *USA*
Two hand
P. Kakousis *GRE*
(111.58 pts)
O. P. Osthoff *USA*
F. Kungler *USA*

WRESTLING: FREESTYLE

Light flyweight
R. Curry *USA*
J. Heim *USA*
G. Thiefenthaler *USA*
Flyweight
G. Mehnert *USA*

G. Bauers *USA*
M. Nelson *USA*
Bantamweight
I. Niflot *USA*
A. Wester *USA*
Z. Strebler *USA*
Featherweight
B. Bradshaw *USA*
T. McLear *USA*
B. C. Clapper *USA*
Lightweight
O. Roehm *USA*
S. R. Tesing *USA*
A. Zirkel *USA*
Welterweight
C. Erikson *USA*
W. Beckman *USA*
J. Winholtz *USA*
Heavyweight
B. Hansen *USA*
F. Kungler *USA*
F. Warmbold *USA*

INTERIM GAMES 1906 ATHENS

ATHLETICS
100 metres
A. Hahn *USA*
(11.2 sec)
F. Moulton *USA*
N. Barker *AUS*
400 metres
P. Pilgrim *USA*
(53.2 sec)
W. Halswelle *GBR*
N. Barker *AUS*
1,500 metres
J. Lightbody *USA*
(4 min 12.0 sec)
J. McGough *GBR*
K. Hellstroem *SWE*
5 miles
H. Hawtrey *GBR*
(26 min 11.8 sec)
J. Svanberg *SWE*
E. Dahl *SWE*
Marathon
W. Sherring *CAN*
(2 hr 51 min 23.6 sec)
J. Svanberg *SWE*
W. Frank *USA*
1,500-metres walk
G. Bonhag *USA*
(7 min 12.6 sec)
D. Linden *CAN*
K. Spetsiotis *GRE*
3,000-metres walk
G. Sztantics *HUN*
(15 min 13.2 sec)
H. Mueller *GER*
G. Saridakis *GRE*
110-metres hurdles
R. Leavitt *USA*
(16.2 sec)
A. Healey *GBR*
V. Duncker *SAF*
High jump
C. Leahy *GBR*
(1.77 m)
L. Gonczy *HUN*
H. Kerrigan *USA* &
T. Diakidis *GRE*
Pole vault
F. Gonder *FRA*
(3.40 m)
B. Soederstroem *SWE*
E. Glover *USA*
Long jump
M. Prinstein *USA*
(7.20 m)
P. O'Connor *GBR*
H. Friend *USA*

Triple jump
P. O'Connor *GBR*
(14.07 m)
C. Leahy *GBR*
T. Cronan *USA*
Standing high jump
R. Ewry *USA*
(1.56 m)
M. Sheridan *USA*
L. Dupont *BEL*
Standing long jump
R. Ewry *USA*
(3.30 m)
M. Sheridan *USA*
L. Robertson *USA*
Shot
M. Sheridan *USA*
(12.32 m)
M. David *HUN*
E. Lemming *SWE*
Discus (freestyle)
M. Sheridan *USA*
(41.46 m)
N. Georgantas *GRE*
W. Jarvinen *FIN*
Discus (Greek style)
W. Jarvinen *FIN*
(35.18 m)
N. Georgantas *GRE*
I. Mudin *HUN*
Javelin
E. Lemming *SWE*
(53.90 m)
K. Lindberg *SWE*
B. Soederstroem *SWE*
Pentathlon
H. Mellander *SWE*
I. Mudin *HUN*
E. Lemming *SWE*
Tug-of-war
GER GRE SWE ·
Throwing the 14-lb stone
N. Georgantas *GRE*
(19.92 m)
M. Sheridan *USA*
M. Dorizas *GRE*

CYCLING

333⅓ metres
F. Verri *ITA*
(22.8 sec)
H. Crowther *GBR*
Menjou *FRA*
1,000 metres
F. Verri *ITA*
(1 min 42.2 sec)
H. Bouffler *GBR*
E. Debougnie *BEL*
5,000 metres
F. Verri *ITA*
(8 min 35.0 sec)
H. Crowther *GBR*
B. Vast *FRA*
2,000-metres tandem
GBR GER GER
(2 min 57.0 sec)
20-kilometres paced race
W. J. Pett *GBR*
(29 min 0 sec)
M. Bardonneau *FRA*
B. Vast *FRA*
Road race (84 km)
B. Vast *FRA*
(2 hr 41 min 28.0 sec)
M. Bardonneau *FRA*
Luget *FRA*

FENCING

Foil
G. Dillon-Kavanagh *FRA*

G. Casmir *GER*
P. d'Hugues *FRA*
Epée
G. de la Falaise *FRA*
G. Dillon-Kavanagh *FRA*
A. van Blijenburgh *HOL*
Team
FRA GBR BEL
Epée for fencing masters
C. Verbrugge *BEL*
M. Gubiani *ITA*
I. Raissis *GRE*
Sabre
J. Georgiadis *GRE*
G. Casmir *GER*
F. Cesarano *ITA*
Sabre for fencing masters
C. Verbrugge *BEL*
I. Raissis *GRE*
Three-cornered sabre
G. Casmir *GER*
G. van Rossam *HOL*
P. Toth *HUN*

GYMNASTICS

Team
NOR DEN ITA
Rope climbing
G. Aliprantis *GRE*
(11.4 sec)
B. Erody *HUN*
K. Kozanitas *GRE*

LAWN TENNIS

Men's singles
M. Decugis *FRA*
M. Germot *FRA*
Z. Zemla *BOH*
Men's doubles
M. Decugis &
M. Germot *FRA*
X. Kasdaglis &
I. Ballis *GRE*
Z. Zemla &
L. Zemla *BOH*
Ladies' singles
E. Semyriotou *GRE*
S. Marinou *GRE*
E. Paspati *GRE*
Mixed doubles
M. Decugis &
Mme Decugis *FRA*
S. Marinou &
G. Simiriotis *GRE*
A. Matsa &
X. Kasdaglis *GRE*

ROWING

Single sculls
G. Delaplane *FRA*
(5 min 53.4 sec)
J. Larran *FRA*
Coxed pairs (1,000 m)
ITA ITA FRA
(4 min 23.0 sec)
Coxed pairs (1,600 m)
ITA BEL FRA
(7 min 32.4 sec)
Coxed fours (2,000 m)
ITA FRA FRA
(8 min 13.0 sec)
Naval rowing boats
ITA GRE GRE
(10 min 45.0 sec)
16-man naval rowing boats
GRE GRE ITA
(16 min 35.0 sec)

SHOOTING

Pistol (50 m)
G. Orphanidis *GRE*
(221 pts)
J. Fouconnier *FRA*
A. Rangavis *GRE*
Rapid-fire pistol
M. Lecoq *FRA*
(250 pts)
L. Moreaux *FRA*
A. Rangavis *GRE*
Free rifle, prone
G. G. Skatteboe *NOR*
Free rifle, kneeling
K. Staeheli *SUI*
Free rifle, standing
G. G. Skatteboe *NOR*
Free rifle, any position
M. M. de Stadelhofen *SUI*
(243 pts)
K. Staeheli *SUI*
L. Moreaux *FRA*
Free rifle, three positions
G. G. Skatteboe *NOR*
(977 pts)
K. Staeheli *SUI*
J. Reich *SUI*
Team
SUI NOR FRA
Military rifle (200 m)
L. Moreaux *FRA*
(187 pts)
L. Richardet *SUI*
J. Reich *SUI*
Military rifle (300 m)
L. Richardet *SUI*
J. Reich *SUI*
R. de Boigne *FRA*
Military revolver (20 m)
L. Richardet *SUI*
(253 pts)
A. Theophilakis *GRE*
G. Skotadis *GRE*
Military revolver, 1873 model
J. Fouconnier *FRA*
(219 pts)
R. de Boigne *FRA*
H. Martin *FRA*
Duelling pistol (20 m)
L. Moreaux *FRA*
(242 pts)
C. Liverziani *ITA*
M. Lecoq *FRA*
Duelling pistol (25 m)
M. Skarlatos *GRE*
(133 pts)
J. H. von Holst *SWE*
W. Carlberg *SWE*

SOCCER

DEN GRE GRE

SWIMMING

100-metres freestyle
C. Daniels *USA*
(1 min 13.4 sec)
Z. von Halmay *HUN*
C. Healy *AUS*
400-metres freestyle
O. Scheff *AUT*
(6 min 23.8 sec)
H. Taylor *GBR*
J. Jarvis *GBR*
1-mile freestyle
H. Taylor *GBR*
(28 min 28.0 sec)

J. Jarvis *GBR*
O. Scheff *AUT*
4 x 250-metres relay
HUN GER GBR
(16 min 52.4 sec)
Platform diving
G. Walz *GER*
(156.00 pts)
G. Hoffmann *GER*
O. Satzinger *AUT*

1908 LONDON

ATHLETICS

100 metres
R. Walker *SAF*
(10.8 sec)
J. Rector *USA*
R. Kerr *CAN*
200 metres
R. Kerr *CAN*
(22.6 sec)
R. Cloughen *USA*
N. Cartmell *USA*
400 metres
W. Halswelle *GBR*
(50.0 sec)

ran final alone
800 metres
M. Sheppard *USA*
(1 min 52.8 sec)
E. Lunghi *ITA*
H. Braun *GER*
1,500 metres
M. Sheppard *USA*
(4 min 03.4 sec)
H. Wilson *GBR*
N. Hallows *GBR*
5 miles
E. Voigt *GBR*
(25 min 11.2 sec)
E. Owen *GBR*
J. Svanberg *SWE*
Marathon
J. Hayes *USA*
(2 hr 55 min 18.4 sec)
C. Hefferon *SAF*
J. Forshaw *USA*
Relay
(2 × 200, 1 × 400, 1 × 800 m)
USA GER HUN
(3 min 29.4 sec)
110-metres hurdles
F. Smithson *USA*
(15.0 sec)
J. Garrels *USA*
A. Shaw *USA*
400-metres hurdles
C. Bacon *USA*
(55.0 sec)
H. Hillman *USA*
L. Tremeer *GBR*

3,200-metres steeplechase
A. Russell *GBR*
(10 min 47.8 sec)
A. Robertson *GBR*
J. Eisele *USA*
3-miles team race
GBR USA FRA
(6 pts)
3,500-metres walk
G. Larner *GBR*
(14 min 55 sec)
E. Webb *GBR*
H. Kerr *NZL*
10-miles walk
G. Larner *GBR*
(1 hr 15 min 57.4 sec)
E. Webb *GBR*
E. Spencer *GBR*
Standing high jump
R. Ewry *USA*
(1.57 m)
K. Tsiklitiras *GRE*
J. Biller *USA*
Standing long jump
R. Ewry *USA*
(3.33 m)
K. Tsiklitiras *GRE*
M. Sheridan *USA*
High jump
H. Porter *USA*
(1.90 m)
C. Leahy *GBR* &
I. Somodi *HUN* &
G. André *FRA*
Pole vault
A. Gilbert *USA* &
E. Cooke *USA*
(3.71 m)
E. Archibald *CAN*
Long jump
F. Irons *USA*
(7.48 m)
D. Kelly *USA*
C. Bricker *CAN*
Triple jump
T. Ahearne *GBR*
(14.91 m)
J. MacDonald *CAN*
E. Larsen *NOR*
Shot
R. Rose *USA*
(14.21 m)
D. Horgan *GBR*
J. Garrels *USA*
Discus (freestyle)
M. Sheridan *USA*
(40.89 m)
M. Giffin *USA*
M. Horr *USA*
Discus (Greek style)
M. Sheridan *USA*
(38.00 m)
M. Horr *USA*
W. Jarvinen *FIN*
Hammer
J. Flanagan *USA*
(51.92 m)

M. McGrath *USA*
C. Walsh *USA*
Javelin (conventional)
E. Lemming *SWE*
(54.83 m)
A. Halse *NOR*
O. Nilsson *SWE*
Javelin (freestyle)
E. Lemming *SWE*
(54.45 m)
M. Dorizas *GRE*
A. Halse *NOR*
Tug-of-war
GBR GBR GBR

ARCHERY
Men
York round
W. Dod *GBR*
(815 pts)
R. B. Brookes-King *GBR*
H. B. Richardson *USA*
50-metres continental
E. Grisot *FRA*
(263 pts)
L. Vernet *FRA*
G. Cabaret *FRA*
Women
Q. Newall *GBR*
(688 pts)
L. Dod *GBR*
Hill-Lowe *GBR*

BOXING
Bantamweight
H. Thomas *GBR*
J. Condon *GBR*
W. Webb *GBR*
Featherweight
R. Gunn *GBR*
C. Morris *GBR*
H. Roddin *GBR*
Lightweight
F. Grace *GBR*
F. Spiller *GBR*
H. Johnson *GBR*
Middleweight
J. Douglas *GBR*
R. Baker *AUS*
W. Philo *GBR*
Heavyweight
A. Oldham *GBR*
S. Evans *GBR*
F. Parks *GBR*

CYCLING
One lap (660 yards)
V. Johnson *GBR*
(51.2 sec)
E. Demangel *FRA*
K. Neumer *GER*
1,000-metres sprint
Void—time exceeded
5,000 metres
B. Jones *GBR*
(8 min 36.2)
M. Schilles *FRA*
A. Auffray *FRA*
20 kilometres
C. Kingsbury *GBR*
(34 min 13.6 sec)
B. Jones *GBR*
J. Werbrouck *BEL*
100 kilometres
C. Bartlett *GBR*
(2 hr 41 min 48.6 sec)
C. Denny *GBR*
O. Lapize *FRA*
Team pursuit (3 laps)
GBR GER CAN
(2 min 18.6 sec)

2,000-metres Tandem
FRA GBR GBR
(3 min 07.6 sec)

FENCING
Epée
G. Alibert *FRA*
(5 wins)
A. Lippmann *FRA*
E. Olivier *FRA*
Team
FRA GBR BEL
Sabre
J. Fuchs *HUN*
(6 wins)
B. Zulavsky *HUN*
V. Goppold de Lobsdorf *BOH*
Team
HUN ITA BOH

FIGURE SKATING
Men
U. Salchow *SWE*
(1,886.5 pts)
R. Johansson *SWE*
P. Thoren *SWE*
Women
E. M. Syers *GBR*
(1,262.5 pts)
E. Rendschmidt *GER*
D. Greenhough-Smith *GBR*
Pairs
A. Heubler &
H. Burger *GER*
(56.0 pts)
P. W. Johnson &
J. H. Johnson *GBR*
M. Syers &
E. Syers *GBR*

GYMNASTICS
Combined
A. Braglia *ITA*
(317 pts)
S. Tysal *GBR*
L. Segura *FRA*
Team
SWE NOR FIN

HOCKEY (FIELD)
ENG IRL SCO & WAL

JEU DE PAUME
Jay Gould *USA*
E. H. Miles *GBR*
N. S. Lytton *GBR*

LACROSSE
CAN GBR

LAWN TENNIS (outdoor)
Men's singles
J. G. Ritchie *GBR*
O. Froitzheim *GER*
W. V. Eaves *GBR*
Women's singles
D. Lambert Chambers *GBR*
D. B. Boothby *GBR*
J. Winch *GBR*
Men's doubles
G. Hillyard &
R. F. Doherty *GBR*

J. G. Ritchie &
J. C. Parke *GBR*
C. Cazalet &
C. P. Dixon *GBR*

LAWN TENNIS (indoor)
Men's singles
A. N. Gore *GBR*
G. A. Caridia *GBR*
J. G. Ritchie *GBR*
Women's singles
G. Eastlake-Smith *GBR*
A. N. Greene *GBR*
M. Adlerstrahle *SWE*
Men's doubles
A. Gore & H. Roper-Barrett *GBR*

MOTORBOATING
Unrestricted
E. Thubron *FRA*
Under 60 feet
T. Thornycoft &
B. Redwood *GBR*
6.5-8 metre cruisers
T. Thornycroft &
B. Redwood *GBR*

POLO
GBR GBR GBR

RACQUETS
Men's singles
E. Noel *GBR*
H. Leaf *GBR*
J. J. Astor *GBR*
Men's doubles
V. Pennell &
J. J. Astor *GBR*
E. Bury &
C. Browning *GBR*
E. Noel &
H. Leaf *GBR*

ROWING
Single sculls
H. Blackstaffe *GBR*
(9 min 26 sec)
A. McCulloch *GBR*
B. von Gaza *GER* &
K. Levitzky *HUN*
Coxless pairs
GBR GBR CAN
(9 min 41.0 sec)
Eights
GBR BEL CAN
(7 min 52 sec)

RUGBY
AUS GBR

SHOOTING
Military rifle teams
USA GBR CAN
Free rifle
A. Helgerud *NOR*
(909 pts)
H. Simon *USA*
O. Saether *NOR*
Military rifle
J. K. Millner *GBR*
(98 pts)
K. K. Casey *USA*
M. Blood *GBR*
Team
NOR SWE FRA

Small-bore rifle
A. Carnell *GBR*
(387 pts)
H. Humby *GBR*
C. Barnes *GBR*
Team
GBR SWE FRA
Small-bore rifle, disappearing target
W. Styles *GBR*
(45 pts)
H. Hawkins *GBR*
E. Amoore *GBR*
Small-bore rifle, moving target
A. Fleming *GBR*
(24 pts)
M. Matthews *GBR*
W. Marsden *GBR*
Rapid-fire pistol
P. van Asbroek *HOL*
(490 pts)
R. Storms *BEL*
J. Gorman *USA*
Team
USA BEL GBR
Running deer, single shot
O. Swahn *SWE*
(25 pts)
T. Ranken *GBR*
A. Rogers *GBR*
Team
SWE GBR
Running deer, double shot
W. Winans *USA*
(46 pts)
T. Ranken *GBR*
O. Swahn *SWE*
Trap shooting
W. Ewing *CAN*
(72 pts)
G. Beattie *CAN*
A. Maunder *GBR* &
A. Metaxas *GRE*
Team
GBR CAN GBR

SOCCER
GBR DEN HOL

SWIMMING
100-metres freestyle
C. Daniels *USA*
(1 min 05.6 sec)

Z. von Halmay *HUN*
H. Julin *SWE*
400-metres freestyle
H. Taylor *GBR*
(5 min 36.8 sec)
F. Beaurepaire *AUS*
O. Scheff *AUT*
1,500-metres freestyle
H. Taylor *GBR*
(22 min 48.4 sec)

T. Battersby *GBR*
F. Beaurepaire *AUS*
200-metres breaststroke
F. Holman *GBR*
(3 min 09.2 sec)
W. Robinson *GBR*
P. Hansson *SWE*
100-metres backstroke
A. Bieberstein *GER*
(1 min 24.6 sec)
L. Dam *DEN*
H. Haresnape *GBR*
4 x 200-metres freestyle relay
GBR HUN USA
(10 min 55.6 sec)
Platform diving
H. Johansson *SWE*
(83.75 pts)
K. Malmstroem *SWE*
A. Spangberg *SWE*
Springboard diving
A. Zuerner *GER*
(85.5 pts)
K. Behrens *GER*
G. Gaidzik *USA*
Water polo
GBR BEL SWE

WRESTLING: FREESTYLE
Bantamweight
G. Mehnert *USA*
W. Press *GBR*
B. Côté *CAN*
Featherweight
G. Dole *USA*
J. Slim *GBR*
W. McKie *GBR*
Lightweight
G. de Relwyskow *GBR*
W. Wood *GBR*
A. Gingell *GBR*
Middleweight
S. Bacon *GBR*
G. de Relwyskow *GBR*
F. Beck *GBR*
Heavyweight
G. O'Kelly *GBR*
J. Gundersen *NOR*
E. Barrett *GBR*

WRESTLING: GRECO-ROMAN
Lightweight
E. Porro *ITA*
N. Orlov *URS*
A. Linden-Linko *FIN*
Middleweight
F. Martensson *SWE*
M. Andersson *SWE*
A. Andersen *DEN*
Light-heavyweight
V. Weckman *FIN*
Y. Saarela *FIN*
C. Jensen *DEN*
Heavyweight
R. Weisz *HUN*
A. Petrov *URS*
S. Jensen *DEN*

YACHTING
6-metre class
GBR BEL FRA
7-metre class
GBR
8-metre class
GBR SWE GBR
12-metre class
GBR GBR

ATHLETICS
100 metres
R. Craig *USA*
(10.8 sec)
A. Meyer *USA*
D. Lippincott *USA*
200 metres
R. Craig *USA*
(21.7 sec)
D. Lippincott *USA*
W. Applegarth *GBR*
400 metres
C. Reidpath *USA*
(48.2 sec)
H. Braun *GER*
E. Lindberg *USA*
800 metres
J. E. Meredith *USA*
(1 min 51.9 sec)
M. Sheppard *USA*
I. Davenport *USA*
1,500 metres
A. Strode-Jackson *GBR*
(3 min 56.8 sec)

A. Kiviat *USA*
N. Taber *USA*
5,000 metres
H. Kolehmainen *FIN*
(14 min 36.6 sec)
J. Bouin *FRA*
G. Hutson *GBR*
10,000 metres
H. Kolehmainen *FIN*
(31 min 20.8 sec)
L. Tewanima *USA*
A. Stenroos *FIN*
Marathon
K. McArthur *SAF*
(2 hr 36 min 54.8 sec)
C. Gitsham *SAF*
G. Strobino *USA*
110-metres hurdles
F. Kelly *USA*
(15.1 sec)
J. Wendell *USA*
M. Hawkins *USA*
4 x 100-metres relay
GBR SWE
(42.4 sec)
4 x 400-metres relay
USA FRA GBR
(3 min 16.6 sec)
Cross-country (12,000 m)
H. Kolehmainen *FIN*
(45 min 11.6 sec)
H. Andersson *SWE*
J. Eke *SWE*
Team
SWE FIN GBR
(10 pts)
3,000-metres team
USA SWE GBR
(9 pts)

10,000-metres walk
G. Goulding *CAN*
(46 min 28.4 sec)
E. Webb *GBR*
F. Altimani *ITA*
High Jump
A. Richards *USA*
(1.93 m)
H. Liesche *GER*
G. Horinne *USA*
Long jump
A. Gutterson *USA*
(7.60 m)
C. Bricker *CAN*
G. Aberg *SWE*
Triple jump
G. Lindblom *SWE*
(14.76 m)
G. Aberg *SWE*
E. Almloef *SWE*
Pole vault
H. Babcock *USA*
(3.95 m)
F. Nelson *USA* &
M. Wright *USA*
Standing high jump
Platt Adams *USA*
(1.63 m)
Benjamin Adams *USA*
K. Tsiklitiras *GRE*
Standing long jump
C. Tsiklitiras *GRE*
(3.37 m)
Platt Adams *USA*
Benjamin Adams *USA*
Shot (one hand)
P. McDonald *USA*
(15.34 m)
R. Rose *USA*
L. Whitney *USA*
Shot (both hands)
R. Rose *USA*
(27.70 m)
P. McDonald *USA*
E. Niklander *FIN*
Discus (one hand)
A. Taipale *FIN*
(45.21 m)
R. Byrd *USA*
J. Duncan *USA*
Discus (both hands)
A. Taipale *FIN*
(82.86 m)
E. Niklander *FIN*
F. Magnussen *SWE*
Javelin (one hand)
E. Lemming *SWE*
(60.64 m)
J. Saaristo *FIN*
M. Koczan *HUN*
Javelin (both hands)
J. Saaristo *FIN*
(109.42 m)
V. Siikaniemi *FIN*
U. Peltonen *FIN*
Hammer
M. McGrath *USA*
(54.74 m)
D. Gillis *CAN*
C. Childs *USA*
Pentathlon
F. Bie *NOR*
(16 pts)
J. Donahue *USA*
F. Lukeman *CAN*
(J. Thorpe (*USA*) won, was disqualified a year later but had his medal restored posthumously in 1982)
Decathlon
H. Wieslander *SWE*
(7,724.495 pts)

C. Lomberg *SWE*
G. Holmer *SWE*
(J. Thorpe (*USA*) won, was disqualified a year later but had his medal restored posthumously in 1982)
Tug-of-war
SWE GBR

CYCLING

Road race (320 km)
R. Lewis *SAF*
(10 hr 42 min 39 sec)
F. Grubb *GBR*
C. Schutte *USA*
Team
SWE GBR USA
(44 hr 35 min 33.6 sec)

EQUESTRIAN

Show jumping
J. Cariou *FRA*
(186 pts)
R. W. von Kroecher *GER*
E. de Blonmaert *BEL*
Team
SWE FRA GER
Dressage
C. Bonde *SWE*
(15 flts)
G. A. Boltenstern *SWE*
H. von Blixen-Finecke *SWE*
Three-day event
A. Nordlander *SWE*
(46.59 pts)
H. von Rochow *GER*
J. Cariou *FRA*
Team
SWE GER USA

FENCING

Foil
N. Nadi *ITA*
(7 wins)
P. Speciale *ITA*
R. Verderber *AUT*
Epée
P. Anspach *BEL*
(6 wins)
I. Osiier *DEN*
P. le Hardy de Beaulieu *BEL*
Team
BEL GBR HOL
Sabre
J. Fuchs *HUN*
(6 wins)
B. Bekessy *HUN*
E. Meszaros *HUN*
Team
HUN AUT HOL

GYMNASTICS

Combined exercises
A. Braglia *ITA*
(135 pts)
L. Ségura *FRA*
A. Tunesi *ITA*
Team
ITA HUN GBR
Combined exercises
Swedish system
SWE DEN NOR
Free exercises
NOR FIN DEN

LAWN TENNIS (outdoor)
Men's singles
C. L. Winslow *SAF*
H. A. Kitson *SAF*
O. Kreuzer *GER*
Women's singles
M. Broquedis *FRA*
D. Koering *GER*
M. Bjurstedt *NOR*
Men's doubles
H. A. Kitson &
C. L. Winslow *SAF*
F. Pipes &
A. Zborzil *AUT*
A. Canet &
M. M. de Marangue *FRA*
Mixed doubles
D. Koering &
H. Schomburgk *GER*
S. Fick &
G. Setterwall *SWE*
M. Broquedis &
A. Canet *FRA*

LAWN TENNIS (indoor)

Men's singles
A. H. Gobert *FRA*
C. P. Dixon *GBR*
A. F. Wilding *NZL*
Women's singles
E. N. Hannam *GBR*
T. Castenschiold *DEN*
M. G. Parton *GBR*
Men's doubles
A. H. Gobert &
M. Germot *FRA*
G. Setterwall &
C. Kempe *SWE*
C. P. Dixon &
A. F. Beamish *GBR*
Mixed doubles
E. N. Hannam &
C. P. Dixon *GBR*
H. Aitchison &
H. R. Barrett *GBR*
S. Fick &
G. Setterwall *SWE*

MODERN PENTATHLON

G. Lilliehook *SWE*
(27 pts)
G. Asbrink *SWE*
G. de Laval *SWE*

ROWING

Single sculls
W. D. Kinnear *GBR*
(7 min 47.6 sec)
P. Vierman *BEL*
E. B. Butler *CAN* &
M. Kusik *URS*
Coxed fours
GER GBR DEN
(6 min 59.4 sec)
Coxed fours with in-riggers
DEN SWE NOR
(7 min 47.0 sec)
Eights
GBR GBR GER
(6 min 15.0 sec)

SHOOTING

Free pistol
A. Lane *USA*
(499 pts)
P. Dolfen *USA*
C. E. Stewart *GBR*

Military revolver (30 m)
Team
SWE URS GBR
Military revolver (50 m)
Team
USA SWE GBR
Rapid-fire pistol
A. Lane *USA*
(287 pts)
P. Palen *SWE*
J. H. von Holst *SWE*
Free rifle
P. Colas *FRA*
(987 pts)
L. J. Madsen *DEN*
N. H. D. Larsen *DEN*
Team
SWE NOR DEN
Military rifle (300 m)
S. Prokopp *HUN*
(97 pts)
C. Osburn *USA*
E. Skogen *NOR*
Military rifle (600 m)
P. Colas *FRA*
(94 pts)
C. Osburn *USA*
J. Jackson *USA*
Team
USA GBR SWE
Small-bore rifle, prone
F. Hird *USA*
(194 pts)
W. Milne *GBR*
H. Burt *GBR*
Team
GBR SWE USA
Small-bore rifle, vanishing target
W. Carlberg *SWE*
(242 pts)
J. H. von Holst *SWE*
G. Ericsson *SWE*
Team
SWE GBR USA
Running deer, single shot
A. Swahn *SWE*
(41 pts)
A. Lundeberg *SWE*
N. Toivonen *FIN*
Team
SWE USA FIN
Running deer, double shot
A. Lundberg *SWE*
(79 pts)
E. Benedicks *SWE*
O. Swahn *SWE*
Trap shooting
J. Graham *USA*
(96 pts)
A. Goeldel *GER*
H. Blau *URS*
Team
USA GBR GER

SOCCER

GBR DEN HOL

SWIMMING

Men
100-metres freestyle
D. P. Kahanamoku *USA*
(1 min 03.4 sec)
C. Healy *AUS*
K. Huszagh *USA*
400-metre freestyle
G. Hodgson *CAN*
(5 min 24.4 sec)
J. Hatfield *GBR*

H. Hardwick *AUS*
1,500-metres freestyle
G. Hodgson *CAN*
(22 min 00.0 sec)
J. Hatfield *GBR*
H. Hardwick *AUS*
100-metres backstroke
H. Hebner *USA*
(1 min 21.2 sec)
O. Fahr *GER*
P. Kellner *GER*
200-metres breaststroke
W. Bathe *GER*
(3 min 01.8 sec)
W. Luetzon *GER*
K. Malisch *GER*
400-metres breaststroke
W. Bathe *GER*
(6 min 29.6 sec)
T. Henning *SWE*
P. Courtman *GBR*
4 x 200-metres freestyle relay
AUS USA GBR
(10 min 11.6 sec)
Highboard diving, plain
E. Adlerz *SWE*
(40 pts)
H. Johansson *SWE*
J. Jansson *SWE*
Highboard diving, fancy
E. Adlerz *SWE*
(73.94 pts)
A. Zuerner *GER*
G. Blomgren *SWE*
Springboard diving
P. Guenther *GER*
(79.23 pts)
H. Luber *GER*
K. Behrens *GER*
Water polo
GBR SWE BEL
Women
100-metres freestyle
F. Durack *AUS*
(1 min 22.2 sec)
W. Wylie *AUS*
J. Fletcher *GBR*
4 x 100-metres freestyle relay
GBR GER AUT
(5 min 52.8 sec)
Highboard diving
G. Johansson *SWE*
(39.90 pts)
L. Regnell *SWE*
I. White *GBR*

WRESTLING: GRECO-ROMAN

Featherweight
K. Koskelo *FIN*
G. Gerstacker *GER*
O. Lasanen *FIN*
Lightweight
E. Ware *FIN*
G. Malmstroem *SWE*
E. Matiasson *SWE*
Middleweight
C. Johansson *SWE*
M. Klein *URS*
A. Asikainen *FIN*
Light-heavyweight
Gold medal not awarded
A. Ahlgren *SWE* &
I. Boehling *FIN*
B. Varga *HUN*

Heavyweight
Y. Saarela *FIN*
J. Olin *FIN*
S. M. Jensen *DEN*

YACHTING

6-metre class
FRA DEN SWE
8-metre class
NOR SWE FIN
10-metre class
SWE FIN URS
12-metre class
NOR SWE FIN

1920 ANTWERP

ATHLETICS

100 metres
C. Paddock *USA*
(10.8 sec)

M. Kirksey *USA*
H. Edward *GBR*
200 metres
A. Woodring *USA*
(22.0 sec)
C. Paddock *USA*
H. Edward *GBR*
400 metres
B. Rudd *SAF*
(49.6 sec)
G. Butler *GBR*
N. Engdahl *SWE*
800 metres
A. Hill *GBR*
(1 min 53.4 sec)
E. Eby *USA*
B. Rudd *SAF*
1,500 metres
A. Hill *GBR*
(4 min 01.8 sec)

P. Noel-Baker *GBR*
L. Shields *USA*
3,000 metres team
USA GBR SWE
(10 pts)

5,000 metres
J. Guillemot *FRA*
(14 min 55.6 sec)
P. Nurmi *FIN*
E. Backman *SWE*
10,000 metres
P. Nurmi *FIN*
(31 min 45.8 sec)

J. Guillemot *FRA*
J. Wilson *GBR*
Marathon
H. Kolehmainen *FIN*
(2 hr 32 min 35.8 sec)
J. Lossman *EST*
V. Arri *ITA*
110-metres hurdles
E. Thomson *CAN*
(14.8 sec)
H. Barron *USA*
F. Murray *USA*
400-metres hurdles
F. Loomis *USA*
(54.0 sec)
J. Norton *USA*
A. Desch *USA*
3000-metres
steeplechase
P. Hodge *GBR*
(10 min 00.4 sec)
P. Flynn *USA*
E. Ambrosini *ITA*
Cross-country
(8,000-metres)
P. Nurmi *FIN*
(27 min 15.00 sec)
E. Backman *SWE*
H. Liimatainen *FIN*
Team
FIN GBR SWE
3,000-metres walk
U. Frigerio *ITA*
(13 min 14.2 sec)
G. Parker *AUS*
R. F. Remer *USA*
10,000-metres walk
U. Frigerio *ITA*
(48 min 06.2 sec)
J. Pearman *USA*
C. Gunn *GBR*
4 x 100-metres relay
USA FRA SWE
(42.2 sec)
4 x 400-metres relay
GBR SAF FRA
(3 min 22.2 sec)
High jump
R. Landon *USA*
(1.94 m)
H. Muller *USA*
B. Ekelund *SWE*
Long jump
W. Pettersson *SWE*
(7.15 m)
C. Johnson *USA*
E. Abrahamsson *SWE*

Triple jump
V. Tuulos *FIN*
(14.50 m)
F. Jansson *SWE*
E. Almloef *SWE*
Pole vault
F. Foss *USA*
(4.09 m)
H. Petersen *DEN*
E. Myers *USA*
Shot
Y. Porhola *FIN*
(14.81 m)
E. Niklander *FIN*
H. Liversedge *USA*
Discus
E. Niklander *FIN*
(44.69 m)
A. Taipale *FIN*
A. Pope *USA*
Hammer
P. Ryan *USA*
(52.88 m)
C. J. Lind *SWE*
B. Bennett *USA*
Javelin
J. Myyra *FIN*
(65.78 m)
U. Peltonen *FIN*
P. Johansson *FIN*
56-lb weight
P. MacDonald *USA*
(11.26 m)
P. Ryan *USA*
C. J. Lind *SWE*
Pentathlon
E. Lehtonen *FIN*
(18 pts)
E. Bradley *USA*
H. Lahtinen *FIN*
Decathlon
H. Lovland *NOR*
(6,803.355 pts)
B. Hamilton *USA*
B. Ohlson *SWE*
Tug-of-war
GBR HOL BEL

ARCHERY

Fixed bird (small)
E. van Moer *BEL*
(11 pts)
L. van der Perck *BEL*
J. Hermans *BEL*
Fixed bird (large)
E. Clostens *BEL*
(13 pts)
L. van der Perck *BEL*
F. Flamand *BEL*
Moving bird (28 m)
H. van Innis *BEL*
(144 pts)
L. C. Quentin *FRA*
Team
HOL BEL FRA
Moving bird (33 m)
H. van Innis *BEL*
(139 pts)
J. L. Brulé *FRA*
Team
BEL FRA
Moving bird (50 m)
J. L. Brulé *FRA*
(134 pts)
H. van Innis *BEL*
Team
BEL FRA
60 and 50-yard,
women
Q. Newall *GBR*
(132 pts)

BOXING

Flyweight
F. de Genaro *USA*
A. Petersen *DEN*
W. Cuthbertson *GBR*
Bantamweight
C. Walker *SAF*
C. J. Graham *CAN*
J. McKenzie *GBR*
Featherweight
P. Fritsch *FRA*
J. Gachet *FRA*
E. Garzena *ITA*
Lightweight
S. Mosbert *USA*
G. Johanssen *DEN*
C. Newton *CAN*
Welterweight
J. Schneider *CAN*
A. Ireland *GBR*
F. Colberg *USA*
Middleweight
H. Mallin *GBR*
G. A. Prud'homme *CAN*
M. H. Herscovitch *CAN*
Light-heavyweight
E. Eagam *USA*
S. Sorsdal *NOR*
H. Franks *GBR*
Heavyweight
R. Rawson *GBR*
S. Petersen *DEN*
X. Eluère *FRA*

CYCLING

1,000-metres sprint
M. Peeters *HOL*
(1 min 38.3 sec)
H. T. Johnson *GBR*
H. Ryan *GBR*
4,000-metres pursuit
Team
ITA GBR SAF
(5 min 20.0 sec)
2,000-metres tandem
GBR SAF HOL
(2 min 49.4 sec)
Track (50 km)
H. George *BEL*
(1 hr 16 min 43.5 sec)
C. A. Alden *GBR*
P. Ikelaar *HOL*
Road race (175 km)
H. Stenqvist *SWE*
(4 hr 40 min 01.8 sec)
H. J. Kaltenbrun *SAF*
F. Canteloube *FRA*
Team
FRA SWE BEL
(19 hr 16 min 43.2 sec)

EQUESTRIAN

Show jumping
T. Lequio *ITA*
(2 flts)
A. Valerio *ITA*
G. Lewenhaupt *SWE*
Team
SWE BEL ITA
Dressage
J. Lundblad *SWE*
(27.937 pts)
B. Sandstroem *SWE*
H. von Rosen *SWE*
Three-day Event
H. Moerner *SWE*
(1,775 pts)
A. Lundstroem *SWE*
E. Caffaratti *ITA*
Team
SWE ITA BEL

FENCING

Foil
N. Nadi *ITA*
(10 wins)
P. Cattiau *FRA*
R. Ducret *FRA*
Team
ITA FRA USA
Epée
A. Massard *FRA*
(9 wins)
A. Lippmann *FRA*
E. Olivier *FRA*
Team
ITA BEL FRA
Sabre
N. Nadi *ITA*
(11 wins)
A. Nadi *ITA*
A. E. W. de Jong *HOL*
Team
ITA FRA HOL

FIGURE SKATING

Men
G. Grafstroem *SWE*
(2,838.50 pts)
W. Boeckl *AUT*
G. Gautschi *SUI*
Women
M. Julin-Mauroy *SWE*
(913.50 pts)
S. Noren *SWE*
T. Weld *USA*
Pairs
L. Jakobsson &
W. Jakobsson *FIN*
(80.75 pts)
A. Bryn &
Y. Bryn *NOR*
P. W. Johnson &
B. Williams *GBR*

GYMNASTICS

Combined exercises
G. Zampori *ITA*
(88.35 pts)
M. Torrès *FRA*
J. Gounot *FRA*
Team
ITA BEL FRA
Combined exercises
Swedish system
SWE DEN BEL
Free exercises
DEN NOR

HOCKEY (FIELD)

ENG DEN BEL

ICE HOCKEY

CAN USA TCH

LAWN TENNIS

Men's singles
L. Raymond *SAF*
I. Kumagae *JPN*
C. L. Winslow *SAF*
Women's singles
S. Lenglen *FRA*
E. D. Holman *GBR*
K. McKane *GBR*
Men's doubles
O. G. Turnbull &
M. Woosnam *GBR*
I. Kumagae &
S. Kashio *JPN*

M. Decugis &
P. Albarran *FRA*
Women's doubles
J. McNair &
K. McKane *GBR*
G. Beamish &
E. D. Holman *GBR*
S. Lenglen &
E. d'Ayen *FRA*
Mixed doubles
M. Decugis &
S. Lenglen *FRA*
K. McKane &
M. Woosnam *GBR*
M. Skrbkova &
L. Zemla *TCH*

MODERN PENTATHLON

G. Dyrssen *SWE*
(18 pts)
E. de Laval *SWE*
G. Runoe *SWE*

POLO

GBR ESP USA

ROWING

Single sculls
J. B. Kelly *USA*
(7 min 35.0 sec)
J. Beresford *GBR*
C. H. d'Arcy *NZL*
Double sculls
USA ITA FRA
(7 min 09.0 sec)
Coxed pairs
ITA FRA SUI
(7 min 56 sec)
Coxed fours
SUI USA NOR
(6 min 54.0 sec)
Eights
USA GBR NOR
(6 min 02.6 sec)

RUGBY

USA FRA

SHOOTING

Free pistol
C. Frederick *USA*
(496 pts)
A. da Costa *BRA*
A. Lane *USA*
Team
USA SWE BRA
Rapid-fire pistol (30 m)
G. Paraense *BRA*
(274 pts)
R. Bracken *USA*
F. Zulauf *SUI*
Team
USA GRE SWE
Running deer, single
shot
O. M. Olsen *NOR*
(43 pts)
A. Swahn *SWE*
H. Natvig *NOR*
Team
NOR FIN USA
Running deer, double
shot
O. Lilloe-Olsen *NOR*
(82 pts)
F. Landelius *SWE*
E. Liberg *NOR*

Team
NOR SWE FIN
Military rifle, two positions
M. Fisher *USA*
(997 pts)
N. H. D. Larsen *DEN*
O. Ostensen *NOR*
Team
USA NOR SUI
Military rifle, standing
C. Osburn *USA*
(36 pts)
L. J. Madsen *DEN*
L. Nuesslein *USA*
Team
DEN USA SWE
Military rifle, prone (300 m)
O. Olsen *NOR*
(60 pts)
L. Johnson *FRA*
F. Kuchen *SUI*
Team
USA FRA FIN
Military rifle, prone (300 and 600 m)
Team
USA NOR SWE
Military rifle, prone (600 m)
C. H. Johansson *SWE*
(58 pts)
M. Eriksson *SWE*
L. Spooner *USA*
Team
USA SAF SWE
Small-bore rifle
L. A. Nuesslein *USA*
(391 pts)
A. Rothrock *USA*
D. Fenton *USA*
Team
USA SWE NOR
Trap shooting
M. Arie *USA*
(95 pts)
F. Troeh *USA*
F. Wright *USA*
Team
USA BEL SWE

SOCCER

BEL ESP HOL

SWIMMING

Men
100-metres freestyle
D. P. Kahanamoko *USA*
(1 min 01.4 sec)
P. K. Kealoha *USA*
W. Harris *USA*
400-metres freestyle
N. Ross *USA*
(5 min 26.8 sec)
L. Langer *USA*
G. Vernot *CAN*
1,500-metres freestyle
N. Ross *USA*
(22 min 23.2 sec)
G. Vernot *CAN*
F. Beaurepaire *AUS*
100-metres backstroke
W. P. Kealoha *USA*
(1 min 15.2 sec)
R. Kegeris *USA*
G. Blitz *BEL*

200-metres breaststroke
H. Malmroth *SWE*
(3 min 04.4 sec)
T. Henning *SWE*
A. Aaltonen *FIN*
400-metres breaststroke
H. Malmroth *SWE*
(6 min 31.8 sec)
T. Henning *SWE*
A. Aaltonen *FIN*
4 x 200-metres freestyle relay
USA AUS GBR
(10 min 04.4 sec)
Highboard diving: fancy
C. Pinkston *USA*
(100.67 pts)
E. Adlerz *SWE*
H. Prieste *USA*
Highboard diving: plain
A. Wallman *SWE*
(183.5 pts)
N. Skoglund *SWE*
J. Jansson *SWE*
Springboard diving
L. Kuehn *USA*
(675.40 pts)
C. Pinkston *USA*
L. Balbach *USA*
Water polo
GBR BEL SWE
Women
100-metres freestyle
E. Bleibtrey *USA*
(1 min 13.6 sec)
I. Guest *USA*
F. Schroth *USA*
300-metres freestyle
E. Bleibtrey *USA*
(4 min 34.0 sec)
M. Woodbridge *USA*
F. Schroth *USA*
4 x 100-metres freestyle relay
USA GBR SWE
(5 min 11.6 sec)
Highboard diving
S. Fryland-Clausen *DEN*
(34.60 pts)
E. Armstrong *GBR*
E. Ollivier *SWE*
Springboard diving
A. Riggin *USA*
(539.90 pts)
H. Wainwright *USA*
T. Payne *USA*

WEIGHTLIFTING

Featherweight
F. de Haes *BEL*
(220.0 kg)
A. Schmidt *EST*
E. Ritter *SUI*
Lightweight
A. Neuland *EST*
(257.5 kg)
L. Williquet *BEL*
F. Rooms *BEL*
Middleweight
H. Gance *FRA*
(245.0 kg)
P. Bianchi *ITA*
A. Pettersson *SWE*
Light-heavyweight
E. Cadine *FRA*
(290.0 kg)
F. Hunenberger *SUI*
E. Pettersson *SWE*

Heavyweight
F. Bottino *ITA*
(270.0 kg)
J. Alzin *LUX*
L. Bernot *FRA*

WRESTLING: FREESTYLE

Featherweight
C. Ackerley *USA*
S. Gerson *USA*
P. W. Bernard *GBR*
Lightweight
K. Anttila *FIN*
G. Svensson *SWE*
P. Wright *GBR*
Middleweight
E. Leino *FIN*
V. Penttala *FIN*
C. Johnson *USA*
Light-heavyweight
A. Larsson *SWE*
C. Courant *SUL*
W. Maurer *USA*
Heavyweight
R. Roth *SUI*
N. Pendleton *USA*
E. Nilsson *SWE* &
F. Meyer *USA*

WRESTLING: GRECO-ROMAN

Featherweight
O. Friman *FIN*
H. Kahkonen *FIN*
F. Svensson *SWE*
Lightweight
E. Ware *FIN*
T. Tamminen *FIN*
F. Andersen *NOR*
Middleweight
C. Westergren *SWE*
A. Lindfors *FIN*
M. Perttila *FIN*
Light-heavyweight
C. Johansson *SWE*
E. Rosenqvist *FIN*
J. Eriksen *DEN*
Heavyweight
A. Lindfors *FIN*
P. Hansen *DEN*
M. Nieminen *FIN*

YACHTING

12-metres (old type)
NOR
12-metres (new type)
NOR
10-metres (old type)
NOR
10-metres (new type)
NOR
8-metres (old type)
NOR NOR
8-metres (new type)
NOR NOR BEL
7-metres (old type)
GBR
6.5 metres
HOL FRA
6-metres (old type)
BEL NOR NOR
6-metres (new type)
NOR BEL
40-metres²
SWE SWE
30-metres²
SWE
12-ft monotype
HOL HOL
18-ft monotype
HOL GBR

NORDIC SKIING

Cross-country (18 km)
T. Haug *NOR*
(1 hr 14 min 31 sec)
J. Grottumsbraaten *NOR*
T. Niku *FIN*
Cross-country (50 km)
T. Haug *NOR*
(3 hr 44 min 32.0 sec)

T. Stromstad *NOR*
J. Grottumsbraaten *NOR*
Ski jumping
J. T. Thams *NOR*
(18.960 pts)
N. Bonna *NOR*
T. Haug *NOR*
Nordic combined
T. Haug *NOR*
(18,906 pts)
T. Stromstad *NOR*
J. Grottumsbraaten *NOR*

FIGURE SKATING

Men
G. Grafstroem *SWE*
(2,575.25 pts)
W. Boeckl *AUT*
G. Gautschi *SUI*
Women
H. Plank-Szabo *AUT*
(2,094.25 pts)
B. S. Loughran *USA*
E. Muckelt *GBR*
Pairs
H. Engelmann &
A. Berger *AUT*
(74.50 pts)
L. Jakobsson &
W. Jakobsson *FIN*
A. Joly &
P. Brunet *FRA*

SPEED SKATING

500 metres
C. Jewtraw *USA*
(44.0 sec)
O. Olsen *NOR*
R. M. Larsen *NOR* &
C. Thunberg *FIN*
1,500 metres
C. Thunberg *FIN*
(2 min 20.8 sec)
R. M. Larsen *NOR*
S. O. Moen *NOR*
5,000 metres
C. Thunberg *FIN*
(8 min 39.0 sec)
J. Skutnabb *FIN*
R. M. Larsen *NOR*
10,000 metres
J. Skutnabb *FIN*
(18 min 04.8 sec)

C. Thunberg *FIN*
R. M. Larsen *NOR*
Combined
C. Thunberg *FIN*
R. Larsen *NOR*
J. Skutnabb *FIN*

BOBSLEIGHING

Four-man bob
SUI II GBR II BEL I
(5 min 45.54 sec)

ICE HOCKEY

CAN USA GBR

ATHLETICS

100 metres
H. Abrahams *GBR*
(10.6 sec)

J. Scholz *USA*
A. Porritt *NZL*
200 metres
J. Scholz *USA*
(21.6 sec)
C. Paddock *USA*
E. Liddell *GBR*
400 metres
E. Liddell *GBR*
(47.6 sec)

H. Fitch *USA*
G. Butler *GBR*
800 metres
D. Lowe *GBR*
(1 min 52.4 sec)
P. Martin *SUI*
S. Enck *USA*
1,500 metres
P. Nurmi *FIN*
(3 min 53.6 sec)
W. Schaerer *SUI*
H. Stallard *GBR*
5,000 metres
P. Nurmi *FIN*
(14 min 31.2 sec)

V. Ritola *FIN*
E. Wide *SWE*
10,000 metres
V. Ritola *FIN*
(30 min 23.2 sec)
E. Wide *SWE*
E. Berg *FIN*
Marathon
A. Stenroos *FIN*
(2 hr 41 min 22.6 sec)
R. Bertini *ITA*
C. DeMar *USA*
3,000 metres team
FIN GBR USA
(8 pts)
110-metres hurdles
D. Kinsey *USA*
(15.0 sec)
S. Atkinson *SAF*
S. Pettersson *SWE*
400-metres hurdles
F. M. Taylor *USA*
(52.6 sec)
E. Vilen *FIN*
I. Riley *USA*
3,000-metres steeplechase
V. Ritola *FIN*
(9 min 33.6 sec)

E. Katz *FIN*
P. Bontemps *FRA*
Cross-country (10,650 m)
P. Nurmi *FIN*
(32 min 54.8 sec)
V. Ritola *FIN*
E. Johnson *USA*
Team
FIN USA FRA
(11 pts)
4 x 100-metres relay
USA GBR HOL
(41.0 sec)
4 x 400-metres relay
USA SWE GBR
(3 min 16.0 sec)
10-kilometres walk
U. Frigerio *ITA*
(47 min 49.0 sec)
G. Goodwin *GBR*
C. C. McMaster *SAF*
High jump
H. Osborn *USA*
(1.98 m)
L. Brown *USA*
P. Lewden *FRA*
Long jump
W. D. H. Hubbard *USA*
(7.44 m)
E. Gourdin *USA*
S. Hansen *NOR*
Triple jump
A. Winter *AUS*
(15.52 m)
L. Bruneto *ARG*
V. Tuulos *FIN*

Pole vault
L. Barnes USA
(3.95 m)
G. Graham USA
J. Brooker USA
Shot
C. Houser USA
(14.99 m)
G. Hartranft USA
R. Hills USA
Discus
C. Houser USA
(46.16 m)
V. Niittymaa Fin
T. Lieb USA
Hammer
F. Tootell USA
(53.30 m)
M. McGrath USA
M. Nokes GBR
Javelin
J. Myyra FIN
(62.96 m)
G. Lindstroem SWE
E. Oberst USA
Pentathlon
E. Lehtonen FIN
(14 pts)
E. Somfay HUN
R. Le Gendre USA
Decathlon
H. Osborn USA
(7,710.775 pts)
E. Norton USA
A. Klumberg EST

BOXING
Flyweight
F. LaBarba USA
J. Mackenzie GBR
R. Fee USA
Bantamweight
W. Smith SAF
S. Tripoli USA
J. Ces FRA
Featherweight
J. Fields USA
J. Salas USA
P. Quartucci ARG
Lightweight
H. Nielsen DEN
A. Copello ARG
F. Boylstein USA
Welterweight
J. Delage BEL
H. Mendez ARG
D. Lewis CAN
Middleweight
H. Mallin GBR
J. Elliott GBR
J. Beecken BEL
Light-heavyweight
H. Mitchell GBR
T. Petersen DEN
S. Sorsdal NOR
Heavyweight
O. von Porat NOR
S. Petersen DEN
A. Porzio ARG

CYCLING
1,000-metres sprint
L. Michard FRA
(12.8 sec)
J. Meijer HOL
J. Cugnot FRA
4,000-metres pursuit team
ITA POL BEL
(5 min 15.0 sec)

2,000-metres tandem
FRA DEN HOL
(2 min 40.0 sec)
Track (50 km)
J. Willems HOL
(1 hr 18 min 24.0 sec)
C. A. Alden GBR
F. H. Wyld GBR
Road race (188 km)
A. Blanchonnet FRA
(6 hr 20 min 48.0 sec)
H. Hoeveraers BEL
R. Hamel FRA
Team
FRA BEL SWE
(19 hr 30 min 14.0 sec)

EQUESTRIAN
Show jumping
A. Gemuseus SUI
(6 flts)
T. Lequio ITA
A. Krolikiewicz POL
Team
SWE SUI POR
Dressage
E. Linder SWE
(276.4 pts)
B. Sandstroem SWE
F. X. Lessage FRA
Three-day event
A. C. D. van der Voort van Zijp HOL
(1,976 pts)
F. Kirkebjerg DEN
S. Doak USA
Team
HOL SWE ITA

FENCING
Men
Foil
R. Ducret FRA
(6 wins)
P. Cattiau FRA
M. van Damme BEL
Team
FRA BEL HUN
Epée
C. Delporte BEL
(8 wins)
R. Ducret FRA
N. Hellsten SWE
Team
FRA BEL ITA
Sabre
S. Posta HUN
(5 wins)
R. Ducret FRA
J. Garai HUN
Team
ITA HUN HOL
Women
Foil
E. Osiier DEN
(5 wins)
G. M. Davis GBR
G. Hecksher DEN

GYMNASTICS
Combined exercises
L. Stukelj YUG
(110.340 pts)
R. Prazak TCH
B. Supcik TCH
Team
ITA FRA SUI
Horizontal bar
L. Stukelj YUG
(19.73 pts)
J. Gutweniger SUI
A. Higelin FRA

Parallel bars
A. Guettinger SUI
(21.63 pts)
R. Prazak TCH
G. Zampori ITA
Pommelled horse
J. Wilhelm SUI
(21.23 pts)
J. Gutweniger SUI
A. Rebetez SUI
Long horse (lengthways)
F. Kriz USA
(9.98 pts)
J. Koutny TCH
B. Morkovsky TCH
Long horse (sideways)
A. Seguin FRA
(10 pts)
J. Gonnot FRA
F. Gangloff FRA
Rings
F. Martino ITA
(21.553 pts)
R. Prazak TCH
L. Vacha TCH
Rope climbing
B. Supcik TCH
(7.2 sec)
A. Sequin FRA
A. Guettinger SUI

LAWN TENNIS
Men's singles
V. Richards USA
H. Cochet FRA
U. L. de Morpurgo ITA
Women's singles
H. Wills USA
J. P. Vlasto FRA
K. McKane GBR
Men's doubles
V. Richards &
F. Hunter USA
J. Brugnon &
H. Cochet FRA
R. Borotra &
R. Lacoste FRA
Women's doubles
H. Wills &
H. Wightman USA
E. Covell &
K. McKane GBR
D. C. Shepherd-Barron &
E. L. Colyer GBR
Mixed doubles
R. N. Williams &
H. Wightman USA
M. Jessup &
V. Richards USA
C. Bouman &
H. Timmer HOL

MODERN PENTATHLON
B. Lindman SWE
(18 pts)
G. Dyrssen SWE
B. Uggla SWE

POLO
ARG USA GBR

ROWING
Single sculls
J. Beresford GBR
(7 min 49.2 sec)
W. E. G. Gilmore USA
J. Schneider SUI

Double sculls
USA FRA SUI
(6 min 34.0 sec)
Coxless pairs
HOL FRA
(8 min 19.4 sec)
Coxed pairs
SUI ITA USA
(8 min 39.0 sec)
Coxless fours
GBR CAN SUI
(7 min 08.6 sec)
Coxed fours
SUI FRA USA
(17 min 18.4 sec)
Eights
USA CAN ITA
(6 min 33.4 sec)

RUGBY
USA FRA ROM

SHOOTING
Rapid-fire pistol
H. N. Bailey USA
(18 pts)
V. Carlberg SWE
L. Hannelius FIN
Free rifle
M. Fisher USA
(95 pts)
C. T. Osburn USA
N. H. D. Larsen DEN
Team
USA FRA HAI
Small-bore rifle, prone
P. C. de Lisle FRA
(398 pts)
M. Dinwiddie USA
J. Hartmann SUI
Running deer, single shot
J. Boles USA
(40 pts)
C. W. Mackworth-Praed GBR
O. M. Olsen Nor
Team
NOR SWE USA
Running deer, double shot
O. Lilloe-Olsen NOR
(76 pts)
C. W. Mackworth-Praed GBR
A. Swahn SWE
Team
GBR NOR SWE
Trap shooting
G. Halasy HUN
(98 pts)
K. Huber FIN
F. Hughes USA
Team
USA CAN FIN

SOCCER
URU SUI SWE

SWIMMING
Men
100-metres freestyle
J. Weissmuller USA
(59.0 sec)
D. P. Kahanamoku USA
S. Kahanamoku USA
400-metres freestyle
J. Weissmuller USA
(5 min 04.2 sec)
A. Borg SWE
A. Charlton AUS

1,500-metres freestyle
A. Charlton AUS
(20 min 06.6 sec)
A. Borg SWE
F. Beaurepaire AUS
100-metres backstroke
W. P. Kealoha USA
(1 min 13.2 sec)
P. Wyatt USA
K. Bartha HUN
200-metres breaststroke
R. Skelton USA
(2 min 56.6 sec)
J. de Combe BEL
W. Kirschbaum USA
4 x 200-metres freestyle relay
USA AUS SWE
(9 min 53.4 sec)
Highboard diving (fancy)
A. White USA
(97.46 pts)
D. Fall USA
C. Pinkston USA
Highboard diving (plain)
R. Eve AUS
(160 pts)
J. Jansson SWE
H. Clarke GBR
Springboard diving
A. White USA
(696.40 pts)
P. Desjardins USA
C. Pinkston USA
Water polo
FRA BEL USA
Women
100-metres freestyle
E. Lackie USA
(1 min 12.4 sec)
M. Wehselau USA
G. Ederle USA
400-metres freestyle
M. Norelius USA
(6 min 02.2 sec)
H. Wainwright USA
G. Ederle USA
100-metres backstroke
S. Bauer USA
(1 min 23.2 sec)
P. Harding GBR
A. Riggin USA
200-metres breaststroke
L. Morton GBR
(3 min 33.2 sec)
A. Geraghty USA
G. Carson USA
4 x 100-metres freestyle relay
USA GBR SWE
(4 min 58.8 sec)
Highboard diving
C. Smith USA
(33.20 pts)
E. Becker USA
H. Toepel SWE
Springboard diving
E. Becker USA
(474.50 pts)
A. Riggin USA
C. Fletcher USA

WEIGHTLIFTING
Featherweight
P. Gabetti ITA
(402.5 kg)
A. Stadler AUT
A. Reinmann SUI

Lightweight
E. Decottignies FRA
(440.0 kg)
A. Zwerina AUT
B. Durdis TCH
Middleweight
C. Galimberti ITA
(492.5 kg)
A. Neuland EST
J. Kikas EST
Light-heavyweight
C. Rigoulet FRA
(502.5 kg)
E. Hunenberger SUI
L. Friedrich AUT
Heavyweight
G. Tonani ITA
(517.5 kg)
F. Aigner AUT
H. Tammer EST

WRESTLING: FREESTYLE
Bantamweight
K. Pihlajamaki FIN
K. E. Makinen FIN
B. Hines USA
Featherweight
B. Reed USA
C. Newton USA
K. Naito JPN
Lightweight
R. Vis USA
V. Vikstroem FIN
A. Haavisto FIN
Welterweight
H. Gehri SUI
E. Leino FIN
O. Mueller SUI
Middleweight
F. Hagmann SUI
P. Ollivier BEL
V. K. Pekkala FIN
Light-heavyweight
J. Spellmann USA
R. Svensson SWE
C. Courant SUI
Heavyweight
H. Steele USA
H. Wernli SUI
A. McDonald GBR

WRESTLING: GRECO-ROMAN
Bantamweight
E. Putsep EST
A. Ahlfors FIN
V. Ikonen FIN
Featherweight
K. Antila FIN
A. Toivola FIN
E. Malmberg SWE
Lightweight
O. Friman FIN
L. Keresztes HUN
K. Westerlund FIN
Middleweight
E. Westerlund FIN
A. Lindfors FIN
R. Steinberg EST
Light-heavyweight
C. Westergren SWE
J. R. Svensson SWE
O. Pellinen FIN
Heavyweight
H. Deglane FRA
E. Rosenqvist FIN
R. Bado HUN

YACHTING
8-metre class
NOR GBR FRA

6-metre class
NOR DEN HOL
12-ft monotype
BEL NOR FIN

1928 ST MORITZ

NORDIC SKIING

Cross-country (18 km)
J. Grottumsbraaten *NOR*
(1 hr 37 min 01.0 sec)

O. Hegge *NOR*
R. Odegaard *NOR*
Cross-country (50 km)
P. E. Hedlund *SWE*
(4 hr 52 min 03.0 sec)
G. Jonsson *SWE*
V. Andersson *SWE*
Ski jumping
A. Andersen *NOR*
(19.208 pts)
S. Ruud *NOR*
R. Burkert *TCH*
Nordic combined
J. Grottumsbraaten *NOR*
(17,833 pts)
H. Vingarengen *NOR*
J. Snersrud *NOR*

FIGURE SKATING

Men
G. Grafstroem *SWE*
(2,698.25 pts)
W. Boeckl *AUT*
R. van Zeebroeck *BEL*
Women
S. Henie *NOR*
(2,452.25 pts)
F. Burger *AUT*
B. S. Loughran *USA*
Pairs
A. Joly &
P. Brunet *FRA*
(100.50 pts)
L. Scholz &
O. Kaiser *AUT*
M. Brunner &
L. Wrede *AUT*

SPEED SKATING

500 metres
C. Thunberg *FIN* &
B. Evensen *NOR*
(43.4 sec)
J. O. Farrell *USA* &
R. M. Larsen *NOR* &
J. Friman *FIN*
1,500 metres
C. Thunberg *FIN*
(2 min 21.1 sec)
B. Evensen *NOR*
I. Ballangrud *NOR*
5,000 metres
I. Ballangrud *NOR*
(8 min 50.5 sec)

J. Skutnabb *FIN*
B. Evensen *NOR*
10,000 metres
Null – bad ice

BOBSLEIGHING

Four-man bob
USA II USA I GER I
(3 min 20.50 sec)

SKELETON TOBOGGANING

Jennison Heaton *USA*
(3 min 1.8 sec)
John R. Heaton *USA*
Earl of Northesk *GBR*

ICE HOCKEY

CAN SWE SUI

1928 AMSTERDAM

ATHLETICS

Men
100 metres
P. Williams *CAN*
(10.8 sec)

J. London *GBR*
G. Lammers *GER*
200 metres
P. Williams *CAN*
(21.8 sec)
W. Rangeley *GBR*
H. Koernig *GER*
400 metres
R. Barbuti *USA*
(47.8 sec)
J. Ball *CAN*
J. Buechner *GER*
800 metres
D. Lowe *GBR*
(1 min 51.8 sec)
E. Bylehn *SWE*
H. Engelhardt *GER*
1,500 metres
H. Larva *FIN*
(3 min 53.2 sec)
J. Ladoumègue *FRA*
E. Purje *FIN*
5,000 metres
V. Ritola *FIN*
(14 min 38 sec)
P. Nurmi *FIN*
E. Wide *SWE*
10,000 metres
P. Nurmi *FIN*
(30 min 18.8 sec)
V. Ritola *FIN*
E. Wide *SWE*
Marathon
EL Boughera Ouafi *FRA*
(2 hr 32 min 57.0 sec)

M. Plaza *CHI*
M. Marttelin *FIN*
110-metres hurdles
S. Atkinson *SAF*
(14.8 sec)
S. Anderson *USA*
J. Collier *USA*
400-metres hurdles
Lord Burghley *GBR*
(53.4 sec)
F. Cuhel *USA*
F. M. Taylor *USA*
3,000-metres steeplechase
T. Loukola *FIN*
(9 min 21.8 sec)
P. Nurmi *FIN*
D. Andersen *FIN*
4 x 100-metres relay
USA GER GBR
(41.0 sec)
4 x 400-metres relay
USA GER CAN
(3 min 14.2 sec)
High jump
R. King *USA*
(1.94 m)
B. Hedges *USA*
C. Ménard *FRA*
Long jump
E. Hamm *USA*
(7.73 m)
S. Cator *HAI*
A. Bates *USA*
Triple jump
M. Oda *JPN*
(15.21 m)
L Casey *USA*
V. Tuulos *FIN*
Pole vault
S. Carr *USA*
(4.20 m)
W. Droegemuller *USA*
C. McGinnis *USA*
Shot
J. Kuck *USA*
(15.87 m)
H. Brix *USA*
E. Hirschfeld *GER*
Discus
C. Houser *USA*
(47.32 m)
A. Kivi *FIN*
J. Corson *USA*
Hammer
P. O'Callaghan *IRL*
(51.39 m)
O. Skiold *SWE*
E. Black *USA*
Javelin
E. Lundkvist *SWE*
(66.60 m)
B. Szepes *HUN*
O. Sunde *NOR*
Decathlon
P. Yrjola *FIN*
(8,053.29 pts)
A. Jarvinen *FIN*
J. K. Doherty *USA*
Women
100 metres
E. Robinson *USA*
(12.2 sec)
F. Rosenfeld *CAN*
E. Smith *CAN*
800 metres
L. Radke *GER*
(2 min 16.8 sec)
K. Hitomi *JPN*
I. Gentzel *SWE*
4 x 100-metres relay
CAN USA GER
(48.4 sec)

High jump
E. Catherwood *CAN*
(1.59 m)
C. Gisolf *HOL*
M. Wiley *USA*
Discus
H. Konopacka *POL*
(39.62 m)
L. Copeland *USA*
R. Svedberg *SWE*

BOXING

Flyweight
A. Kocsis *HUN*
A. Appel *FRA*
C. Cavagnoli *ITA*
Bantamweight
V. Tamagnini *ITA*
J. Daley *USA*
H. Isaacs *SAF*
Featherweight
L. van Klaveren *HOL*
V. Peralta *ARG*
H. Devine *USA*
Lightweight
C. Orlandi *ITA*
S. Halaiko *USA*
G. Berggren *SWE*
Welterweight
E. Morgan *NZL*
R. Landini *ARG*
R. Smillie *CAN*
Middleweight
P. Toscani *ITA*
J. Hermanek *TCH*
L. Steyaert *BEL*
Light-heavyweight
V. Avendano *ARG*
E. Pistulla *GER*
K. L. Miljon *HOL*
Heavyweight
A. R. Jurado *ARG*
N. Ramm *SWE*
M. J. Michaelsen *DEN*

CYCLING

1,000-metres sprint
R. Beaufrand *FRA*
(13.2 sec)
A. Mazairac *HOL*
W. Falck-Hansen *DEN*
1,000-metres time trial
W. Falck-Hansen *DEN*
(1 min 14.4 sec)
G. D. H. Bosch van Drakestein *HOL*
E. Gray *AUS*
4,000-metres team pursuit
ITA HOL GBR
(5 min 01.8 sec)
2,000-metres tandem
HOL GBR GER
(11.8 sec)
Road race
H. Hansen *DEN*
(4 hrs 47 min 18.0 sec)
F. W. Southall *GBR*
G. Carlsson *SWE*
Team
DEN GBR SWE
(15 hr 09 min 14.0 sec)

EQUESTRIAN

Show jumping
F. Ventura *TCH*
P. Bertram de Balanda *FRA*
C. Kuhn *SUI*

Team
ESP POL SWE
Dressage
C. F. von Langen *GER*
(237.42 pts)
P. Marion *FRA*
R. Olson *SWE*
Team
GER SWE HOL
Three-day event
C. F. Pahud de Mortanges *HOL*
(1,969.82 pts)
G. P. de Kruyff *HOL*
B. Neumann *GER*
Team
HOL NOR POL

FENCING

Men
Foil
L. Gaudin *FRA*
(9 wins)
E. Casmir *GER*
G. Gaudini *ITA*
Team
ITA FRA ARG
Epée
L. Gaudin *FRA*
(8 wins)
G. Buchard *FRA*
G. Calnan *USA*
Team
ITA FRA POR
Sabre
O. Tersztyanszky *HUN*
(9 wins)
A. Petschauer *AUT*
B. Bini *Ita*
Team
HUN ITA POL
Women
Foil
H. Mayer *GER*
(7 wins)
M. Freeman *GBR*
O. Oelkers *GER*

GYMNASTICS

Men
Combined exercises
G. Miez *SUI*
(247.500 pts)
H. Haenggi *SUI*
L. Stukelj *YUG*
Team
SUI TCH YUG
Horizontal bar
G. Miez *SUI*
(19.17 pts)
R. Neri *ITA*
E. Mack *SUI*
Parallel bars
L. Vacha *TCH*
(18.83 pts)
J. Primozic *YUG*
H. Haenggi *SUI*
Pommelled horse
H. Haenggi *SUI*
(19.75 pts)
G. Miez *SUI*
H. Savolainen *FIN*
Long horse
E. Mack *SUI*
(9.58 pts)
E. Loeffler *TCH*
S. Derganc *YUG*
Rings
L. Stukelj *YUG*
(19.25 pts)

L. Vacha *TCH*
E. Loeffler *TCH*
Women
Combined exercises
Team
HOL ITA GBR

HOCKEY (FIELD)

IND HOL GER

MODERN PENTATHLON

S. Thofelt *SWE*
(47 pts)
B. Lindmann *SWE*
H. Kahl *GER*

ROWING

Single sculls
H. Pearce *AUS*
(7 min 11.0 sec)
K. Myers *USA*
T. D. Collett *GBR*
Double sculls
USA CAN AUT
(6 min 41.4 sec)
Coxless pairs
GER GBR USA
(7 min 06.4 sec)
Coxed pairs
SUI FRA BEL
(7 min 42.6 sec)
Coxless fours
GBR USA ITA
(6 min 36.0 sec)
Coxed fours
ITA SUI POL
(6 min 47.8 sec)
Eights
USA GBR CAN
(6 min 03.2 sec)

SOCCER

URU ARG ITA

SWIMMING

Men
100-metres freestyle
J. Weissmuller *USA*
(58.6 sec)

I. Barany *HUN*
K. Takaishi *JPN*
400-metres freestyle
A. Zorilla *ARG*
(5 min 01.6 sec)
A. Charlton *AUS*
A. Borg *SWE*
1,500-metres freestyle
A. Borg *SWE*
(19 min 51.8 sec)

A. Charlton *AUS*
C. Crabbe *USA*
100-metres backstroke
G. Kojac *USA*
(1 min 08.2 sec)
W. Laufer *USA*
P. Wyatt *USA*
200-metres breaststroke
Y. Tsuruta *JPN*
(2 min 48.8 sec)
E. Rademacher *GER*
T. Yidifonso *PHI*
4 x 200-metres freestyle relay
USA JPN CAN
(9 min 36.2 sec)
Highboard diving
P. Desjardins *USA*
(98.74 pts)
F. Simaika *EGY*
M. Galitzen *USA*
Springboard diving
P. Desjardins *USA*
(185.04 pts)
M. Galitzen *USA*
F. Simaika *EGY*
Water polo
GER HUN FRA
Women
100-metres freestyle
A. Osipowich *USA*
(1 min 11.0 sec)
E. Garatti *USA*
J. Cooper *GBR*
400-metres freestyle
M. Norelius *USA*
(5 min 42.8 sec)
M. J. Braun *HOL*
J. McKim *USA*
100-metres backstroke
M. J. Braun *HOL*
(1 min 22.0 sec)
E. E. King *GBR*
J. Cooper *GBR*
200-metres breaststroke
H. Schrader *GER*
(3 min 12.6 sec)
M. Baron *HOL*
L. Muehe *GER*
4 x 100-metres freestyle relay
USA GBR SAF
(4 min 47.6 sec)
Highboard diving
E. (Becker) Pinkston *USA*
(31.60 pts)
G. Coleman *USA*
L. Sjoqvist *SWE*
Springboard diving
H. Meany *USA*
(78.62 pts)
D. Poynton *USA*
G. Coleman *USA*

WEIGHTLIFTING

Featherweight
F. Andrysek *AUT*
(287.5 kg)
P. Gabetti *ITA*
H. Woelpert *GER*
Lightweight
K. Helbig *GER* &
H. Haas *AUT*
(322.5 kg)
F. Arnout *FRA*
Middleweight
R. François *FRA*
(335.0 kg)
C. Galimberti *ITA*
A. Scheffer *HOL*

Light-heavyweight
S. Nosseir *EGY*
(365.0 kg)
L. Hostin *FRA*
J. Verheijen *HOL*
Heavyweight
J. Strassberger *GER*
(372.5 kg)
A. Luhaar *EST*
J. Skobla *TCH*

WRESTLING: FREESTYLE

Bantamweight
K. E. Makinen *FIN*
E. Spapen *BEL*
J. Trifunov *CAN*
Featherweight
A. Morrison *USA*
K. Pihajamaki *FIN*
H. Minder *SUI*
Lightweight
O. Kapp *EST*
C. Pàcome *FRA*
E. Leino *FIN*
Welterweight
A. J. Haavisto *FIN*
L. O. Appleton *USA*
M. E. Letchford *CAN*
Middleweight
E. Kyburz *SUI*
D. P. Stockton *CAN*
S. Rabin *GBR*
Light-heavyweight
T. Sjostedt *SWE*
A. Bogli *SUI*
H. Lefebvre *FRA*
Heavyweight
J. Richthoff *SWE*
A. Sihvola *FIN*
E. Dame *FRA*

WRESTLING: GRECO-ROMAN

Bantamweight
K. Leucht *GER*
J. Maudr *TCH*
G. Gozzi *ITA*
Featherweight
W. Vali *EST*
E. Malmberg *SWE*
G. Quaglia *ITA*
Lightweight
L. Keresztes *HUN*
E. Sperling *GER*
E. Westerlund *FIN*
Middleweight
V. Kokkinen *FIN*
L. Papp *HUN*
A. Kuznets *EST*
Light-heavyweight
I. Mustafa *EGY*
A. Rieger *GER*
O. Pellinen *FIN*
Heavyweight
J. R. Svensson *SWE*
H. E. Nystroem *FIN*
G. Gehring *GER*

YACHTING

6-metre class
NOR DEN EST
8-metre class
FRA HOL SWE
12-ft monotype
SWE NOR FIN

NORDIC SKIING

Cross-country (18 km)
S. Utterstroem *SWE*
(1 hr 23 min 07.0 sec)
A. T. Wilkstroem *SWE*
V. Saarinen *FIN*
Cross-country (50 km)
V. Saarinen *FIN*
(4 hr 28 min 00.0 sec)
V. Likkanen *FIN*
A. Rustadstven *NOR*
Ski jumping
B. Ruud *NOR*
(228.1 pts)
H. Beck *NOR*
K' Wahlberg *NOR*
Nordic combination
J. Grottumsbraaten *NOR*
(446.00 pts)
O. Stenen *NOR*
H. Vinjarengen *NOR*

FIGURE SKATING

Men
K. Schaefer *AUT*
(2,602.0 pts)
G. Grafstroem *SWE*
M. Wilson *CAN*
Women
S. Henie *NOR*
(2,302.5 pts)
F. Burger *AUT*
M. Vinson *USA*
Pairs
A. Brunet &
P. Brunet *FRA*
(76.7 pts)
B. Loughran &
S. Badger *USA*
E. Rotter &
L. Szollas *HUN*

SPEED SKATING

500 metres
J. A. Shea *USA*
(43.4 sec)
B. Evensen *NOR*
A. Hurd *CAN*
1,500 metres
J. A. Shea *USA*
(2 min 57.7 sec)
A. Hurd *CAN*
W. F. Logan *CAN*
5,000 metres
I. Jaffee *USA*
(9 min 40.8 sec)
E. S. Murphy *USA*
W. F. Logan *CAN*
10,000 metres
I. Jaffee *USA*
(19 min 13.6 sec)
I. Ballangrud *NOR*
F. Stack *CAN*

BOBSLEIGHING

Two-man
USA I SUI II USA II
(8 min 14.74 sec)
Four-man
USA I USA II GER I
(7 min 53.68 sec)

ICE HOCKEY

CAN USA GER

ATHLETICS

Men
100 metres
E. Tolan *USA*
(10.3 sec)
R. Metcalfe *USA*
A. Jonath *GER*
200 metres
E. Tolan *USA*
(21.2 sec)
G. Simpson *USA*
R. Metcalfe *USA*
400 metres
W. Carr *USA*
(46.2 sec)
B. Eastman *USA*
A. Wilson *CAN*
800 metres
T. A. Hampson *GBR*
(1 min 49.7 sec)
A. Wilson *CAN*
P. Edwards *CAN*
1,500 metres
L. Beccali *ITA*
(3 min 51.2 sec)
J. Cornes *GBR*
P. Edwards *CAN*
5,000 metres
L. Lehtinen *FIN*
(14 min 30.0 sec)
R. Hill *USA*
L. Virtanen *FIN*
10,000 metres
J. Kusocinski *POL*
(30 min 11.4 sec)
V. Iso-Hollo *FIN*
L. Virtanen *FIN*
Marathon
J. Zabala *ARG*
(2 hr 31 min 36.0 sec)
S. Ferris *GBR*
A. Toivonen *FIN*
110-metres hurdles
G. Saling *USA*
(14.6 sec)
P. Beard *USA*
D. Finlay *GBR*
400-metres hurdles
R. Tisdall *IRL*
(51.7 sec)
G. Hardin *USA*
F. M. Taylor *USA*
3,000-metres steeplechase
V. Iso-Hollo *FIN*
(10 min 33.4 sec)
T. Evenson *GBR*
J. McCluskey *USA*
(*extra lap run in error*)
4 x 100-metres relay
USA GER ITA
(40.0 sec)
4 x 400-metres relay
USA GBR CAN
(3 min 08.2 sec)
50-kilometres walk
T. Green *GBR*
(4 hr 50 min 10 sec)
J. Dalinsh *LAT*
U. Frigerio *ITA*
High jump
D. McNaughton *CAN*
(1.97 m)
R. Van Osdel *USA*
S. Toribio *PHI*
Long jump
E. Gordon *USA*
(7.64 m)
C. L. Redd *USA*

C. Nambu *JPN*
Triple jump
C. Nambu *JPN*
(15.72 m)
E. Svensson *SWE*
K. Oshima *JPN*
Pole vault
W. Miller *USA*
(4.32 m)
S. Nishida *JPN*
G. Jefferson *USA*
Shot
L. Sexton *USA*
(16.01 m)
H. Rothert *USA*
F. Douda *TCH*
Discus
J. Anderson *USA*
(49.49 m)
H. J. Laborde *FRA*
P. Winter *FRA*
Hammer
P. O'Callaghan *IRL*
(53.92 m)
V. Porhola *FIN*
P. Zaremba *USA*
Javelin
M. Jarvinen *FIN*
(72.71 m)
M. Sippala *FIN*
E. Penttila *FIN*
Decathlon
J. Bausch *USA*
(8,462.230 pts)
A. Jarvinen *FIN*
W. Eberle *GER*
Women
100 metres
S. Walasiewicz *POL*
(11.9 sec)
H. Strike *CAN*
W. von Bremen *USA*
80-metres hurdles
M. Didrikson *USA*
(11.7 sec)
E. Hall *USA*
M. Clark *SAF*
4 x 100-metres relay
USA CAN GBR
(47.0 sec)
High jump
J. Shiley *USA*
(1.65 m)
M. Didrikson *USA*
E. Dawes *CAN*
Discus
L. Copeland *USA*
(40.58 m)
R. Osburn *USA*
J. Wajsowna *POL*
Javelin
M. Didrikson *USA*
(43.68 m)
E. Braumueller *GER*
T. Fleischer *GER*

BOXING

Flyweight
I. Enekes *HUN*
F. Cabanas *MEX*
L. Salica *USA*
Bantamweight
H. Gwynne *CAN*
H. Ziglarski *GER*
J. Villanueva *PHI*
Featherweight
C. Robledo *ARG*
J. Schleinkofer *GER*
G. Carlsson *SWE*
Lightweight
L. Stevens *SAF*
T. Ahlqvist *SWE*

N. Bor *USA*
Welterweight
E. Flynn *USA*
E. Campe *GER*
B. Ahlberg *FIN*
Middleweight
C. Barth *USA*
A. Azar *ARG*
E. Pierce *SAF*
Light-heavyweight
D. Carstens *SAF*
G. Rossi *ITA*
P. Jorgensen *DEN*
Heavyweight
S. Lovell *ARG*
L. Rovati *ITA*
F. Feary *USA*

CYCLING

1,000-metres sprint
J. van Egmond *HOL*
(12.6 sec)
L. Chaillot *FRA*
B. Pellizzari *ITA*
1,000-metres time trial
E. Gray *AUS*
(1 min 13.0 sec)
J. van Egmond *HOL*
G. Rampelberg *FRA*
4,000-metres team pursuit
ITA FRA GBR
(4 min 53.0 sec)
2,000-metres tandem
FRA GBR DEN
(12.0 sec)
Road race (100 km)
A. Pavesi *ITA*
(2 hr 28 min 05.6 sec)
G. Segato *ITA*
B. Britz *SWE*
Team
ITA DEN SWE
(7 hr 27 min 15.2 sec)

EQUESTRIAN

Show jumping
T. Nishi *JPN*
(8 flts)
H. Chamberlin *USA*
C. von Rosen *SWE*
Team
All teams eliminated
Dressage
F. X. Lesage *FRA*
(343.75 pts)
P. Marion *FRA*
H. Tuttle *USA*
Team
FRA SWE USA
Three-day event
C. F. Pahud de Mortanges *HOL*
(1,813.83 pts)
E. F. Thomson *USA*
C. von Rosen *SWE*
Team
USA HOL

FENCING

Men
Foil
G. Marzi *ITA*
(9 wins)
J. Levis *USA*
G. Gaudini *ITA*
Team
FRA ITA USA
Epée
G. Cornaggia-Medici *ITA*
(8 wins)
G. Buchard *FRA*

G. Calnan USA
Team
FRA ITA USA
Sabre
G. Piller *HUN*
(8 wins)
G. Gaudini *ITA*
E. Kabos *HUN*
Team
HUN ITA POL
Women
Foil
E. Preis *AUT*
(8 wins)
J. H. Guiness *GBR*
E. Bogen *HUN*

GYMNASTICS

Combined exercises
R. Neri *ITA*
(140.625 pts)
I. Pelle *HUN*
H. Savolainen *FIN*
Team
ITA USA FIN
Floor
I. Pelle *HUN*
(9.60 pts)
G. Miez *SUI*
M. Lertora *ITA*
Horizontal bar
D. Bixler *USA*
(18.33 pts)
H. Savolainen *FIN*
E. Terasvirta *FIN*
Parallel bars
R. Neri *ITA*
(18.97 pts)
I. Pelle *HUN*
H. Savolainen *FIN*
Pommelled horse
I. Pelle *HUN*
(19.07 pts)
O. Bonoli *ITA*
F. Haubold *USA*
Long horse
S. Guglielmetti *ITA*
(18.03 pts)
A. Jochim *GER*
E. Carmichael *USA*
Rings
G. Gulack *USA*
(18.97 pts)
W. Denton *USA*
G. Lattuada *ITA*
Rope climbing
R. Bass *USA*
(6.7 sec)
W. Galbraith *USA*
T. Connelly *USA*
Tumbling
R. Wolfe *USA*
(18.90 m)
E. Gross *USA*
W. Herrmann *USA*
Indian club swinging
G. Roth *USA*
(8.97 m)
P. Erenberg *USA*
W. Kuhlmeier *USA*

HOCKEY (FIELD)

IND JPN USA

MODERN PENTATHLON

J. Oxenstierna *SWE*
(32 pts)
B. Lindman *SWE*
R. Mayo *USA*

ROWING

Single sculls
H. Pearce *AUS*
(7 min 44.4 sec)
W. Miller *USA*
G. Douglas *URU*
Double sculls
USA GER CAN
(7 min 17.4 sec)
Coxless pairs
GBR NZL POL
(8 min 00.0 sec)
Coxed pairs
USA POL FRA
(8 min 25.8 sec)
Coxless fours
GBR GER ITA
(6 min 58.2 sec)
Coxed fours
GER ITA POL
(7 min 19.0 sec)
Eights
USA ITA CAN
(6 min 37.6 sec)

SHOOTING

Rapid-fire pistol
R. Morigi *ITA*
(36 pts)
H. Hax *GER*
D. Matteucci *ITA*
Small-bore rifle, prone
B. Ronnmark *SWE*
(294 pts)
G. Huet *MEX*
Y. Hradetzky-Soos *HUN*

SWIMMING

Men
100-metres freestyle
Y. Miyazaki *JPN*
(58.2 sec)
T. Kawaishi *JPN*
A. Schwartz *USA*
400-metres freestyle
C. Crabbe *USA*
(4 min 48.4 sec)
J. Taris *FRA*
T. Oyokota *JPN*
1,500-metres freestyle
K. Kitamura *JPN*
(19 min 12.4 sec)
S. Makino *JPN*
J. Cristy *USA*
100-metres backstroke
M. Kiyokawa *JPN*
(1 min 08.6 sec)
T. Irie *JPN*
K. Kawatsu *JPN*
200-metres breaststroke
Y. Tsuruta *JPN*
(2 min 45.4 sec)
R. Koike *JPN*
T. Yldefonso *PHI*
4 x 200-metres freestyle relay
JPN USA HUN
(8 min 58.4 sec)
Highboard diving
H. Smith *USA*
(124.80 pts)
M. Galitzen *USA*
F. Kurtz *USA*
Springboard diving
M. Galitzen *USA*
(161.38 pts)
H. Smith *USA*
R. Degener *USA*
Water polo
HUN GER USA

Women
100-metres freestyle
H. Madison *USA*
(1 min 06.8 sec)
W. den Ouden *HOL*
E. (Garatti) Saville *USA*
400-metres freestyle
H. Madison *USA*
(5 min 28.5 sec)
L. Kight *USA*
J. Makaal *SAF*
100-metres backstroke
E. Holm *USA*
(1 min 19.4 sec)
P. Mealing *AUS*
V. Davies *GBR*
200-metres breaststroke
C. Dennis *AUS*
(3 min 06.3 sec)
H. Maehata *JPN*
E. Jacobsen *DEN*
4 x 100-metres freestyle relay
USE HOL GBR
(4 min 38.0 sec)
Highboard diving
D. Poynton *USA*
(40.26 pts)

G. Coleman *USA*
L. Sjoqvist *SWE*
Springboard diving
G. Coleman *USA*
(87.52 pts)
K. Rawls *USA*
J. Fauntz *USA*

WEIGHTLIFTING

Featherweight
R. Suvigny *FRA*
(287.5 kg)
H. Woelpert *GER*
A. Terlazzo *USA*
Lightweight
R. Duverger *FRA*
(325.0 kg)
H. Haas *AUT*
G. Pierini *ITA*
Middleweight
R. Ismayr *GER*
(345.0 kg)
G. Calimberti *ITA*
K. Hipfinger *AUT*
Light-heavyweight
L. Hostin *FRA*
(365.0 kg)
S. Olsen *DEN*
H. Duey *USA*
Heavyweight
J. Skobla *TCH*
(380.0 kg)
V. Psenicka *TCH*
J. Strassberger *GER*

WRESTLING: FREESTYLE

Bantamweight
R. Pearce *USA*
O. Zombori *HUN*
A. Jaskari *FIN*
Featherweight
K. Pihlajamaki *FIN*
E. Nemir *USA*
E. Karlsson *SWE*
Lightweight
C. Pacôme *FRA*
K. Karpati *HUN*
G. Klaren *SWE*
Welterweight
J. Van Bebber *USA*
D. MacDonald *CAN*
E. Leino *FIN*
Middleweight
I. Johansson *SWE*
K. Luukko *FIN*
J. Tunyogi *HUN*
Light-heavyweight
P. Mehringer *USA*
T. Sjostedt *SWE*
E. Scarf *AUS*
Heavyweight
J. Richthoff *SWE*
J. Riley *FIN*
N. Hirschl *AUT*

WRESTLING: GRECO-ROMAN

Bantamweight
J. Brendel *GER*
M. Nizzola *ITA*
L. François *FRA*
Featherweight
G. Gozzi *ITA*
W. Ehrl *GER*
L. Koskela *FIN*
Lightweight
E. Malmberg *SWE*
A. Kurland *DEN*
E. Sperling *GER*
Welterweight
I. Johansson *SWE*
V. Kajander *FIN*
E. Gallegati *ITA*
Middleweight
V. Kokkinen *FIN*
L. Papp *HUN*
A. Kuznets *EST*
Light-heavyweight
R. Svensson *SWE*
O. Pellinen *FIN*
M. Gruppioni *ITA*
Heavyweight
C. Westergren *SWE*
J. Urban *TCH*
N. Hirschl *AUT*

YACHTING

Monotype
J. Lebrun *FRA*
A. L. J. Maas *HOL*
S. A. Cansino *ESP*
6-metre class
SWE USA CAN
8-metre class
USA CAN
12-foot monotype
FRA HOL ESP
Star
USA GBR SWE

1936 GARMISCH-PARTENKIRCHEN

NORDIC SKIING

Cross-country (18 km)
E. A. Larsson *SWE*
(1 hr 14 min 38.0 sec)
O. Hagen *NOR*
P. Niemi *FIN*
Cross-country (50 km)
E. Wiklund *SWE*
(3 hr 30 min 11.0 sec)
A. Wikstroem *SWE*
N. J. Englund *SWE*
4 x 10-kilometres relay
FIN NOR SWE
(2 hr 41 min 33.0 sec)
Ski jumping
B. Ruud *NOR*
(232.0 pts)
S. Eriksson *SWE*
R. Andersen *NOR*
Nordic combined
O. Hagen *NOR*
(430.30 pts)
O. Hoffsbakken *NOR*
S. Brodahl *NOR*

ALPINE SKIING

Men's combined
F. Pfnuer *GER*
(99.25 pts)
G. Lantschner *GER*
E. Allais *FRA*
Women's combined
C. Cranz *GER*
(97.06 pts)
K. Grasegger *GER*
L. S. Nilson *NOR*

FIGURE SKATING

Men
K. Schaefer *AUT*
(2,959.0 pts)
E. Baier *GER*
F. Kaspar *AUT*
Women
S. Henie *NOR*
(2,971.4 pts)
C. Colledge *GBR*
V. A. Hulten *SWE*
Pairs
M. Herber &
E. Baier *GER*
I. Pausin &
E. Pausin *AUT*
E. Rotter &
L. Szollas *HUN*

SPEED SKATING

500 metres
I. Ballangrud *NOR*
(43.4 sec)
G. Krog *NOR*
L. Freisinger *USA*
1,500 metres
C. Mathiesen *NOR*
(2 min 19.2 sec)
I. Ballangrud *NOR*
B. Wasenius *FIN*
5,000 metres
I. Ballangrud *NOR*
(8 min 19.6 sec)
B. Wasenius *FIN*
A. Ojala *FIN*
10,000 metres
I. Ballangrud *NOR*
(17 min 24.3 sec)
B. Wasenius *FIN*
M. Stiepel *AUT*

BOBSLEIGHING

Two-man
USA I SUI II USA II
(5 min 29.29 sec)
Four-man
SUI II SUI I GBR I
(5 min 19.85 sec)

ICE HOCKEY

GBR CAN USA

1936 BERLIN

ATHLETICS

Men
100 metres
J. C. Owens *USA*
(10.3 sec)

R. Metcalfe *USA*
M. Osendarp *HOL*
200 metres
J. C. Owens *USA*
(20.7 sec)
M. Robinson *USA*
M. Osendarp *HOL*
400 metres
A. Williams *USA*
(46.5 sec)
A. G. Brown *GBR*
J. LuValle *USA*
800 metres
J. Woodruff *USA*
(1 min 52.9 sec)
M. Lanzi *ITA*
P. Edwards *CAN*
1,500 metres
J. Lovelock *NZL*
(3 min 47.8 sec)

G. Cunningham *USA*
L. Beccali *ITA*
5,000 metres
G. Hoeckert *FIN*
(14 min 22.2 sec)

L. Lehtinen *FIN*
H. Jonsson *SWE*
10,000 metres
I. Salminen *FIN*
(30 min 15.4 sec)
A. Askola *FIN*
V. Iso-Hollo *FIN*
Marathon
K. Son *JPN*
(2 hr 29 min 19.2 sec)
E. Harper *GBR*
S. Nan *JPN*
110-metres hurdles
F. Towns *USA*
(14.2 sec)
D. Finlay *GBR*
F. Pollard *USA*
400-metres hurdles
G. Hardin *USA*
(52.4 sec)
J. Loaring *CAN*
M. White *PHI*
3,000-metres steeplechase
V. Iso-Hollo *FIN*
(9 min 03.8 sec)
K. Tuominen *FIN*
A. Dompert *GER*
4 x 100-metres relay
USA ITA GER
(39.8 sec)
4 x 400-metres relay
GBR USA GER
(3 min 09.0 sec)
50-kilometres walk
H. Whitlock *GBR*
(4 hr 30 min 41.1 sec)

A. Schwab *SUI*
A. Bubenko *LAT*
High jump
C. Johnson *USA*
(2.03 m)
D. Albritton *USA*
D. Thurber *USA*
Long jump
J. C. Owens *USA*
(8.06 m)

L. Long *GER*
N. Tajima *JPN*
Triple jump
N. Tajima *JPN*
(16.00 m)
M. Harada *JPN*
J. P. Metcalfe *AUS*
Pole vault
E. Meadows *USA*
(4.35 m)
S. Nishida *JPN*
S. Oe *JPN*
Shot
H. Woellke *GER*
(16.20 m)
S. Barlund *FIN*
G. Stoeck *GER*
Discus
K. Carpenter *USA*
(50.48 m)

G. Dunn *USA*
G. Oberweger *ITA*
Hammer
K. Hein *GER*
(56.49 m)
E. Blask *GER*
F. Warngard *SWE*
Javelin
G. Stoeck *GER*
(71.84 m)
Y. Nikkanen *FIN*
K. Toivonen *FIN*
Decathlon
G. Morris *USA*
(7,900 pts)
R. Clark *USA*
J. Parker *USA*
Women
100 metres
H. Stephens *USA*
(11.5 sec)
S. Walasiewicz *POL*
K. Krauss *GER*
80-metres hurdles
T. Valla *ITA*
(11.7 sec)
A. Steuer *GER*
E. Taylor *CAN*
4 x 100-metres relay
USA GBR CAN
(46.9 sec)
High jump
I. Csak *HUN*
(1.60 m)
D. Odam *GBR*
E. Kaun *GER*
Discus
G. Mauermayer *GER*
(47.63 m)
J. Wajsowna *POL*
P. Mollenhauer *GER*
Javelin
T. Fleischer *GER*
(45.18 m)
L. Krueger *GER*
M. Kwasniewska *POL*

BASKETBALL

USA CAN MEX

BOXING

Flyweight
W. Kaiser *GER*
G. Matta *ITA*
L. Laurie *USA*
Bantamweight
U. Sergo *ITA*
J. Wilson *USA*
F. Ortiz *MEX*
Featherweight
O. Casanovas *ARG*
C. Catterall *SAF*
J. Miner *GER*
Lightweight
I. Harangi *HUN*
N. Stepulov *EST*
E. Agren *SWE*
Welterweight
S. Suvio *FIN*
M. Murach *GER*
G. Petersen *DEN*
Middleweight
J. Despeaux *FRA*
H. Tiller *NOR*
R. Villareal *ARG*
Light-heavyweight
R. Michelot *FRA*
R. Voigt *GER*
F. Risiglione *ARG*
Heavyweight
H. Runge *GER*
G. Lovell *ARG*
E. Nilsen *NOR*

CANOEING

Canadian singles
F. Amyot *CAN*
(5 min 32.1 sec)
B. Karlik *TCH*
E. Koschik *GER*
Canadian pairs
TCH AUT CAN
(4 min 50.1 sec)
Kayak singles
G. Hradetzky *AUT*
(4 min 22.9 sec)
H. Caemmerer *GER*
J. Kraaier *HOL*
Kayak pairs
AUT GER HOL
(4 min 03.8 sec)
10,000-metres folding kayak singles
G. Hradetzky *AUT*
(50 min 01.2 sec)
F. Eberhardt *FRA*
X. Hoermann *GER*
10,000-metres folding kayak pairs
SWE GER HOL
(45 min 49.8 sec)
10,000-metres kayak singles
E. Krebs *GER*
(46 min 01.7 sec)
F. Landertinger *AUT*
E. Riedel *USA*
10,000-metres kayak pairs
GER AUT SWE
(41 min 45.0 sec)
10,000-metres Canadian pairs
TCH CAN AUT
(50 min 33.8 sec)

CYCLING

1,000-metres sprint
T. Merkens *GER*
(11.8 sec)
A. van Vliet *HOL*
L. Chaillot *FRA*
1,000-metres time trial
A. van Vliet *HOL*
(1 min 12.0 sec)
P. Georget *FRA*
R. Karsch *GER*
4,000-metres team pursuit
FRA ITA GBR
(4 min 45.0 sec)
2,000-metres tandem
GER HOL FRA
(11.8 sec)
Road race (100 km)
R. Charpentier *FRA*
(2 hr 33 min 05.0 sec)
G. Lapébie *FRA*
E. Nievergelt *SUI*
Tcam
FRA SUI BEL
(7 hr 39 min 16.2 sec)

EQUESTRIAN

Show jumping
K. Hasse *GER*
(4 flts)
H. Rang *ROM*
J. von Platthy *HUN*
Team
GER HOL POR
Dressage
H. Pollay *GER*
(1,760.0 pts)
F. Gerhard *GER*
A. Podhajsky *AUT*
Team
GER FRA SWE
Three-day event
L. Stubbendorf *GER*
(37.70 flts)
E. F. Thomson *USA*
H. M. Lunding *DEN*
Team
GER POL GBR

FENCING

Men
Foil
G. Gaudini *ITA*
(7 wins)
E. Gardère *FRA*
G. Bocchino *ITA*
Team
ITA FRA GER
Epée
F. Riccardi *ITA*
(5 wins)
S. Ragno *ITA*
G. Cornaggia-Medici *ITA*
Team
ITA SWE FRA
Sabre
E. Kabos *HUN*
(7 wins)
G. Marzi *ITA*
A. Gerevich *HUN*
Team
HUN ITA GER
Women
Foil
I. Elek *HUN*
(6 wins)
H. Mayer *GER*
E. Preis *AUT*

GYMNASTICS

Men
Combined exercises
A. Schwarzmann *GER*
(133.100 pts)
E. Mack *SUI*
K. Frey *GER*
Team
GER SUI FIN
Floor
G. Miez *SUI*
(18.666 pts)
J. Walter *SUI*
K. Frey *GER* &
E. Mack *SUI*
Horizontal bar
A. Saarvala *FIN*
(19.367 pts)
K. Frey *GER*
A. Schwarzmann *GER*
Parallel bars
K. Frey *GER*
(19.067 pts)
M. Reusch *SUI*
A. Schwarzmann *GER*
Pommelled horse
K. Frey *GER*
(19.333 pts)
E. Mack *SUI*
A. Bachmann *SUI*
Long horse
A. Schwarzmann *GER*
(19.20 pts)
E. Mack *SUI*
M. Volz *GER*
Rings
A. Hudec *TCH*
(19.433 pts)
L. Stukelj *YUG*
M. Volz *GER*
Women
Combined exercises team
GER TCH HUN

HANDBALL (outdoor)

GER AUT SUI

HOCKEY (FIELD)

IND GER HOL

MODERN PENTATHLON

G. Handrick *GER*
(31.5 pts)
C. Leonard *USA*
S. Abba *ITA*

POLO

ARG GBR MEX

ROWING

Single sculls
G. Schaefer *GER*
(8 min 21.5 sec)
J. Hasenoehrl *AUT*
D. Barrow *USA*
Double sculls
GBR GER POL
(8 min 00.0 sec)
Coxless pairs
GER DEN ARG
(8 min 16.1 sec)
Coxed pairs
GER ITA FRA
(8 min 36.9 sec)
Coxless fours
GER GBR SUI
(7 min 01.8 sec)

Coxed fours
GER SUI FRA
(7 min 16.2 sec)
Eights
USA ITA GER
(6 min 25.4 sec)

SHOOTING

Free pistol
T. Ullman *SWE*
(559 pts)
E. Krempel *GER*
C. des Jammonières *FRA*
Rapid-fire pistol
C. van Oyen *GER*
(36 pts)
H. Hax *GER*
T. Ullman *SWE*
Small-bore rifle, prone
W. Rogeberg *NOR*
(300 pts)
R. Berzsenyi *HUN*
W. Karas *POL*

SOCCER

ITA AUT NOR

SWIMMING

Men
100-metres freestyle
F. Czik *HUN*
(57.6 sec)
M. Yusa *JPN*
S. Arai *JPN*
400-metres freestyle
J. Medica *USA*
(4 min 44.5 sec)
S. Uto *JPN*
S. Makino *JPN*
1,500-metres freestyle
N. Terada *JPN*
(19 min 13.7 sec)
J. Medica *USA*
S. Uto *JPN*
100-metres backstroke
A. Kiefer *USA*
(1 min 05.9 sec)
A. Van de Weghe *USA*
M. Kiyokawa *JPN*
200-metres breaststroke
T. Hamuro *JPN*
(2 min 41.5 sec)
E. Sietas *GER*
R. Koike *JPN*
4 x 200-metres freestyle relay
JPN USA HUN
(8 min 51.5 sec)
Highboard diving
M. Wayne *USA*
(113.58 pts)
E. Root *USA*
H. Stork *GER*
Springboard diving
R. Degener *USA*
(163.57 pts)
M. Wayne *USA*
A. Greene *USA*
Water polo
HUN GER BEL
Women
100-metres freestyle
H. Mastenbroek *HOL*
(1 min 05.9 sec)
J. Campbell *ARG*
G. Arendt *GER*
400-metres freestyle
H. Mastenbroek *HOL*
(5 min 26.4 sec)

R. Hveger *DEN*
L. (Kight) Wingard *USA*
100-metres backstroke
D. Senff *HOL*
(1 min 18.9 sec)
H. Mastenbroek *HOL*
A. Bridges *USA*
200-metres breaststroke
H. Maehata *JPN*
(3 min 03.6 sec)
M. Genenger *GER*
I. Sorensen *DEN*
4 x 100-metres freestyle relay
HOL GER USA
(4 min 36.0 sec)
Highboard diving
D. (Poynton) Hill *USA*
(33.93 pts)
V. Dunn *USA*
K. Koehler *GER*
Springboard diving
M. Gestring *USA*
(89.27 pts)
K. Rawls *USA*
D. (Poynton) Hill *USA*

WEIGHTLIFTING

Featherweight
A. Terlazzo *USA*
(312.5 kg)
S. Soliman *EGY*
I. H. Shams *EGY*
Lightweight
A. M. Mesbah *EGY* &
R. Fein *AUT*
(342.5 kg)
K. Jansen *GER*
Middleweight
K. S. el Touni *EGY*
(387.5 kg)
R. Ismayr *GER*
A. Wagner *GER*
Light-heavyweight
L. Hostin *FRA*
(372.5 kg)
E. Deutsch *GER*
I. Wasif *EGY*
Heavyweight
J. Manger *GER*
(410.0 kg)
V. Psenicka *TCH*
A. Luhaaar *EST*

WRESTLING: FREESTYLE

Bantamweight
O. Zombori *HUN*
R. Flood *USA*
J. Herbert *GER*
Featherweight
K. Pihlajamaki *FIN*
F. Millard *USA*
G. Jonsson *SWE*
Lightweight
K. Karpati *HUN*
W. Ehrl *FIN*
H. Pihlajamaki *FIN*
Welterweight
F. Lewis *USA*
T. Andersson *SWE*
J. Schleimer *CAN*
Middleweight
E. Poilvé *FRA*
R. Voliva *USA*
A. Kirecci *TUR*
Light-heavyweight
K. Fridell *SWE*
A. Neo *ESt*
E. Siebert *GER*

Heavyweight
K. Palusalu *EST*
J. Klapuch *TCH*
H. Nystroem *FIN*

WRESTLING: GRECO-ROMAN

Bantamweight
M. Lorincz *HUN*
E. Svensson *SWE*
J. Brendel *GER*
Featherweight
Y. Erkan *TUR*
A. Reini *FIN*
E. Karlsson *SWE*
Lightweight
E. Koskela *FIN*
J. Herda *TCH*
V. Vali *EST*
Welterweight
R. Svedberg *SWE*
F. Schaefer *GER*
E. Virtanen *FIN*
Middleweight
I. Johansson *SWE*
L. Schweikert *GER*
J. Palotas *HUN*
Light-heavyweight
A. Cadier *SWE*
E. Bietags *LIT*
A. Neo *EST*
Heavyweight
K. Palusalu *EST*
J. Nyman *SWE*
K. Hornfischer *GER*

YACHTING

6-metre class
GBR NOR SWE
8-metre class
ITA NOR GER
12-foot monotype
HOL GER GBR
Star
GER SWE HOL
Olympic monotype
D. M. J. Kagchelland *HOL*
W. Krogmann *GER*
P. M. Scott *GBR*

1948 ST. MORITZ

NORDIC SKIING

Cross-country (18 km)
M. Lundstroem *SWE*
(1 hr 13 min 50.0 sec)
N. Ostensson *SWE*
G. Eriksson *SWE*
Cross-country (50 km)
N. Karlsson *SWE*
(3 hr 47 min 48.0 sec)
H. Eriksson *SWE*
B. Vanninen *FIN*
4 x 10-kilometres relay
SWE FIN NOR
(2 hr 32 min 08.0 sec)
Ski jumping
P. Hugsted *NOR*
(228.1 pts)
B. Ruud *NOR*
T. Schjelderup *NOR*
Nordic combined
H. Hasu *FIN*
(448.80 pts)
M. Huhtala *FIN*
S. Israelsson *SWE*

ALPINE SKIING

Men
Downhill
H. Oreiller *FRA*
(2 min 55.0 sec)
F. Gabl *AUT*
K. Molitor *SUI* &
R. Olinger *SUI*
Slalom
E. Reinalter *SUI*
(2 min 10.3 sec)
J. Couttet *FRA*
H. Oreiller *FRA*
Combined
H. Oreiller *FRA*
(3.27 pts)
K. Molitor *SUI*
J. Couttet *FRA*
Women
Downhill
H. Schlunegger *SUI*
(2 min 28.3 sec)
T. Beiser *AUT*
R. Hammerer *AUT*
Slalom
G. Fraser *USA*
(1 min 57.2 sec)
A. Meyer *SUI*
E. Mahringer *AUT*
Combined
T. Beiser *AUT*
(6.58 pts)
G. Fraser *USA*
E. Mahringer *AUT*

FIGURE SKATING

Men
R. Button *USA*
(1,720.6 pts)
H. Gerschwiler *SUI*
E. Rada *AUT*
Women
B. A. Scott *CAN*
(1,467.7 pts)
E. Pawlik *AUT*
J. Altwegg *GBR*
Pairs
M. Lannoy &
P. Baugniet *BEL*
A. Kekessy &
E. Kiraly *HUN*
S. Morrow &
W. Diestelmeyer *CAN*

SPEED SKATING

500 metres
F. Helgesen *NOR*
(43.1 sec)
K. Bartholomew *USA* &
T. Byberg *NOR* &
R. Fitzgerald *USA*
1,500 metres
S. Farstad *NOR*
(2 min 17.6 sec)
A. Seyffarth *SWE*
O. Lundberg *NOR*
5,000 metres
R. Liaklev *NOR*
(8 min 29.4 sec)
O. Lundberg *NOR*
G. Hedlund *SWE*
10,000 metres
A. Seyffarth *SWE*
(17 min 26.3 sec)
L. Parkkinen *FIN*
P. Lammio *FIN*

BOBSLEIGHING

Two-man
SUI II SUI I USA II
(5 min 29.20 sec)

Four-man
USA II BEL I USA 1
(5 min 20.10 sec)
SKELETON TOBOGGANING
N. Bibbia *ITA*
(5 min 23.20 sec
John R. Heaton *USA*
J. G. Crammond *GBR*

ICE HOCKEY
CAN TCH SUI

1948 LONDON

ATHLETICS

Men
100 metres
W. H. Dillard *USA*
(10.3 sec)
H. N. Ewell *USA*
L. La Beach *PAN*
200 metres
M. Patton *USA*
(21.1 sec)
H. N. Ewell *USA*
L. La Beach *PAN*
400 metres
A. Wint *JAM*
(46.2 sec)
H. McKenley *JAM*
M. Whitfield *USA*
800 metres
M. Whitfield *USA*
(1 min 49.2 sec)

A. Wint *JAM*
M. Hansenne *FRA*
1,500 metres
H. Eriksson *SWE*
(3 min 49.8 sec)
L. Strand *SWE*
W. Slijkhuis *HOL*
5,000 metres
G. Reiff *BEL*
(14 min 17.6 sec)

E. Zatopek *TCH*
W. Slijkhuis *HOL*

10,000 metres
E. Zatopek *TCH*
(29 min 59.6 sec)
A. Mimoun *FRA*
B. Albertsson *SWE*
Marathon
D. Cabrera *ARG*
(2 hr 34 min 51.6 sec)
T. Richards *GBR*
E. Gailly *BEL*
110-metres hurdles
W. Porter *USA*
(13.9 sec)
C. Scott *USA*
C. Dixon *USA*
400-metres hurdles
R. Cochran *USA*
(51.1 sec)
D. White *CEY*
R. Larsson *SWE*
3,000-metres steeplechase
T. Sjostrand *SWE*
(9 min 04.6 sec)

E. Elmsater *SWE*
G. Hagstroem *SWE*
4 x 100-metres relay
USA GBR ITA
(40.6 secs)
4 x 400-metres relay
USA FRA SWE
(3 min 10.4 sec)
10-kilometres walk
J. Mikaelsson *SWE*
(45 min 13.2 sec)
I. Johansson *SWE*
F. Schwab *SUI*
50-kilometres walk
J. Ljunggren *SWE*
(4 hr 41 min 52.0 sec)
G. Godel *SUI*
T. Johnson *GBR*
High jump
J. Winter *AUS*
(1.98 m)
B. Paulsen *NOR*
G. Stanich *USA*
Long jump
W. Steele *USA*
(7.82 m)
T. Bruce *AUS*
H. Douglas *USA*
Triple jump
A. Ahman *SWE*
(15.40 m)
G. Avery *AUS*
R. Sarialp *TUR*
Pole vault
O. G. Smith *USA*
(4.30 m)
E. Kataja *FIN*
R. Richards *USA*
Shot
W. Thompson *USA*
(17.12 m)
J. Delaney *USA*

J. Fuchs *USA*
Discus
A. Consolini *ITA*
(52.78 m)
G. Tosi *ITA*
F. Gordien *USA*
Hammer
I. Nemeth *HUN*
(56.07 m)
I. Gubijan *YUG*
R. Bennett *USA*
Javelin
T. Rautavaara *FIN*
(69.77 m)
S. Seymour *USA*
J. Varszegi *HUN*
Decathlon
R. Mathias *USA*
(7.139 pts)
I. Heinrich *FRA*
F. Simmons *USA*
Women
100 metres
F. Blankers-Koen *HOL*
(11.9 sec)
D. Manley *GBR*
S. Strickland *AUS*
200 metres
F. Blankers-Koen *HOL*
(24.4 sec)
A. Williamson *GBR*
A. Patterson *USA*
80-metres hurdles
F. Blankers-Koen *HOL*
(11.2 sec)

M. Gardner *GBR*
S. Strickland *AUS*
4 x 100-metres relay
HOL AUS CAN
(47.5 sec)
High jump
A. Coachman *USA*
(1.68 m)
D. (Odam) Tyler *GBR*
M. Ostermeyer *FRA*
Long jump
O. Gyarmati *HUN*
(5.70 m)
N. S. de Portela *ARG*
A. B. Leyman *SWE*
Shot
M. Ostermeyer *FRA*
(13.75 m)
A. Piccinini *ITA*
I. Schaeffer *AUT*
Discus
M. Ostermeyer *FRA*
(41.92 m)
E. Gentile Cordiale *ITA*
J. Mazeas *FRA*
Javelin
H. Bauma *AUT*
(45.57 m)
K. Parvianen *FIN*
L. Carlstedt *DEN*

BASKETBALL

USA FRA BRA

BOXING

Flyweight
P. Perez *ARG*
S. Bandinelli *ITA*
S. A. Han *KOR*
Bantamweight
T. Csik *HUN*
G. Zuddas *ITA*
J. Venegas *PUR*
Featherweight
E. Formenti *ITA*
D. Shepherd *SAF*
A. Antkiewicz *POL*
Lightweight
G. Dreyer *SAF*
J. Vissers *BEL*
S. Wad *DEN*
Welterweight
J. Torma *TCH*
H. Herring *USA*
A. d'Ottavio *ITA*
Middleweight
L. Papp *HUN*
J. Wright *GBR*
I. Fontana *ITA*
Light-heavyweight
G. Hunter *SAF*
D. Scott *GBR*
M. Cia *ARG*
Heavyweight
R. Iglesias *ARG*
G. Nilsson *SWE*
J. Arthur *SAF*

CANOEING

Men
Canadian singles
J. Holecek *TCH*
(5 min 42.0 sec)
D. Bennett *CAN*
R. Boutigny *FRA*
Canadian pairs
TCH USA FRA
(5 min 07.1 sec)
Kayak singles
G. Fredriksson *SWE*
(4 min 33.2 sec)
J. F. Kobberup Andersen *DEN*
H. Eberhardt *FRA*
Kayak pairs
SWE DEN FIN
(4 min 07.3 sec)
10,000-metres
Canadian singles
F. Capek *TCH*
(1 hr 2 min 5.2 sec)
F. Havens *USA*
N. Lane *CAN*
10,000-metres
Canadian pairs
USA TCH FRA
(55 min 55.4 sec)
10,000-metres kayak singles
G. Fredriksson *SWE*
(50 min 47.7 sec)
K. Wires *FIN*
E. Skabo *NOR*
10,000-metres kayak pairs
SWE NOR FIN
(46 min 9.4 sec)
Women
Kayak singles
K. Hoff *DEN*
(2 min 31.9 sec)

A. van der Anker-Doedans *HOL*
F. Schwingl *AUT*

CYCLING

1,000-metres sprint
M. Ghella *ITA*
(12.0 sec)
R. Harris *GBR*
A. Schandorff *DEN*
1,000-metres time trial
J. Dupont *FRA*
(1 min 13.5 sec)
P. Nihant *BEL*
T. Godwin *GBR*
4,000-metres team pursuit
FRA ITA GBR
(4 min 57.8 sec)
2,000-metres tandem
ITA GBR FRA
(11.3 sec)
Road race (199.6-km)
J. Beyaert *FRA*
(5 hr 18 min 12.6 sec)
G. P. Voorting *HOL*
L. Wouters *BEL*
Team
BEL GBR FRA

EQUESTRIAN

Show jumping
H. Mariles-Cortes *MEX*
(6.25 flts)
R. Uriza *MEX*
J. F. d'Orgeix *FRA*
Team
MEX ESP GBR
Dressage
H. Moser *SUI*
(492.5 pts)
A. Jousseaume *FRA*
G. A. Boltenstern *SWE*
Team
FRA USA POR
Three-day event
B. Chevalier *FRA*
(I 4 pts)
F. Henry *USA*
R. Selfelt *SWE*
Team
USA SWE MEX

FENCING

Men
Foil
J. Buhan *FRA*
(7 wins)
C. d'Oriola *FRA*
L. Maszlay *HUN*
Team
FRA ITA BEL
Epée
L. Cantone *ITA*
(7 wins)
O. Zappelli *SUI*
E. Mangiarotti *ITA*
Team
FRA ITA SWE
Sabre
A. Gerevich *HUN*
(7 wins)
V. Pinton *ITA*
P. Kovacs *HUN*
Team
HUN ITA USA
Women
Foil
I. Elek *HUN*
(6 wins)

K. Lachmann *DEN*
E. Mueller-Preis *AUT*

GYMNASTICS

Men
Combined exercises
V. Huhtanen *FIN*
(229.7 pts)
W. Lehmann *SUI*
P. Aaltonen *FIN*
Team
FIN SUI HUN
Floor
F. Pataki *HUN*
(38.70 pts)
J. Mogyorosi-Klencs *HUN*
Z. Ruzicka *TCH*
Horizontal bar
J. Stalder *SUI*
(39.7 pts)
W. Lehmann *SUI*
V. Huhtanen *FIN*
Parallel bars
M. Reusch *SUI*
(39.50 pts)
V. Huhtanen *FIN*
C. Kipfer *SUI* &
J. Stalder *SUI*
Pommelled horse
P. Aaltonen *FIN* &
V. Huhtanen *FIN* &
H. Savolainen *FIN*
(38.7 pts)
L. Zanetti *ITA*
G. Vigone *ITA*
Long horse
P. Aaltonen *FIN*
(39.1 pts)
O. Rove *FIN*
J. Mogyorosi-Klencs *HUN* &
F. Pataki *HUN* &
L. Sotornik *TCH*
Rings
K. Frei *SUI*
M. Reusch *SUI*
Y. Ruzicka *TCH*
Women
Combined exercises team
TCH HUN USA

HOCKEY (FIELD)

IND GBR HOL

MODERN PENTATHLON

W. Grut *SWE*
(16 pts)
G. Moore *USA*
G. Gardin *SWE*

ROWING

Single sculls
M. Wood *AUS*
(7 min 24.4 sec)
E. Risso *URU*
R. Catasta *ITA*
Double sculls
GBR DEN URU
(6 min 51.3 sec)
Coxless pairs
GBR SUI ITA
(7 min 21.1 sec)
Coxed pairs
DEN ITA HUN
(8 min 05.0 sec)

Coxless fours
ITA DEN USA
(6 min 39.0 sec)
Coxed fours
USA SUI DEN
(6 min 50.3 sec)
Eights
USA GBR NOR
(5 min 56.7 sec)

SHOOTING

Free pistol
E. Vasquez Cam *PER*
(545 pts)
R. Schnyder *SUI*
T. Ullman *SWE*
Rapid-fire pistol
K. Takacs *HUN*
(580 pts)
C. E. Diaz Saenz Valiente *ARG*
S. Lundqvist *SWE*
Free rifle
E. Grunig *SUI*
(1,120 pts)
P. Janhonen *FIN*
W. Rogeberg *NOR*
Small-bore rifle, prone
A. Cook *USA*
(599 pts)
W. Tomsen *USA*
I. Jonsson *SWE*

SOCCER

SWE YUG DEN

SWIMMING

Men
100-metres freestyle
W. Ris *USA*
(57.3 sec)
A. Ford *USA*
G. Kadas *HUN*
400-metres freestyle
W. Smith *USA*
(4 min 41.0 sec)
J. McLane *USA*
J. Marshall *AUS*
1,500-metres freestyle
J. McLane *USA*
(19 min 18.5 sec)
J. Marshall *AUS*
G. Mitro *HUN*
100-metres backstroke
A. Stack *USA*
(1 min 06.4 sec)
R. Cowell *USA*
G. Vallerey *FRA*
200-metres breaststroke
J. Verdeur *USA*
(2 min 39.3 sec)
K. Carter *USA*
R. Sohl
4 x 200-metres freestyle relay
USA HUN FRA
(8 min 46.0 sec)
Highboard diving
S. Lee *USA*
(130.05 pts)
B. Harlan *USA*
J. Capilla Perez *MEX*
Springboard diving
B. Harlan *USA*
(163.64 pts)
M. Anderson *USA*
S. Lee *USA*
Water polo
ITA HUN HOL

Women
100-metres freestyle
G. Andersen *DEN*
(1 min 06.3 sec)
A. Curtis *USA*
M. L. Vaessen *HOL*
400-metres freestyle
A. Curtis *USA*
(5 min 17.8 sec)
K. M. Harup *DEN*
C. Gibson *GBR*
100-metres backstroke
K. M. Harup *DEN*
(1 min 14.4 sec)
S. Zimmerman *USA*
J. J. Davis *AUS*
200-metres breaststroke
P. van Vliet *HOL*
(2 min 57.2 sec)
B. Lyons *AUS*
E. Novak *HUN*
4 x 100-metres relay
USA DEN HOL
(4 min 29.2 sec)
Highboard diving
V. Draves *USA*
(68.87 pts)
P. Elsener *USA*
B. Christoffersen *DEN*
Springboard diving
V. Draves *USA*
(108.74 pts)
Y. A. Olsen *USA*
P. Elsener *USA*

WEIGHTLIFTING

Bantamweight
J. De Pietro *USA*
(307.5 kg)
J. Creus *GBR*
R. Tom *USA*
Featherweight
M. Fayad *EGY*
(332.5 kg)
R. Wilkes *TRI*
J. Salmassi *IRN*
Lightweight
I. H. Shams *EGY*
(360.0 kg)
A. Hamouda *EGY*
J. Halliday *GBR*
Middleweight
F. Spellman *USA*
(390.0 kg)
P. George *USA*
S. J. Kim *KOR*
Light-heavyweight
S. Stanczyk *USA*
(417.5 kg)
H. Sakata *USA*
G. Magnusson *SWE*
Heavyweight
J. Davis *USA*
(452.5 kg)
N. Schemansky *USA*
A. Charité *HOL*

WRESTLING: FREESTYLE

Flyweight
L. Viitala *FIN*
H. Balamir *TUR*
T. Johansson *SWE*
Bantamweight
N. Akkar *TUN*
G. Leeman *USA*
C. Kouyos *FRA*
Featherweight
G. Bilge *TUR*
I. Sjolin *SWE*
A. Mueller *SUI*

Lightweight
C. Atik *TUR*
G. Frandfors *SWE*
H. Baumann *SUI*
Welterweight
Y. Dogu *TUR*
R. Garrard *AUS*
L. Merrill *USA*
Middleweight
G. Brand *USA*
A. Candemir *TUR*
E. Linden *SWE*
Light-heavyweight
H. Wittenberg *USA*
F. Stoeckli *SUI*
B. Fahlkvist *SWE*
Heavyweight
G. Bobis *HUN*
B. Antonsson *SWE*
J. Armstrong *AUS*

WRESTLING: GRECO-ROMAN

Flyweight
P. Lombardi *ITA*
K. Olcay *TUR*
R. Kangasmaki *FIN*
Bantamweight
K. Pettersen *SWE*
A. M. Hassan *EGY*
H. Kaya *TUR*
Featherweight
M. Oktav *TUR*
O. Anderberg *SWE*
F. Toth *HUN*
Lightweight
G. Freij *SWE*
A. Eriksen *NOR*
K. Ferencz *HUN*
Welterweight
G. Andersson *SWE*
M. Szilvasi *HUN*
H. Hansen *DEN*
Middleweight
A. Groenberg *SWE*
M. Tayfur *TUR*
E. Gallegati *ITA*
Light-heavyweight
K. E. Nilsson *SWE*
K. Groendahl *FIN*
I. Orabi *EGY*
Heavyweight
A. Kirecci *TUR*
T. Nilsson *SWE*
G. Fantoni *ITA*

YACHTING

6-metre class
USA ARG SWE
Dragon
NOR SWE DEN
Star
USA CUB HOL
Swallow
GBR POR USA
Firefly
P. Elvstrom *DEN*
R. Evans *USA*
J. H. de Jong *HOL*

1952 OSLO

NORDIC SKIING

Men
Cross-country (18 km)
H. Brenden *NOR*
(1 hr 1 min 34.0 sec)
T. Makela *FIN*
P. Lonkila *FIN*

Cross-country (50 km)
V. Hakulinen *FIN*
(3 hr 33 min 33.0 sec)
E. Kolehmainen *FIN*
M. Estenstad *NOR*
4 x 10-kilometres relay
FIN NOR SWE
(2 hr 20 min 16 sec)
Ski jumping
A. Bergmann *NOR*
(226.0 pts)
T. Falkanger *NOR*
K. Holmstroem *SWE*
Nordic combined
S. Slattvik *NOR*
(451.621 pts)
H. Hasu *FIN*
S. Stenersen *NOR*
Women
Cross-country (10 km)
L. Wideman *FIN*
(41 min 40.0 sec)
M. Hietamies *FIN*
S. Rantanen *FIN*

ALPINE SKIING

Men
Downhill
Z. Colo *ITA*
(2 min 30.8 sec)
O. Schneider *AUT*
C. Pravda *AUT*
Giant slalom
S. Eriksen *NOR*
(2 min 25.0 sec)
C. Pravda *AUT*
T. Spiess *AUT*
Slalom
O. Schneider *AUT*
(2 min 00.0 sec)
S. Eriksen *NOR*
G. Berge *NOR*
Women
Downhill
T. Jochum-Beiser *AUT*
(1 min 47.1 sec)
A. Buchner *GER*
G. Minuzzo *ITA*
Giant slalom
A. Mead-Lawrence *USA*
(2 min 06.8 sec)
D. Rom *AUT*
A. Buchner *GER*
Slalom
A. Mead-Lawrence *USA*
(2 min 10.6 sec)
O. Reichert *GER*
A. Buchner *GER*

FIGURE SKATING

Men
R. Button *USA*
(1,730.3 pts)
H. Seibt *AUT*
J. Grogan *USA*
Women
J. Altwegg *GBR*
(1,455.8 pts)
T. Albright *USA*
J. du Bief *FRA*
Pairs
R. Falk &
P. Falk *GER*
(102.6 pts)
K. E. Kennedy &
M. Kennedy *USA*
M. Nagy &
L. Nagy *HUN*

SPEED SKATING

500 metres
K. Henry *USA*
(43.2 sec)
D. McDermott *USA*
A. Johansen *NOR* &
G. Audley *CAN*
1,500 metres
H. Andersen *NOR*
(2 min 20.4 sec)
W. van der Voort *HOL*
R. Aas *NOR*
5,000 metres
H. Andersen *NOR*
(8 min 10.6 sec)
K. Broekman *HOL*
S. Haugli *NOR*
10,000 metres
H. Andersen *NOR*
(16 min 45.8 sec)

K. Broekman *HOL*
C. E. Asplund *SWE*

BOBSLEIGHING

Two-man
GER I USA I SUI I
(5 min 24.54 sec)
Four-man
GER I USA I SUI I
(5 min 07.84 sec)

ICE HOCKEY

CAN USA SWE

1952 HELSINKI

ATHLETICS

Men
100 metres
L. Remigino *USA*
(10.4 sec)
H. McKenley *JAM*
E. McDonald Bailey *GBR*
200 metres
A. Stanfield *USA*
(20.7 sec)
W. T. Baker *USA*
J. Gathers *USA*
400 metres
G. Rhoden *JAM*
(45.9 sec)
H. McKenley *JAM*
O. Matson *USA*
800 metres
M. Whitfield *USA*
(1 min 49.2 sec)
A. Wint *JAM*
H. Ulzheimer *GER*
1,500 metres
J. Barthel *LUX*
(3 min 45.1 sec)

R. McMillen *USA*
W. Lueg *GER*
5,000 metres
E. Zatopek *TCH*
(14 min 06.6 sec)
A. Mimoun *FRA*
H. Schade *GER*
10,000 metres
E. Zatopek *TCH*
(29 min 17.0 sec)
A. Mimoun *FRA*
A. Anufriev *URS*
Marathon
E. Zatopek *TCH*
(2 hr 33 min 03.2 sec)
R. Gorno *ARG*
G. Jansson *SWE*
110-metres hurdles
W. H. Dillard *USA*
(13.7 sec)
J. Davis *USA*
A. Barnard *USA*
400-metres hurdles
C. Moore *USA*
(50.8 sec)
Y. Lituyev *URS*
J. Holland *NZL*
3,000-metres steeplechase
H. Ashenfelter *USA*
(8 min 45.4 sec)
V. Kazantsev *USA*
J. Disley *GBR*
4 x 100-metres relay
USA URS HUN
(40.1 sec)
4 x 400-metres relay
JAM USA GER
(3 min 03.9 sec)
10-kilometres walk
J. Mikaelsson *SWE*
(45 min 02.8 sec)
F. Schwab *SUL*
B. Yunk *URS*
50-kilometres walk
G. Dordoni *ITA*
(4 hr 28 min 07.8 sec)
J. Dolezal *TCH*
A. Roka *HUN*
High Jump
W. Davis *USA*
(2.04 m)
K. Wiesner *USA*
J. Telles de Conceiçao *BRA*
Long jump
J. Biffle *USA*
(7.57 m)
M. Gourdine *USA*
O. Foldessy *HUN*
Triple jump
A. F. da Silva *BRA*
(16.22 m)

V. Einarsson *ISL*
V. Kreyer *URS*

Pole vault
R. Richards *USA*
(4.55 m)
D. Laz *USA*
R. Lundberg *SWE*
Shot
P. O'Brien *USA*
(17.41 m)
D. Hooper *USA*
J. Fuchs *USA*
Discus
S. Iness *USA*
(55.03 m)
A. Consolini *ITA*
J. Dillion *USA*
Hammer
J. Csermak *HUN*
(60.34 m)
K. Storch *GER*
I. Nemeth *HUN*
Javelin
C. Young *USA*
(73.78 m)
W. Miller *USA*
T. Hyytiainen *FIN*
Decathlon
R. Mathias *USA*
(7,887 pts)

M. Campbell *USA*
F. Simmons *USA*
Women
100 metres
M. Jackson *AUS*
(11.5 sec)
D. Hasenjager *SAF*
S. Strickland *AUS*
200 metres
M. Jackson *AUS*
(23.7 sec)
B. Brouwer *HOL*
N. Khnykina *URS*
80-metres hurdles
S. Strickland *AUS*
(10.9 sec)
M. Golubnichaya *URS*
M. Sander *GER*
4×100-metres relay
USA GER GBR
(45.9 sec)
High jump
E. Brand *SAF*
(1.67 m)
S. Lerwill *GBR*
A. Chudina *URS*
Long jump
Y. Williams *NZL*
(6.24 m)
A. Chudina *URS*
S. Cawley *GBR*
Shot
G. Zybina *URS*
(15.28 m)
M. Werner *GER*
K. Tochenova *URS*
Discus
N. Romashkova *URS*

(51.42 m)
Y. Bagryantseva *URS*
N. Dumbadze *URS*
Javelin
D. Zatopkova *TCH*
(50.47 m)
A. Chudina *URS*
Y. Gorchakova *URS*

BASKETBALL

USA URS URU

BOXING

Flyweight
N. Brooks *USA*
E. Basel *GER*
A. Bulakov *URS* &
W. Toweel *SAF*
Bantamweight
P. Hamalainen *FIN*
J. McNally *IRL*
G. Garbuzov *URS* &
J. H. Kang *KOR*
Featherweight
J. Zachara *TCH*
S. Caprari *ITA*
L. Leisching *SAF* &
J. Ventaja *FRA*
Lightweight
A. Bolognesi *ITA*
A. Antkiewicz *POL*
G. Fiat *ROM* &
E. Pakkanen *FIN*
Light-welterweight
C. Adkins *USA*
V. Mednov *URS*
E. Mallenius *FIN* &
B. Visintin *ITA*
Welterweight
Z. Chychia *POL*
S. Shcherbakov *URS*
V. Jorgensen *DEN* &
G. Heidemann *GER*
Light-middleweight
L. Papp *HUN*
T. van Schalkwyk *SAF*
B. Tishin *URS* &
E. Herrara *ARG*
Middleweight
F. Patterson *USA*
V. Tita *ROM*
B. Nikolov *BUL* &
K. Sjoelin *SWE*
Light-heavyweight
N. Lee *USA*
A. Pacenza *ARG*
A. Perov *URS* &
H. Siljander *FIN*
Heavyweight
H. E. Sanders *USA*
silver medal not awarded
A. Nieman *SAF* &
I. Koski *FIN*

CANOEING

Men
Canadian singles
J. Holecek *TCH*
(4 min 56.3 sec)
J. Parti *HUN*
O. Ojanpera *FIN*
Canadian pairs
DEN TCH GER
(4 min 38.3 sec)
Kayak singles
G. Fredriksson *SWE*
(4 min 07.9 sec)
T. Stroemberg *FIN*
L. Gantois *FRA*

Kayak pairs
FIN SWE AUT
(3 min 51.1 sec)
10,000-metres Canadian singles
F. Havens *USA*
(57 min 41.1 sec)
G. Novak *HUN*
A. Jindra *TCH*
10,000-metres Canadian pairs
FRA CAN GER
(54 min 08.3 sec)
10,000-metres kayak singles
T. Stroemberg *FIN*
(47 min 22.8 sec)
G. Fredriksson *SWE*
M. Scheuer *GER*
10,000-metres kayak pairs
FIN SWE HUN
(44 min 21.3 sec)
Women
Kayak singles
S. Saimo *FIN*
(2 min 18.4 sec)
G. Liebhart *AUT*
N. Savina *URS*

CYCLING

1,000-metres sprint
E. Sacchi *ITA*
(12.0 sec)
L. Cox *AUS*
W. Potzernheim *GER*
1,000-metres time trial
R. Mockridge *AUS*
(1 min 11.1 sec)
M. Morettini *ITA*
R. Robinson *SAF*
4,000-metres team pursuit
ITA SAF GBR
(4 min 46.1 sec)
2,000-metres tandem
AUS SAF ITA
(11.0 sec)
Road race (190.4 km)
A. Noyelle *BEL*
(5 hr 06 min 03.4 sec)
R. Grondalaers *BEL*
E. Ziegler *GER*
Team
BEL ITA FRA
(15 hr 20 min 46.6 sec)

EQUESTRIAN

Show jumping
P. J. d'Oriola *FRA*
(8 flts)
O. Cristi *CHI*
F. Thiedemann *GER*
Team
GBR CHI GER
Dressage
H. St. Cyr *SWE*
(860 pts)
L. Hartel *DEN*
A. Jousseaume *FRA*
Team
SWE SUI GER
Three-day event
H. von Blixen-Finecke *SWE*
(28.33 flts)
G. Lefrant *FRA*
W. Buesing *GER*
Team
SWE GER USA

FENCING

Men
Foil
C. d'Oriola *FRA*
(8 wins)
E. Mangiarotti *ITA*
M. di Rosa *ITA*
Team
FRA ITA HUN
Epée
E. Mangiarotti *ITA*
(7 wins)
D. Mangiarotti *ITA*
O. Zappeli *SUI*
Team
ITA SWE SUI
Sabre
P. Kovacs *HUN*
(8 wins)
A. Gerevich *HUN*
T. Berczelly *HUN*
Team
HUN ITA FRA
Women
Foil
I. Camber *ITA*
(5 wins)
I. Elek *HUN*
K. Lachmann *DEN*

GYMNASTICS

Men
Combined exercises
V. Chukarin *URS*
(115.70 pts)
G. Shaginyan *URS*
J. Stalder *SUI*
Team
URS SUI FIN
Floor
W. Thoresson *SWE*
(19.25 pts)
I. Uesako *JPN* &
J. Jokiel *POL*
Horizontal bar
J. Guenthard *SUI*
(19.55 pts)
J. Stalder *SUI* &
A. Schwarzmann *GER*
Parallel bars
H. Eugster *SUI*
(19.65 pts)
V. Chukarin *URS*
J. Stalder *SUI*
Pommelled horse
V. Chukarin *URS*
(19.50 pts)
Y. Korolkov *URS* &
G. Shaginyan *URS*
Long horse
V. Chukarin *URS*
(19.20 pts)
M. Takemoto *JPN* &
T. Uesako *JPN* &
T. Ono *JPN*
Rings
G. Shaginyan *URS*
(19.75 pts)
V. Chukarin *URS*
D. Leonkin *URS* &
H. Eugster *SUI*
Women
Combined exercises
M. Gorokhovskaya *URS*
(76.78 pts)
N. Bocharova *URs*
M. Korondi *HUN*
Team
URS HUN TCH

Team exercises
(with portable
apparatus)
SWE URS HUN
Floor
A. Keleti *HUN*
(19.36 pts)
M. Gorokhovskaya *URS*
M. Korondi *HUN*
Beam
N. Bocharova *URs*
M. Gorokhovskaya *URS*
M. Korondi *HUN*
Asymmetrical bars
M. Korondi *HUN*
(19.40 pts)
M. Gorokhovskaya *URS*
A. Keleti *HUN*
Horse
Y. Kalinchuk *URS*
(19.20 pts)
M. Gorokhovskaya *URS*
G. Minaicheva *URS*

HOCKEY (FIELD)

IND HOL GBR

MODERN PENTATHLON

L. Hall *SWE*
(32 pts)
G. Benedek *HUN*
I. Szondi *HUN*
Team
HUN SWE FIN

ROWING

Single sculls
Y. Tyukalov *URS*
(8 min 12.8 sec)
M. Wood *AUS*
I. Kocerka *POL*
Double sculls
ARG URS URU
(7 min 32.2 sec)
Coxless pairs
USA BEL SUI
(8 min 20.7 sec)
Coxed pairs
FRA GER DEN
(8 min 28.6 sec)
Coxless fours
YUG FRA FIN
(7 min 16.0 sec)
Coxed fours
TCH SUI USA
(7 min 33.4 sec)
Eights
USA URS AUS
(6 min 25.9 sec)

SHOOTING

Free Pistol
H. Benner *USA*
(553 pts)
A. Leon Gozalo *ESP*
A. Balogh *HUN*
Rapid-fire pistol
K. Takacs *HUN*
(579 pts)
S. Kun *HUN*
G. Lichiardopol *ROM*
Free rifle
A. Bogdanov *URS*
(1,123 pts)
R. Buechler *SUI*
L. Vainshtain *URS*
Small-bore rifle, prone
I. Sarbu *ROM*
(400 pts)
B. Andreev *URS*
A. Jackson *USA*

Small-bore rifle, three positions
E. Kongshaug *NOR*
(1,164 pts)
V. Yloenen *FIN*
B. Andreev *URS*
Trap shooting
G. P. Généreux *CAN*
(192 pts)
K. Holmqvist *SWE*
H. Liljedahl *SWE*
Running deer, single and double shot
J. Larsen *NOR*
(413 pts)
P. O. Skoeldberg *SWE*
T. Maeki *FIN*

SOCCER

HUN YUG SWE

SWIMMING

Men
100-metres freestyle
C. Scholes *USA*
(57.4 sec)
H. Suzuki *JPN*
G. Larsson *SWE*
400-metres freestyle
J. Boiteux *FRA*
(4 min 30.7 sec)
F. Konno *USA*
P. O. Ostrand *SWE*
1,500-metres freestyle
F. Konno *USA*
(18 min 30.3 sec)
S. Hashizume *JPN*
T. Okamoto *BRA*
100-metres backstroke
Y. Oyakawa *JPN*
(1 min 05.4 sec)
G. Buzon *FRA*
J. Taylor *USA*
200-metres breaststroke
J. Davies *AUS*
(2 min 34.4 sec)
B. Stassforth *USA*
H. Klein *GER*
4×200-metres freestyle relay
USA JPN FRA
(8 min 31.1 sec)

HIGHBOARD DIVING

S. Lee *USA*
(156.28 pts)
J. Capilla Perez *MEX*
G. Haase *GER*
Springboard diving
D. Browning *USA*
(205.29 pts)
M. Anderson *USA*
S. Lee *USA*
Water polo
HUN YUG ITA
Women
100-metres freestyle
K. Szoke *HUN*
(1 min 06.8 sec)
J. Termeulen *HOL*
J. Temes *HUN*
400-metres freestyle
V. Gyenge *HUN*
(5 min 12.1 sec)
E. Novak *HUN*
E. Kawamoto *USA*
100-metres backstroke
J. Harrison *SAF*
(1 min 14.3 sec)
G. Wielema *HOL*
J. Stewart *NZL*

200-metres breaststroke
E. Szekely *HUN*
(2 min 51.7 sec)
E. Novak *HUN*
H. Gordon *GBR*
4×100-metres freestyle relay
HUN HOL USA
(4 min 24.4 sec)
Highboard diving
P. McCormick *USA*
(79.37 pts)
P. J. Myers *USA*
J. Irwin *USA*
Springboard diving
P. McCormick *USA*
(147.30 pts)
M. Moreau *FRA*
Z. A. (Olsen) Jensen *USA*

WEIGHTLIFTING

Bantamweight
I. Udodov *URS*
(315.0 kg)
M. Namdjou *IRN*
A. Mirzai *IRN*
Featherweight
R. Chimishkian *URS*
(337.5 kg)
N. Saksonov *URS*
R. Wilkes *TRI*
Lightweight
T. Kono *USA*
(362.5 kg)
Y. Lopatin *URS*
V. Barberis *AUT*
Middleweight
P. George *USA*
(400.0 kg)
G. Gratton *CAN*
S. J. Kim *KOR*
Light-heavyweight
T. Lomakhin *URS*
(417.5 kg)
S. Stanczyk *USA*
A. Vorobev *URS*
Middle-heavyweight
N. Schemansky *USA*
(445.0 kg)
G. Novak *URS*
L. Kilgour *TRI*
Heavyweight
J. Davis *USA*
(460.0 kg)
J. Bradford *USA*
H. Selvetti *ARG*

WRESTLING: FREESTYLE

Flyweight
H. Gemici *TUR*
Y. Kitano *JPN*
M. Mollaghassemi *IRN*
Bantamweight
S. Ishii *JPN*
R. Marmedbekov *URS*
K. S. Jadav *IND*
Featherweight
B. Sit *TUR*
N. Guivehtchi *IRN*
J. Henson *USA*
Lightweight
O. Anderberg *SWE*
J. T. Evans *USA*
D. Tovfighe *IRN*
Welterweight
W. Smith *USA*
P. Berlin *SWE*
A. Modjtabavi *IRN*
Middleweight
D. Tsimakuridze *URS*
G. R. Takhti *IRN*

G. Gurics *HUN*
Light heavyweight
V. Palm *SWE*
H. Wittenberg *USA*
A. Atan *TUR*
Heavyweight
A. Mekokishvili *URS*
B. Antonsson *SWE*
K. Richmond *GBR*

WRESTLING: GRECO-ROMAN

Flyweight
B. Gurevich *URS*
I. Fabra *ITA*
L. Honkala *FIN*
Bantamweight
I. Hodes *HUN*
Z. Khihab *LIB*
A. Terian *URS*
Featherweight
Y. Punkin *URS*
I. Polyak *HUN*
A. Rashed *EGY*
Lightweight
S. Safin *URS*
G. Freij *SWE*
M. Athanasov *TCH*
Welterweight
M. Szilvasi *HUN*
G. Andersson *SWE*
K. Taha *LIB*
Middleweight
A. Groenberg *SWE*
K. Rauhala *FIN*
N. Belov *URS*
Light-heavyweight
K. Groendahl *FIN*
S. Shikhladze *URS*
K. E. Nilsson *SWE*
Heavyweight
Y. Kotkas *URS*
J. Ruzicka *TCH*
T. Kovanen *FIN*

YACHTING

5.5-metre class
USA NOR SWE
6-metre class
USA NOR FIN
Dragon
NOR SWE GER
Star
ITA USA POR
Finn
P. Elvstrom *DEN*
(8,209 pts)
C. Currey *GBR*
R. Sarby *SWE*

1956 CORTINA

NORDIC SKIING

Men
Cross-country (15 km)
H. Brenden *NOR*
(49 min 39.0 sec)
S. Jernberg *SWE*
P. Kolchin *URS*
Cross-country (30 km)
V. Hakulinen *FIN*
(1 hr 44 min 06.0 sec)
S. Jernberg *SWE*
P. Kolchin *URS*
Cross-country (50 km)
S. Jernberg *SWE*
(2 hr 50 min 27.0 sec)
V. Hakulinen *FIN*
F. Terentyev *URS*

4 x 10-kilometres relay
URS FIN SWE
(2 hr 15 min 30.0 sec)
Ski jumping
A. Hyvarinen *FIN*
(227.0 pts)
A. Kallakorpi *FIN*
H. Glass *GER*
Nordic combined
S. Stenersen *NOR*
(455.0 pts)
B. Eriksson *SWE*
F. Gron-Gasienica *POL*
Women
Cross-country (10 km)
L. Kozyreva *URS*
(38 min 11.0 sec)
R. Yeroshina *URS*
S. Edstroem *SWE*
3 x 5-kilometres relay
FIN URS SWE
(1 hr 09 min 01.0 sec)

ALPINE SKIING

Men
Downhill
A. Sailer *AUT*
(2 min 52.2 sec)

R. Fellay *SUI*
A. Molterer *AUT*
Giant Slalom
A. Sailer *AUT*
(3 min 00.1 sec)
A. Molterer *AUT*
W. Schuster *AUT*
Slalom
A. Sailer *AUT*
(3 min 14.7 sec)
C. Igaya *JPN*
S. Sollander *SWE*
Women
Downhill
M. Berthod *SUI*
(1 min 40.7 sec)
F. Daenzer *SUI*
L. Wheeler *CAN*
Giant slalom
O. Reichert *GER*
(1 min 56.5 sec)
J. Frandl *AUT*
D. Hochleitner *AUT*
Slalom
R. Colliard *SUI*
(1 min 52.3 sec)
R. Schoepf *AUT*
Y. Sidorova *URS*

FIGURE SKATING

Men
H. A. Jenkins *USA*
(1,497.75 pts)
R. Robertson *USA*
D. Jenkins *USA*

Women
T. Albright USA
(1,866.39 pts)
C. Heiss USA
I. Wendl AUT
Pairs
E. Schwarz &
K. Oppelt AUT
F. Dafoe &
N. Bowden CAN
M. Nagy &
L. Nagy HUN

SPEED SKATING

500 metres
Y. Grischin URS
(40.2 sec)
R. Grach URS
A. Gjestvang NOR
1,500 metres
Y. Grischin URS &
J. Mikailov URS
T. Salonen FIN
5,000 metres
B. Schilkov URS
(7 min 48.7 sec)
S. Ericsson SWE
O. Goncharenko URS
10,000 metres
S. Ericsson SWE
(16 min 35.9 sec)
K. Johannesen NOR
O. Goncharenko URS

BOBSLEIGHING

Two-man
ITA I ITA II SUI I
(5 min 30.14 sec)
Four-man
SUI I ITA II USA I
(5 min 10.44 sec)

ICE HOCKEY

URS USA CAN

1956 MELBOURNE

ATHLETICS

Men
100 metres
B. Morrow USA
(10.5 sec)
W. T. Baker USA
H. Hogan AUS
200 metres
B. Morrow USA
(20.6 sec)
A. Stanfield USA
W. T. Baker USA
400 metres
C. Jenkins USA
(46.7 sec)
K. F. Haas GER
V. Hellsten FIN &
A. Ignatiev URS
800 metres
T. Courtney USA
(1 min 47.7 sec)
D. Johnson GBR
A. Boysen NOR
1,500 metres
R. Delany IRL
(3 min 41.2 sec)
K. Richtzenhain GER
J. Landy AUS
5,000 metres
V. Kuts URS
(13 min 39.6 sec)
G. Pirie GBR
D. Ibbotson GBR

10,000 metres
V. Kuts URS
(28 min 45.6 sec)

J. Kovacs HUN
A. Lawrence AUS
Marathon
A. Mimoun FRA
(2 hr 25 min 00.0 sec)
F. Mihalic YUG
V. Karvonen FIN
110-metres hurdles
L. Calhoun USA
(13.5 sec)
J. Davis USA
A. Barnard USA
400-metres hurdles
G. Davis USA
(50.1 sec)
E. Southern USA
J. Culbreath USA
3,000-metres steeplechase
C. Brasher GBR
(8 min 41.2 sec)

S. Rozsnyoi HUN
E. Larsen NOR
4 x 100-metres relay
USA URS GER
(39.5 sec)
4 x 400-metres relay
USA AUS GBR
(3 min 04.8 sec)
20-kilometres walk
L. Spirin URS
(1 hr 31 min 27.4 sec)
A. Mikenas URS
B. Yunk URS
50-kilometres walk
N. Read NZL
(4 hr 30 min 42.8 sec)
Y. Maskinskov URS
J. Ljunggren SWE
High jump
C. Dumas USA
(2.12 m)
C. Porter AUS
I. Kashkarov USA
Long jump
G. Bell USA   (7.83 m)

J. Bennett USA
J. Valkama FIN
Triple jump
A. F. da Silva BRA
(16.35 m)
V. Einarsson ISL
V. Kreyer URS
Pole vault
R. Richards USA
(4.56 m)
R. Gotowski USA
G. Roubanis GRE
Shot
P. O'Brien USA
(18.57 m)
W. Nieder USA
J. Skobla TCH
Discus
A. Oerter USA
(56.36 m)
F. Gordien USA
D. Koch USA
Hammer
H. Connolly USA
(63.19 m)

M. Krivonosov URS
A. Samotsvetov URS
Javelin
E. Danielsen NOR
(85.71 m)
J. Sidlo POL
V. Tsibulenko URS
Decathlon
M. Campbell USA
(7,937 pts)
R. Johnson USA
V. Kuznetsov URS
Women
100 metres
B. Cuthbert AUS
(11.5 sec)
C. Stubnick GER
M. Mathews AUS
200 metres
B. Cuthbert AUS
(23.4 sec)
C. Stubnick GER
M. Mathews AUS
80-metres hurdles
S. (Strickland) de la Hunty AUS
(10.7 sec)
G. Koehler GER
N. Thrower AUS
4 x 100-metres relay
AUS GBR USA
(44.5 sec)
High jump
M. McDaniel USA
(1.76 m)
T. Hopkins GBR &
M. Pisaryera URS
Long jump
E. Krzesinska POL
(6.35 m)
W. White USA

N. (Khnykina) Dvalishvili URS
Shot
T. Tyshkyevich URS
(16.59 m)
G. Zybina URS
M. Werner GER
Discus
O. Fikotova TCH
(53.69 m)
I. Beglyakova URS
N. (Romashkova) Ponomaryeva URS
Javelin
I. Jaunzeme URS
(53.86 m)
M. Ahrens CHI
N. Konyaeva URS

BASKETBALL

USA URS URU

BOXING

Flyweight
T. Spinks GBR
M. Dobrescu ROM
J. Caldwell IRL &
R. Libeer FRA
Bantamweight
W. Behrendt GER
S. C. Song KOR
F. Gilroy IRL &
C. Barrientos CHI
Featherweight
V. Safronov URS
T. Nicholls GBR
H. Niedzwiedzki POL &
P. Hamalainen FIN
Lightweight
R. McTaggart GBR
H. Kurschat GER
A. Byrne IRL &
A. Lagetko URS
Light-welterweight
V. Yengibaryan URS
F. Nenci ITA
H. Loubscher SAF &
C. Dumitrescu ROM
Welterweight
N. Linca ROM
F. Tiedt IRL
K. Hogarth AUS &
N. Gargano GBR
Light-middleweight
L. Papp HUN
J. Torres USA
J. McCormack GBR &
Y. Pietrzykowski POL
Middleweight
G. Shatkov URS
R. Tapia CHI
G. Chapron FRA &
V. Zalazar ARG
Light-heavyweight
J. F. Boyd USA
G. Negrea ROM
C. Lucas CHI &
R. Murauskas URS
Heavyweight
T. P. Rademacher USA
L. Mukhin URS
D. Bekker SAF &
G. Bozzano ITA

CANOEING

Men
Canadian singles
L. Rotman ROM
(5 min 05.3 sec)
I. Hernek HUN
G. Bukharin URS

Canadian pairs
ROM URS HUN
(4 min 47.4 sec)
Kayak singles
G. Fredriksson SWE
(4 min 12.8 sec)
I. Pisarev URS
L. Kiss HUN
Kayak pairs
GER URS AUT
(3 min 49.6 sec)
10,000-metres
Canadian singles
L. Rotman ROM
(56 min 41.0 sec)
J. Parti HUN
G. Bukharin URS
10,000-metres
Canadian pairs
URS FRA HUN
(54 min 02.4 sec)
10,000-metres kayak singles
G. Fredriksson SWE
(47 min 43.4 sec)
F. Hatlaczky HUN
M. Scheuer GER
10,000-metres kayak pairs
HUN GER AUS
(43 min 37.0 sec)
Women
Kayak singles
E. Dementieva URS
(2 min 18.9 sec)
T. Zenz GER
T. Soby DEN

CYCLING

1,000-metres sprint
M. Rousseau FRA
(11.4 sec)
G. Pesenti ITA
R. Ploog AUS
1,000-metres time trial
L. Faggin ITA
(1 min 09.8 sec)
L. Fovcek TCH
A. Swift SAF
4,000-metres team pursuit
ITA FRA GBR
(4 min 37.4 sec)
2,000-metres tandem
AUS TCH ITA
(10.8 sec)
Road race (187.7 km)
E. Baldini ITA
(5 hr 21 min 17.0 sec)
A. Geyre FRA
A. Jackson GBR
Team
FRA GBR GER
(16 hr 10 min 36 sec)

EQUESTRIAN

Show jumping
H. G. Winkler GER
(4 flts)
R. d'Inzeo ITA
P. d'Inzeo ITA
Team
GER ITA GBR
Dressage
H. St. Cyr SWE
(860 pts)
L. Hartel DEN
L. Linsenhoff GER
Team
SWE GER SUI

Three-day event
P. Kastenman SWE
(66.53 flts)
A. Luetke-Westhues GER
F. Weldon GBR
Team
GBR GER CAN

FENCING

Men
Foil
C. d'Oriola FRA
(6 wins)
G. Bergamini ITA
A. Spallino ITA
Team
ITA FRA HUN
Epée
C. Pavesi ITA
(5 wins)
G. Delfino ITA
E. Mangiarotti ITA
Team
ITA HUN FRA
Sabre
R. Karpati HUN
(6 wins)
J. Pawlowski POL
L. Kuznetsov URS
Team
HUN POL URS
Women
Foil
G. Sheen GBR
(6 wins)

O. Orban ROM
R. Garilhe FRA

GYMNASTICS

Men
Combined exercises
V. Chukarin URS
(114.25 pts)
T. Ono JPN
Y. Titov URS
Team
URS JPN FIN
Floor
V. Muratov URS
(19.20 pts)
N. Aihara JPN &
W. Thoresson SWE &
V. Chukarin URS
Horizontal bar
T. Ono JPN
(19.60 pts)
Y. Titov URS
M. Takemoto JPN
Parallel bars
V. Chukarin URS
(19.20 pts)
M. Kubota JPN
T. Ono JPN &
Pommelled horse
B. Shakhlin URS
(19.25 pts)

T. Ono *JPN*
V. Chukarin *URS*
Long horse
H. Bantz *GER* &
V. Muratov *URS*
(18.85 pts)
Y. Titov *URS*
Rings
A. Azarian *URS*
(19.35 pts)
V. Muratov *URS*
M. Takemoto *JPN* &
M. Kubota *JPN*
Women
Combined exercises
L. Latynina *URS*
(74.933 pts)
A. Keleti *HUN*
S. Muratova *URS*
Team
URS HUN ROM
Team exercises
(with portable apparatus)
HUN SWE POL
Beam
A. Keleti *HUN*
(18.800 pts)
E. Bosakova *TCH* &
T. Manina *URS*
Asymmetrical bars
A. Keleti *HUN*
(18.966 pts)
L. Latynina *URS*
S. Muratova *URS*
Horse
L. Latynina *URS*
(18.833 pts)
T. Manina *URS*
A. S. Colling *SWE* &
O. Tass *HUN*
Floor
L. Latynina *URS* &
A. Keleti *HUN*
(18.733 pts)
E. Leustean *ROM*
Portable apparatus team event
URS

HOCKEY (FIELD)

IND PAK GER

MODERN PENTATHLON

L. Hall *SWE*
(4,833 pts)
O. Mannonen *FIN*
V. Korhonen *FIN*
Team
URS USA FIN

ROWING

Single sculls
V. Ivanov *URS*
(8 min 02.5 sec)
S. Mackenzie *AUS*
J. Kelly *USA*
Double sculls
URS USA AUS
(7 min 24.0 sec)
Coxless pairs
USA URS AUT
(7 min 55.4 sec)
Coxed pairs
USA GER URS
(8 min 26.1 sec)
Coxless fours
CAN USA FRA
(7 min 08.8 sec)

Coxed fours
ITA SWE FIN
(7 min 19.4 sec)
Eights
USA CAN AUS
(6 min 35.2 sec)

SHOOTING

Free pistol
P. Linnosvuo *FIN*
(556 pts)
M. Umarov *URS*
O. Pinnion *USA*
Rapid-fire pistol
S. Petrescu *ROM*
(587 pts)
Y. Cherkassov *URS*
G. Lichiardopol *ROM*
Free rifle
V. Borisov *URS*
(1,138 pts)
A. Erdman *URS*
V. Ylonen *FIN*
Small-bore rifle, prone
G. R. Ouellette *CAN*
(600 pts)
V. Borisov *URS*
G. S. Boa *CAN*
Small-bore rifle, three positions
A. Bogdanov *USA*
(1,172 pts)
O. Horinek *TCH*
N. J. Sundberg *SWE*
Trap shooting
G. Rossini *ITA*
(195 pts)
A. Smelczynski *POL*
A. Ciceri *ITA*
Running deer, single and double shot
V. Romanenko *URS*
P. O. Skoeldberg *SWE*
V. Sevryugin *URS*

SOCCER

URS YUG BEL

SWIMMING

Men
100-metres freestyle
J. Henricks *AUS*
(55.4 sec)
J. Devitt *AUS*
G. Chapman *AUS*
400-metres freestyle
M. Rose *AUS*
(4 min 27.3 sec)
T. Yamanaka *JPN*
G. Breen *USA*
1,500-metres freestyle
M. Rose *AUS*
(17 min 58.9 sec)
T. Yamanaka *JPN*
G. Breen *USA*
100-metres backstroke
D. Theile *AUS*
(1 min 02.2 sec)
J. Monckton *AUS*
F. McKinney *USA*
200-metres breaststroke
M. Furukawa *JPN*
(2 min 34.7 sec)
M. Yoshimura *JPN*
K. Yunichev *URS*
200-metres butterfly
W. Yorzyk *USA*
(2 min 19.3 sec)
T. Ishimoto *JPN*
G. Tumpek *HUN*

4 x 200-metres freestyle relay
AUS USA URS
(8 min 23.6 sec)
Highboard diving
J. Capilla Perez *MEX*
(152.44 pts)
G. Tobian *USA*
R. Connor *USA*
Springboard diving
R. Clotworthy *USA*
(159.56 pts)
D. Harper *USA*
J. Capilla Perez *MEX*
Water polo
HUN YUG URS
Women
100-metres freestyle
D. Fraser *AUS*
(1 min 02.0 sec)
L. Crapp *AUS*
F. Leech *AUS*
400-metres freestyle
L. Crapp *AUS*
(4 min 54.6 sec)
D. Fraser *AUS*
S. Ruuska *USA*
100-metres backstroke
J. Grinham *GBR*
(1 min 12.9 sec)
C. Cone *USA*
M. Edwards *GBR*
200-metres breaststroke
U. Happe *GER*
(2 min 53.1 sec)
E. Szekely *HUN*
E. M. Ten Elsen *GER*
100-metres butterfly
S. Mann *USA*
(1 min 11.0 sec)
N. Ramey *USA*
M. J. Sears *USA*
4 x 100-metres freestyle relay
AUS USA SAF
(4 min 17.1 sec)
Highboard diving
P. McCormick *USA*
(84.85 pts)
J. Irwin *USA*
P. J. Myers *USA*
Springboard diving
P. McCormick *USA*
(142.36 pts)
J. Stunyo *USA*
I. MacDonald *CAN*

WEIGHTLIFTING

Bantamweight
C. Vinci *USA*
(342.5 kg)
V. Stogov *URS*
M. Namdjou *IRN*
Featherweight
I. Berger *USA*
(352.5 kg)
Y. Minaev *URS*
M. Zielinski *POL*
Lightweight
I. Rybak *URS*
(380.0 kg)
R. Khabutdinov *URS*
C. H. Kim *KOR*
Middleweight
F. Bogdanovski *URS*
(420.0 kg)
P. George *USA*
E. Pignatti *ITA*
Light-heavyweight
T. Kono *USA*
(447.5 kg)

V. Stepanov *URS*
J. George *USA*
Middle-heavyweight
A. Vorobev *URS*
(472.5 kg)
D. Sheppard *USA*
J. Debuf *FRA*
Heavyweight
P. Anderson *USA*
(500.0 kg)
H. Selvetti *ARG*
A. Pigaiani *ITA*

WRESTLING: FREESTYLE

Flyweight
M. Tsalkalamanidze *URS*
M. Khojastehpour *IRN*
H. Akbas *TUR*
Bantamweight
M. Dagistanli *TUR*
M. Yaghoubi *IRN*
M. Shakhov *URS*
Featherweight
S. Sasahara *JPN*
J. Mewis *BEL*
E. Penttila *FIN*
Lightweight
E. Habibi *IRN*
S. Kasahara *JPN*
A. Bestaev *URS*
Welterweight
M. Ikeda *JPN*
I. Zengin *TUR*
V. Balavadze *URS*
Middleweight
N. Sranchev *BUL*
D. Hodge *USA*
G. Skhirtladze *URS*
Light-heavyweight
G. R. Takhti *IRN*
B. Kulaev *URS*
P. S. Blair *USA*
Heavyweight
H. Kaplan *TUR*
H. Mekhmedov *BUL*
T. Kangasniemi *FIN*

WRESTLING: GRECO-ROMAN

Flyweight
N. Solovyev *URS*
I. Fabra *ITA*
D. A. Egribas *TUR*
Bantamweight
K. Vyrupaev *URS*
E. Vesterby *SWE*
F. Horvat *ROM*
Featherweight
R. Makinen *FIN*
I. Polyak *HUN*
R. Zhneladze *URS*
Lightweight
K. Lehtonen *FIN*
R. Dogan *TUR*
G. Toth *HUN*
Welterweight
M. Bayrak *TUR*
V. Maneev *URS*
P. Berlin *SWE*
Middleweight
G. Kartozia *URS*
D. Dobrev *BUL*
R. Jansson *SWE*
Light-heavyweight
V. Nikolaev *URS*
P. Sirakov *BUL*
K. E. Nilsson *SWE*
Heavyweight
A. Parfenov *URS*
W. Dietrich *GER*
A. Bulgarelli *ITA*

YACHTING

5.5-metre class
SWE GBR AUS
Dragon
SWE DEN GBR
Star
USA ITA BAH
Finn
P. Elvstrom *DEN*
(7,509 pts)
A. Nelis *BEL*
J. Marvin *USA*
12-metre sharpie
NZL AUS GBR

1960 SQUAW VALLEY

NORDIC SKIING

Men
Cross-country (15 km)
H. Brusveen *NOR*
(51 min 55.5 sec)
S. Jernberg *SWE*
V. Hakulinen *FIN*
Cross-country (30 km)
S. Jernberg *SWE*
(1 hr 51 min 03.9 sec)
R. Ramgard *SWE*
N. Anikin *URS*
Cross-country (50 km)
K. Hamalainen *FIN*
(2 hr 59 min 06.3 sec)
V. Hakulinen *FIN*
R. Ramgard *SUI*
4 x 10-kilometres
FIN NOR URS
(2 hr 18 min 45.6 sec)
Ski jumping
H. Recknagel *GER*
(227.2 pts)
N. Halonen *FIN*
O. Leodolter *AUT*
Nordic combined
G. Thoma *GER*
(457.952 pts)
T. Knutsen *NOR*
N. Gusakov *URS*
Biathlon
K. Lestander *SWE*
(1 hr 33 min 21.6 sec)
A. Tyrvainen *FIN*
A. Privalov *URS*
Women
Cross-country (10 km)
M. Gusakova *URS*
(39 min 46.6 sec)
L. (Kosyreva) Baranova *URS*
R. Yeroshina *URS*
3 x 5-kilometres relay
SWE URS FIN
(1 hr 4 min 21.4 sec)

ALPINE SKIING

Men
Downhill
J. Vuarnet *FRA*
(2 min 06.0 sec)
H. P. Lanig *GER*
G. Perillat *FRA*
Giant slalom
R. Staub *SUI*
(1 min 48.3 sec)
J. Stiegler *AUT*
E. Hinterseer *AUT*
Slalom
E. Hinterseer *AUT*
(2 min 08.9 sec)

M. Leitner *AUT*
C. Bozon *FRA*
Women
Downhill
H. Biebl *GER*
(1 min 37.6 sec)
P. Pitou *USA*
G. Hecher *AUT*
Giant slalom
Y. Ruegg *SUI*
(1 min 39.9 sec)
P. Pitou *USA*
G. Chenal-Minuzzo *ITA*
Slalom
A. Heggtveit *CAN*
(1 min 49.6 sec)
B. Snite *USA*
B. Henneberger *GER*

FIGURE SKATING

Men
D. Jenkins *USA*
(1,440.2 pts)

J. Divin *TCH*
D. Jackson *CAN*
Women
C. Heiss *USA*
(1,490.1 pts)

S. Dijkstra *HOL*
B. Roles *USA*
Pairs
B. Wagner &
R. Paul *CAN*
M. Kilius &
H. J. Bauemler *GER*
N. Ludington &
R. Ludington *USA*
Speed skating
Men
500 metres
Y. Grischin *URS*
(40.2 sec)
W. Disney *USA*
R. Grach *URS*
1,500 metres
R. Aas *NOR* &
Y. Grischin *URS*
(2 min 10.4 sec)

B. Stenin *URS*
5,000 metres
V. Kositschkin *URS*
(7 min 51.3 sec)
K. Johannesen *NOR*
J. Pesman *HOL*
10,000 metres
K. Johannesen *NOR*
(15 min 46.6 sec)
V. Kositschkin *URS*
K. Backman *SWE*
Women
500 metres
H. Haase *GER*
(45.9 sec)
N. Donchenko *URS*
J. Ashworth *USA*
1,000 metres
K. Guseva *URS*
(1 min 34.1 sec)
H. Haase *GER*
T. Rylova *URS*
1,500 metres
L. Skoblikova *URS*
(2 min 25.2 sec)
E. Seroczynska *POL*
H. Pilejczyk *POL*
3,000 metres
L. Skoblikova *URS*
(5 min 14.3 sec)
V. Stenina *URA*
E. Huttunen *FIN*

ICE HOCKEY

USA CAN URS

1960 ROME

Athletics

Men
100 metres
A. Hary *GER*
(10.2 sec)

D. Sime *USA*
P. Radford *GBR*
200 metres
L. Berutti *ITA*
(20.5 sec)
L. Carney *USA*
A. Seye *FRA*
400 metres
O. Davis *USA*
(44.9 sec)
K. Kaufmann *GER*
M. Spence *SAF*
800 metres
P. Snell *NZL*
(1 min 46.3 sec)
R. Moens *BEL*
G. Kerr *JAM*
1,500 metres
H. Elliott *AUS*
(3 min 35.6 sec)

M. Jazy *FRA*
I. Rozsavolgyi *HUN*
5,000 metres
M. Halberg *NZL*
(13 min 43.4 sec)
H. Grodotzki *GER*
K. Zimny *POL*
10,000 metres
P. Bolotnikov *URS*
(28 min 32.2 sec)
H. Grodotzki *GER*
D. Power *AUS*
Marathon
A. Bikila *ETH*
(2 hr 15 min 16.2 sec)

R. Ben Abdesselem *MAR*
B. Magee *NZL*
110-metres hurdles
L. Calhoun *USA*
(13.8 sec)
W. May *USA*
H. Jones *USA*
400-metres hurdles
G. Davis *USA*
(49.3 sec)
C. Cushman *USA*
R. Howard *USA*
3,000-metres steeplechase
Z. Krzyszkowiak *POL*
(8 min 34.2 sec)
N. Sokolov *URS*
S. Rzhishchin *URS*
4 x 100-metres relay
GER URS GBR
(39.5 sec)
4 x 400-metres relay
USA GER ANT
(3 min 02.2 sec)
20-kilometre walk
V. Golubnichiy *URS*
(1 hr 34 min 07.2 sec)
N. Freeman *AUS*
S. Vickers *GBR*
50-kilometres walk
D. Thompson *GBR*
(4 hr 25 min 30.0 sec)
J. Ljunggren *SWE*
A. Pamich *ITA*

High jump
R. Shavlakadze *URS*
(2.16 m)
V. Brumel *URS*
J. Thomas *USA*
Long jump
R. Boston *USA*
(8.12 m)
I. Robertson *USA*
I. Ter-Ovanesyan *URS*
Triple jump
J. Schmidt *POL*
(16.81 m)
V. Goryayev *URS*
V. Kreyer *URS*
Pole vault
D. Bragg *USA*
(4.70 m)
R. Morris *USA*
E. Landstroem *FIN*
Shot
W. Nieder *USA*
(19.68 m)
P. O'Brien *USA*
D. Long *USA*
Discus
A. Oerter *USA*
(59.18 m)
R. Babka *USA*
R. Cochran *USA*
Hammer
V. Rudenkov *URS*
(67.10 m)
G. Zsivotzky *HUN*
T. Rut *POL*
Javelin
V. Tsibulenko *URS*
(84.64 m)
W. Krueger *GER*
G. Kulcsar *HUN*
Decathlon
R. Johnson *USA*
(8,392 pts)
C. K. Yang *ROC*
V. Kuznetsov *URS*
Women
100 metres
W. Rudolph *USA*
(11.0 sec)
D. Hyman *GBR*
G. Leone *ITA*
200 metres
W. Rudolph *USA*
(24.0 sec)
J. Heine *GBR*
D. Hyman *GBR*
800 metres
L. Shevtsova *URS*
(2 min 04.3 sec)
B. Jones *AUS*
U. Donath *GER*
80-metres hurdles
I. Press *URS*
(10.8 sec)
C. Quinton *GBR*
G. (Koehler) Birkemeyer *GER*
4 x 100-metres relay
USA GER POL
(44.5 sec)
High jump
I. Balas *ROM*
(1.85 m)
J. Jozwiakowska *POL* &
D. Shirley *GBR*
Long jump
V. Krepkina *URS*
(6.37 m)
E. Krzesinska *POL*
H. Claus *GER*
Shot
T. Press *URS*
(17.32 m)

J. Luettge *GER*
E. Brown *USA*
Discus
N. Ponomaryeva *URS*
(55.10 m)
T. Press *URS*
L. Manoliu *ROM*
Javelin
E. Ozolina *URS*
(55.98 m)
D. Zatopkova *TCH*
B. Kalediene *URS*

BASKETBALL

USA URS BRA

BOXING

Flyweight
G. Torok *HUN*
S. Sivko *URS*
K. Tanabe *JPN* &
A. Elgvindi *UAR*
Bantamweight
O. Grigoriev *URS*
P. Zamparini *ITA*
O. Taylor *AUS* &
B. Bendig *POL*
Featherweight
F. Musso *ITA*
J. Adamskli *POL*
W. Meyers *SAF* &
J. Limmonen *FIN*
Lightweight
K. Pazdzior *POL*
S. Lopopolo *ITA*
R. McTaggart *GBR* &
A. Laudonio *ARG*
Light-welterweight
B. Nemecek *TCH*
C. Quartey *GHA*
Q. Daniels *USA* &
M. Kasprzyk *POL*
Welterweight
G. Benvenuti *ITA*
Y. Radonyak *URS*
L. Drogosz *POL* &
James Lloyd *GBR*
Light-middleweight
W. McClure *USA*
C. Bossi *ITA*
B. Lagutin *URS* &
W. Fisher *GBR*
Middleweight
E. Crook *USA*
T. Walasek *POL*
I. Monea *ROM* &
Y. Feofanov *URS*
Light-heavyweight
C. Clay *USA*

C. Pietrzykowski *POL*
A. Madigan *AUS* &
G. Saraudi *ITA*

Heavyweight
F. de Piccoli *ITA*
D. Bekker *SAF*
J. Nemec *TCH* &
G. Siegmund *GER*

CANOEING

Men
Canadian singles
J. Parti *HUN*
(4 min 33.93 sec)
A. Silayer *URS*
L. Rotman *ROM*
Canadian pairs
URS ITA HUN
(4 min 17.94 sec)
Kayak singles
E. Hansen *DEN*
(3 min 53.0 sec)
I. Szollosi *HUN*
G. Fredriksson *SWE*
Kayak pairs
SWE HUN POL
(3 min 34.73 sec)
4 × 500-metres kayak singles relay
GER HUN DEN
(7 min 39.43 sec)
Women
Kayak singles
A. Seredina *URS*
(2 min 08.08 sec)
T. Zenz *GER*
D. Pilecka *POL*
Kayak pairs
URS GER HUN
(1 min 54.76 sec)

CYCLING

1,000-metres sprint
S. Gaiardoni *ITA*
(11.1 sec)
L. Sterckz *BEL*
V. Gasparella *ITA*
1,000-metres time trial
S. Gaiardoni *ITA*
(1 min 07.27 sec)
D. Gieseler *GER*
R. Vargashkin *URS*
4,000-metres team pursuit
ITA GER URS
(4 min 30.90 sec)
2,000-metres tandem
ITA GER URS
(10.7 sec)
Road race (175.4 km)
V. Kapitonov *URS*
(4 hr 20 min 37.0 sec)
L. Trapè *ITA*
W. van den Berghen *BEL*
Team
ITA GER URS
(2 hr 14 min 33.53 sec)

EQUESTRIAN

Show jumping
R. d'Inzeo *ITA*
(12 flts)
P. d'Inzeo *ITA*
D. Broome *GBR*
Team
GER USA ITA
Dressage
S. Filatov *URS*
(2,144 pts)

G. Fischer *SUI*
J. Neckermann *GER*
Team *not held*
Three-day event
L. Morgan *AUS*
(+7.15 pts)
N. Lavis *AUS*
A. Buehler *SUI*
Team
AUS SUI FRA

FENCING

Men
Foil
V. Zhadonich *URS*
(7 wins)
Y. Sisikin *URS*
A. Axelrod *USA*
Team
URS ITA GER
Epée
G. Delfino *ITA*
(5 wins)
A. Jay *GBR*
B. Khabarov *URS*
Team
ITA GBR URS
Sabre
R. Karpati *HUN*
(5 wins)

Z. Horvath *HUN*
W. Calarese *ITA*
Team
HUN POL ITA
Women
Foil
H. Schmid *GER*
(6 wins)
V. Rastvorova *URS*
M. Vicol *ROM*
Team
URS HUN ITA

GYMNASTICS

Men
Combined exercises
B. Shakhlin *URS*
(115.95 pts)

T. Ono *JPN*
Y. Titov *URS*
Team
JPN URS ITA
Floor
N. Aihara *JPN*
(19.45 pts)
Y. Titov *URS*
F. Menichelli *ITA*
Horizontal bar
T. Ono *JPN*
(19.60 pts)
M. Takemoto *JPN*
B. Shakhlin *URS*
Parallel bars
B. Shakhlin *URS*
(19.40 pts)
G. Carminucci *ITA*
T. Ono *JPN*
Pommelled horse
E. Ekman *FIN* &
B. Shakhlin *URS*
(19.375 pts)
S. Tsurumi *JPN*
Long horse
T. Ono *JPN* &
B. Shakhlin *URS*
(19.340 pts)
V. Portnoi *URS*
Rings
A. Azarian *URS*
(19.725 pts)
B. Shakhlin *URS*
Y. Kapsazov *BUL* &
T. Ono *JPN*
Women
Combined exercises
L. Latynina *URS*
(77.031 pts)
S. Muratova *URS*
P. Astakhova *URS*
Team
URS TCH ROM
Beam
E. Bosakova *TCH*
(19.283 pts)
L. Latynina *URS*
S. Muratova *URS*
Asymmetrical bars
P. Astakhova *URS*
(19.616 pts)
L. Latynina *URS*
T. Lyukhina *URS*
Horse
M. Nikolaeva *URS*
(19.316 pts)
S. Muratova *URS*
L. Latynina *URS*
Floor
L. Latynina *URA*
(19.583 pts)
P. Astakhova *URS*
T. Lyukhina *URS*

HOCKEY (FIELD)

PAK IND ESP

MODERN PENTATHLON

F. Nemeth *HUN*
(5,024 pts)
I. Nagy *HUN*
R. Beck *USA*
Team
HUN URS USA

ROWING

Single sculls
V. Ivanov *URS*
(7 min 13.96 sec)

A. Hill *GER*
T. Kocerka *POL*
Double sculls
TCH URS SUI
(6 min 47.50 sec)
Coxless pairs
URS AUT FIN
(7 min 02.00 sec)
Coxed pairs
GER URS USA
(7 min 29.14 sec)
Coxless fours
USA ITA URS
(6 min 26.26 sec)
Coxed fours
GER FRA ITA
(6 min 39.12 sec)
Eights
GER CAN TCH
(5 min 57.18 sec)

SHOOTING

Free pistol
A. Gushchin *URS*
(560 pts)
M. Umarov *URS*
Y. Yoshikawa *JPN*
Rapid-fire pistol
W. McMillan *USA*
(587 pts)
P. Linnosvuo *FIN*
A. Zabelin *URS*
Free rifle
H. Hammerer *AUT*
(1,129 pts)
H. Spillmann *SUI*
V. Borisov *URS*
Small-bore rifle, prone
P. Kohnke *GER*
(590 pts)
J. Hill *USA*
E. Forcella Pelliccioni *VEN*
Small-bore rifle, three positions
V. Shamburkin *URS*
(1,149 pts)
M. Niasov *URS*
K. Zaehringer *GEWR*
Trap shooting
I. Dumitrescu *ROM*
(192 pts)
G. Rossini *ITA*
S. Kalinin *URS*

SOCCER

YUG DEN HUN

SWIMMING

Men
100-metres freestyle
J. Devitt *AUS*
(55.2 sec)
L. Larson *USA*
M. Dos Santos *BRA*
400-metres freestyle
M. Rose *AUS*
(4 min 18.3 sec)
T. Yamanaka *JPN*
J. Konrads *AUS*
1,500-metres freestyle
J. Konrads *AUS*
(17 min 19.6 sec)
M. Rose *AUS*
G. Breen *USA*
100-metres backstroke
D. Theile *AUS*
(1 min 01.9 sec)
F. McKinney *USA*
R. Bennett *USA*

200-metres breaststroke
W. Mulliken *USA*
(2 min 37.4 sec)
Y. Osaki *JPN*
W. Mensonides *HOL*
200-metres butterfly
M. Troy *USA*
(2 min 12.8 sec)
N. Hayes *AUS*
D. Gillanders *USA*
4 x 200-metres freestyle relay
USA JPN AUS
(8 min 10.2 sec)
4 x 100-metres medley relay
USA AUS JPN
(4 min 05.4 sec)
Highboard diving
R. Webster *USA*
165.56 pts)
G. Tobian *USA*
B. Phelps *GBR*
Springboard diving
G. Tobian *USA*
(170.00 pts)
S. Hall *USA*
J. Botella *MEX*
Water polo
ITA URS HUN
Women
100-metres freestyle
D. Fraser *AUS*
(1 min 01.2 sec)
C. Von Saltza *USA*
N. Steward *GBR*
400-metres freestyle
C. Von Saltza *USA*
(4 min 50.6 sec)
J. Cederqvist *SWE*
C. Lagerberg *HOL*
100-metres backstroke
L. Burke *USA*
(1 min 09.3 sec)
N. Steward *GBR*
S. Tanaka *JPN*
200-metres breaststroke
A. Lonsborough *GBR*
(2 min 49.5 sec)

W. Urselmann *GER*
B. Gobel *GER*
100-metres butterfly
C. Schuler *USA*
(1 min 09.5 sec)
M. Heemskerk *HOL*
J. Andrew *AUS*
4 x 100-metres freestyle relay
USA AUS GER
(4 min 08.9 sec)
4 x 100-metres medley relay
USA AUS GER
(4 min 08.9 sec)

Highboard diving
I. Kraemer *GER*
(91.28 pts)
P. J. (Myers) Pope *USA*
N. Krutova *USA*
Springboard diving
I. Kraemer *GER*
(155.8 pts)
P. J. (Myers) Pope *USA*
E. Ferris *GBR*

WEIGHTLIFTING

Bantamweight
C. Vinci *USA*
(345.0 kg)
Yoshinobu Miyake *JPN*
E. Elmkhah *IRN*
Featherweight
Y. Minaev *URS*
(372.5 kg)
I. Berger *USA*
S. Mannironi *ITA*
Lightweight
V. Bushuev *URS*
(397.5 kg)
H. L. Tan *SIN*
A. W. Aziz *IRQ*
Middleweight
A. Kurinov *URS*
(437.5 kg)
T. Kono *URS*
G. Veres *HUN*
Light-heavyweight
I. Palinski *POL*
(442.5 kg)
S. George *USA*
J. Bochenek *POL*
Middle-heavyweight
A. Vorobev *URS*
(472.5 kg)
T. Lomakhin *URS*
L. Martin *GBR*
Heavyweight
Y. Vlassov *URS*
(537.5 kg)
J. Bradford *USA*
N. Schemansky *USA*

WRESTLING: FREESTYLE

Flyweight
A. Bilek *TUR*
M. Matsubara *JPN*
M. Saifpour Saldabadi *IRN*
Bantamweight
T. McCann *USA*
N. Zalev *BUL*
T. Trojanowski *POL*
Featherweight
M. Dagistanli *TUR*
S. Ivanov *BUL*
V. Rubashvili *URS*
Lightweight
S. Wilson *USA*
V. Sinyarski *URS*
E. Dimov *BUL*
Welterweight
D. Blubaugh *USA*
I. Ogan *TUR*
M. Bashir *PAK*
Middleweight
H. Gungor *TUR*
G. Skhirtladze *URS*
H. Y. Antonsson *SWE*
Light-heavyweight
A. Atli *TUR*
G. R. Takhti *IRN*
A. Albul *URS*
Heavyweight
W. Dietrich *GER*
H. Kaplan *TUR*
S. Tsarasov *URS*

WRESTLING: GRECO-ROMAN

Flyweight
D. Pirvulescu *ROM*
O. Sayed *EGY*
M. Paziraye *IRN*
Bantamweight
O. Karavaev *URS*
I. Cernea *ROM*
P. Dinko *BUL*
Featherweight
M. Sille *TUR*
I. Polyak *HUN*
K. Vyrupaev *URS*
Lightweight
A. Koridze *URS*
B. Martinovic *YUG*
G. Freij *SWE*
Welterweight
M. Bayrak *TUR*
G. Maritschnigg *GER*
R. Schiermeyer *FRA*
Middleweight
D. Dobrev *BUL*
L. Metz *GER*
I. Taranu *RUM*
Light-heavyweight
T. Kis *TUR*
K. Bimbalov *BUL*
G. Kartozia *USA*
Heavyweight
I. Bogdan *URS*
W. Dietrich *GER*
B. Kubat *TCH*

YACHTING

5.5-metre class
USA DEN SUI
Flying Dutchman
NOR DEN GER
Dragon
GRE ARG ITA
Star
URS POR USA
Finn
P. Elvstrom *DEN*
(8,171 pts)
A. Chuchelov *URS*
A. Nelis *BEL*

1964 INNSBRUCK

NORDIC SKIING

Men
Cross-country (15 km)
E. Mantyranta *FIN*
(50 min 54.1 sec)
H. Gronningen *NOR*
S. Jernberg *SWE*
Cross-country (30 km)
E. Mantyranta *FIN*
(1 hr 30 min 50.7 sec)
H. Gronningen *NOR*
I. Voronchikhin *URS*
Cross-country (50 km)
S. Jernberg *SWE*
(2 hr 43 min 52.6 sec)

A. Ronnlund *SWE*
A. Tiainen *FIN*
4 x 10-kilometres relay
SWE FIN URS
(2 hr 18 min 34.6 sec)
Ski jumping (70 m)
V. Kankkonen *FIN*
(229.9 pts)
T. Engan *NOR*
T. Brandtzag *NOR*
Ski jumping (90 m)
T. Engan *NOR*
(230.7 pts)
V. Kankkonen *FIN*
T. Brandtzag *NOR*
Nordic combined
T. Knutsen *NOR*
(469.28 pts)
N. Kiselev *URS*
G. Thoma *GER*
Biathlon
V. Melanin *URS*
(1 hr 20 min 26.8 sec)
A. Privalov *URS*
O. Jordet *NOR*
Women
Cross-country (5 km)
K. Boyarskikh *URS*
(17 min 50.5 sec)
M. Lehtonen *FIN*
A. Kolchina *URS*
Cross-country (10 km)
K. Boyarskikh *URS*
(40 min 24.3 sec)
E. Mekshilo *URS*
M. Gusakova *URS*
3 × 5-kilometres relay
URS SWE FIN
(59 min 20.2 sec)

ALPINE SKIING

Men
Downhill
E. Zimmermann *AUT*
(2 min 18.1 sec)
L. Lacroix *FRA*
W. Bartels *GER*
Giant slalom
F. Bonlieu *FRA*
(1 min 46.71 sec)
K. Schranz *AUT*
J. Stiegler *AUT*
Slalom
J. Stiegler *AUT*
(2 min 11.13 sec)

W. W. Kidd *USA*
J. F. Heuga *USA*
Women
Downhill
C. Haas *AUT*
(1 min 55.39 sec)
E. Zimmermann *AUT*
G. Hecher *AUT*

Giant slalom
M. Goitschel *FRA*
(1 min 52.24 sec)

C. Goitschel *FRA* &
J. Saubert *USA*
Slalom
C. Goitschel *FRA*
(1 min 29.86 sec)

M. Goitschel *FRA*
J. Saubert *USA*

FIGURE SKATING

Men
M. Schnelldorfer *GER*
(1,916.9 pts)

A. Calmat *FRA*
S. Allen *USA*
Women
S. Dijkstra *HOL*
(2,018.5 pts)
R. Heitzer *AUT*
P. Burka *CAN*
Pairs
L. Belousova &
O. Protopopov *URS*
(104.4 pts)
M. Kilius &
H. J. Bauemler *GER*
D. Wilkes &
J. Revell *CAN*

SPEED SKATING

Men
500 metres
R. McDermott *USA*
(40.1 sec)
Y. Grischin *URS* &
V. Orlov *URS* &
A. Gjestvang *NOR*
1,500 metres
A. Antson *URS*
(2 min 10.3 sec)
C. Verkerk *HOL*
V. Haugen *NOR*
5,000 metres
K. Johannesen *NOR*
(7 min 38.4 sec)

P. I. Moe *NOR*
F. A. Maier *NOR*
10,000 metres
J. Nilsson *SWE*
(15 min 50.1 sec)
F. A. Maier *NOR*
K. Johannesen *NOR*
Women
500 metres
L. Skoblikova *URS*
(45.0 sec)
I. Yegorova *URS*
T. Sidorova *URS*
1,000 metres
L. Skoblikova *URS*
(1 min 33.2 sec)
I. Yegorova *URS*
K. Mustonen *FIN*
1,500 metres
L. Skoblikova *URS*
(2 min 22.6 sec)
K. Mustonen *FIN*
B. Kolokoltseva *URS*
3,000 metres
L. Skoblikova *URS*
(5 min 14.9 sec)
V. Stenina *URS* &
P. H. Han *PRK*

BOBSLEIGHING

Two-man
GBR I ITA II ITA I
(4 min 21.90 sec)
Four-man
CAN I AUT I ITA II
(4 min 14.46 sec)

LUGE TOBOGGANING

Men
Single-seater
T. Koehler *GER*
(3 min 26.77 sec)
K. Bonsack *GER*
H. Plenk *GER*
Two-seater
AUT AUT ITA
(1 min 41.62 sec)

Women
Single-seater
O. Enderlein *GER*
(3 min 24.67 sec)
I. Geisler *GER*
H. Thurner *AUT*

ICE HOCKEY

URS SWE TCH

1964 TOKYO

ATHLETICS

Men
100 metres
R. Hayes *USA*
(10.0 sec)
E. Figuerola *CUB*
H. Jerome *CAN*
200 metres
H. Carr *USA*
(20.3 sec)
P. Drayton *USA*
E. Roberts *TRI*
400 metres
M. Larrabee *USA*
(45.1 sec)

W. Mottley *TRI*
A. Badenski *POL*
800 metres
P. Snell *NZL*
(1 min 45.1 sec)
W. Crothers *CAN*
W. Kiprugut *KEN*
1,500 metres
P. Snell *NZL*
(3 min 38.1 sec)

J. Odlozil *TCH*
J. Davies *NZL*
5,000 metres
R. Schul *USA*
(13 min 48.8 sec)
H. Norpoth *GER*
W. Dellinger *USA*
10,000 metres
W. Mills *USA*
(28 min 24.4 sec)

M. Gammoudi *TUN*
R. Clarke *AUS*
Marathon
A. Bikila *ETH*
(2 hr 12 min 11.2 sec)
B. Heatley *GBR*
K. Tsuburaya *JPN*
110-metres hurdles
H. Jones *USA*
(13.6 sec)
H. B. Lindgren *USA*
A. Mikhailov *URS*
400-metres hurdles
R. W. Cawley *USA*
(49.6 sec)
J. Cooper *GBR*
S. Morale *ITA*
**3,000-metres
steeplechase**
G. Roelants *BEL*
(8 min 30.8 sec)

M. Herriott *GBR*
I. Belyayev *URS*
4 x 100-metres relay
USA POL FRA
(39.0 sec)
4 x 400-metres relay
USA GBR TRI
(3 min 00.7 sec)
20-kilometres walk
K. Matthews *GBR*
(1 hr 29 min 34.0 sec)
D. Linder *GER*
V. Golubnichiy *URS*
50-kilometres walk
A. Pamich *ITA*
(4 hr 11 min 12.4 sec)
P. Nihill *GBR*
I. Pettersson *SWE*
High jump
V. Brumel *URS*
(2.18 m)
J. Thomas *USA*
J. Rambo *USA*
Long jump
L. Davies *GBR*
(8.07 m)
R. Boston *USA*
I. Ter-Ovanesyan *URS*
Triple jump
J. Schmidt *POL*
(16.85 m)
O. Fedoseyev *URS*
V. Kravchenko *URS*
Pole vault
F. Hansen *USA*
(5.10 m)
W. Reinhardt *GER*
K. Lehnertz *GER*
Shot
D. Long *USA*
(20.33 m)
R. Matson *USA*
V. Varju *HUN*
Discus
A. Oerter *USA*
(61.00 m)

L. Danek *TCH*
D. Weill *USA*
Hammer
R. Klim *URS*
(69.74 m)
G. Zsivotzky *HUN*
T. Rut *POL*
Javelin
P. Nevala *FIN*
(82.66 m)
G. Kulcsar *HUN*
J. Lusis *URS*
Decathlon
W. Holdorf *GER*
(7,887 pts)
R. Aun *URS*
H. J. Walde *GER*
Women
100 metres
W. Tyus *USA*
(11.4 sec)
E. Maguire *USA*
E. Kobukowska *POL*
200 metres
E. Maguire *USA*
(23.0 sec)
I. Kirszentein *POL*
M. Black *AUS*
400 metres
B. Cuthbert *AUS*
(52.0 sec)
A. Packer *GBR*
J. Amoore *AUS*
800 metres
A. Packer *GBR*
(2 min 01.1 sec)
M. Dupureur *FRA*
A. Chamberlain *NZL*
80-metres hurdles
K. Balzer *GER*
(10.5 sec)
T. Ciepla *POL*
P. Kilborn *AUS*
4 x 100-metres relay
POL USA GBR
(43.6 sec)
Pentathlon
I. Press *URS*
(5,246 pts)
M. Rand *GBR*
G. Bystrova *URS*
High jump
I. Balas *ROM*
(1.90 m)
M. Brown *AUS*
T. Chenchik *URS*
Long jump
M. Rand *GBR*
(6.76 m)
I. Kirzenstein *POL*
T. Shchelkanova *URS*
Shot
T. Press *URS*
(18.14 m)

R. Garisch *GER*
G. Zybina *URS*

Discus
T. Press *URS*
(57.27 m)
I. Lotz *GER*
L. Manoliv *ROM*
Javelin
M. Penes *ROM*
(60.54 m)
M. Rudas *HUN*
Y. Gorchakova *URS*

BASKETBALL

USA URS BRA

BOXING

Flyweight
F. Atzori *ITA*
A. Olech *POL*
S. Sorokin *URS* &
R. Carmody *USA*
Bantamweight
T. Sakurai *JPN*
S. C. Chung *KOR*
B. J. Fabila *MEX* &
W. Rodriguez *URU*
Featherweight
S. Stepashkin *URS*
A. Villeneuva *VEN*
C. Brown *USA* &
H. Schulz *GER*
Lightweight
J. Grudzien *POL*
V. Baranikov *URS*
R. Harris *USA* &
J. McCourt *IRL*
Light-welterweight
J. Kulej *POL*
Y. Frolov *URS*
E. Blay *GHA* &
H. Galhia *TUN*
Welterweight
M. Kasprzyk *POL*
R. Tamulis *URS*
P. Purhonen *FIN* &
S. Bertini *ITA*
Light-middleweight
B. Lagutin *URS*
J. Gonzales *FRA*
N. Maiyegun *NGR* &
J. Grzesiak *POL*
Middleweight
V. Popenchenko *URS*
E. Schulz *GER*
F. Valla *ITA* &
T. Walasek *POL*
Light-heavyweight
C. Pinto *ITA*
A. Kiselyov *URS*
A. Nicolov *BUL* &
Z. Pietrzykowski *POL*
Heavyweight
J. Frazier *USA*
H. Huber *GER*
G. Ros *ITA* &
V. Yemelyanov *URS*

CANOEING

Canadian singles
J. Eschert *GER*
(4 min 35.14 sec)
A. Igorov *ROM*
Y. Penyaev *URS*
Canadian pairs
URS FRA DEN
(4 min 04.64 sec)
Kayak singles
R. Peterson *SWE*
(3 min 47.13 sec)
M. Hesz *HUN*
A. Vernescu *ROM*

Kayak pairs
SWE HOL GER
(3 min 38.54 sec)
Kayak fours
URS GER ROM
(3 min 14.67 sec)
Women
Kayak singles
L. Khvedosyuk *URS*
(2 min 12.87 sec)
H. Lauer *ROM*
M. Jones *USA*
Kayak pairs
GER USA ROM
(1 min 56.95 sec)

CYCLING

1,000-metres sprint
G. Pettenella *ITA*
(13.69 sec)
S. Bianchetto *ITA*
D. Morelon *GBR*
**1,000-metres time
trial**
P. Sercu *BEL*
(1 min 09.59 sec)
G. Pettenella *ITA*
P. Trentin *FRA*
**4,000-metres team
pursuit**
J. Daler *TCH*
(5 min 04.75 sec)
G. Ursi *ITA*
P. Isaksson *DEN*
Team
GER ITA HOL
(4 min 35.67 sec)
2,000-metres tandem
ITA URS GER
(10.75 sec)
Road race (194.8 km)
M. Zanin *ITA*
(4 hr 39 min 51.63 sec)
K. A. Rodian *DEN*
W. Godcfroot *BEL*
Team
HOL ITA SWE
(2 hr 26 min 31.19 sec)

EQUESTRIAN

Show jumping
P. J. d'Oriola *FRA*
(9 flts)
H. Schridde *GER*
P. Robeson *GBR*
Team
GER FRA ITA
Dressage
H. Chammartin *SUI*
(1,504 pts)
H. Boldt *GER*
S. Filatov *URS*
Team
GER SUI URS
Three-day event
M. Checcoli *ITA*
(64.40 pts)
C. Moratorio *ARG*
F. Ligges *GER*
Team
ITA USA GER

FENCING

Men
Foil
E. Franke *POL*
(3 wins)
J. C. Magnan *FRA*
D. Revenu *FRA*
Team
URS POL FRA

Epée
G. Kriss *URS*
(2 wins)
W. Hoskyns *GBR*
G. Kostava *URS*
Team
HUN ITA FRA
Sabre
T. Pesza *HUN*
(2 wins)
C. Arabo *FRA*
V. Mavlikhanov *URS*
Team
URS ITA POL
Women
Foil
I. Ujlaki-Rejto *HUN*
(2 wins)
H. Mees *GER*
A. Ragno *ITA*
Team
HUN URS GER

GYMNASTICS

Men
Combined exercises
Y. Endo *JPN*
(115.95 pts)
S. Tsurumi *JPN* &
B. Shakhlin *URS* &
V. Lisitski *URS*
Team
JPN URS GER
Floor
F. Menichelli *ITA*
(19.45 pts)
V. Lisitski *URS*
Y. Endo *JPN*
Horizontal bar
B. Shakhlin *URS*
(19.625 pts)
Y. Titov *URS*
M. Cerar *YUG*
Parallel bars
Y. Endo *JPN*
(19.675 pts)
S. Tsurumi *JPN*
F. Menichelli *ITA*
Pommelled horse
M. Cerar *YUG*
(19.525 pts)
S. Tsurumi *JPN*
Y. Tsapenko *URS*
Long horse
H. Yamashita *JPN*
(19,660 pts)
V. Lisitski *URS*
H. Rantakari *FIN*
Rings
T. Hayata *JPN*
(19,475 pts)
F. Menichelli *ITA*
B. Shakhlin *URS*
Women
Combined exercises
V. Caslavska *TCH*
(77.564 pts)
L. Latynina *URS*
P. Astakhova *URS*
Team
URS TCH JPN
Beam
V. Caslavska *TCH*
(19.449 pts)
T. Manina *URS*
L. Latynina *URS*
Asymmetrical bars
P. Astakhova *URS*
(19.332 pts)
K. Makray *HUN*
L. Latynina *URS*

Horse vault
V. Caslavska *TCH*
(19.483 pts)
L. Latynina *URS*
B. Radochla *GER*
Floor
L. Latynina *URS*
(19.599 pts)
P. Astakhova *URS*
A. Janosi *HUN*

HOCKEY (FIELD)

IND PAK AUS

JUDO

Lightweight
T. Nakatani *JPN*
E. Hanni *SUI*
O. Stepanov *URS* &
A. Bogolubov *URS*
Middleweight
I. Okano *JPN*
W. Hofmann *GER*
J. Bregman *USA* &
E. T. Kim *KOR*
Heavyweight
I. Inokuma *JPN*
A. H. Rogers *CAN*
A. Kiknadze *URS* &
P. Chikviladze *URS*
Open
A. Geesink *HOL*
A. Kaminaga *JPN*
K. Glahn *GER* &
T. Boronovskis *AUS*

MODERN PENTATHLON

F. Torok *HUN*
(5,116 pts)
I. Novikov *URS*
A. Mokoyev *URS*
Team
URS USA HUN

ROWING

Single sculls
V. Ivanov *URS*
(8 min 22.51 sec)
A. Hill *GER*
G. Kottman *SUI*
Double sculls
URS USA TCH
(7 min 10.66 sec)
Coxless pairs
CAN HOL GER
(7 min 32.94 sec)
Coxed pairs
USA FRA HOL
(8 min 21.23 sec)
Coxless fours
DEN GBR USA
(6 min 59.30 sec)
Coxed fours
GER ITA HOL
(7 min 00.44 sec)
Eights
USA GER TCH
(6 min 18.23 sec)

SHOOTING

Free pistol
V. Markkanen *FIN*
(560 pts)
F. Green *USA*
Y. Yoshikawa *JPN*
Rapid-fire pistol
P. Linnosvuo *FIN*
(592 pts)

I. Tripsa *ROM*
L. Nacovsky *TCH*
Free rifle
G. Anderson *USA*
(1,153 pts)
S. Kveliashvili *URS*
M. Gunnarsson *USA*
Small-bore rifle, prone
L. Hammerl *HUN*
(597 pts)
L. Wigger *USA*
T. Pool *USA*
**Small-bore rifle, three
positions**
L. Wigger *USA*
(1,164 pts)
V. Khristov *BUL*
L. Hammerl *HUN*
Trap shooting
E. Mattareli *ITA*
(198 pts)
P. Senichev *URS*
W. Morris *USA*

SOCCER

HUN TCH GER

SWIMMING

Men
100-metres freestyle
D. Schollander *USA*
(53.4 sec)
R. McGregor *GBR*
N. J. Klein *GER*
400-metres freestyle
D. Schollander *USA*
(4 min 12.2 sec)

F. Wiegand *GER*
A. Wood *AUS*
1,500-metres freestyle
R. Windle *AUS*
(17 min 01.7 sec)
J. Nelson *USA*
A. Wood *AUS*
200-metres backstroke
J. Graef *USA*
(2 min 10.3 sec)
G. Dilley *USA*
R. Bennett *USA*
**200-metres
breaststroke**
I. O'Brien *AUS*
(2 min 27.8 sec)
G. Propopenko *URS*
C. Jastremski *USA*
200-metres butterfly
K. Berry *AUS*
(2 min 06.6 sec)
C. Robie *USA*
F. Schmidt *USA*
400-metres medley
R. Roth *USA*
(4 min 45.4 sec)
R. Saari *USA*

G. Hetz *GER*
**4 x 100-metres
freestyle relay**
USA GER AUS
(3 min 33.2 sec)
**4 x 200-metres
freestyle relay**
USA GER JPN
(7 min 52.1 sec)
**4 x 100-metres medley
relay**
USA GER AUS
(3 min 58.5 sec)
Highboard diving
R. Webster *USA*
(148.58 pts)
K. Dibiasi *ITA*
T. Gompf *USA*
Springboard diving
K. Sitzberger *USA*
(159.90 pts)
F. Gorman *USA*
L. Andreasen *USA*
Water polo
HUN YUG URS
Women
100-metres freestyle
D. Fraser *AUS*
(59.5 sec)

S. Stouder *USA*
K. Ellis *USA*
400-metres freestyle
V. Duenkel *USA*
(4 min 43.3 sec)
M. Ramenofsky *USA*
T. L. Stickles *USA*
100-metres backstroke
C. Ferguson *USA*
(1 min 07.7 sec)
C. Caron *FRA*
V. Duenkel *USA*
**200-metres
breaststroke**
G. Prosumenshchikova
URS
(2 min 46.4 sec)
C. Kolb *USA*
S. Babanina *URS*
100-metres butterfly
S. Stouder *USA*
(1 min 04.7 sec)
A. Kuk *HOL*
K. Ellis *USA*
400-metres medley
D. De Varona *USA*
(5 min 18.7 sec)
S. Finneran *USA*
M. Randall *USA*
**4 x 100-metres
freestyle relay**
USA AUS HOL
(4 min 03.8 sec)
**4 x 100-metres medley
relay**
USA HOL URS
(4 min 33.9 sec)

Highboard diving
L. Bush *USA*
(99.80 pts)
I. Kraemer-Engel *GER*
G. Alekseeva *URS*
Springboard diving
I. Kraemer-Engel *GER*
(145.00 pts)
J. Collier *USA*
P. Willard *USA*

VOLLEYBALL

Men
URS TCH JPN
Women
JPN URS POL

WEIGHTLIFTING

Bantamweight
A. Vakhonin *URS*
(357.5 kg)
I. Foldi *HUN*
S. Inchinoseki *JPN*
Featherweight
Yoshinobu Miyake *JPN*
(397.5 kg)
I. Berger *USA*
M. Nowak *POL*
Lightweight
W. Baszanowski *POL*
(432.5 kg)
V. Kaplunov *URS*
M. Zielinski *POL*
Middleweight
H. Zdrazila *TCH*
(445.0 kg)
V. Kurentsov *URS*
M. Ohuchi *JPN*
Light-heavyweight
R. Plyukfelder *URS*
(475.0 kg)
G. Toth *HUN*
G. Veres *HUN*
Middle-heavyweight
V. Golovanov *URS*
(487.5 kg)
L. Martin *GBR*
I. Palinski *POL*
Heavyweight
L. Zhabotinsky *URS*
(572.5 kg)
Y. Vlassov *URS*
N. Schemansky *USA*

WRESTLING: FREESTYLE

Flyweight
Y. Yoshida *JPN*
C. S. Chang *KOR*
S. Aliaakbor Haydari
IRN
Bantamweight
Y. Uetake *JPN*
H. Akbas *TUR*
A. Abragimov *URS*
Featherweight
O. Watanabe *JPN*
S. Ivanov *BUL*
N. Khokhashvili *URS*
Lightweight
E. Valchev *BUL*
K. J. Rost *GER*
I. Horiuchi *JPN*
Welterweight
I. Ogan *TUR*
G. Sagaradze *URS*
M. A. Sanatkaran *IRN*
Middleweight
P. Gardshev *BUL*
H. Gungor *TUR*
D. Brand *USA*

Light-heavyweight
A. Medved *TUR*
A. Ayik *TUR*
S. Mustafov *BUL*
Heavyweight
A. Ivanitski *URS*
L. Djiber *BUL*
H. Kaplan *TUR*

WRESTLING: GRECO-ROMAN

Flyweight
T. Hanahara *JPN*
A. Kerezov *BUL*
D. Pirvulescu *ROM*
Bantamweight
M. Ichiguchi *JPN*
V. Trostyanski *URS*
I. Cernea *ROM*
Featherweight
I. Polyak *HUN*
R. Rurura *URS*
B. Martinovic *YUG*
Lightweight
K. Ayvaz *TUR*
V. Bularca *ROM*
D. Grantseladze *URS*
Welterweight
A. Koleslov *URS*
C. Todorov *BUL*
B. Nystroem *SWE*
Middleweight
B. Simic *YUG*
J. Kormanik *TCH*
L. Metz *GER*
Light-heavyweight
B. Rader *BUL*
P. Svensson *SWE*
H. Kiehl *GER*
Heavyweight
I. Kozma *HUN*
A. Roschin *URS*
W. Dietrich *GER*

YACHTING

5.5-metre class
AUS SWE USA
Flying Dutchman
NZL GBR USA
Dragon
DEN GER USA
Star
BAH USA SWE
Finn
W. Kuhweide *GER*
(7,638 pts)
P. Barrett *USA*
H. Wind *DEN*

1968 GRENOBLE

NORDIC SKIING

Men
Cross-country (15 km)
H. Gronningen *NOR*
(47 min 54.2 sec)
E. Mantyranta *FIN*
G. Larsson *SWE*
Cross-country (30 km)
F. Nones *ITA*
(1 hr 35 min 39.2 sec)
O. Martinsen *NOR*
E. Mantyranta *FIN*
Cross-country (50 km)
O. Ellefsaeter *NOR*
(2 hr 28 min 45.8 sec)
V. Vedenin *URS*
J. Haas *SWE*

4 x 10-kilometres relay
NOR FIN SWE
(2 hr 08 min 33.5 sec)
Ski jumping (70 m)
J. Raska *TCH*
(216.5 pts)
B. Bachler *AUT*
B. Preiml *AUT*
Ski jumping (90 m)
V. Beloussov *URS*
(231.3 pts)
J. Raska *TCH*
L. Grini *NOR*
Nordic combined
F. Keller *GER*
(449.04 pts)
A. Kaelin *SUI*
A. Kunz *GDR*
Biathlon
M. Solberg *NOR*
(1 hr 13 min 45.9 sec)
A. Tikhonov *URS*
V. Gundartsev *URS*
Biathlon relay
URS NOR SWE
(2 hr 13 min 02.4 sec)
Women
Cross-country (5 km)
T. Gustafsson *SWE*
(16 min 45.2 sec)
G. Kulakova *URS*
A. Kolchina *URS*
Cross-country (10 km)
T. Gustafsson *SWE*
(36 min 46.5 sec)
B. Mordre *NOR*
I. Aufles *NOR*
3 x 5-kilometres relay
NOR SWE URS
(57 min 30.0 sec)

ALPINE SKIING

Men
Downhill
J.-C. Killy *FRA*
(1 min 59.85 sec)

G. Perillat *FRA*
J. D. Daetwyler *SUI*
Giant slalom
J.-C. Killy *FRA*
(3 min 29.28 sec)
W. Favre *SUI*
H. Messner *AUT*
Slalom
J.-C. Killy *FRA*
(1 min 39.73 sec)
H. Huber *AUT*
A. Matt *AUT*
Women
Downhill
O. Pall *AUT*
(1 min 40.87 sec)
I. Mir *FRA*
C. Haas *AUT*

Giant slalom
N. Greene *CAN*
(1 min 51.97 sec)

A. Famose *FRA*
F. Bochatay *SUI*
Slalom
M. Goitschel *FRA*
(1 min 25.86 sec)

N. Greene *CAN*
A. Famose *FRA*

FIGURE SKATING

Men
W. Schwarz *AUT*
(1,904.1 pts)
T. Wood *USA*
P. Pera *FRA*
Women
P. Fleming *USA*
(1,970.5 pts)
G. Seyfert *GDR*
H. Maskova *TCH*
Pairs
L. Belousova &
O. Protopopov *URS*
(315.2 pts)
T. Yukchesternava &
A. Gorelik *URS*
M. Glockshuber &
W. Danne *GER*

SPEED SKATING

Men
500 metres
E. Keller *GER*
(40.3 sec)
M. Thomassen *NOR* &
R. McDermott *USA*
1,500 metres
C. Verkerk *HOL*
(2 min 03.4 sec)
A. Schenk *HOL* &
I. Eriksen *NOR*
5,000 metres
F. A. Maier *NOR*
(7 min 22.4 sec)
C. Verkerk *HOL*
P. Nottet *HOL*

10,000 metres
J. Hoglin *SWE*
(15 min 23.6 sec)
F. A. Maier *NOR*
O. Sandler *SWE*
Women
500 metres
L. Titova *URS*
(46.1 sec)
M. Meyers *USA* &
D. Holum *USA* &
J. Fish *USA*
1,000 metres
C. Geijssen *HOL*
(1 min 32.6 sec)
L. Titova *URS*
D. Holum *USA*
1,500 metres
K. Mustonen *FIN*
(2 min 22.4 sec)
C. Geijssen *HOL*
C. Kaiser *HOL*
3,000 metres
J. Schut *HOL*
(4 min 56.2 sec)
K. Mustonen *FIN*
C. Kaiser *HOL*

BOBSLEIGHING

Two-man
ITA I GER I ROM I
(4 min 41.54 sec)
Four-man
ITA I AUT I SUI I
(2 min 17.39 sec)

LUGE TOBOGGANING

Men
Single-seater
M. Schmid *AUT*
(2 min 52.48 sec)
T. Koehler *GDR*
K. Bonsack *GDR*
Two-seater
GDR AUT GER
(1 min 35.85 sec)
Women
Single-seater
E. Lechner *ITA*
(2 min 28.66 sec)
C. Schmuck *GER*
A. Duenhaupt *GER*

ICE HOCKEY

URS TCH CAN

1968 MEXICO CITY

ATHLETICS

Men
100 metres
J. Hines *USA*
(9.9 sec)
L. Miller *JAM*
C. Greene *USA*
200 metres
T. Smith *USA*
(19.8 sec)
P. Norman *AUS*
J. Carlos *USA*
400 metres
L. Evans *USA*
(43.8 sec)
L. James *USA*
R. Freeman *USA*
800 metres
R. Doubell *AUS*
(1 min 44.3 sec)
W. Kiprugut *KEN*
T. Farrell *USA*

1,500 metres
K. Keino *KEN*
(3 min 34.9 sec)

J. Ryun *USA*
B. Tuemmler *GER*
5,000 metres
M. Gammoudi *TUN*
(14 min 05.0 sec)
K. Keino *KEN*
N. Temu *KEN*
10,000 metres
N. Temu *KEN*
(29 min 27.4 sec)
M. Wolde *ETH*
M. Gammoudi *TUN*
Marathon
M. Wolde *ETH*
(2 hr 20 min 26.4 sec)
K. Kimihara *JPN*
M. Ryan *NZL*
110-metres hurdles
W. Davenport *USA*
(13.3 sec)
E. Hall *USA*
E. Ottoz *ITA*
400-metres hurdles
D. Hemery *GBR*
(48.1 sec)

G. Hennige *GER*
J. Sherwood *GBR*
3,000-metres steeplechase
A. Biwott *KEN*
(8 min 51.0 sec)
B. Kogo *KEN*
G. Young *USA*
4 x 100-metres relay
USA CUB FRA
(38.2 sec)
4 x 400-metres relay
USA KEN GER
(2 min 56.1 sec)
20-kilometres walk
V. Golubnichiy *URS*
(1 hr 33 min 58.4 sec)
J. Pedraza *MEX*
N. Smaga *URS*
50-kilometres walk
C. Hoehne *GDR*
(4 hr 20 min 30.6 sec)

A. Kiss *HUN*
L. Young *USA*
High jump
R. Fosbury *USA*
(2.24 m)
E. Caruthers *USA*
V. Gavrilov *URS*
Long jump
R. Beamon *USA*
(8.90 m)
K. Beer *GDR*
R. Boston *USA*
Triple jump
V. Saneyev *URS*
(17.39 m)
N. Prudencio *BRA*
G. Gentile *ITA*
Pole vault
R. Seagren *USA*
(5.40 m)
C. Schiprowski *GER*
W. Nordwig *GDR*
Shot
R. Matson *USA*
(20.54 m)
G. Woods *USA*
E. Gushchin *URS*
Discus
A. Oerter *USA*
(64.78 m)
L. Milde *GDR*
L. Danek *TCH*
Hammer
G. Zsivotzky *HUN*
(73.36 m)
R. Klim *URS*
L. Lovasc *HUN*
Javelin
J. Lusis *URS*
(90.10 m)
J. Kinnunen *FIN*
G. Kulcsar *HUN*
Decathlon
W. Toomey *USA*
(8,193 pts)
H.-J. Walde *GER*
K. Bendlin *GER*
Women
100 metres
W. Tyus *USA*
(11.0 sec)
B. Ferrell *USA*
I. Szewinska
(Kirszenstein) *POL*
200 metres
I. Szewinska
(Kirszenstein) *POL*
(22.5 sec)
R. Boyle *AUS*
J. Lamy *AUS*
400 metres
C. Besson *FRA*
(52.0 sec)
L. Board *GBR*
N. Pechenkina *URS*
800 metres
M. Manning *USA*
(2 min 00.9 sec)

I. Silai ROM
M. Gommers HOL
80-metres hurdles
M. Caird AUS
(10.3 sec)
P. Kilborn AUS
C. Cheng ROC
4 x 100-metres relay
USA CUB URS
(42.8 sec)
Pentathlon
I. Becker GER
(5,098 pts)

L. Prokop AUT
A. T. Kovacs HUN
High jump
M. Rezkova TCH
(1.82 m)
A. Okorokova URS
V. Kozyr URS
Long jump
V. Viscopoleanu ROM
(6.82 m)
S. Sherwood GBR
T. Talysheva URS
Shot
M. Gummel GDR
(19.61 m)
M. Lange GDR
N. Chizhova URS
Discus
L. Manoliu ROM
(58.28 m)
L. Westermann GER
J. Kleiber HUN
Javelin
A. Nemeth HUN
(60.36 m)
M. Penes ROM
E. Janko AUT

BASKETBALL
USA YUG URS

BOXING
Light-flyweight
F. Rodriguez VEN
Y. J. Jee KOR
H. Marbley USA &
H. Skrzypczak POL
Flyweight
R. Delgado MEX
A. Olech POL
S. de Oliveira BRA &
L. Rwabwogo UGA
Bantamweight
V. Sokolov URS
E. Mukwanga UGA
E. Morioka JPN &
K. C. Chang KOR
Featherweight
A. Roldan MEX
A. Robinson USA
P. Waruinge KEN &
I. Mikhailov BUL

Lightweight
R. Harris USA
J. Grudzien POL
C. Cutov ROM &
Y. Vujin YUG
Light-welterweight
J. Kulej POL
E. Regueiferos CUB
A. Nilsson FIN &
J. Wallington USA
Welterweight
M. Wolke GDR
J. Bessala CMR
V. Masalimov URS &
M. Guilloti Gonzalez ARG
Light-middleweight
B. Lagutin URS
R. Garbey CUB
J. Baldwin USA &
G. Meier GER
Middleweight
C. Finnegan GBR
A. Kiselyov URS
A. Zaragoza MEX &
A. Jones USA
Light-heavyweight
D. Poznyak URS
I. Monea ROM
G. Stankov BUL &
S. Dragan POL
Heavyweight
G. Foreman USA
I. Chepulis URS
G. Bambini ITA &
J. Rocha MEX

CANOEING
Men
Canadian singles
T. Tatai HUN
(4 min 36.4 sec)
D. Lewe GER
V. Galkov URS
Canadian pairs
ROM HUN URS
(4 min 07.18 sec)
Kayak singles
M. Hesz HUN
(4 min 02.63 sec)
A. Shaparenko URS
E. Hansen DEN
Kayak pairs
URS HUN AUT
(3 min 37.54 sec)
Kayak fours
NOR ROM HUN
(3 min 14.38 sec)
Women
Kayak singles
L. Pinaeva URS
(2 min 11.09 sec)
R. Breuer GER
V. Dumitru ROM
Kayak pairs
GER HUN URS
(1 min 56.44 sec)

CYCLING
1,000-metres sprint
D. Morelon FRA
(10.68 sec)
G. Turrini ITA
P. Trentin FRA
1,000-metres time trial
P. Trentin FRA
(1 min 03.91 sec)
N. C. Fredborg DEN
J. Kierzkowski POL

4,000-metres pursuit
D. Rebillard FRA
(4 min 41.71 sec)
M. F. Jensen DEN
X. Kurmann SUI
Team
DEN GER ITA
(4 min 22.44 sec)
2,000-metres tandem
FRA HOL BEL
(9.83 sec)
Road race (196.2 km)
P. Vianelli ITA
(4 hr 41 min 25.24 sec)
L. Mortensen DEN
G. Pettersson SWE
Team
HOL SWE ITA

EQUESTRIAN
Show jumping
W. Steinkraus USA
(4 flts)
M. Coakes GBR
D. Broome GBR
Team
CAN FRA GER
Dressage
I. Kizimov URS
(1,572 pts)
J. Neckermann GER
R. Klimke GER
Team
GER URS SWE
Three-day event
J. J. Guyon FRA
(38.86 flts)
D. Allhusen GBR
M. Page USA
Team
GBR USA AUS

FENCING
Men
Foil
I. Drimba ROM
(4 wins)
J. Kamuti HUN
D. Revenu FRA
Team
FRA URS POL
Epée
G. Kulcsar HUN
(4 wins)
G. Kriss URS
G. Sacca'o ITA
Team
HUN URS POL
Sabre
J. Pawlowski POL
(4 wins)
M. Rakita URS
T. Pesza HUN
Team
URS ITA HUN
Women
Foil
Y. Novikova URS
(4 wins)
P. Roldan MEX
I. Rejto HUN
Team
URS HUN ROM

GYMNASTICS
Men
Combined exercises
S. Kato JPN
(115.90 pts)
M. Voronin URS
A. Nakayama JPN

Team
JPN URS GDR
Floor
S. Kato JPN
(19.475 pts)
A. Nakayama JPN
T. Kato JPN
Horizontal bar
M. Voronin URS &
A. Nakayama JPN
(19.550 pts)
E. Kenmotsu JPN
Parallel bars
A. Nakayama JPN
(19.475 pts)
M. Voronin URS
V. Klimenko URS
Pommelled horse
M. Cerar YUG
(19.325 pts)
O. E. Laiho FIN
M. Voronin URS
Long horse
M. Voronin URS
(19.000 pts)
Y. Endo JPN
S. Diomidov URS
Rings
A. Nakayama JPN
(19.450 pts)
M. Voronin URS
M. Tsukahara JPN
Women
Combined exercises
V. Caslavska TCH
(78.25 pts)
Z. Voronina URS
N. Kuchinskaya URS
Team
URS TCH GDR
Beam
N. Kuchinskaya URS
(19.650 pts)
V. Caslavska TCH
L. Petrik URS
Asymmetrical bars
V. Caslavska TCH
(19.650 pts)
K. Janz GDR
Z. Voronina URS
Horse vault
V. Caslavska TCH
(19.775 pts)
E. Zuchold GDR
Z. Voronina URS
Floor
V. Caslavska TCH &
L. Petrik URS
(19.675 pts)
N. Kuchinskaya URS

HOCKEY (FIELD)
PAK AUS IND

MODERN PENTATHLON
B. Ferm SWE
(4,964 pts)
A. Balczo HUN
P. Lednev URS
Team
HUN URS FRA

ROWING
Single sculls
H. J. Wienese HOL
(7 min 47.80 sec)
J. Meissner GER
A. Demiddi ARG
Double sculls
URS HOL USA
(6 min 51.82 sec)

Coxless pairs
GDR USA DEN
(7 min 26.56 sec)
Coxed pairs
ITA HOL DEN
(8 min 04.81 sec)
Coxless fours
GDR HUN ITA
(6 min 39.18 sec)
Coxed fours
NZL GDR SUI
(6 min 45.62 sec)
Eights
GER AUS URS
(6 min 07.00 sec)

SHOOTING
Free pistol
G. Kosykh URS
(562 pts)
H. Mertel GER
H. Vollmar GDR
Rapid-fire pistol
J. Zapedski POL
(593 pts)
M. Rosca ROM
R. Suleimanov URS
Free rifle
G. Anderson USA
(1,157 pts)
V. Kornev URS
K. Mueller SUI
Small-bore rifle, prone
J. Kurka TCH
(598 pts)
L. Hammerl HUN
I. Ballinger NZL
Small-bore rifle, three positions
B. Klingner GER
(1,157 pts)
J. Writer USA
V. Parkhimovich URS
Trap shooting
J. R. Braithwaite GBR
(198 pts)
T. Garrigus USA
K. Czekalla GDR
Skeet
Y. Petrov URS
(198 pts)
R. Garagnani ITA
K. Wirnhier GER

SOCCER
HUN BUL JPN

SWIMMING
Men
100-metres freestyle
M. Wenden AUS
(52.2 sec)
K. Walsh USA
M. Spitz USA
200-metres freestyle
M. Wenden AUS
(1 min 55.2 sec)
D. Schollander USA
J. Nelson USA
400-metres freestyle
M. Burton USA
(4 min 09.0 sec)
R. Hutton CAN
A. Mosconi FRA
1,500-metres freestyle
M. Burton USA
(16 min 38.9 sec)
J. Kinsella USA
G. Brough AUS

100-metres backstroke
R. Matthes GDR
(58.7 sec)
C. Hickcox USA
R. Mills USA
200-metres backstroke
R. Matthes GDR
(2 min 09.6 sec)
M. Ivey USA
J. Horsley USA
100-metres breaststroke
D. McKenzie USA
(1 min 07.7 sec)
V. Kosinski URS
N. Pankin URS
200-metres breaststroke
F. Munoz MEX
(2 min 28.7 sec)
V. Kosinski URS
B. Job USA
100-metres butterfly
D. Russell USA
(55.9 sec)
M. Spitz USA
R. Wales USA
200-metres butterfly
C. Robie USA
(2 min 08.7 sec)
M. Woodroffe GBR
J. Ferris USA
200-metres medley
C. Hickcox USA
(2 min 12.0 sec)
G. Buckingham USA
J. Ferris USA
400-metres medley
C. Hickcox USA
(4 min 48.4 sec)
G. Hall USA
M. Holthaus GER
4 x 100-metres freestyle relay
USA URS AUS
(3 min 31.7 sec)
4 x 200-metres freestyle relay
USA AUS URS
(7 min 52.3 sec)
4 x 100-metres medley relay
USA GDR URS
(3 min 54.9 sec)
Highboard diving
K. Dibiasi ITA
(164.18 pts)
A. Gaxiola MEX
E. Young USA
Springboard diving
B. Wrightson USA
(170.15 pts)
K. Dibiasi ITA
J. Henry USA
Water polo
YUG URS HUN
Women
100-metres freestyle
J. Henne USA
(1 min 0.0 sec)
S. Pedersen USA
L. Gustavson USA
200-metres freestyle
D. Meyer USA
(2 min 10.5 sec)
J. Henne USA
J. Barkman USA
400-metres freestyle
D. Meyer USA
(4 min 31.8 sec)
L. Gustavson USA
K. Moras AUS

800-metres freestyle
D. Meyer USA
(9 min 24.0 sec)
P. Kruse USA
M. T. Ramirez MEX
100-metres backstroke
K. Hall USA
(1 min 6.2 sec)
E. B. Tanner CAN
J. Swaggerty USA
200-metres backstroke
L. D. Watson USA
(2 min 24.8 sec)
E. B. Tanner CAN
K. Hall USA
100-metres breaststroke
D. Bjedov YUG
(1 min 15.8 sec)
G. Prozumenshchikova URS
S. Wichman USA
200-metres breaststroke
S. Wichman USA
(2 min 44.4 sec)
D. Bjedov YUG
G. Prozumenshchikova URS
100-metres butterfly
L. McClements AUS
(1 min 5.5 sec)
E. Daniel USA
S. Shields USA
200-metres butterfly
A. Kok HOL
(2 min 24.7 sec)
H. Lindner GDR
E. Daniel USA
200-metres medley
C. Kolb USA
(2 min 24.7 sec)
S. Pedersen USA
J. Henne USA
400-metres medley
C. Kolb USA
(5 min 8.5 sec)
L. Vidali USA
S. Steinbach GDR
4 x 100-metres freestyle relay
USA GDR CAN
4 x 100-metres medley relay
USA AUS GER
Highboard diving
M. Duchkova TCH
(109.59 pts)
N. Lobanova URS
A. Peterson USA
Springboard diving
S. Gossick USA
(150.77 pts)
T. Pogozheva URS
K. O'Sullivan USA

VOLLEYBALL

Men
URS JPN TCH
Women
URS JPN POL

WEIGHTLIFTING

Bantamweight
M. Nassiri IRN
(367.5 kg)
I. Foldi HUN
H. Trebicki POL
Featherweight
Yoshinobu Miyake JPN
(392.5 kg)
D. Zhanidze URS
Yoshuyike Miyake JPN

Lightweight
W. Baszanowski POL
(437.5 kg)
P. Jalayer IRN
M. Zielinski POL
Middleweight
V. Kurentsov URS
(475.0 kg)
M. Ohuchi JPN
K. Bakos HUN
Light-heavyweight
B. Selitski URS
(485.0 kg)
V. Belyaev URS
N. Ozimek POL
Middle-heavyweight
K. Kangasniemi FIN
(517.5 kg)
Y. Talts URS
M. Golab POL
Heavyweight
L. Zhabotinsky URS
(572.5 kg)
S. Reding BEL
J. Dube USA

WRESTLING: FREESTYLE

Flyweight
S. Nakata JPN
R. Sanders USA
S. Sukhbaatar MGL
Bantamweight
Y. Uetake JPN
D. Behm USA
A. Gorgori IRN
Featherweight
M. Kaneko JPN
E. Todorov BUL
S. Seyed-Abassy IRN
Lightweight
A. Movahed Ardabili IRN
E. Valchev JPN
S. Danzandarjaa MGL
Welterweight
M. Atalay TUR
D. Robin FRA
D. Purev MGL
Middleweight
B. Gurevich URS
M. Jigjid MGL
P. Gardshev BUL
Light-heavyweight
A. Ayik TUR
S. Lomidze URS
J. Csatari HUN
Heavyweight
A. Medved URS
O. Duralyev BUL
W. Dietrich GER

WRESTLING: GRECO-ROMAN

Flyweight
P. Kirov BUL
V. Bakulin URS
M. Zeman TCH
Bantamweight
J. Varga HUN
I. Baciu ROM
I. Kochergin URS
Featherweight
R. Rurura URS
H. Fujimoto JPN
S. Popescu ROM
Lightweight
M. Munemura JPN
S. Horvath YUG
P. Galaktopoulos GRE
Welterweight
R. Vesper GDR
D. Robin FRA
K. Bajko HUN

Middleweight
L. Metz GDR
V. Olenik URS
B. Simic YUG
Light-heavyweight
B. Radev BUL
N. Yakovenko URS
N. Martinescu ROM
Heavyweight
I. Kozma HUN
A. Roshchin URS
P. Kment TCH

YACHTING

5.5-metre class
SWE SUI GBR
Flying Dutchman
GBR GER BRA
Dragon
USA DEN GDR
Star
USA NOR ITA
Finn
V. Mankin URS
(11.7 pts)
H. Raudaschl AUT
F. Albarelli AUT

1972 SAPPORO

NORDIC SKIING

Men
Cross-country (15 km)
S. A. Lundback SWE
(45 min 28.24 sec)
F. Simashov URS
I. Formo NOR
Cross-country (30 km)
V. Vedenine URS
(1 hr 36 min 31.15 sec)
P. Tyldum NOR
J. Harviken NOR
Cross-country (50 km)
P. Tyldum NOR
(2 hr 43 min 14.75 sec)
M. Myrmo NOR
V. Vedenine URS
4 x 10-kilometres relay
URS NOR SUI
(2 hr 04 min 47.94 sec)
Ski jumping (70 m)
Y. Kasaya JPN
(244.2 pts)
A. Konno JPN
S. Aochi JPN
Ski jumping (90 m)
W. Fortuna POL
(219.9 pts)
W. Steiner SUI
R. Schmidt GDR
Nordic combined
U. Wehling GDR
(413.340 pts)
R. Miettinen FIN
K. H. Luck GDR
Biathlon
M. Solberg NOR
(1 hr 15 min 55.50 sec)
H. Knauthe GDR
L. Arwidson SWE
Biathlon relay
URS FIN GDR
(1 hr 51 min 44.92 sec)
Women
Cross-country (5 km)
G. Kulakova URS
(17 min 00.50 sec)
M. Kajosmaa FIN
H. Sikolova TCH

Cross-country (10 km)
G. Kulakova URS
(34 min 17.82 sec)
A. Olunina URS
M. Kajosmaa FIN
3 x 5-kilometres relay
URS FIN NOR
(48 min 46.15 sec)

ALPINE SKIING

Men
Downhill
B. Russi SUI
(1 min 51.43 sec)
R. Collombin SUI
H. Messner AUT
Giant slalom
G. Thoeni ITA
(3 min 09.62 sec)
E. Bruggmann SUI
W. Mattle SUI
Slalom
F. F. Fernandez-Ochoa ESP
(1 min 49.27 sec)
G. Thoeni ITA
R. Thoeni ITA
Women
Downhill
M.-T. Nadig SUI
(1 min 36.68 sec)
A. Proell AUT
S. Corrock USA
Giant slalom
M.-T. Nadig SUI
(1 min 29.90 sec)
A. Proell AUT
W. Drexel AUT
Slalom
B. Cochran USA
(1 min 31.24 sec)
D. Debernard FRA
F. Steurer FRA

FIGURE SKATING

Men
O. Nepela TCH
(2,739.1 pts)
S. Chetverukhin URS
P. Pera FRA
Women
B. Schuba AUT
(2,751.5 pts)
K. Magnussen CAN
J. Lynn USA
Pairs
I. Rodnina &
A. Ulanov URS
(420.4 pts)
L. Smirnova &
A. Suraikin URS
M. Gross &
U. Kagelmann GDR

SPEED SKATING

Men
500 metres
E. Keller GER
(39.44 sec)
H. Borjes SWE
V. Muratov URS
1,500 metres
A. Schenk HOL
(2 min 02.96 sec)
R. Gronvold NOR
G. Claesson SWE
5,000 metres
A. Schenk HOL
(7 min 23.61 sec)
R. Gronvold NOR
S. Stensen NOR

10,000 metres
A. Schenk HOL
(15 min 01.35 sec)
C. Verkerk HOL
S. Stensen NOR
Women
500 metres
A. Henning USA
(43.33 sec)
V. Krasnova URS
L. Titova URS
1,000 metres
M. Pflug GER
(1 min 31.40 sec)
A. Keulen-Deelstra HOL
A. Henning USA
1,500 metres
D. Holum USA
(2 min 20.85 sec)
C. Baas-Kaiser HOL
A. Keulen-Deelstra HOL
3,000 metres
C. Baas-Kaiser HOL
(4 min 52.14 sec)
D. Holum USA
A. Keulen-Deelstra HOL

BOBSLEIGHING

Two-man
GER II GER II SUI I
(4 min 57.07 sec)
Four-man
SUI I ITA I GER I
(4 min 43.07 sec)

LUGE TOBOGGANING

Men
Single-seater
W. Scheidel GDR
(3 min 27.58 sec)
H. Ehrig GDR
W. Fiedler GDR
Two-seater
ITA & GDR GDR
(1 min 28.35 sec)
Women
Single-seater
A. A. Mueller GDR
(2 min 59.18 sec)
U. Ruehrhold GDR
M. Schumann GDR

ICE HOCKEY

URS USA TCH

1972 MUNICH

ATHLETICS

Men
100 metres
V. Borsov URS
(10.14 sec)
R. Taylor USA
L. Miller JAM
200 metres
V. Borsov URS
(20.00 sec)
L. Black USA
P. Mennea ITA
400 metres
V. Matthews USA
(44.66 sec)
W. Collett USA
J. Sang KEN
800 metres
D. Wottle USA
(1 min 45.9 sec)
Y. Arzhanov URS
M. Boit KEN

1,500 metres
P. Vasala FIN
(3 min 36.3 sec)
K. Keino KEN
R. Dixon NZL
5,000 metres
L. Viren FIN
(13 min 26.4 sec)
M. Gammoudi TUN
I. Stewart GBR
10,000 metres
L. Viren FIN
(27 min 38.4 sec)
E. Puttemans BEL
M. Yifter ETH
Marathon
F. Shorter USA
(2 hr 12 min 19.8 sec)

K. Lismont BEL
M. Wolde ETH
110-metres hurdles
R. Milburn USA
(13.24 sec)
G. Drut FRA
T. Hill USA
400-metres hurdles
J. Akii-bua UGA
(47.82 sec)
R. Mann USA
D. Hemery GBR
3,000-metres steeplechase
K. Keino KEN
(8 min 23.6 sec)
B. Jipcho KEN
T. Kantanen FIN
4 x 100-metres relay
USA URS GER
(38.19 sec)
4 x 400-metres relay
KEN GBR FRA
(2 min 59.8 sec)
20-kilometres walk
P. Frenkel GDR
(1 hr 26 min 42.4 sec)
V. Golubnichiy URS
H. Reimann GDR
50-kilometres walk
B. Kannenberg GER
(3 hr 56 min 11.6 sec)
V. Soldatenko URS
L. Young USA
High jump
Y. Tarmak URS
(2.23 m)
S. Junge GDR
D. Stones USA
Long jump
R. Williams USA
(8.24 m)
H. Baumgartner GER
A. Robinson USA
Triple jump
V. Saneyev URS
(17.39 m)
J. Drehmel GDR

246

N. Prudencio *BRA*
Pole vault
W. Nordwig *GDR*
(5.50 m)
R. Seagren *USA*
J. Johnson *USA*
Shot
W. Komar *POL*
(21.18 m)
G. Woods *USA*
H. Briesenik *GDR*
Discus
L. Danek *TCH*
(64.40 m)
L. J. Silvester *USA*
R. Bruch *SWE*
Hammer
A. Bondarchuk *URS*
(75.50 m)
J. Sachse *GDR*
V. Khmelevski *URS*
Javelin
K. Wolfermann *GER*
(90.48 m)
J. Lusis *URS*
W. Schmidt *USA*
Decathlon
N. Avilov *URS*
(8,454 pts)
L. Litvenko *URS*
R. Katus *POL*
Women
100 metres
R. Stecher *GDR*
(11.07 sec)
R. Boyle *AUS*
S. Chivas .*CUB*
200 metres
R. Stecher *GDR*
(22.40 sec)
R. Boyle *AUS*
I. Szewinska
(Kirszenstein) *POL*
400 metres
M. Zehrt *GDR*
(51.08 sec)
R. Wilden *GER*
K. Hammond *USA*
800 metres
H. Falck *GER*
(1 min 58.6 sec)
N. Sabaite *URS*
G. Hoffmeister *GDR*
1,500 metres
L. Bragina *URS*
(4 min 01.4 sec)

G. Hoffmeister *GDR*
P. Cacchi *ITA*
100-metres hurdles
A. Ehrhardt *GDR*
(12.59 sec)
V. Bufabu *ROM*
K. Balzer *GDR*
4 x 100-metres relay
GER GDR CUB
(42.81 sec)

4 x 400-metres relay
GDR USA GER
(3 min 23.0 sec)
Pentathlon
M. Peters *GBR*
(4,801 pts)

H. Rosendahl *GER*
B. Pollak *GDR*
High jump
U. Meyfarth *GER*
(1.92 m)
Y. Blagoyeva *BUL*
I. Gusenbauer *AUT*
Long jump
H. Rosendahl *GER*
(6.78 m)

D. Yorgova *BUL*
E. Suranova *TCH*
Shot
N. Chizhova *URS*
(21.03 m)
M. Gummel *GDR*
I. Khristova *BUL*
Discus
F. Melnik *URS*
(66.62 m)
A. Menis *ROM*
V. Stoeva *BUL*
Javelin
R. Fuchs *GDR*
(63.88 m)
J. Todten *GDR*
K. Schmidt *USA*

ARCHERY

Men
J. Williams *USA*
(2,528 pts)
G. Jervill *SWE*
K. Laasonen *FIN*
Women
D. Wilber *USA*
(2,424 pts)
I. Szydlowska *POL*
E. Gapchencko *URS*

BASKETBALL

URS USA CUB

BOXING

Light-flyweight
G. Gedo *HUN*
U. G. Kim *PRK*
R. Evans *GBR* &
E. Rodriquez *ESP*
Flyweight
G. Kostadinov *BUL*
L. Rwabwogo *UGA*
I. Blazynski *POL* &
D. Rodriguez *CUb*
Bantamweight
O. Martinez *CUB*
A. Zamora *MEX*
G. Turpin *GBR* &
R. Carreras *USA*
Featherweight
B. Kusnetsov *URS*
P. Waruinge *KEN*
C. Rojas *COL* &
A. Botos *HUN*
Lightweight
J. Szczepanski *POL*
L. Orban *HUN*
S. Mbugua *KEN* &
A. Perez *COL*
Light-welterweight
R. Seales *USA*
A. Anghelov *BUL*
Z. Vujin *YUG* &
I. Daborg *NIG*
Welterweight
E. Correa *CUB*
J. Kajdi *HUN*
D. Murunga *KEN* &
J. Valdez *USA*
Light-middleweight
D. Kottysch *GER*
W. Rudkowski *POL*
A. Minter *GBR* &
P. Tiepold *GDR*
Middleweight
V. Lemechev *URS*
R. Virtanen *FIN*
P. Amartey *GHA* &
M. Johnson *USA*
Light-heavyweight
M. Parlov *YUG*
G. Carrillo *CUB*
I. Ikhouria *NGR* &
J. Gortat *POL*
Heavyweight
T. Stevenson *CUB*
I. Alexe *ROM*
P. Hussing *GER* &
H. Thomsen *SWE*

CANOEING

Men
Canadian singles
I. Patzaichin *ROM*
(4 min 08.94 sec)
T. Wichmann *HUN*
D. Lewe *GER*
Canadian pairs
URS ROM BUL
(3 min 52.60 sec)
Kayak singles
A. Shaparenko *URS*
(3 min 48.06 sec)
R. Peterson *SWE*
G. Csapo *HUN*
Kayak pairs
URS HUN POL
(3 min 31.23 sec)
Kayak fours
URS ROM NOR
(3 min 14.02 sec)
Slalom: Canadian singles
R. Eiben *GDR*
(315.84 pts)

R. Kauder *GER*
J. McEwan *USA*
Slalom: Canadian pairs
GDR GER FRA
(310.68 pts)
Slalom: kayak singles
S. Horn *GDR*
(268.56 pts)
N. Sattier *AUT*
H. Gimpel *GDR*
Women
Kayak singles
Y. Ryabchinskaya *URS*
(2 min 03.17 sec)
M. Jaapies *HOL*
A. Pfeffer *HUN*
Kayak pairs
URS GDR ROM
(1 min 53.50 sec)
Slalom: kayak singles
A. Bahmann *GDR*
(364.50 pts)
G. Grothaus *GER*
M. Wunderlich *GER*

CYCLING

1,000-metres sprint
D. Morelon *FRA*
(11.69 sec)
J. M. Nicholson *AUS*
O. Pkhakadze *URS*
1,000-metres time trial
N. C. Fredborg *DEN*
(1 min 06.44 sec)
D. Clark *AUS*
J. Schutze *GDR*
4,000-metres pursuit
K. Knudsen *NOR*
(4 min 45.74 sec)
X. Kurmann *SUI*
H. Lutz *GER*
Team
GER GDR GBR
(4 min 22.14 sec)
2,000-metres tandem
URS GDR POL
Road race (182.4 km)
H. Kuiper *HOL*
(4 hr 14 min 37 sec)
K. C. Sefton *AUS*
Team
URS POL
(2 hr 11 min 17.8 sec)
Bronze medals not awarded

EQUESTRIAN

Show jumping
G. Mancinelli *ITA*
(8 flts)
A. Moore *GBR*
N. Shapiro *USA*
Team
GER USA ITA
Dressage
L. Linsenhoff *GER*
(1,229 pts)
E. Petushkova *URS*
J. Neckermann *GER*
Team
URS GER SWE
(5,095 pts)
Three-day event
R. Meade *GBR*
(57.73 pts)
A. Argenton *ITA*
S. Jonsson *SWE*

Team
GBR USA GER

FENCING

Men
Foil
W. Woyda *POL*
(5 wins)
J. Kamuti *HUN*
C. Noel *FRA*
Team
POL URS FRA
Epée
C. Fenyvesi *HUN*
(4 wins)
J. La Degaillerie *FRA*
G. Kulcsar *HUN*
Team
HUN SUI URS
Sabre
V. Sidiak *URS*
(4 wins)
P. Maroth *HUN*
V. Nazlymov *URS*
Team
ITA URS HUN
Women
A. (Ragno) Lonzi *ITA*
(4 wins)
I. Bobis *HUN*
G. Gorokhova *URS*
Team
URS HUN ROM

GYMNASTICS

Men
Combined exercises
S. Kato *JPN*
(114.650 pts)
E. Kenmotsu *JPN*
A. Nakayama *JPN*
Team
JPN URS GDR
Floor
N. Andrianov *URS*
(19.175 pts)
A. Nakayama *JPN*
S. Kasamatsu *JPN*
Horizontal bar
M. Tsukahara *JPN*
(19.725 pts)
S. Kato *JPN*
S. Kasamatsu *JPN*
Parallel bars
S. Kato *JPN*
(19.475 pts)
S. Kasamatsu *JPN*
E. Kenmotsu *JPN*
Pommelled horse
V. Klimenko *URS*
(19.125 pts)
S. Kato *JPN*
E. Kenmotsu *JPN*
Long horse
K. Koeste *GDR*
(18.850 pts)
V. Klimenko *URS*
N. Andrianov *URS*
Rings
A. Nakayama *JPN*
(19.350 pts)
M. Voronin *URS*
M. Tsukahara *JPN*
Women
Combined exercises
L. Tourischeva *URS*
(77.025 pts)
K. Janz *GDR*
T. Lasakovich *URS*
Team
URS GDR HUN

Beam
O. Korbut *URS*
(19.400 pts)
T. Lazakovich *URS*
K. Janz *GDR*
Asymmetrical bars
K. Janz *GDR*
(19.675 pts)
O. Korbut *URS* &
E. Zuchold *GDR*
Horse vault
K. Janz *GDR*
(19.525 pts)
E. Zuchold *GDR*
L. Tourischeva *URS*
Floor
O. Korbut *URS*
(19.575 pts)
L. Tourischeva *URS*
L. Lazakovich *URS*

HANDBALL

YUG TCH ROM

HOCKEY (FIELD)

GER PAK IND

JUDO

Lightweight
T. Kawaguchi *JPN*
Silver not awarded
Y. I. Kim *PRK* &
I. Mounier *FRA*
Welterweight
T. Nomura *JPN*
A. Zajkowski *POL*
D. Hoetger *GDR* &
A. Novikov *URS*
Middleweight
S. Sekine *JPN*
S. L. Oh *PRK*
B. Jacks *GBR* &
J. P. Cochet *FRA*
Light-heavyweight
S. Khokhoshvili *URS*
D. C. Starbrook *GBR*
P. Barth *GER* &
C. Ishii *BRA*
Heavyweight
W. Ruska *HOL*
K. Glahn *GER*
G. Onashvili *URS* &
M. Nishimura *JPN*
Open
W. Ruska *HOL*
V. Kusnetsov *URS*
A. Parisi *GBR* &
J. C. Brondani *FRA*

MODERN PENTATHLON

A. Balczo *HUN*
(5,412 pts)
B. Onishenko *URS*
P. Lednev *URS*
Team
URS HUN FIN

ROWING

Single sculls
Y. Malyshev *URS*
(7 min 10.12 sec)
A. Demiddi *ARG*
W. Gueldenpfennig *GDR*
Double sculls
URS NOR GDR
(7 min 01.77 sec)
Coxless pairs
GDR SUI HOL

(6 min 53.16 sec)
Coxed pairs
GDR TCH ROM
(7 min 17.25 sec)
Coxless fours
GDR NZL GER
(6 min 24.27 sec)
Coxed fours
GER GDR TCH
(6 min 31.85 sec)
Eights
NZL USA GDR
(6 min 08.94 sec)

SHOOTING

Free pistol
R. Skanaker *SWE*
(567 pts)
D. Iuga *ROM*
R. Dollinger *AUT*
Rapid-fire pistol
J. Zapedski *POL*
(595 pts)
L. Falta *TCH*
V. Torshin *URS*
**Moving target
(running bear)**
L. Zhelezniak *URS*
(596 pts)
H. Bellingrodt *COL*
K. Kynoch *GBR*
Free rifle
L. Wigger *USA*
(1,155 pts)
B. Melnik *URS*
L. Pap *HUN*
Small-bore rifle, prone
H. J. Li *PRK*
(599 pts)
V. Auer *USA*
N. Rotaru *ROM*
Small-bore rifle, three positions
J. Writer *USA*
(1,166 pts)
L. Bassham *USA*
W. Lippoldt *GDR*
Trap shooting
A. Scalzone *ITA*
(199 pts)
M. Carrega *FRA*
S. Basagni *ITA*
Skeet
K. Wirnhier *GER*
(195 pts)
Y. Petrov *URS*
M. Buchheim *GDR*

SOCCER

POL HUN GDR & URS

SWIMMING

Men
100-metres freestyle
M. Spitz *USA*
(51.122 sec)
J. Heidenreich *USA*
V. Bure *URS*
200-metres freestyle
M. Spitz *USA*
(1 min 52.78 sec)
S. Genter *USA*
W. Lampe *GER*
400-metres freestyle
B. Cooper *AUS*
(4 min 00.27 sec)
S. Genter *USA*
T. McBreen *USA*
1,500-metres freestyle
M. Burton *USA*
(15 min 52.58 sec)

G. Windeatt *AUS*
D. Northway *USA*
100-metres backstroke
R. Matthes *GDR*
(56.58 sec)
M. Stamm *USA*
J. Murphy *USA*
200-metres backstroke
R. Matthes *GDR*
(2 min 02.82 sec)
M. Stamm *USA*
M. Ivey *USA*
100-metres breaststroke
N. Taguchi *JPN*
(1 min 04.94 sec)
T. Bruce *USA*
J. Hencken *USA*
200-metres breaststroke
J. Hencken *USA*
(2 min 21.55 sec)
D. Wilkie *GBR*
N. Taguchi *JPN*
100-metres butterfly
M. Spitz *USA*
(54.27 sec)

B. Robertson *CAN*
J. Heidenreich *USA*
200-metres butterfly
M. Spitz *USA*
(2 min 00.70 sec)
G. Hall *USA*
R. Backhaus *USA*
200-metres medley
G. Larsson *SWE*
(2 min 07.17 sec)
T. McKee *USA*
S. Furniss *USA*
400-metres medley
G. Larsson *SWE*
(4 min 31.98 sec)
T. McKee *USA*
A. Hargitay *HUN*
4 x 100-metres freestyle relay
USA URS GDR
(3 min 26.42 sec)
4 x 200-metres freestyle relay
USA GER URS
(7 min 35.78 sec)
4 x 100-metres medley relay
USA GDR CAN
(3 min 48.16 sec)
Highboard diving
K. Dibiasi *ITA*
(504.12 pts)
R. Rydze *USA*
F. Cagnotto *ITA*
Springboard diving
V. Vasin *URS*
(594.09 pts)

F. Cagnotto *ITA*
C. Lincoln *USA*
Water polo
URS HUN USA
Women
100-metres freestyle
S. Neilson *USA*
(58.59 sec)
S. Babashoff *USA*
S. Gould *AUS*
200-metres freestyle
S. Gould *AUS*
(2 min 03.56 sec)

S. Babashoff *USA*
K. Rothhammer *USA*
400-metres freestyle
S. Gould *AUS*
(4 min 19.04 sec)
N. Calligaris *ITA*
G. Wegner *GDR*
800-metres freestyle
K. Rothhammer *USA*
(8 min 53.68 sec)
S. Gould *USA*
N. Calligaris *ITA*
100-metres backstroke
M. Belote *USA*
(2 min 19.19 sec)
A. Gyarmati *HUN*
S. Atwood *USA*
200-metres backstroke
M. Belote *USA*
(2 min 19.19 sec)
S. Atwood *USA*
D. M. Gurr *CAN*
100-metres breaststroke
C. Carr *USA*
(1 min 13.58 sec)
G. Stepanova *URS*
B. Whitfield *AUS*
200-metres breaststroke
B. Whitfield *AUS*
(2 min 41.71 sec)
D. Schoenfield *USA*
G. Stepanova *URS*
100-metres butterfly
M. Aoki *JPN*
(1 min 03.34 sec)
R. Beier *GDR*
A. Gyarmati *HUN*
200-metres butterfly
K. Moe *USA*
(2 min 15.57 sec)
L. Colella *USA*
E. Daniel *USA*
200-metres medley
S. Gould *AUS*
(2 min 23.07 sec)
K. Ender *GDR*
L. Vidali *USA*
400-metres medley
G. Neall *AUS*
(5 min 02.97 sec)
L. Cliff *CAN*

N. Calligaris *ITA*
4 x 100-metres freestyle relay
USA GDR GER
(3 min 55.19 sec)
4 x 100-metres medley relay
USA GDR GER
(4 min 20.75 sec)
Highboard diving
U. Knape *SWE*
(390.00 pts)
M. Duchkova *TCH*
M. Janicke *GDR*
Springboard diving
M. King *USA*
(450.03 pts)
U. Knape *SWE*
M. Janicke *GDR*

VOLLEYBALL

Men
JPN GDR URS
Women
URS JPN PRK

WEIGHTLIFTING

Flyweight
Z. Smalcerz *POL*
(337.5 kg)
L. Szucs *HUN*
S. Holczreiter *HUN*
Bantamweight
I. Foldi *HUN*
(377.5 kg)
M. Nassiri *IRN*
G. Chetin *URS*
Featherweight
N. Nurikyan *BUL*
(402.5 kg)
D. Zhanidze *URS*
J. Benedek *HUN*
Lightweight
M. Kirzhinov *URS*
(460.0 kg)
M. Kuchev *BUL*
Z. Kaczmarek *POL*
Middleweight
Y. Bikov *BUL*
(485 kg)
M. Trabulsi *LIB*
A. Silvino *ITA*
Light-heavyweight
L. Jensen *NOR*
(507.5 kg)
N. Ozimek *POL*
G. Horvath *HUN*
Middle-heavyweight
A. Nikolov *BUL*
(525.0 kg)
A. Shoppov *BUL*
H. Bettemborg *SWE*
Heavyweight
Y. Talts *URS*
(580.0 kg)

A. Kraichev *BUL*
G. Gruetzner *GDR*

Super-heavyweight
(*previously called heavyweight*)
V. Alexeyev *URS*
(640.0 kg)
R. Mang *GER*
G. Bonk *GDR*

WRESTLING: FREESTYLE

Light-flyweight
R. Dmitriev *URS*
O. Nikolov *BUL*
E. Javadpour *IRN*
Flyweight
K. Kato *JPN*
A. Alakhverdiev *URS*
H. K. Gwong *PRK*
Bantamweight
H. Yanagida *JPN*
R. Sanders *USA*
L. Klinga *HUN*
Featherweight
Z. Abdulbekov *URS*
V. Akdag *TUR*
I. Krastev *BUL*
Lightweight
D. Gable *USA*
K. Wada *JPN*
R. Ashuraliev *URS*
Welterweight
W. Wells *USA*
J. Karlsson *SWE*
A. Seger *GER*
Middleweight
L. Tediashvili *URS*
J. Peterson *USA*
V. Jorga *ROM*
Light-heavyweight
B. Peterson *USA*
G. Strakhov *URS*
K. Bajko *HUN*
Heavyweight
I. Yaragin *URS*
K. Baianmunkh *MGL*
J. Csatari *HUN*
Super-heavyweight
A. Medved *URS*
O. Duralyev *BUL*
C. Taylor *USA*

WRESTLING: GRECO-ROMAN

Light-flyweight
G. Berceanu *ROM*
R. Aliabadi *IRN*
S. Anghelov *BUL*
Flyweight
P. Kirov *BUL*
K. Hirayama *JPN*
G. Bognanni *ITA*
Bantamweight
P. Kazakov *URS*
H. J. Veil *GER*
R. Bjoerlin *FIN*
Featherweight
G. Markov *BUL*
H. H. Wehling *GDR*
K. Lipien *POL*
Lightweight
S. Khisamutdinov *URS*
S. Apostolov *BUL*
G. M. Ranzi *ITA*
Welterweight
V. Macha *TCH*
P. Galaktopoulos *GRE*
J. Karlsson *SWE*

Middleweight
C. Hegedus *HUN*
A. Narazenko *HUN*
M. Nenadic *YUG*
Light-heavyweight
V. Rezantsev *URS*
J. Corak *YUG*
C. Kwiecinski *POL*
Heavyweight
N. Martinescu *ROM*
N. Iakovenko *URS*
F. Kiss *HUN*
Super-heavyweight
A. Roshchin *URS*
A. Tomov *BUL*
V. Dolipschi *ROM*

YACHTING

Tempest
URS GBR USA
Soling
USA SWE CAN
Flying Dutchman
GBR FRA GER
Dragon
AUS GDR USA
Star
AUS SWE GER
Finn
S. Maury *FRA*
(58.0 pts)
I. Hatzipavlis *GRE*
V. Potapov *URS*

1976 INNSBRUCK

NORDIC SKIING

Men
Cross-country (15 km)
N. Bajukov *URS*
(43 min 58.47 sec)
E. Beliaev *URS*
A. Koivisto *FIN*
Cross-country (30 km)
S. Saveliev *URS*
(1 hr 30 min 29.38 sec)
W. Koch *USA*
I. Garanin *URS*
Cross-country (50 km)
I. Formo *NOR*
(2 hr 37 min 30.05 sec)
G.-D. Klause *GDR*
B. Sodergren *SWE*
4 x 10-kilometres relay
FIN NOR URS
(2 hr 07 min 59.72 sec)
Ski jumping (70 m)
H.-G. Aschenbach *GDR*
(252.0 pts)
J. Danneberg *GDR*
K. Schnabl *AUT*
Ski jumping (90 m)
K. Schnabl *AUT*
(234.8 pts)

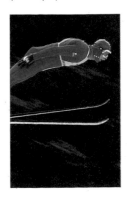

A. Innauer *AUT*
H. Glass *GDR*
Nordic combined
U. Wehling *GDR*
(423.39 pts)
U. Hettich *GER*
K. Winkler *GDR*
Biathlon
N. Kruglov *URS*
(1 hr 14 min 12.26 sec)
H. Ikola *FIN*
A. Elizarov *URS*
Biathlon relay
URS FIN GDR
(1 hr 57 min 55.64 sec)
Women
Cross-country (5 km)
H. Takalo *FIN*
(15 min 48.69 sec)
R. Smetanina *URS*
N. Baldicheva *URS*
Cross-country (10 km)
R. Smetanina *URS*
(30 min 13.41 sec)
H. Takalo *FIN*
G. Kulakova *URS*
4 x 5-kilometres relay
URS FIN GDR
(1 hr 07 min 49.75 sec)

ALPINE SKIING

Men
Downhill
F. Klammer *AUT*
(1 min 45.73 sec)
B. Russi *SUI*
H. Plank *ITA*
Giant slalom
H. Hemmi *SUI*
(3 min 26.97 scc)
E. Good *SUI*
I. Stenmark *SWE*
Slalom
P. Gros *ITA*
(2 hrs 03.29 sec)
G. Thoeni *ITA*
W. Frommelt *LIE*
Women
Downhill
R. Mittermaier *GER*
(1 min 46.16 sec)
B. Totschnig *AUT*
C. Nelson *USA*
Giant Slalom
K. Kreiner *CAN*
(1 min 29.13 sec)
R. Mittermaier *GER*
D. Debernard *FRA*
Slalom
R. Mittermaier *GER*
(1 min 46.16 sec)
G. Giordani *ITA*
H. Wenzel *LIE*

FIGURE SKATING

Men
J. Curry *GBR*
(192.74 pts)
V. Kovalev *URS*
T. Cranston *CAN*
Women
D. Hamill *USA*
(193.80 pts)

D. de Leeuw *HOL*
C. Errath *GDR*
Pairs
I. Rodnina &
A. Zaitsev *URS*
(140.54 pts)

R. Kermer &
R. Oesterreich *GDR*
M. Gross &
U. Kagelmann *GDR*
Ice dancing
L. Pakhomova &
A. Gorshkov *URS*
(209.92 pts)
I. Moiseeva &
A. Minenkov *URS*
C. O'Connor &
J. Millns *USA*

SPEED SKATING

Men
500 metres
E. Kulikov *URS*
(39.17 sec)
V. Muratov *URS*
D. Immerfall *USA*
1,000 metres
P. Mueller *USA*
(1 min 19.32 sec)
J. Didriksen *NOR*
V. Muratov *URS*
1,500 metres
J. Storholt *NOR*
(1 min 59.38 sec)
J. Kondakov *URS*
H. van Helden *HOL*
5,000 metres
S. Stensen *NOR*
(7 min 24.48 sec)

P. Kleine *HOL*
H. van Helden *HOL*
10,000 metres
P. Kleine *HOL*
(14 min 50.59 sec)
S. Stensen *NOR*
H. van Helden *HOL*
Women
500 metres
S. Young *USA*
(42.76 sec)
C. Priestner *CAN*
T. Averina *URS*
1,000 metres
T. Averina *URS*
(1 min 28.43 sec)
L. Poulos *USA*
S. Young *USA*
1,500 metres
G. Stepanskaya *URS*
(2 min 16.58 sec)
S. Young *USA*
T. Averina *URS*
3,000 metres
T. Averina *URS*
(4 min 45.19 sec)
A. Mitscherlich *GDR*
L. Korsmo *NOR*

BOBSLEIGHING

Two-man
GDR II GER I SUI I
(3 min 44.42 sec)
Four-man
GDR I SUI II GER I
(3 min 40.43 sec)

LUGE TOBOGGANING

Men
Single-seater
D. Guenther *GDR*
(3 min 27.688 sec)
J. Fendt *GER*
H. Rinn *GDR*
Two-seater
GDR GER AUT
(1 min 25.604 sec)
Women
Single-seater
M. Schumann *GDR*
(2 min 50.621 sec)
U. Ruehrold *GDR*
E. Demleitner *GER*

ICE HOCKEY

URS TCH GER

1976 MONTREAL

ATHLETICS

Men
100 metres
H. Crawford *TRI*
(10.06 sec)
D. Quarrie *JAM*
V. Borsov *URS*
200 metres
D. Quarrie *JAM*
(20.23 sec)
M. Hampton *USA*
D. Evans *USA*
400 metres
A. Juantorena *CUB*
(44.26 sec)
F. Newhouse *USA*
H. Frazier *USA*
800 metres
A. Juantorena *CUB*
(1 min 43.50 sec)

I. Van Damme *BEL*
R. Wohlhutter *USA*
1,500 metres
J. Walker *NZL*
(3 min 39.17 sec)
I. Van Damme *BEL*
P.-H. Wellmann *GER*
5,000 metres
L. Viren *FIN*
(13 min 24.76 sec)

D. Quax *NZL*
K.-P. Hildenbrand *GER*
10,000 metres
L. Viren *FIN*
(27 min 40.38 sec)
C. S. Lopes *POR*
B. Foster *GBR*
Marathon
W. Cierpinski *GDR*
(2 hr 09 min 55.0 sec)
F. Shorter *USA*
K. Lismont *BEL*
110-metres hurdles
G. Drut *FRA*
(13.30 sec)
A. Casanas *CUB*
W. Davenport *USA*
400-metres hurdles
E. Moses *USA*
(47.64 sec)
M. Shine *USA*
E. Gavrilenko *URS*
3,000-metres steeplechase
A. Garderud *SWE*
(8 min 08.02 sec)

B. Malinowski *POL*
F. Baumgartl *GDR*
20-kilometres walk
D. Bautista *MEX*
(1 hr 24 min 40.60 sec)
H. Reimann *GDR*
P. Frenkel *GDR*
4 x 100-metres relay
USA GDR URS
(38.33 sec)
4 x 400-metres relay
USA POL GER
(2 min 58.65 sec)

High jump
J. Wszola *POL*
(2.25 m)
G. Joy *CAN*
D. Stones *USA*
Long jump
A. Robinson *USA*
(8.35 m)
R. Williams *USA*
F. Wartenberg *GDR*
Triple jump
V. Saneyev *URS*
(17.29 m)
J. Butts *USA*
J. C. de Oliviera *BRA*
Pole vault
T. Slusarski *POL*
(5.50 m)
A. Kalliomaki *FIN*
D. Roberts *USA*
Shot
U. Beyer *GDR*
(21.05 m)
E. Mironov *URS*
A. Baryshnikov *URS*
Discus
M. Wilkins *USA*
(67.50 m)

W. Schmidt *GDR*
J. Powell *USA*
Hammer
Y. Sedykh *URS*
(77.52 m)
A. Spiridonov *URS*
A. Bondarchuk *URS*
Javelin
M. Nemeth *HUN*
(94.58 m)
H. Siitonen *FIN*
G. Megelea *ROM*
Decathlon
B. Jenner *USA*
(8,618 pts)
G. Kratschmer *GER*
N. Avilov *URS*
Women
100 metres
A. Richter *GER*
(11.08 sec)
R. Stecher *GDR*
I. Helten *GER*
200 metres
B. Eckert *GDR*
(22.37 sec)
A. Richter *GER*
R. Stecher *GDR*
400 metres
I. Szewinska (Kirszenstein) *POL*
(49.29 sec)
C. Brehmer *GDR*
E. Streidt *GDR*
800 metres
T. Kazankina *URS*
(1 min 54.94 sec)
N. Chtereva *BUL*

E. Zinn *GDR*
1,500 metres
T. Kazankina *URS*
(4 min 05.48 sec)
G. Hoffmeister *GDR*
U. Klapezynski *GDR*
100-metres hurdles
J. Schaller *GDR*
(12.77 sec)
T. Anisimova *URS*
N. Lebedeva *URS*
4 x 100-metres relay
GDR GER URS
(42.55 sec)
4 x 400-metres relay
GDR USA URS
(3 min 19.23 sec)
High jump
R. Ackermann *GDR*
(1.93 m)
S. Simeoni *ITA*
Y. Blagoeva *BUL*
Long jump
A. Voigt *GDR*
(6.72 m)
K. McMillan *USA*
L. Alfeeva *URS*
Shot
I. Khristova *BUL*
(21.16 m)
N. Chizhova *URS*
H. Fibingerova *TCH*
Discus
E. Schlaak *GDR*
(69.00 m)
M. Vergova *BUL*
G. Hinzmann *GDR*
Javelin
R. Fuchs *GDR*
(65.94 m)
M. Becker *GER*
K. Schmidt *USA*
Pentathlon
S. Siegl *GDR*
(4,745 pts)

C. Laser *GDR*
B. Pollak *GDR*

ARCHERY

Men
D. Pace *USA*
(2,571 pts)
H. Michinaga *JPN*
G. C. Ferrari *ITA*
Women
L. Ryon *USA*
(2,499 pts)
V. Kovpan *URS*
Z. Rustamova *URS*

BASKETBALL

Men
USA YUG URS
Women
URS USA BUL

BOXING

Light-flyweight
J. Hernandez *CUB*
B. U. Li *PRK*
P. Pooltarat *THA* &
O. Maldonado *PUR*
Flyweight
L. Randolph *USA*
R. Duvalong *CUB*
D. Torosyan *URS* &
L. Blazynski *POL*
Bantamweight
Y. J. Gu *PRK*
C. Mooney *USA*
P. Cowdell *GBR* &
C. Hwang *KOR*
Featherweight
A. Herrera *CUB*
R. Nowakowski *GDR*
J. Paredes *MEX* &
L. Kosedowski *POL*
Lightweight
H. Davis *USA*
S. Cutov *ROM*
A. Rusevski *YUG* &
V. Solomin *URS*
Light-welterweight
R. Leonard *USA*
A. Aldama *CUB*
V. Kolev *BUL* &
K. Szczerba *POL*
Welterweight
J. Bachfeld *GDR*
P. J. Gamarro *VEN*
R. Skricek *GER* &
V. Zilberman *ROM*
Light-middleweight
J. Rybicki *POL*
T. Kacar *YUG*
V. Savchenko *URS* &
R. Garbey *CUB*
Middleweight
M. Spinks *USA*
R. Riskiev *URS*
A. Nastac *ROM* &
L. Martinez *CUB*
Light-heavyweight
L. Spinks *USA*
S. Soria *CUB*
C. Dafinoiu *ROM* &
J. Gortat *POL*
Heavyweight
T. Stevenson *CUB*
M. Simon *ROM*
J. Tate *USA* &
C. Hill *BER*

CANOEING

Men
500-metres Canadian singles
A. Rogov *URS*
(1 min 59.23 sec)
J. Wood *CAN*
M. Ljubek *YUG*
1,000-metres Canadian singles
M. Ljubek *YUG*
(4 min 09.51 sec)
V. Urchenko *URS*
T. Wichmann *HUN*
500-metres Canadian pairs
URS POL HUN
(1 min 45.81 sec)
1,000-metres Canadian pairs
URS ROM HUN
(3 min 52.76 sec)

500-metres kayak singles
V. Diba *ROM*
(1 min 46.41 sec)
Z. Sztanity *HUN*
R. Helm *GDR*
1,000-metres kayak singles
R. Helm *GDR*
(3 min 48.20 sec)
G. Csapo *HUN*
V. Diba *ROM*
500-metres kayak pairs
GDR URS ROM
(1 min 35.87 sec)
1,000-metres kayak pairs
URS GDR HUN
(3 min 29.01 sec)
1,000-metres kayak fours
URS ESP GDR
(3 min 08.69 sec)
Women
Kayak singles
C. Zirzow *GDR*
(2 min 01.05 sec)
T. Korshunova *URS*
K. Rajnai *HUN*
Kayak pairs
URS HUN GDR
(1 min 51.15 sec)

CYCLING

1,000-metres sprint
A. Tkac *TCH*
(10.78 sec)
D. Morelon *FRA*
H.-J. Geschke *GDR*
1,000-metres time trial
K.-J. Grunke *GDR*
(1 min 05.93 sec)
M. Vaarten *BEL*
N. Fredborg *DEN*
4,000-metres pursuit
G. Braun *GDR*
(9 min 47.6 sec)
H. Ponsteen *HOL*
T. Huschke *GDR*
Team
GER URS GBR
(4 min 21.06 sec)
Road race
B. Johansson *SWE*
(4 hr 46 min 52.0 sec)
G. Martinelli *ITA*
M. Nowicki *POL*
Team
URS POL DEN
(2 hr 08 min 53.0 sec)

EQUESTRIAN

Show jumping
A. Schockemoehle *GER*
(0 flts)

M. Vaillancourt *CAN*
F. Mathy *BEL*
Team
FRA GER BEL
Dressage
C. Stueckelberger *SUI*
(1,486 pts)
H. Boldt *GER*
R. Klimke *GER*
Team
GER SUI USA
Three-day event
E. Coffin *USA*
(114.99 pts)
J. Plumb *USA*
K. Schultz *GER*

FENCING

Men
Foil
F. Dal Zotto *ITA*
(4 wins)
A. Romankov *URS*
B. Talvard *FRA*
Team
GER ITA FRA
Epée
A. Pusch *GER*
(3 wins)
J. Hehn *GER*
G. Kulcsar *HUN*
Team
SWE GER SUI
Sabre
V. Krovopouskov *URS*
(5 wins)
V. Nazlimov *URS*
V. Sidiak *URS*
Team
URS ITA ROM
Women
Foil
I. Schwarczenberger *HUN*
(4 wins)
M. C. Collino *ITA*
E. (Novikova) Belova *URS*
Team
URS FRA HUN

GYMNASTICS

Men
Combined exercises
N. Andrianov *URS*
(116.650 pts)
S. Kato *JPN*
M. Tsukahara *JPN*
Team
URS POL DEN
(2 hr 08 min 53.0 sec)

Team
JPN URS GDR
Floor
N. Andrianov *URS*
(19.450 pts)
V. Marchenko *URS*
P. Kormann *USA*
Horizontal bar
M. Tsukahara *JPN*
(19.675 pts)
E. Kenmotsu *JPN*
E. Gienger *GER*
Parallel bars
S. Kato *JPN*
(19.675 pts)
N. Andrianov *URS*
M. Tsukahara *JPN*
Pommelled horse
Z. Magyar *HUN*
(19.700 pts)
E. Kenmotsu *JPN*
N. Andrianov *URS*
Long horse
N. Andrianov *URS*
(19.540 pts)

M. Tsukuhara *JPN*
H. Kajiyama *JPN*
Rings
N. Andrianov *URS*
(19.650 pts)
A. Ditiatin *URS*
D. Grecu *ROM*
Women
Combined exercises
N. Comaneci *ROM*
(79.275 pts)
N. Kim *URS*
L. Tourischeva *URS*
Team
URS ROM GDR
Beam
N. Comaneci *ROM*
(19.950 pts)
O. Korbut *URS*
M. Egervari *HUN*
Asymmetrical bars
N. Comaneci *ROM*
(20.000 pts)

T. Ungureanu *ROM*
M. Egervari *HUN*
Horse vault
N. Kim *URS*
(19.800 pts)
L. Tourischeva *URS*
C. Dombeck *GDR*
Floor
N. Kim *URS*
(19.850 pts)
L. Tourischeva *URS*
N. Comaneci *ROM*

HANDBALL

Men
URS ROM POL
Women
URS GDR HUN

HOCKEY (FIELD)

NZL AUS PAK

JUDO

Lightweight
H. Rodriguez *CUB*
E. Chang *KOR*
F. Mariani *ITA* &
J. Tuncsik *HUN*
Light-middleweight
V. Nevzorov *URS*
K. Kuramoto *JPN*
P. Vial *FRA* &
M. Talaj *POL*
Middleweight
I. Sonoda *JPN*
V. Dvoinikov *URS*
S. Obadov *YUG* &
Y. Park *KOR*

Light-heavyweight
K. Nimomiya *JPN*
R. Harshiladze *URS*
D. Starbrook *GBR* &
J. Roethlisberger *SUI*
Heavyweight
S. Novikov *URS*
G. Neureuther *GER*
S. Endo *JPN* &
A. Coage *USA*
Open
H. Uemura *JPN*
K. Remfry *GBR*
S. Chochishvili *URS* &
J. Cho *KOR*

MODERN PENTATHLON

J. Pyciak-Peciak *POL*
(5,520 pts)
P. Lednev *URS*
J. Bartu *TCH*
Team
GBR TCH HUN

ROWING

Men
Single sculls
P. Karppinen *FIN*
(7 min 29.03 sec)

P.-M. Kolbe *GER*
J. Dreifke *GDR*
Double sculls
NOR GBR GDR
(7 min 13.20 sec)
Quadruple sculls
GDR URS TCH
(6 min 18.65 sec)
Coxless pairs
GDR USA GER
(7 min 23.31 sec)
Coxed pairs
GDR URS TCH
(7 min 58.99 sec)
Coxless fours
GDR NOR URS
(6 min 37.42 sec)
Coxed fours
URS GDR GER
(6 min 40.22 sec)
Eights
GDR GBR NZL
(5 min 58.29 sec)
Women
Single sculls
C. Scheiblich *GDR*
(4 min 05.56 sec)
J. Lind *USA*
E. Antonova *URS*
Double sculls
BUL GDR URS
(3 min 44.36 sec)
Quadruple sculls
GDR URS BUL
(3 min 29.99 sec)

Coxless pairs
BUL GDR GER
(4 min 01.22 sec)
Coxed pairs
GDR BUL URS
(3 min 45.08 sec)
Eights
GDR URS USA
(3 min 33.32 sec)

SHOOTING

Free pistol
U. Potteck *GDR*
(573 pts)
H. Vollmar *GDR*
R. Dollinger *AUT*
Rpaid-fire pistol
N. Klaar *GDR*
(597 pts)
J. Wiefel *GDR*
R. Ferraris *ITA*
Small-bore rifle, prone
K. Smieszek *GER*
(599 pts)
U. Lind *GER*
G. Lushchikov *URS*
Small-bore rifle, three positions
L. Bassham *USA*
(1,162 pts)
M. Murdock *USA*
W. Seibold *GER*
Running game
A. Gazov *URS*
(579 pts)
A. Kedyarov *URS*
J. Greszkiewicz *POL*
Trap shooting
D. Haldeman *USA*
(190 pts)
A. Silva Marques *POR*
U. Baldi *ITA*
Skeet
J. Panacek *TCH*
(198 pts)
E. Swinkels *HOL*
W. Gawlowski *POL*

SOCCER

GDR POL URS

SWIMMING

Men
100-metres freestyle
J. Montgomery *USA*
(49.99 sec)
J. Babashoff *USA*
P. Nocke *GER*
200-metres freestyle
B. Furniss *USA*
(1 min 50.29 sec)
J. Naber *USA*
J. Montgomery *USA*
400-metres freestyle
B. Goodell *USA*
(3 min 51.93 sec)

T. Shaw *USA*
V. Raskatov *URS*
1,500-metres freestyle
B. Goodell *USA*
(15 min 02.40 sec)
B. Hackett *USA*
S. Holland *AUS*
100-metres backstroke
J. Naber *USA*
(55.49 sec)

P. Rocca *USA*
R. Matthes *GDR*
200-metres backstroke
J. Naber *USA*
(1 min 59.19 sec)
P. Rocca *USA*
D. Harrigan *USA*
100-metres breaststroke
J. Hencken *USA*
(1 min 03.11 sec)
D. Wilkie *GBR*
A. Iuozaytis *URS*
200-metres breaststroke
D. Wilkie *GBR*
(2 min 15.11 sec)

J. Hencken *USA*
R. Colella *USA*
100-metres butterfly
M. Vogel *USA*
(54.35 sec)
J. Bottom *USA*
G. Hall *USA*
200-metres butterfly
M. Bruner *USA*
(1 min 59.23 sec)
S. Gregg *USA*
B. Forrester *USA*
400-metres medley
R. Strachan *USA*
(4 min 23.68 sec)
T. McKee *USA*
A. Smirnov *URS*
2 x 200-metres freestyle relay
USA URS GBR
(7 min 23.22 sec)

4 x 100-metres medley relay
USA CAN GER
(3 min 42.22 sec)
Highboard diving
K. Dibiasi *ITA*
(600.51 pts)
G. Louganis *USA*
V. Aleynik *URS*
Springboard diving
P. Boggs *USA*
(619.05 pts)
F. Cagnotto *ITA*
A. Kosenkov *URS*
Water polo
HUN ITA HOL
Women
100-metres freestyle
K. Ender *GDR*
(55.65 pts)
P. Priemer *GDR*
E. Brigitha *HOL*
200-metres freestyle
K. Ender *GDR*
(1 min 59.26 sec)
S. Babashoff *USA*
E. Brigitha *HOL*
400-metres freestyle
P. Thuemer *GDR*
(4 min 09.89 sec)
S. Babashoff *USA*
S. Smith *CAN*
800-metres freestyle
P. Thwemer *GDR*
(8 min 37.14 sec)
S. Babashoff *USA*
W. Weinberg *USA*
100-metres backstroke
V. Richter *GDR*
(1 min 01.83 sec)
B. Treiber *GDR*
N. Garapick *CAN*
200-metres backstroke
V. Richter *GDR*
(2 min 13.43 sec)
B. Treiber *GDR*
N. Garapick *CAN*
100-metres breaststroke
H. Anke *GDR*
(1 min 11.16 sec)
L. Rusanova *URS*
M. Koshevaia *URS*
200-metres breaststroke
M. Koshevaia *URS*
(2 min 33.35 sec)
M. Iurchenia *URS*
L. Rusanova *URS*
100-metres butterfly
K. Ender *GDR*
(1 min 00.13 sec)
A. Pollack *GDR*
W. Boglioli *USA*
200-metres butterfly
A. Pollack *GDR*
(2 min 11.41 sec)
U. Tauber *GDR*
R. Gabriel *GDR*
400-metres medley
U. Tauber *GDR*
(4 min 42.77 sec)
C. Gibson *CAN*
B. Smith *CAN*
4 x 100-metres freestyle relay
USA GDR CAN
(3 min 44.82 sec)
4 x 100-metres medley relay
GDR USA CAN
(4 min 07.95 sec)

Highboard diving
E. Vaytsekhovskaia *URS*
(406.59 pts)
U. Knape *SWE*
D. Wilson *USA*
Springboard diving
J. Chandler *USA*
(506.19 pts)
C. Koehler *GDR*
C. McIngvale *USA*

VOLLEYBALL

Men
POL URS CUB
Women
JPN URS KOR

WEIGHTLIFTING

Flyweight
A. Voronin *URS*
(242.5 kg)
G. Koszegi *HUN*
M. Nassiri *IRN*
Bantamweight
N. Nurikyam *BUL*
(262.5 kg)
G. Cziura *POL*
K. Ando *JPN*
Featherweight
N. Kolesnikov *URS*
(285 kg)
G. Todorov *BUL*
K. Hirai *JPN*
Lightweight
Z. Kaczmarek *POL*
(307.5 kg)
P. Korul *URS*
D. Senet *FRA*
Middleweight
Y. Mitkov *BUL*
(335.0 kg)
V. Militosyan *URS*
P. Wenzel *GDR*
Light-heavyweight
V. Shary *URS*
(365.0 kg)
B. Blagoev *BUL*
T. Stoichev *BUL*
Middle-heavyweight
D. Rigert *URS*
(382.5 kg)
L. James *USA*
A. Shopov *BUL*
Heavyweight
V. Khristov *BUL*
(400.0 kg)
Y. Zaitsev *URS*
K. Semerdjiev *BUL*
Super heavyweight
V. Alexeyev *URS*
(440.0 kg)
G. Bonk *GDR*
H. Losch *GDR*

WRESTLING: FREESTYLE

Light-flyweight
K. Issaev *BUL*
R. Dmitriev *URS*
A. Kudo *JPN*
Flyweight
Y. Takada *JPN*
A. Ivanov *URS*
H.-S. Jean *KOR*
Bantamweight
V. Umin *URS*
H.-D. Bruchert *GDR*
M. Arai *JPN*

Featherweight
J.-M. Yang *KOR*
Z. Oidov *MGL*
G. Davis *USA*
Welterweight
J. Date *JPN*
L. Keaser *USA*
Y. Sugawara *JPN*
Middleweight
J. Peterson *USA*
V. Novojilov *URS*
A. Seger *GER*
Light-heavyweight
L. Tediashvili *URS*
B. Peterson *USA*
S. Morcov *ROM*
Heavyweight
I. Yarygin *URS*
R. Hellickson *USA*
D. Kostov *Bul*
Super heavyweight
S. Andiev *URS*
J. Balla *HUN*
L. Simon *ROM*

WRESTLING: GRECO-ROMAN

Light-flyweight
A. Shumakov *URS*
G. Berceanu *ROM*
S. Anghelov *BUL*
Flyweight
V. Kostantinov *URS*
N. Ginga *ROM*
K. Hirayama *JPN*
Bantamweight
P. Ukkola *FIN*
I. Frgic *YUG*
F. Mustafin *URS*
Featherweight
K. Lipien *POL*
N. Davidian *URS*
L. Reczi *HUN*
Lightweight
S. Nalbandyan *URS*
S. Rusu *ROM*
H. H. Wehling *GDR*
Welterweight
A. Bykov *URS*
V. Macha *TCH*
K. Helbing *GER*
Middleweight
M. Petkovic *YUG*
V. Cheboksarov *URS*
I. Kolev *BUL*
Light-heavyweight
V. Rezantsev *URS*
S. Ivanov *BUL*
C. Kwiecinski *POL*
Heavyweight
N. Bolboshin *URS*
K. Goranov *BUL*
A. Skrzylewski *POL*
Super heavyweight
A. Kolchinski *URS*
A. Tomov *BUL*
B. Codreanu *ROM*

YACHTING

Tempest
SWE URS USA
(14.0 pts)
Soiling
DEN USA GDR
(46.7 pts)
Flying Dutchman
GER GBR BRA
(34.7 pts)
Tornado
GBR USA GER
(18.0 pts)

470
GER ESP AUS
(42.4 pts)
Finn
J. Schumann *GDR*
(35.4 pts)
A. Belashov *URS*
J. Bertrand *AUS*

1980 LAKE PLACID

NORDIC SKIING

Men
Cross-country (15 km)
T. Wassberg *SWE*
(41 min 57.63 sec)
J. Mieto *FIN*
O. Aunli *NOR*
Cross-country (30 km)
N. Zimjatov *URS*
(1 hr 27 min 02.80 sec)
R. Vasili *URS*
I. Lebanov *BUL*
Cross-country (50 km)
N. Zimjatov *URS*
(2 hr 27 min 24.60 sec)
J. Mieto *FIN*
A. Zavjalov *URS*
4 x 10-kilometres relay
URS NOR FIN
(1 hr 57 min 03.46 sec)
Ski jumping (70 km)
A. Innauer *AUT*
(266.3 pts)
M. Deckert *GDR*
H. Yagi *JPN*
Ski jumping (90 m)
T. Tormanen *FIN*
(271.0 pts)
H. Neuper *AUT*
J. Puikkonen *FIN*
Nordic combined
U. Wehling *GDR*
(432.200 pts)
J. Karjalainen *FIN*
K. Winkler *GDR*
Biathlon (10 km)
F. Ullrich *GDR*
(32 min 10.69 sec)
V. Alikin *URS*
A. Aljabiev *URS*
Biathlon (20 km)
A. Aljabiev *URS*
(1 hr 08 min 16.31 sec)
F. Ullrich *GDR*
E. Roesch *GDR*
4 x 7.5 kilometres
URS GDR GER
Women
Cross-country (5 km)
R. Smetanina *URS*
(15 min 06.92 sec)

H. Riihivouri *FIN*
K. Jeriova *TCH*

Cross-country (10 km)
B. Petzold *GDR*
(30 min 31.54 sec)
H. Riihivouri *FIN*
H. Takalo *FIN*
4 x 5-kilometres relay
GDR URS NOR

ALPINE SKIING

Men
Downhill
L. Stock *AUT*
(1 min 45.50 sec)

P. Wirnsberger *AUT*
S. Podborski *CAN*
Giant slalom
I. Stenmark *SWE*
(2 min 40.74 sec)
A. Wenzel *LIE*
H. Enn *AUT*
Slalom
I. Stenmark *SWE*
(1 min 44.26 sec)
P. Mahre *USA*
J. Luethy *SUI*
Women
Downhill
A. Moser (Proell) *AUT*
(1 min 37.52 sec)
H. Wenzel *LIE*
M.-T. Nadig *SUI*
Giant slalom
H. Wenzel *LIE*
(2 min 41.66 sec)
I. Epple *GER*
P. Pelen *FRA*
Slalom
H. Wenzel *LIE*
(1 min 25.09 sec)
C. Kinshofer *GER*
E. Hess *SUI*

FIGURE SKATING

Men
R. Cousins *GBR*
(189.48 pts)

J. Hoffmann *GDR*
C. Tickner *USA*
Women
A. Poetzsch *GDR*
(189.00 pts)
L. Fratianne *USA*
D. Lurz *GER*
Pairs
I. Rodnina &
A. Zaitsev *URS*
(147.26 pts)
M. Cherkosova &
S. Shakrai *URS*
M. Mager &
U. Bewersdorff *GDR*
Ice dancing
N. Limichuk &
G. Karponosov *URS*
(205.48 pts)
K. Regoczy &
A. Sallay *HUN*
I. Moiseeva &
A. Minenkov *URS*

SPEED SKATING

Men
500 metres
E. Heiden *USA*
(38.03 sec)

E. Kulikov *URS*
L. de Boer *HOL*
1,000 metres
E. Heiden *USA*
(1 min 15.18 sec)
G. Boucher *CAN*
F. Roenning *NOR*
1,500 metres
E. Heiden *USA*
(1 min 55.44 sec)
K. Stenshjemmet *NOR*
T. Andersen *NOR*
5,000 metres
E. Heiden *USA*
(7 min 02.29 sec)
K. Stenshjemmet *NOR*
T. Oxholm *NOR*
10,000 metres
E. Heiden *USA*
(14 min 28.13 sec)
P. Kleine *HOL*
T. Oxholm *NOR*
Women
500 metres
K. Enke *GDR*
(41.78 sec)
L. Mueller *USA*
N. Petruseva *URS*
1,000 metres
N. Petruseva *URS*
(1 min 24.10 sec)
L. Mueller *USA*
S. Albrecht *GDR*
1,500 metres
A. Borckink *HOL*
(2 min 10.95 sec)

R. Visser *HOL*
S. Becker *GDR*
3,000 metres
B. Jensen *NOR*
(4 min 32.13 sec)
S. Becker *GDR*
B. Heiden *USA*

BOBSLEIGHING

Two-man
SUI II GDR II GDR I
(4 min 09.36 sec)
Four-man
GDR I SUI I GDR II
(3 min 59.92 sec)

LUGE TOBOGGANING

Men
Single-seater
B. Glass *GDR*
(2 min 54.796 sec)
P. Hildgartner *ITA*
A. Winkler *GER*
Two-seater
GDR ITA AUT
(1 min 19.331 sec)
Women
Single-seater
V. Zozulia *URS*
(2 min 36.537 sec)
M. Sollmann *GDR*
I. Amantova *URS*

ICE HOCKEY

USA URS SWE

1980 MOSCOW

ATHLETICS

Men
100 metres
A. Wells *GBR*
(10.25 sec)

S. Leonard *UVB*
P. Petrov *BUL*

200 metres
P. Mennea *ITA*
(20.19 sec)
A. Wells *GBR*
D. Quarrie *JAM*
400 metres
V. Markin *URS*
(44.60 sec)
R. Mitchell *AUS*
F. Schaffer *GDR*
800 metres
S. Ovett *GBR*
(1 min 45.4 sec)

S. Coe *GBR*
N. Kirov *URS*
1,500 metres
S. Coe *GBR*
(3 min 38.4 sec)

J. Straub *GDR*
S. Ovett *GBR*
5,000 metres
M. Yifter *ETH*
(13 min 21.0 sec)
S. Nyambui *TAN*
K. Maaninka *FIN*
10,000 metres
M. Yifter *ETH*
(27 min 42.7 sec)
K. Maaninka *FIN*
M. Kedir *ETH*
Marathon
W. Cierpinski *GDR*
(2 hr 11 min 03 sec)
C. Nijboer *HOL*
S. Dzhumanazarov *URS*
110-metres hurdles
T. Munkelt *GDR*
(13.39 sec)
A. Casanas *CUB*
A. Puchkov *URS*
400-metres hurdles
V. Beck *GDR*
(48.70 sec)
V. Arkhipenko *URS*
G. Oakes *GBR*
**3,000-metres
steeplechase**
B. Malinowski *POL*
(8 min 09.7 sec)

F. Bayi *TAN*
E. Tura *ETH*
20-kilometres walk
M. Damilano *ITA*
(1 hr 23 min 35.5 sec)
P. Pochinchuk *URS*
R. Wieser *GDR*
50-kilometres walk
H. Gauder *GDR*
(3 hr 49 min 24.0 sec)
J. Llopart *ESP*
Y. Ivchenko *URS*
4 x 100-metres relay
URS POL FRA
(38.26 sec)
4 x 400-metres relay
URS GDR ITA
(3 min 01.1 sec)
High jump
G. Wessig *GDR*
(2.36 m)

J. Wszola *POL*
J. Freimuth *GDR*
Long jump
L. Dombrowski *GDR*
(8.54 m)
F. Paschek *GDR*
V. Podlozhnyi *URS*
Triple jump
J. Uudmae *URS*
(17.35 m)
V. Saneyev *URS*
J. de Oliveira *BRA*
Pole Vault
W. Kozakiewicz *POL*
(5.78 m)

K. Volkov *URS*
T. Slusarski *POL*
Shot
V. Kiselyou *URS*
(21.35 m)
A. Baryshnikov *URS*
U. Beyer *GDR*
Discus
V. Rasshchupkin *URS*
(66.64 m)
I. Bugar *TCH*
L. Delis *CUB*
Javelin
D. Kula *URS*

(91.20 m)
A. Marakov *URS*
W. Hanisch *GDR*
Hammer
V. Sedykh *URS*
(81.80 m)
S. Litvonic *URS*
Y. Tamm *URS*
Decathlon
D. Thompson *GBR*
(8,495 pts)

Y. Kutsenko *URS*
S. Zhelanov *URS*
Women
100 metres
L. Kondratyeva *URS*
(11.06 sec)
M. Gohr *GDR*
I. Auerswald *GDR*
200 metres
B. Woeckel *GDR*
(22.03 sec)
N. Bochina *URS*
M. Ottey *JAM*
400 metres
M. Koch *GDR*
(48.88 sec)

J. Kratochvilova *TCH*
C. Lathan *GDR*
800 metres
N. Olizarenko *URS*
(1 min 53.5 sec)
O. Mineyeva *URS*
T. Providokhina *URS*
1,500 metres
T. Kazankina *URS*
(3 min 56.6 sec)
C. Wartenberg *GDR*
N. Olizarenko *URS*
100-metres hurdles
V. Komisova *URS*
(12.56 sec)
J. Klier *GDR*
L. Langer *POL*
4 x 100-metres relay
GDR URS GBR
(41.60 sec)
4 x 400-metres relay
URS GDR GBR

(3 min 20.2 sec)
High jump
S. Simeoni *ITA*
(1.97 m)
U. Kielan *POL*
J. Kirst *GDR*
Long jump
T. Kolpakova *URS*
(7.06 m)
B. Wujak *GDR*
T. Skachko *URS*
Shot
I. Slupianek *GDR*
(22.41 m)
S. Krachevskaya *URS*
M. Pufe *GDR*
Discus
E. Jahl *GDR*
(69.96 m)
M. Petkova *BUL*
T. Lesovaya *URS*
Javelin
M. Colon *CUB*
(68.40 m)
S. Gunba *URS*
V. Hommola *GDR*
Penthathlon
N. Tkachenko *URS*
(5,083 pts)
O. Rukavishnikova *URS*
O. Kuragina *URS*

ARCHERY

Men
T. Poikolainen *FIN*
(2,455 pts)
B. Isachenko *URS*
G. Ferrari *ITA*
Women
K. Losaberidze *URS*
(2,491 pts)
N. Butuzova *URS*
P. Meriluoto *FIN*

BASKETBALL

Men
YUG ITA URS
Women
URS BUL YUG

BOXING

Light-flyweight
S. Sabyrov *URS*
H. Ramos *CUB*
I. Moustafov *BUL* &
Byong Uk Li *PRK*
Flyweight
P. Lessov *BUL*
V. Miroshnichenko *URS*
J. Varadi *HUN* &
H. Russell *IRL*
Bantamweight
J. Hernandez *CUB*
B. J. Pinango *VEN*
M. Anthony *GUY* &
D. Cipere *ROM*
Featherweight
R. Fink *GDR*
A. Horta *CUB*
V. Rybakov *URS* &
K. Kosedowski *POL*
Lightweight
A. Herrera *CUB*
V. Demianenko *URS*
R. Nowakowski *GDR* &
K. Adach *POL*
Light-welterweight
P. Oliva *ITA*
S. Konakbiev *URS*
A. Willis *GBR* &

J. Aguilar *CUB*
Welterweight
A. Aldama *CUB*
J. Mugabi *UGA*
K.-H. Krueger *GDR* &
K. Szczerbo *POL*
Light-middleweight
A. Martinez *CUB*
A. Koshkin *URS*
J. Franek *TCH* &
D. Kastner *GDR*
Middleweight
J. Gomez *CUB*
V. Savchenko *URS*
V. Silaghi *ROM* &
J. Rybicki *POL*
Light-heavyweight
S. Kacar *YUG*
P. Skrzecz *POL*
H. Bauch *GDR* &
R. Rojas *CUB*
Heavyweight
T. Stevenson *CUB*

P. Zacv *URS*
I. Levai *HUN* &
J. Fanghanel *GDR*

CANOEING

Men
500-metres Canadian singles
S. Postrekhin *URS*
(1 min 53.37 sec)
L. Lubenov *BUL*
O. Heukroot *GDR*
500-metres Canadian pairs
HUN ROM BUL
(1 min 43.39 sec)
1,000-metres Canadian singles
L. Lubenov *BUL*
(4 min 12.38 sec)
S. Postrekhin *URS*
E. Leve *GDR*
1,000-metres Canadian pairs
ROM GDR URS
(3 min 47.65 sec)
500-metres kayak singles
V. Parfenovich *URS*
(1 min 43.43 sec)
J. Sumegi *AUS*
V. Diba *ROM*
500-metres kayak pairs
URS ESP GDR
(1 min 32.38 sec)
1,000-metres kayak singles
R. Helm *GDR*
(3 min 48.77 sec)
A. Lebas *FRA*
I. Birladeanu *ROM*

1,000-metres kayak pairs
URS HUN ESP
(3 min 26.72 sec)
Kayak fours
GDR ROM BUL
(3 min 13.76 sec)
Women
Kayak singles
B. Fischer *GDR*
(1 min 57.96 sec)
V. Ghecheva *BUL*
A. Melnikova *URS*
Kayak pairs
GDR URS HUN
(1 min 43.88 sec)

CYCLING

1,000-metres sprint
L. Hesslich *GDR*
Y. Cahard *FRA*
S. Kopylov *URS*
1,000-metres time trial
L. Thoms *GDR*
(1 min 02.955 sec)
A. Panfilov *URS*
D. Weller *JAM*
4,000-metres pursuit
R. Dill-Bundi *SUI*
A. Bondue *FRA*
H.-H. Orsted *DEN*
Team
URS GDR TCH
Road race
S. Sukhoruchenkov *URS*
(4 hr 48 min 28.9 sec)
C. Lang *POL*
Y. Barinov *URS*
101-kilometres team time trial
URS GDR TCH
(2 hr 01 min 21.7 sec)

EQUESTRIAN

Show jumping
J. Kowalczyk *POL*
(8 flts)
N. Korolkov *URS*
J. Perez Heras *MEX*
Team
URS POL MEX
Dressage
E. Theurer *AUS*
(1,370 pts)
Y. Kovshov *URS*
V. Ugryumov *URS*
Team
URS BUL ROM
Three-day event
F. E. Roman *ITA*
(108.60 pts)
A. Blinov *URS*
Y. Salnikov *URS*
Teams
URS ITA MEX

FENCING

Men
Foil
V. Smirnov *URS*
(4 wins)
P. Jolyot *FRA*
A. Romankov *URS*
Team
FRA URS POL
Epée
J. Harmenberg *SWE*
(4 wins)
E. Kolczonay *HUN*

P. Riboud *FRA*
Team
FRA POL URS
Sabre
V. Korvopuskov *URS*
(4 wins)
M. Burtsev *URS*
I. Gedovari *HUN*
Women
Foil
P. Trinquet *FRA*
(4 wins)
M. Maros *HUN*
B. Wysoczanska *POL*
Team
FRA URS HUN

GYMNASTICS

Men
Combined exercises
A. Dityatin *URS*
(118.650 pts)
N. Andrianov *URS*
S. Deltchev *BUL*
Team
URS GDR HUN
Floor
R. Bruckner *GDR*
(19.750 pts)
N. Andrianov *URS*
A. Dityatin *URS*
Horizontal bars
S. Deltchev *BUL*
(19.825 pts)
A. Dityatin *URS*
N. Andrianov *URS*
Parallel bars
A. Tkachyov *URS*
(19.775 pts)
A. Dityatin *URS*
R. Bruckner *GDR*
Pommelled horse
Z. Magyar *HUN*
(19.925 pts)
A. Dityatin *URS*
M. Nikolay *GDR*
Long horse
N. Andrianov *URS*
(19.825 pts)
A. Dityatin *URS* R.
Bruckner *GDR*
Rings
A. Dityatin *URS*
(19.875 pts)
A. Tkachyov *URS*
J. Tabak *TCH*
Women
Combined exercises
Y. Davydova *URS*
(79.150 pts)
M. Gnauck *GDR* &
N. Comaneci *ROM*
Team
URS ROM GDR
Beam
N. Comaneci *ROM*
(19.800 pts)
Y. Davydova *URS*
N. Shaposhnikova *URS*
Asymmetric bars
M. Gnauck *GDR*
(19.875 pts)
E. Eberle *ROM*
S. Kraeker *GDR* &
M. Ruhn *ROM*
Horse
N. Shaposhnikova *URS*
(19.725 pts)
S. Kraeker *GDR*
M. Ruhn *ROM*
Floor
N. Kimm *URS* &

N. Comaneci *ROM*
(19.875 pts)
N. Shaposhnikova *URS*
& M. Gnauck *GDR*

HANDBALL

Men
GDR URS ROM
Women
URS YUG GDR

HOCKEY (FIELD)

Men
IND ESP URS
Women
ZIM TCH URS

JUDO

60-kilograms
T. Rey *FRA*
J. Rodriquez *POR*
T. Kincses *HUN* &
A. Emizh *URS*
65-kilograms
N. Solodukhin *URS*
T. Damdin *MGL*
I. Nedkov *BUL* &
J. Pawlowski *POL*
71-kilograms
E. Gamba *ITA*
N. Adams *GBR*
K.-H. Lehmann *GDR* &
R. Davaadalai *MGL*
78-kilograms
S. Khabareli *URS*
J. Ferrer *CUB*
B. Tchoullouyan *FRA* &
M. Fratica *ROM*
86-kilograms
J. Roethlisberger *SUI*
I. Azcuy *CUB*
A. Iatskevich *URS* &
D. Ultsch *GDR*
95-kilograms
R. van de Walle *BEL*
T. Khubuluri *URS*
D. Lorenz *GDR* &
N. Numan *HOL*
Over 95-kilograms
A. Parisi *FRA*

D. Zaprianov *BUL*
V. Kocman *TCH* &
R. Kovacevic *YUG*
Open
D. Lorenz *GDR*
A. Parisi *FRA*
A. Mapp *GBR* &
A. Ozsvar *HUN*

MODERN PENTATHLON

A. Starostin *URS*

(5,568 pts)
T. Szombathelyi *HUN*
P. Lednev *URS*
Team
URS HUN SWE

ROWING

Men
Single sculls
P. Karppinen *FIN*
(7 min 09.61 sec)
V. Yakusha *URS*
P. Kersten *GDR*
Double sculls
GDR YUG TCH
(6 min 24.33 sec)
Quadruple sculls
GDR URS BUL
(5 min 49.81 sec)
Coxless pairs
GDR URS GBR
(6 min 48.01 sec)
Coxed pairs
GDR URS YUG
(7 min 02.54 sec)
Coxless fours
GDR URS GBR
(6 min 08.17 sec)
Eights
GDR GBR URS
(5 min 49.05 sec)
Women
Single sculls
S. Toma *ROM*
(3 min 40.69 sec)
A. Makhina *URS*
M. Schroter *GDR*
Double sculls
URS GDR ROM
(3 min 16.27 sec)
Quadruple sculls
GDR URS BUL
(3 min 15.32 sec)
Coxless pairs
GDR POL BUL
(3 min 30.49 sec)
Coxed fours
GDR BUL URS
(3 min 19.27 sec)
Eights
GDR URS ROM
(3 min 03.32 sec)

SHOOTING

Free pistol
A. Melentov *URS*
(581 pts)
H. Vollmar *GDR*
L. Diakov *BUL*
Rapid fire pistol
C. Ion *ROM*
(596 pts)
J. Wiefel *GDR*
G. Petritsch *AUT*
Small-bore rifle, prone
K. Varga *HUN*
(599 pts)
H. Heilfort *GDR*
P. Zaprianov *BUL*
Small-bore rifle, three positions
V. Vlasov *URS*
(1,173 pts)
B. Hartstein *GDR*
S. Johansson *SWE*
Running game
I. Sokolov *URS*
(589 pts)
T. Pfeffler *GDR*
A. Gazon *URS*

Trap shooting
L. Giovannetti *ITA*
(198 pts)
R. Yambulatov *URS*
J. Damme *GDR*
Skeet
H. Rasmussen *DEN*
(196 pts)
L. Carlsson *SWE*
R. Castrillo *CUB*

SOCCER

TCH GDR YUG

SWIMMING

Men
100-metres freestyle
J. Woithe *GDR*
(50.40 sec)
P. Holmertz *SWE*
P. Johansson *SWE*
200-metres freestyle
S. Kopliakov *URS*
(1 min 49.81 sec)
A. Krylov *URS*
G. Brewer *AUS*
400-metres freestyle
V. Salnikov *URS*
(3 min 51.31 sec)

A. Krylov *URS*
I. Stukolin *URS*
1,500-metres freestyle
V. Salnikov *URS*
(15 min 08.25 sec)
R. Strohbach *GBR*
100-metres backstroke
B. Baron *SWE*
(56.53 sec)
V. Kuznetsov *URS*
V. Dolgov *URS*
200-metres backstroke
S. Wladar *HUN*
(2 min 01.93 sec)
Z. Verrasz *HUN*
M. Kerry *AUS*
100-metres breaststroke
D. Goodhew *GBR*
(1 min 03.34 sec)
A. Miskarov *URS*
P. Evans *AUS*
200-metres breaststroke
R. Zulpa *URS*
(2 min 15.85 sec)
A. Vermes *HUN*
A. Miskarov *URS*
100-metres butterfly
P. Arvidsson *SWE*
(54.92 sec)
R. Pyttel *GDR*
D. Lopez *ESP*

200-metres butterfly
S. Fesenko *URS*
(1 min 59.76 sec)
P. Hubble *GBR*
R. Pyttel *GDR*
400-metres medley
A. Sidorenko *URS*
(4 min 28.02 sec)
S. Fesenko *URS*
Z. Verraszto *HUN*
4 x 200-metres
freestyle relay
URS GDR BRA
(7 min 23.50 sec)
4 x 100-metres medley
relay
AUS URS GBR
(3 min 45.70 sec)
Highboard diving
F. Hoffmann *GDR*
(835.650 pts)
V. Aleinik *URS*
D. Ambartsumyan *URS*
Springboard diving
A. Portnov *URS*
(905.025 pts)
C. Giron *MEX*
F. Cagnotto *ITA*
Water polo
URS YUG HUN
Women
100-metres freestyle
B. Krause *GDR*
(54.79 sec)
C. Metschuk *GDR*
I. Diers *GDR*
200-metres freestyle
B. Krause *GDR*
(1 min 58.33 sec)
I. Diers *GDR*
C. Schmidt *GDR*
400-metres freestyle
I. Diers *GDR*
(4 min 08.76 sec)
P. Schneider *GDR*

P. Schmidt *GDR*
800-metres freestyle
M. Ford *AUS*
(8 min 28.90 sec)
I. Diers *GDR*
H. Dahne *GDR*
100-metres backstroke
R. Reinisch *GDR*
(1 min 00.86 sec)
I. Kleber *GDR*
P. Reidel *GDR*
200-metres backstroke
R. Reinisch *GDR*
(2 min 11.77 sec)
C. Polit *GDR*
B. Treiber *GDR*
100-metres
breaststroke
V. Geweniger *GDR*
(1 min 10.22 sec)
E. Vasikova *URS*
S. Nielsson *DEN*
200-metres
breaststroke
L. Kachushite *URS*
(2 min 29.54 sec)
S. Varganova *URS*
Y. Bogdanova *URS*
100-metres butterfly
C. Metschuk *GDR*
(1 min 00.42 sec)
A. Pollack *GDR*
C. Knacke *GDR*
400-metres medley
P. Schneider *GDR*
(4 min 36.29 sec)
S. Davies *GBR*
A. Czopek *HOL*
4 x 100-metres
freestyle relay
GDR SWE HOL
(3 min 42.71 sec)
4 x 100-metres medley
relay
GDR GBR URS

(4 min 06.67 sec)
Highboard diving
M. Jaschke *GDR*
(596.250 pts)
S. Emirzyan *URS*
L. Tsotadze *URS*
Springboard diving
I. Kalinina *URS*
(725.910 pts)
M. Proeber *GDR*
K. Guthke *GDR*

VOLLEYBALL

Men
URS BUL ROM
Women
URS GDR BUL

WEIGHTLIFTING

Flyweight
K. Osmanoliev *URS*
(245.0 kg)
B. C. Ho *PRK*
G. S. Han *PRK*
Bantamweight
D. Nunez *CUB*
(275.0 kg)
Y. Sarkisyan *URS*
T. Dembonczyk *POL*
Featherweight
V. Mazin *URS*
(290 kg)
S. Dimitrov *BUL*
M. Seweryn *POL*
Lightweight
Y. Roussev *BUL*
(342.5 kg)
J. Kunz *GDR*
M. Pachov *BUL*
Middleweight
A. Zlatev *BUL*
(360.0 kg)
A. Pervy *URS*
N. Kolev *BUL*

Light-heavyweight
Y. Vardanyan *URS*
(400.0 kg)
D. Blagoev *BUL*
D. Poliacik *TCH*
Middle-heavyweight
D. Paczabo *HUN*
(377.5 kg)
R. Alexandrov *BUL*
F. Mantek *GDR*
100-kilograms
O. Zaremba *TCH*
(395.0 kg)
I. Nikitin *URS*
A. Blanco *CUB*
Heavyweight
L. Taranenko *URS*
(422.5 kg)
V. Christov *BUL*
G. Szalai *HUN*
Super heavyweight
S. Rakhmanov *URS*
(440.0 kg)
J. Heuser *GDR*
J. Rutkowski *POL*

WRESTLING: FREESTYLE

Light-flyweight
C. Pollio *ITA*
S. Jang *PRK*
S. Kornilaev *URS*
Flyweight
A. Beloglazov *URS*
W. Stecyk *POL*
N. Selimov *BUL*
Bantamweight
S. Beloglazov *URS*
H. P. Li *PRK*
D. Quinbold *MGL*
Featherweight
M. Abushev *URS*
M. Doukov *BUL*
G. Hadjiioannidis *GRE*

Lightweight
S. Absaidov *URS*
I. Yankov *BUL*
S. Sejdi *YUG*
Welterweight
V. Raitchev *BUL*
J. Davaajav *MGL*
D. Karabin *TCH*
Middleweight
I. Abilov *BUL*
M. Aratsilov *URS*
I. Kovacs *HUN*
Light-heavyweight
S. Oganesyan *URS*
U. Neupert *GDR*
A. Cichon *POL*
Heavyweight
I. Mate *URS*
S. Tchervenkov *BUL*
J. Strnisko *TCH*
Super heavyweight
S. Andiev *URS*
J. Balla *HUN*
A. Sandurski *POL*

WRESTLING: GRECO-ROMAN

Light-flyweight
Z. Ushkempirov *URS*
C. Alexandru *ROM*
F. Seres *HUN*
Flyweight
V. Blagidze *URS*
L. Racz *HUN*
M. Mladenov *BUL*
Bantamweight
S. Serikov *URS*
J. Lipien *POL*
B. Ljungbeck *SWE*
Featherweight
S. Migiakis *GRE*
I. Toth *HUN*
B. Kramorenko *URS*

Lightweight
S. Rusu *ROM*
A. Supron *POL*
L.-E. Skiold *SWE*
Welterweight
F. Kocsis *HUN*
A. Bykov *URS*
M. Huhtala *FIN*
Middleweight
G. Korban *URS*
J. Dolgowicz *POL*
P. Pavlov *BUL*
Light-heavyweight
N. Nottny *HUN*
I. Kanygin *URS*
P. Dicu *ROM*
Heavyweight
G. Raikov *BUL*
R. Bierla *POL*
V. Andrei *ROM*
Super heavyweight
A. Kolchinsky *URS*
A. Tomov *BUL*
H. Bchara *LEB*

YACHTING

Star
URS AUT ITA
Soling
DEN URS GRE
Flying Dutchman
ESP IRL HUN
Tornado
BRA DEN SWE
470
BRA GDR FIN
Finn
E. Rechardt *FIN*
(36.70 pts)
W. Mahrhofer *AUT*
A. Balashov *URS*
(*Pictures of some of the gold medalists appear next to their names.*)

Notes on Measurements and Abbreviations

For the benefit of those readers who visualize distances in feet and inches, a short conversion table showing distances of events follows. Exceptional performances are given an exact conversion when descibed in the text.

The list of abbreviations for countries is that used by the International Olympic Committee.

A few early records are incomplete. Some information about early results is not known; in other cases the name of a second or third does not appear because there were only one or two competitors.

When women competitors have married during their careers, and might thus appear in the records under two names, no rigid style has been used. Where a competitor (such as I. Kirszenstein) later became better known under her married name (Szewinska), the later records give the married name with the single name in brackets to remind readers of the competitor's earlier name. Thus, the above example becomes I. Szewinska (Kirszenstein). Where, however, the competitor became best known with her married name hyphenated to her single name, this style is used; thus I. Kraemer becomes I. Kraemer–Engel for subsequent entries.

Conversions of distances of events

metres	miles	yards	feet	inches	metres	miles	yards	feet	inches
70		76	1	8	4,000 (4 km)	2	854	1	4
80		87	1	6	5,000 (5 km)	3	188	0	2
90		98	1	3	10,000 (10 km)	6	376	0	4
100		109	1	1	15,000 (15 km)	9	564	0	7
110		120	0	11	18,000 (18 km)	11	325	1	2
200		218	2	2	20,000 (20 km)	12	752	0	10
400		437	1	4	30,000 (30 km)	18	1,128	1	2
500		546	2	5	50,000 (50 km)	31	120	2	0
800		874	2	8	100,000 (100 km)	62	241	0	11
1,000		1,093	1	10					
1,500		1,640	1	3					
3,000 (3 km)	1	1,520	2	6					

Marathon 42,195 metres or 26 miles 385 yards

Abbreviations of Countries

The following list is of the official Olympic abbreviations. However it includes some abbreviations, such as *BOH* for Bohemia, not now used in the Olympic Games, and others, such as *QAT* for Qatar, which have not yet been used but which might occur in 1984 results.

AFG	Afghanistan	*CHI*	Chile	*GER*	Germany (from	*JPN*	Japan	*NGU*	Papua-New	*SWE*	Sweden
AHO	Antilles	*CIV*	Ivory Coast		1968 German	*KEN*	Kenya		Guinea	*SWZ*	Swaziland
	(Holland)	*CMR*	Cameroon		Federal	*KHM*	Cambodia	*NOR*	Norway	*SYR*	Syria
ALB	Albania		Republic		Republic or		(Khmere	*NZL*	New Zealand	*TAN*	Tanzania
ALG	Algeria	*COK*	Congo Kinshasa		West Germany)		Republic)	*PAK*	Pakistan	*TCH*	Czechoslovakia
AND	Andorra	*COL*	Colombia	*GHA*	Ghana	*KOR*	Korea	*PAN*	Panama	*THA*	Thailand
ANT	Antigua	*CRC*	Costa Rica	*GRE*	Greece	*KUW*	Kuwait	*PAR*	Paraguay	*TOG*	Togoland
ARG	Argentina	*CUB*	Cuba	*GRN*	Grenada	*LAO*	Laos	*PER*	Peru	*TPE*	Chinese Taipei
AUS	Australia	*CYP*	Cyprus	*GUA*	Guatemala	*LAT*	Latvia	*PHI*	Philippines	*TRI*	Trinidad and
	(Australasia	*DAH*	Dahomey	*GUI*	Guinea	*LBA*	Libya	*POL*	Poland		Tobago
	1896–1912)	*DEN*	Denmark	*GUY*	Guyana	*LBR*	Liberia	*POR*	Portugal	*TUN*	Tunisia
AUT	Austria	*DOM*	Dominican	*HAI*	Haiti	*LES*	Lesotho	*PRK*	North Korea	*TUR*	Turkey
BAH	Bahamas		Republic	*HBR*	British	*LIB*	Lebanon	*PUR*	Puerto Rico	*UAE*	United Arab
BAN	Bangladesh	*ECU*	Ecuador		Honduras	*LIE*	Liechtenstein	*QAT*	Qatar		Emirates
BAR	Barbados	*EGY*	Egypt, United	*HKG*	Hong Kong	*LIT*	Lithuania	*RHO*	Rhodesia	*UGA*	Uganda
BEL	Belgium		Arab Republic	*HOL*	Holland	*LUX*	Luxembourg	*ROC*	Republic of	*URS*	USSR
BEN	Benin	*ENG*	England		(Netherlands)	*MAD*	Madagascar		China	*URU*	Uruguay
BER	Bermuda	*ESP*	Spain	*HON*	Honduras	*MAL*	Malaysia	*ROM*	Rumania	*USA*	United States
BIR	Burma	*EST*	Estonia	*HUN*	Hungary	*MAR*	Morocco	*SAF*	South Africa		of America
BIZ	Belize	*ETH*	Ethiopia	*INA*	Indonesia	*MAW*	Malawi	*SAL*	El Salvador	*VEN*	Venezuela
BOH	Bohemia	*FIJ*	Fiji	*IND*	India	*MEX*	Mexico	*SAU*	Saudi Arabia	*VIE*	Vietnam
BOL	Bolivia	*FIN*	Finland	*IRL*	Ireland	*MGL*	Mongolia	*SCO*	Scotland	*VOL*	Upper Volta
BOT	Botswana	*FRA*	France	*IRN*	Iran	*MLI*	Mali	*SEN*	Senegal	*WAL*	Wales
BRA	Brazil	*FRG*	West Germany	*IRQ*	Iraq	*MLT*	Malta	*SEY*	Seychelles	*YAR*	Yemen Arab
BRN	Bahrain		(*see also GER*)	*ISL*	Iceland	*MON*	Monaco	*SIN*	Singapore		Republic
BUL	Bulgaria	*GAB*	Gabon	*ISR*	Israel	*MOZ*	Mozambique	*SLC*	Sierra Leone	*YMD*	Yemen
CAF	Central Africa	*GAM*	Gambia	*ISV*	Virgin Isles	*MRI*	Mauritius	*SMR*	San Marino		Democratic
CAN	Canada	*GBR*	Great Britain	*ITA*	Italy	*MTN*	Mauritania	*SOM*	Somali Republic		Republic
CAY	Cayman Islands	*GDR*	German	*IVB*	British Virgin	*NCA*	Nicaragua	*SRI*	Sri Lanka	*YUG*	Yugoslavia
CEY	Ceylon		Democratic		Islands	*NEP*	Nepal	*SUD*	Sudan	*ZAI*	Zaire
CGO	Congo Republic		Republic (East	*JAM*	Jamaica	*NGR*	Nigeria	*SUI*	Switzerland	*ZAM*	Zambia
CHA	Chad		Germany)	*JOR*	Jordan			*SUR*	Surinam	*ZIM*	Zimbabwe

Acknowledgements

No book such as this could be attempted without constant checking against those books produced earlier. The author acknowledges his debt to several of these, notably the following:
Encyclopedia of the Olympic Games by Erich Kamper (Harenberg, Dortmund, 1972). This book contains a complete list of results of the summer Games until 1972, and is indispensible to anybody studying the full history of the Games.
The Guinness Book of Olympic Records, edited by Norris McWhirter and Stan Greenberg (Penguin Books, Harmondsworth, Middlesex, 1980), contains results and other statistics of all events currently in the Olympic programme.
The Guinness Book of Athletic Facts and Feats by Peter Matthews (Guinness Superlatives, Enfield, Middlesex, 1982) gives details of all athletic feats, including much information on the Olympic Games.
Encyclopedia of Track and Field Athletics by Mel Watman (Robert Hale, London, and St. Martins Press, New York, 5th edition 1981) is a good general encyclopedia on athletics.
The partwork *The Game* (in 112 parts, Marshall Cavendish, 1971) includes brief descriptions of each Olympic Games, and the book made from it, *The History of the Olympics*, edited by Martin Tyler and Phil Soar (Marshall Cavendish, London, New York, Sydney, 1975) also contains a list of medal winners.
The 1980 Olympics Handbook by Norman Giller (Arthur Barker, London, 1980) contains descriptions of each of the summer Games till 1976.
An Illustrated History of the Olympics by Richard Schaap (Alfred A. Knopf, New York, 3rd edition 1975) gives a good account of each Games, particularly from the point of view of the United States of America.
The Modern Olympic Games by John Lucas (A. S. Barnes, South Brunswick and New York, and Thomas Yoseloff, London, 1980) is particularly good on the political problems that have bedevilled the Olympic Games.
The Olympic Games edited by Lord Killanin and John Rodda (Barrie and Jenkins, London, 1976) contains results, biographies and numerous background articles by distinguished contributors on all aspects of the Olympic Games.
The author also thanks those librarians who kindly lent books, and in particular Carole Hampton of the Hamlyn Group Library who co-ordinated the efforts to acquire them.
The Official Reports of the British Olympic Association were also of great help, and thanks are due to the staff members of the British Olympic Association for their generous assistance.
The Los Angeles Olympic Organizing Committee in the person of John A. Fransen, Director of Public Relations, was also most helpful, and supplied much of the information for the chapter dealing with the plans for the 1984 Games.
Finally the author apologizes to readers who would normally spell 'metres' as 'meters', who would never refer to 'track and field' as 'athletics', and who know the 'long jump' as the 'broad jump'. Their consolation is that their athletes figure prominently throughout.